# Fair and Affordable Housing in the U.S.

# Studies in Critical Social Sciences

*Series Editor*
David Fasenfest
Wayne State University

*Editorial Board*

The titles published in this series are listed at brill.nl/scss.

# Fair and Affordable Housing in the U.S.
## Trends, Outcomes, Future Directions

Edited by Robert Mark Silverman
and Kelly L. Patterson

Haymarket Books
Chicago, IL

First published in 2011 by Brill Academic Publishers, The Netherlands
© 2011 Koninklijke Brill NV, Leiden, The Netherlands

Published in paperback in 2012 by
Haymarket Books
P.O. Box 180165
Chicago, IL 60618
773-583-7884
www.haymarketbooks.org

ISBN: 978-1-60846-238-4

Trade distribution:
In the US, Consortium Book Sales, www.cbsd.com
In Canada, Publishers Group Canada, www.pgcbooks.ca
In the UK, Turnaround Publisher Services, www.turnaround-psl.com
In Australia, Palgrave Macmillan, www.palgravemacmillan.com.au
In all other countries, Publishers Group Worldwide, www.pgw.com

Cover design by Ragina Johnson.

This book was published with the generous support of Lannan Foundation
and the Wallace Global Fund.

Printed in the United States.


Library of Congress Cataloging-in-Publication data is available.

# CONTENTS

# LIST OF FIGURES AND TABLES

## Figures

*Tables*

# ACKNOWLEDGEMENTS

This edited book would not have been possible without the support of several individuals. We would like to thank the series editor, David Fasenfest, for his input during the conceptualization and subsequent stages of this endeavor. We also thank Boris van Gool, Rosanna Woensdregt, Michael Mozina, and other members of the team at Brill for their work on this project. We are appreciative for Lesley Kenny's copyediting of draft chapters. We thank the Baldy Center for Law & Social Policy at the University at Buffalo for the Small Research grant that partially funded this effort. In addition, we thank the Center for Urban Studies at the University at Buffalo for funding that partially supported this effort. Finally, we thank each of the contributors to this edited book for responding to our initial call for chapters and submitting their original work.

# NOTES ON CONTRIBUTORS

GEORGE C. GALSTER is a Distinguished Professor and the Clarence Hilberry Professor of Urban Affairs in the Department of Urban Studies and Planning at Wayne State University. He earned his Ph.D. in Economics from M.I.T., with undergraduate degrees from Wittenberg and Case Western Reserve Universities. He has published over 100 scholarly articles and book chapters, primarily on the topics of metropolitan housing markets, racial discrimination and segregation, neighborhood dynamics, residential reinvestment, community lending and insurance patterns, and urban poverty.

ANGELA A. KAISER is an Assistant Professor in the Department of Social Work at Oakland University. She received her MSW and Ph.D. at Wayne State University.

DENNIS KEATING is Professor of Urban Planning and Law in the Levin College of Urban Affairs and the Cleveland-Marshall College of Law at Cleveland State University. He directs the Master of Urban Planning, Design and Development Program. His teaching and research interests include housing and urban policy, neighborhood development, land use law and planning, housing law, and fair housing. He has published widely on these subjects, including six books and numerous articles. He is a past president of the housing research council of the International Sociological Association and has served on the board of the Urban Affairs Association.

CHARLES M. LAMB is a Professor in the Department of Political Science, University at Buffalo, SUNY. His research includes work on fair housing policy, presidential and bureaucratic politics, and judicial decision making. He is the author of *Housing Segregation in Suburban America since 1960: Presidential and Judicial Politics* (New York: Cambridge University Press, 2005).

KIRK MCCLURE is a Professor with the Department of Urban Planning at the University of Kansas where he teaches and conducts research in the areas of affordable housing, economic development and real estate development. His research evaluates the workings of the nation's housing assistance programs, including programs for low-income renters as well as low-income homebuyers, and the behavior of the nation's housing markets. His research is found in dozens of articles and reports published in many of the leading journals in the field of urban planning. He has received multiple awards for his research. His research has been sponsored by the U.S. Department of Housing and Urban Development, the Fannie Mae Foundation, the Lincoln Land Institute plus many other organizations. He is on the Board of Editors for multiple leading journals that are national and international in scope. McClure holds two bachelor degrees from the University of Kansas plus a Master of City Planning from the Massachusetts Institute of Technology and a Ph.D. in city planning from the University of California, Berkeley.

KELLY L. PATTERSON is an Assistant Professor in the School of Social Work at the University at Buffalo. She holds a Ph.D. in Urban Studies from the University of Wisconsin-Milwaukee, a Masters in Public Affairs from the University at Buffalo, and a B.A. in Sociology from North Carolina Central University. Her research focuses on housing policy, residential segregation, fair and affordable housing, and rent vouchers. She has published in *Housing and Society, Critical Sociology, Housing Policy Debate,* and other peer reviewed journals.

ANNA MARIA SANTIAGO is the Leona Bevis & Marguerite Haynam Professor in Community Development in the Mandel School of Applied Social Sciences at Case Western Reserve University. Her research focuses on a number of topics, including social capital formation and asset building in low-income families; neighborhood effects on the health and well-being of low-income, minority children; the short- and long-term effects of housing and social welfare programs and policies as anti-poverty strategies; low-income homeownership and predatory lending; poverty and welfare dependency; residential segregation and housing discrimination in U.S. metropolitan areas; intimate violence in minority families; minority access to social service delivery systems; the social and economic consequences of disability status; and spirituality and social work.

ANA H. SANTIAGO-SAN ROMAN received a MSW in social work from Wayne State University in 2002 and a BA in history of art from the

University of Michigan in 1999. She is the Managing Editor for the *Journal of Community Practice*. She is also the Project Manager for the Denver Housing Study, funded by the Ford and MacArthur Foundations.

ALEX SCHWARTZ is an Associate Professor at Milano The New School for Management and Urban Policy, and Chairman of the School's Department of Urban Policy Analysis and Management. He is also Senior Research Associate at the Community Development Research Center (CDRC). He holds a Ph.D. in Urban Planning and Policy Development from Rutgers University. His principal area of research centers on housing and community development, including affordable housing programs, community reinvestment, and community development corporations. His most recent publication is *Housing Policy in the United States* (Routledge 2010). His research has appeared in such journals as *Cityscape, Economic Development Quarterly, Housing Policy Debate, Housing Studies, International Journal of Urban and Regional Research, Journal of Urban Affairs*, and *Journal of the American Planning Association*.

NICHOLAS R. SEABROOK received his Ph.D. from the University at Buffalo in 2010 and is currently an Assistant Professor in the Department of Political Science and Public Administration at the University of North Florida. He specializes in American Politics and Public Law. His research focuses on fair housing policy, money in politics, election administration, redistricting, and political geography. It has been published in *Social Science Quarterly, American Politics Research*, and *The Forum*.

ROBERT MARK SILVERMAN is an Associate Professor in the Department of Urban and Regional Planning at the University at Buffalo. He holds a Ph.D. in Urban Studies from the University of Wisconsin-Milwaukee. He also holds a B.S. in Political Science and a Masters in Public Administration from Arizona State University. His research focuses on community development, the nonprofit sector, community-based organizations, and inequality in inner city housing markets. He has published in *Urban Affairs Review, Urban Studies, National Civic Review, Action Research, Community Development, Journal of Black Studies, Journal of Social History*, and other peer reviewed journals.

GREGORY D. SQUIRES is a Professor of Sociology and Public Policy and Public Administration at George Washington University. Currently he is a member of the Advisory Board of the John Marshall Law School Fair Housing Legal Support Center in Chicago, Illinois, and the Social Science Advisory Board of the Poverty & Race Research Action Council in Washington, D.C. and he previously served as a member of the Federal Reserve Board's Consumer Advisory Council. He has written for several academic journals and general interest publications including *Housing Policy Debate, Urban Studies, New York Times*, and *Washington Post*. His recent books include *Privileged Places: Race, Residence and the Structure of Opportunity* (with Charis E. Kubrin – Lynne Rienner 2006), *There is No Such Thing as a Natural Disaster: Race, Class, and Hurricane Katrina* (with Chester Hartman – Routledge 2006) and *The Integration Debate: Competing Futures for American Cities* (with Chester Hartman – Routledge 2010).

HENRY LOUIS TAYLOR, JR. is a Professor in the Department of Urban and Regional Planning at the University at Buffalo and founding director of the U.B. Center for Urban Studies. He is the author of more than 80 articles, essays and technical reports and has written and edited five books and monographs. His latest book is *Inside El Barrio: A Bottom-Up View of Life in Castro's Cuba*. Taylor is currently working on a manuscript that examines the relationship between the city planning movement and black residential development in the urban metropolis.

J. ROSIE TIGHE is a faculty member in the Department of Geography and Planning at Appalachian State University. She holds a Ph.D. in Community and Regional Planning from the University of Texas at Austin and a Master's Degree in Urban and Environmental Policy and Planning from Tufts University. She currently lives in Boone, North Carolina with her husband and hounds. Her research focuses on fair housing, race and class, public opinion, and housing affordability.

CRISTINA M. TUCKER is a lecturer in the School of Social Work at the University of Pennsylvania. She received a MSW and a master's in Hispanic Studies from California State University, Sacramento. She received her Ph.D. from the School of Social Work at Wayne State University.

DAVID VARADY is a Professor of Planning at the University of Cincinnati, he has published six books and over sixty articles on housing issues (vouchers, public housing, neighborhood upgrading) and urban segregation. His most recent book, *Neighborhood Choices: Section 8 Housing Vouchers and Residential Mobility*, coauthored with Carole C. Walker was published by the Center for Urban Policy Research, Rutgers University, in 2007. Between March and November, 2010, he was a visiting scholar at OTB Research Institute for the Built Environment, Delft University of Technology in the Netherlands.

ERIC M. WILK is a lecturer in the Department of Political Science, University of Georgia. His research focuses on voting behavior, political parties in Congress, elections, federalism, and fair housing policy. He has published articles on fair housing policy (coauthored with Charles M. Lamb) that have appeared in the *Political Research Quarterly*, *Politics and Policy*, and the *Public Administration Review*.

# MAKING HOUSING POLICY FAIRER AND MORE AFFORDABLE IN THE U.S.

Robert Mark Silverman and Kelly L. Patterson

## Fair and Affordable Housing in the U.S.

From its inception, U.S. fair and affordable housing policy has been constrained by neoliberal ideologies that emphasize market-based approaches to program implementation. Public policy aimed at ameliorating housing discrimination and expanding low-income groups' access to housing markets has remained underdeveloped, underfunded, and poorly implemented. Policymakers have been reluctant to look beyond individual experiences in housing markets. Most policy is designed to address immediate barriers that individuals face in their search for housing. Legislation routinely falls short of recognizing obstacles that groups and classes in society face in housing markets. The identification of housing as a basic human right is not clearly articulated in U.S. policy.

Symbolically, U.S. housing policy has included stated goals which suggest that American's embrace rights to fair and affordable housing. For instance, the Housing Act of 1949 articulated the goal of providing a "decent home in a suitable living environment for every American family." In practice, this goal was never realized. One of the more lasting effects of the 1949 Act was the wide scale displacement of minorities and the urban poor caused by the *urban renewal* program. This program established a pattern in U.S. housing policy which has ensued for decades. Under the guise of providing decent and suitable living environments for American families, urban renewal resulted in the systematic displacement of minorities and the poor, and the wholesale denial of fair and affordable housing rights. The impact of urban renewal was so severe in minority communities that it earned the moniker *Negro removal* (Anderson 1964).

The period following urban renewal was characterized by short-lived attempts at policy reform that were labeled by their detractors as inefficient, overly bureaucratic, and incompatible with American values. One example of such an effort to reform housing and community development policy was the Model Cities initiative. This initiative was created in 1966 and terminated in 1974. It attempted to empower residents in the housing and community development process through "maximum feasibility participation." From its inception, the program faced resistance from elected officials at the state and local levels, and it was aggressively scuttled. In 1974, Model Cities was replaced with a less ambitious set of policies based on formula-based block grants and public-private partnerships. These policies have dominated the landscape into the contemporary period. Under their logic, fair and affordable housing policy has incrementally gone through the processes of devolution and nonprofitization (Swantrom 1999, Bockmeyer 2003).

The retrenchment of housing policy was an outgrowth of the general ethos of "privatism" (Hayes 1995). Consequently, U.S. housing policy has been heavily influenced by the belief that government should facilitate and support private sector activities in housing markets. Under this logic, individual transactions in a self-regulating private market are viewed as the most efficient and effective mechanisms for providing fair and affordable housing. Since the 1980s, the devolution and nonprofitization of housing policy has accelerated as neoliberal ideologies have taken hold at the national and global levels (Thibault 2007, Purcell 2008). Direct federal implementation of fair and affordable housing policy has incrementally given way to an increased emphasis on program implementation by local governments and nonprofits. While this shift has occurred, there has been an unwavering emphasis on institutionalizing market-based approaches to fair and affordable housing. These trends, and the neoliberal undercurrents that drive them, constitute the parameters in which U.S. fair and affordable housing policy has been shaped.

*The Parameters of Fair Housing Policy*

Privatism and neoliberal ideology have been imprinted on all four aspects of fair housing policy examined in this edited book. U.S. fair housing policy has been circumscribed by these ideological leanings. Housing discrimination was not addressed by federal legislation until the Fair Housing Act of 1968 prohibited discrimination at any point in the sale or rental of housing on the basis of race, color, religion, sex, and national origin. The 1968 Act designated the U.S. Department of Housing and Urban Development (HUD) as the federal agency to administer programs related to fair housing. HUD was authorized to *affirmatively* further fair housing in all of its programs and funded activities. As a political statement, the 1968 Act represented a monumental shift in US housing policy. Prior to its passage, there was virtually no legal recourse for individuals facing discrimination in housing markets. After the 1968 Act's passage, individuals could file complaints with HUD and had standing to sue when they felt they were discriminated against in their search for housing. However, this legislative milestone was narrowly constructed and focused exclusively on providing remedies to individuals who experienced discrimination.

The 1968 Act did not provide remedies for structural forms of discrimination faced by ascribed groups or classes in society. Instead, the burden of proving that acts of discrimination had occurred was firmly placed on those who had been victimized. The 1968 Act was narrowly constructed in a number of other ways (Yinger 1999, Landis and McClure 2010). For instance, it did not apply to a substantial proportion of properties. The 1968 Act did not apply to rental properties with four or fewer units, and it did not apply to home sales unless real estate agents were used. Consequently, many renters and homebuyers remained unprotected from housing discrimination. When the 1968 Act did apply, mechanisms for fair housing enforcement were extraordinarily weak. HUD had no enforcement powers when fair housing violations were identified. Instead, the agency filled a conciliation role. In extreme cases of discrimination, HUD could notify the U.S. Department of Justice (DOJ) about suspected violations. Typically, the DOJ would take action on a small number of highly egregious instances of housing discrimination. Enforcement was further hampered since individuals only had 180 days to file a lawsuit related to fair housing and they were responsible for all court costs and attorneys' fees (unless a court waived them due to economic hardship). In addition, punitive damages were capped at $1000.

It took two decades for significant reforms in fair housing legislation to occur. In 1988, several amendments to the 1968 Act were adopted. The amendments expanded fair housing protections to those facing housing discrimination based on disability and family status (e.g., pregnant women and households with children under the age of 18). The amendments empowered HUD to hold administrative hearings and impose fines and damages for violations. HUD was required to address complaints within four months, and the time limit for individuals to file civil suits was extended from 180 days to two years. In addition, caps on damages were significantly increased. The 1988 amendments augmented other programs designed to address short-comings in fair housing enforcement. These included the fair housing assistance program (FHAP) which was created in 1979 and the fair housing initiatives program (FHIP) which was created in 1986.

Under the FHAP program, grants are awarded annually on a non-competitive basis to state and local fair housing agencies. FHAP agencies are referred complaints from two sources, HUD and other organizations charged with the task of investigating instances of housing discrimination in their jurisdiction. Based on those investigations, complaints referred to FHAP agencies can be dismissed, conciliated/settled, or referred to the DOJ or the courts for litigation. In principle, the FHAP is designed to decentralize the process of investigating and enforcing fair housing policy. In practice, the program has suffered from chronic underfunding, uneven administration across states and agencies, and inconsistent reporting of case outcomes (U.S. General Accounting Office 2004).

Under the FHIP program, grants are awarded to nonprofit housing organizations on a competitive basis. FHIP Organizations undertake activities to enhance compliance with fair housing law. These activities include education, monitoring, routing complaints to other agencies for action, and fair housing compliance programs. The FHIP is designed to complement and support investigative activities of HUD, FHAP agencies, and the DOJ. FHIP organizations educate the public about fair housing law, screen complaints at the local level, attempt to foster voluntary compliance, and encourage informal resolutions of fair housing violations. In 2009, FHIP organizations processed 66% of all fair housing complaints (National Fair Housing Alliance 2010). The FHIP also represents an additional layer of devolution in fair housing policy. The program contracts out key elements of policy implementation to nonprofit organizations. The incremental expansion of the FHIP has formalized the nonprofitization of fair housing policy. Like the FHAP, the FHIP has suffered from chronic underfunding, uneven administration across states and agencies, and inconsistent reporting of case outcomes.

Since the 1988 amendments, federal fair housing policy has remained relatively static. It has been over 20 years since fair housing protections were extended to additional groups or classes. Under current federal law, there is still no fair housing protection based on marital status, sources of income, sexual orientation, gender identification, political affiliation, Housing Choice Voucher (HCV) status, or other characteristics. The 1968 Act (as amended) also remains focused on individual complaints and lacks remedies for structural forms of discrimination. Moreover, rental properties with four or fewer units and home sales where real estate agents are not used remain exempt from the 1968 Act (as amended).

Despite an unequivocal federal mandate to *affirmatively* further fair housing, many states and localities consistently fall short of this legal obligation. The outcome of acute underfunding and the inconsistent implementation of fair housing policy are clear when one considers that, of the estimated four million instances of housing discrimination annually, the combined caseload of all agencies and organizations across the country involved a record high of 30,758 complaints in 2008 (National Fair Housing Alliance 2010). That was only 0.76% of the estimated instances of discrimination. Of those complaints, approximately 1/3 resulted in some form of settlement or conciliation. In essence, 0.76% of all instances of discrimination result in a complaint being filed with a FHAP agency, a FHIP organization, or the DOJ, and only 1/3 of those complaints result in a legal remedy.

## The Parameters of Affordable Housing Finance and Land Use Policy

Two areas of policy epitomize the degree to which privatism and neoliberal ideology have imprinted upon affordable housing finance and land use policies. The first is the low-income housing tax credit program (LIHTC) and the second involves the limited application of inclusionary zoning. The LIHTC program epitomizes the wedding of policy devolution, nonprofitization, and privatism. The program, which was part of the Tax Reform Act of 1986, provided for the syndication of LIHTCs (Schwartz 2006). Through this process, tax credits are sold to private investors by the federal government at a discount. This means that investors pay less than the face value of the tax credits they receive. The proceeds from the discounted sales of tax credits are syndicated by intermediary organizations who also charge a fee for this service. After the syndication process is complete, the remaining funds are transferred through state governments to public and nonprofit sponsors of LIHTC projects. After discounting the price of LIHTCs and accounting for syndication fees, developers received approximately $0.80 for every dollar of tax credits allocated in 2009 (Schwartz 2010). The level of proceeds going to developers has fluctuated during the life of the program, ranging from $0.60 per dollar to

$0.99 per dollar.[1] Currently, the value of LIHTCs has been on a downward trajectory in response to lower demand from investors and a weakened U.S. housing market.

The program requires that housing units built with LIHTC remain rental properties occupied by low-income households for at least 15 years. The program also requires that 10% of each state's LIHTC allocation be set aside for projects with nonprofit sponsors. Since its inception, approximately $5 billion dollars have been authorized for the program annually. Today, the LIHTC program has become the largest single federal subsidy for affordable housing development. It also remains distinct since it is part of the federal tax code and administered by state governments rather than HUD (Jolin 2000, Orlebeke 2000).

Over the years, a body of research has emerged which examines and critiques the LIHTC program. Much of this research focuses on program outcomes related to: the supply of affordable housing, the geographic distribution of LIHTC projects, the impact of tax credits on overall project funding, and the degree to which LIHTC funding is used to target specific populations in need of affordable housing. A core criticism that has emerged in relation to the LIHTC program is that projects receiving tax credits tend to cluster in low-income, racially concentrated areas (Cummings and DiPasquale 1999, Muralidhara 2006, McClure 2008). Roisman (1998) and two subsequent studies by the Poverty & Race Research Action Council (2004, 2008) have indicated that this situation has been exasperated by a lack of mandates from the U.S. Department of Treasury and a lack of comprehensiveness in states' LIHTC Qualified Allocation Plans.

In addition to concerns about the geographic distribution of LIHTC projects, researchers have critiqued the financial stability of affordable housing funded by the program. Wallace (1998) and Deng (2005) question the cost-effectiveness of LIHTC projects in comparison to the use of market-based rent vouchers. They argue that affordable housing development is feasible in tight housing markets, but in other areas the use of rental vouchers is more cost-effective. McClure (1990, 2000)

---

[1] This represented a 20% decline in average developer proceeds from the LIHTC since 2006. Much of this decline has been attributed to reduced investor demand for LIHTCs since the recent financial crisis. Declining developer proceeds from the LIHTC program suggest a return to historic levels of approximately $0.60 per dollar that were common in the 1980s and early 1990s.

and Schwartz (2006) add that the LIHTC program by itself does not cover all the costs of affordable housing development. As a result, sponsors of projects using LIHTCs must find additional funding to leverage development. Schwartz and Melendez (2008) also point out that the long-term sustainability of LIHTC projects is further threatened by the lack of funding for unit maintenance and upgrading after tax credits expire.

Despite its emergence as the largest single federal subsidy for affordable housing development, the LIHTC is hampered by resource constraints, a lack of coordination, and disparate impacts on minorities and poor communities. In part, these outcomes can be attributed to the tendency of policies, based on the logic of privatism and neoliberalism, to prioritize subsidizing private markets over promoting social equity. By design, advocacy for expanded housing rights for minorities and the poor is trumped by policies wedded to privatism and neoliberal ideologies.

The LIHTC program also suffers from a lack of comprehensiveness and linkage to supportive land use policies. The ability to link land use policies to other aspects of affordable housing has been hampered by privatism and neoliberalism. These ideologies prioritize the protection of private property rights over equity concerns in society. As a result, any efforts to regulate land use in order to forward a social goal are thwarted. In the U.S., ardent support for privatism and neoliberalism is clearly articulated in the level of resistance to inclusionary zoning policies. Typically, such policies require that new housing subdivisions include set asides for affordable housing and link other concessions to promote fair housing goals. In most states and localities across the U.S., there are no provisions for inclusionary zoning. Despite efforts by fair and affordable housing advocates, the adoption of inclusionary zoning has been blocked by lobbying efforts of real estate developers and other private sector interests.

Faced with opposition from real estate developers and other private interests, only a small number of cities have managed to enact inclusionary zoning to ensure that fair and affordable housing is a component of new development projects. When placed in the context of U.S. housing markets on the whole, cities with inclusionary zoning ordinances are truly anomalies. In these rare instances, inclusionary zoning has been enacted after extended legal and political challenges. Often, the scope of inclusionary zoning provisions is relatively limited and provides developers and private interests with flexibility in how set asides for affordable housing are applied. For example Boston, MA and Denver, CO adopted inclusionary zoning in 2000 and 2002 respectively (Frug and Barron 2008). Boston's inclusionary zoning ordinance requires a 15% set aside for affordable housing in new developments. Denver's inclusionary zoning ordinance requires a 10% set aside. In these cities and others, inclusionary zoning is often accompanied by provisions for density bonuses and other incentives for developers.

There have also been a few instances where land use tools like inclusionary zoning have been used at the regional and state levels. One tool available to metropolitan areas are regional fair-share housing allocation plans. These plans create a regional framework for the development and distribution of affordable housing. They use mechanisms like inclusionary zoning, density bonuses, developer subsidies, and the development of regional housing trust funds to implement fair housing strategies. The viability of regional fair-share housing allocation plans hinges on the coordination of land use and affordable housing policy across municipalities at the regional level. New Jersey has one of the more aggressive stances toward the promotion of affordable housing (National Neighborhood Coalition 2001). In 1983, the State of New Jersey passed its Fair Housing Act and created the state's Council on Affordable Housing (COAH) to oversee its implementation. Under the New Jersey Fair Housing Act, municipalities with approved affordable housing plans became eligible for a variety of funding benefits. However, New Jersey's Fair Housing Act has faced challenges from local governments and the private sector since its adoption. Recently, efforts have been stepped up to rescind the law and devolve decision-making power related to inclusionary zoning (Augenstein 2010). As in the past, the interests of private developers and a preference for market-based subsidies have been juxtaposed against existing fair and affordable housing policies.

Municipalities and states that have adopted land use policies that complement efforts to promote fair and affordable housing have become lightening rods for proponents of privatism and neoliberalism. The prospect of becoming embattled in perpetual legal and political challenges over such policies serves as a deterrent to their broader adoption. In a climate dominated by ideologies driven by privatism and neoliberalism, U.S. affordable housing finance and land use policies remain highly circumscribed.

*The Parameters of Rental Assistance Programs*

The evolution of rental assistance programs in the U.S. epitomizes the institutionalization of privatism and neoliberal ideologies in public policy. The Housing Choice Voucher program (HCV) is the largest affordable housing program in the country (Schwartz 2006, 2010). Through the program, more than 2 million households receive rent vouchers on an annual basis.[2] By design, the HCV program is market-based. Qualified households receive a rent voucher that can be applied to available housing units on the private market. It operates under the assumption that there is an ample supply of rental property available on the private market, but average rents exceed low-income house-holds' ability to pay. Vouchers are designed to bridge the gap between what renters can afford to pay and the rents landlords demand. Instead of building affordable units in the public sector, the policy is designed to subsidize private landlords.

The HCV program originated as part of the Housing and Community Development Act of 1974. At its inception, the HCV program was called the Section 8 Certificate program. It provided local housing authorities with vouchers to distribute within their jurisdictional boundaries. HUD distributed vouchers to housing authorities on a formula bases. Formulas were based on population, poverty rates, housing costs, and other local conditions. Households receiving Section 8 certificates were only allowed to use them to subsidize rents within the issuing housing authority's boundaries. This restriction on the use of Section 8 certificates blocked low-income renters from pursuing housing opportunities across the metropolitan areas where they were located. Instead of dispersing, these households tended to cluster in low rent areas located within a housing authority's boundaries (Schwartz 2010).

---

[2] According to Schwartz (2010), the number of HCV holders eclipsed the number of available public housing units in the U.S. in the early 1990s. In 1994, there were approximately 1.4 million public housing units. The inventory of public housing began to decline rapidly with the implementation of the HOPE VI program. By 2008, it had dropped to approximately 1.1 million units. The implementation of HOPE VI also resulted in the transition of over 260,000 former public housing tenants to the HVC program. These trends corresponded with the more general expansion of the HCV program, which grew from approximately 1.4 million vouchers in 1994 to over 2 million in 2009.

In an effort to address the tendency for certificates to concentrate in poor neighborhoods, Congress created the Section 8 voucher program in 1983. The Section 8 voucher program began as a demonstration program and was incrementally expanded. Its main distinction from the earlier Section 8 certificate program was that it allowed vouchers to be used anywhere in a metropolitan area, rather than restricting their use to a housing authority's boundaries. Despite this change in policy, Section 8 certificate and voucher holders continued to concentrate in poor neighborhoods, and minority households were more likely to remain segregated in low-income areas (Pendall 2000). The Section 8 certificate and voucher programs were merged as part of the Quality Housing and Work Responsibility Act of 1998. The programs were renamed the HCV program and all vouchers became portable when the merger was implemented in 1999. However, concerns about the concentration of households in low-income communities remain salient.

The HCV program is also hindered by a variety of other structural weaknesses in its design and implementation. The most daunting weakness of the program is that it is acutely underfunded. The demand for vouchers far exceeds the supply of vouchers in the current system. Local housing authorities routinely maintain long waiting lists where households must wait several years to receive rental assistance (DiPasquale et al. 2003). The underfunding of the HCV program has also limited the availability of staff to inspect rental properties, provide mobility counseling, and other supportive services (Shlay 1993, Varady and Walker 2001). This has resulted in delays in the identification of housing and limits on the geographic area where renters can realistically search for housing. Although the current program allows renters to search for housing across the metropolitan areas where they are located, time limits on the use of vouchers, limited information about available rental units, work commitments, family considerations, and other obligations can narrow housing options. In many respects, households lucky enough to receive HCVs are still constrained in their housing choices and continue to concentrate in low-income neighborhoods.

In large part, the market-based orientation of the HCV program is to blame for the lack of attention paid to the needs of low-income renters. By design, the program primarily serves as a subsidy for private landlords. A secondary goal of the HCV program is its role as a mobility program for low-income households. Landlords are not mandated to accept HCVs, participation in the program is voluntary. However, many landlords do participate in the program because it guarantees that rents will be paid on time. The main obligation for landlords participating in the program is to ensure their properties pass inspection and are maintained at minimum occupancy standards. While the HCV program plays an important role in propping up inner-city rental markets, it has a limited impact on promoting geographic and socioeconomic mobility for the poor. In fact, these two goals are somewhat contradictory. The emphasis on subsidizing markets, cornerstones of privatism and neoliberalism, undercuts the equity and social justice goals of the program.

*The Parameters of Homeownership*

In the contemporary period, the thrust of U.S. housing policy has been on subsidizing private homeownership. This policy was institutionalized following the Great Depression and expanded after the Second World War. Two key elements of homeownership policy came out of the New Deal. They involved the creation of the Federal Home Owners' Loan Corporation (FHOLC) and the Federal Housing Administration (FHA). These two agencies created an environment where future housing policies would be guided by privatism and neoliberal ideologies. In essence, the federal government adopted a policy based on private mortgages which were guaranteed by public agencies, and complementary property appraisal and land use policies. Following the New Deal, additional policies were adopted to expand homeownership. They included a variety of tax incentives and deductions for interest paid on mortgages, as well as expanded subsidies for the development of single family homes.

Historically, access to homeownership has been unequal. Minorities and low-income groups have been systematically denied credit and housing opportunities (Lipsitz 1995). As a result, whites have had greater access to housing opportunities in the suburbs and the economic benefits of homeownership. After decades of discrimination, minorities began to make inroads (Squires 1992). The Home Mortgage Disclosure Act of 1975 (HMDA) required financial institutions to report on their lending patterns by race, income, and geographic location. The Community Reinvestment Act of 1977 (CRA) allowed communities to use HMDA data to challenge bank mergers. Those challenges resulted in CRA agreements to correct for existing discrimination in community lending and related financial activities. Despite these gains, a substantial gap remained between white and minority homeownership rates. In 2007, homeownership reached 75.2% for white households, while it peaked at 47.8% for black households (Landis and McClure 2010). Between 1980 and 2007, that represented an 8.2% increase in homeownership rates for whites and a 5.9% increase for blacks. Although minorities have made gains in homeownership since the 1980s, they still lag behind whites.

There is also mounting evidence that recent growth in homeownership rates has been stimulated by the deregulation of financial markets and the proliferation of subprime lending in low-income segments of housing markets (Shlay 2006). Minority borrowers have comprised a disproportionate component of this segment of the homeownership market, and subsequently these borrowers have faced high rates of foreclosures during the current financial crisis. Ironically, when the financial crisis hit, and low-income homeowners faced foreclosure, many remained supportive of privatism and neoliberal homeownership policies (Saegert et al. 2009). Privatism and neoliberal ideologies remain driving principles in U.S. housing policy. When these underlying principles prove to be flawed, society tends to attribute their failings to individual shortcomings. Calls for institutional reform are often rebuffed with calls for individual sacrifice and personal responsibility.

Despite these tendencies, there is a need for reforms to housing policy to be guided by systematic analysis of institutional barriers to fair and affordable housing. One of the key issues to address is the imbalance between subsidizing markets and promoting social justice. The emphasis on market-based approaches to addressing housing inequality has made fair housing the ugly stepchild of U.S. housing policy. This is evidenced by the dearth of funding for programs designed to address housing discrimination and the lack of fair housing enforcement. Similarly, the development and provision of low-income housing had been subsumed in the politics of privatism and neoliberalism. The LIHTC program subsidizes affordable housing development through tax expenditures. In the short term, corporations benefit from LIHTCs and communities add affordable rental properties to their inventories of housing. In the long term, many LIHTC units remain concentrated in poor neighborhoods and access to resources for their maintenance and upkeep is uncertain. The HCV program faces a comparable dilemma. Landlords benefit from the predictability of rental payments,

while renters remain concentrated in poor neighborhoods with limited access to vouchers and mobility counseling. While these programs constitute the bulk of fair and affordable housing activities in
the U.S., the thrust of housing policy remains focused on promoting
homeownership. In 2008, over 79% of all federal expenditures for
housing were used to subsidize and promote homeownership, while
the remainder of expenditures focused on the needs of low-income
households and renters (Landis and McClure 2010).[3]

*Outline of the Book*

This edited book adds to our understanding of the trends, outcomes
and future directions of fair and affordable housing policy. It is divided
into four parts examining issues of interest to housing scholars and
practitioners. The sections include discussions of fair housing policy,
affordable housing finance and land use, rent vouchers, and homeownership policy. Part one of the book examines fair housing policy and
perception of its implementation. The first chapter, by Eric Wilk,
Charles Lamb, and Nicholas Seabrook, examines FHAP outcomes over
a 25 year period. They find that FHAP enforcement has gone through
a process of devolution to states and localities. Although enforcement
has increased over time, rates of change have fluctuated with the political climate, and FHAP funding has remained inadequate to address all
instances of housing discrimination. The second chapter, by Nicholas
Seabrook, Charles Lamb and Eric Wilk, discusses how the federal
courts have interpreted fair housing policy. They find that the Supreme
Court has assumed a relatively limited role with respect to fair housing
cases. For the most part, the Court has been inactive in fair housing
cases and this trend is expected to continue, given the Courts current
composition and ideological leanings. However, the lower courts have
incrementally expanded fair housing rights, particularly in the
Northeast and Midwest. This suggests that a critical mass of fair housing precedents is accumulating in case law. The third chapter, by Robert
Silverman, examines attitudes about fair housing. Specifically, this
chapter focuses on black real estate professionals' perceptions of fair

---

[3] Sixty-seven percent of total expenditure included mortgage interest deductions
and other tax expenditures designed to subsidize homeownership.

housing policy. Although these individuals perceived a gradual decline in discrimination, specific barriers persisted in housing markets. A need for increased fair housing education and minority employment in the real estate industry is identified. In addition, the poor and disabled are perceived as groups facing the most discrimination. This is particularly true for those in the rental market.

Part two of the book examines finance and land use issues that impact affordable housing development. The first chapter, by Rosie Tighe, provides an overview of affordable housing policy in the U.S., as well as a discussion of land use issues that promote and impede efforts to enhance housing options for the poor. Her chapter also examines public opposition to fair housing and the obligation of professional planners to mitigate it. The second chapter, by Alex Schwartz, assesses the strengths and weaknesses of the LIHTC program over the last quarter century. His analysis describes how the program has emerged as the largest subsidy for affordable rental housing development in the U.S.. Yet, he also cautions readers about the program's vulnerability due to weakening housing markets and the ensuing financial crisis that emerged in recent years. The third chapter, by Dennis Keating, reviews the state of inclusionary housing policy. He reviews experiments in the U.S. with HUD's Move to Opportunity program (MTO), as well as state and local inclusionary zoning laws. The chapter also explores the implications of framing inclusionary housing policy as an issue linked to affordability in the suburbs, rather than an issue of racial discrimination.

Part three of the book turns to the use of rent vouchers as a tool to address concentrated poverty in inner-city neighborhoods. The first chapter, by David Varady, examines the ability of rent voucher programs to promote poverty deconcentration and family self-sufficiency. He finds evidence that voucher recipients cluster spatially and that this promotes social decline in neighborhoods already vulnerable to change. The second chapter, by Kelly Patterson, analyzes the degree to which HCVs are spatially concentrated in Buffalo, NY. This is a critical case analysis since the metropolitan area surrounding Buffalo has an ample supply of affordable rental units and voucher recipients have access to other resources such as mobility counseling. Despite the characteristics of Buffalo's rental market, Patterson finds that voucher recipients remain concentrated in inner-city neighborhoods. These outcomes are more acute for black voucher holders than whites. The third chapter, by Kirk McClure, proposes a new direction in affordable housing policy. This proposal entails making funds for HCVs and LIHTCs fungible. He argues that some communities would benefit from a merger of the two programs and the ability to intermingle their funds. In essence, McClure argues for a more holistic approach to affordable housing policy which considers the income constraints of renters and development needs in concert.

Part four of the book serves to remind readers of the backdrop for fair and affordable housing policy in the U.S.. It explores the segment of affordable housing policy that focuses on the promotion of universal homeownership. The first chapter, by Henry Taylor, examines the development of housing markets in the U.S. and the commoditization of housing during the early 20<sup>th</sup> century. He argues that innovations in housing finance and land use have been driven by real estate developers, financial institutions, and professional planners. He concludes that the commoditization of housing and the promotion of private homeownership resulted in the establishment of contemporary residential segregation patterns, and that reform across the institutions that spawned the contemporary milieu is necessary to address the crisis of housing affordability. The second chapter, by Gregory Squires, discusses the nexus between racial segregation and subprime lending. He explains how subprime lending has had an acute impact on a specific housing submarket in the U.S., the segment composed of low-income and minority homeowners. Several options for reforming affordable housing finance and development are identified. An emphasis is placed on reforms designed to stabilize minority homeownership and address racial segregation. The third chapter is by Anna Santiago, George Galster, Cristina Tucker, Angela Kaiser, and Ana Santiago-San Roman. These authors examine homeowners' experiences with the Denver Housing Authority's Homeownership program (HOP). The HOP program provided minority and first-time homebuyers with wrap-around services, including pre-purchase counseling and homeownership training. Most of the participants in the HOP program were rental voucher recipients transitioning to homeownership. Overall, they found that Latino and black homeowners in the HOP program avoided many of the pitfalls associated with minority homeownership, such as: purchasing of homes in declining neighborhoods, depreciating property values, higher than average mortgage default rates, victimization by predatory lenders, and difficulty in maintaining properties. Yet, even with the benefits of participation in the HOP program, Latino and black homebuyers indicated that the transition from subsidized tenant to homeowner was challenging. The authors stress the need for additional post-purchase follow-up, training in home maintenance techniques, and ongoing financial counseling in order to ensure that the benefits of homeownership are sustainable for minority and low-income purchasers.

*References*

Anderson, Martin. 1964. *The Federal Bulldozer: A Critical Analysis of Urban Renewal.* Cambridge, MA: MIT Press.
Augenstein, Seth. 2010. "N.J. Affordable Housing Overhaul Advances." *New Jersey Hearld Online* 10 June: < http://www.njherald.com/story/news/11scrapcoah>.
Bockmeyer, Janice L. 2003. "Devolution and the Transformation of Community Housing Activism." *The Social Science Journal* 40:175–188.
Cummings, Jean L. amd Denise D. DiPasquale. 1999. "The Low-Income Housing Tax Credit: An Analysis of the First Ten Years." *Housing Policy Debate* 10(2): 251–307.
Deng, Lan. 2005. "The Cost-Effectiveness of the Low-Income Housing Tax Credit Relative to Vouchers: Evidence from Six Metropolitan Areas." *Housing Policy Debate* 16(3/4): 469–511.
DiPasquale, Denise, Dennis Fricke and Daniel Garcia-Diaz. 2003. "Comparing the Costs of Federal Housing Assistance Programs." *Economic Policy Review* 9(2): 147–166.
Frug, Gerald E. and David J. Barron. 2008. *City Bound: How States Stifle Urban Innovation.* Ithaca, NY: Cornell University Press.
Hayes, R Allen. 1995. *The Federal Government and Urban Housing: Ideology and Change in Public Policy.* Albany, NY: State University of New York Press.
Jolin, Marc. 2000. "Good Cause Eviction and the Low-Income Housing Tax Credit." *The University of Chicago Law Review* 67(2): 521–546.
Landis, John D. and Kirk McClure. 2010. "Rethinking Federal Housing Policy." *Journal of the American Planning Association* 76(3): 319–348.
Lipsitz, George. 1995. "The Possessive Investment in Whiteness: Racialized Social Democracy and the 'White' Problem in American Studies." *American Quarterly* 47(3): 369–387.
McClure, Kirk. 1990. "Low and Moderate Income Housing Tax Credits." *Journal of the American Planning Association* 56(3): 363–369.
McClure, Kirk. 2000. "The Low-Income Housing Tax Credit as an Aid to Housing Finance: How Well Has It Worked?" *Housing Policy Debate* 11(1): 91–114.
McClure, Kirk. 2008. "Deconcentrating Poverty with Housing Programs." *Journal of the American Planning Association* 74(1): 90–99.
Muralidhara, Shilesh. 2006. "Deficiencies in the Low-Income Housing Tax Credit in Targeting the Lowest-Income Households and in Promoting Concentrated Poverty and Segregation." *Law and Inequality* 24: 353–374.
National Fair Housing Alliance. 2010. *Fair Housing Enforcement: Time for a Change.* Washington, DC: National Fair Housing Alliance.
National Neighborhood Coalition. 2001. *Affordable Housing and Smart Growth: Making the Connection.* Washington, DC: National Neighborhood Coalition.
Orlebeke, Charles J. 2000. "The Evolution of Low-Income Housing Policy, 1949 to 1999." *Housing Policy Debate* 11(2): 489–520.
Pendall, Rolf. 2000. "Why Voucher and Certificate Users Live in Distressed Neighborhoods." *Housing Policy Debate* 11(4): 881–910.
Poverty & Race Research Action Council. 2004. *Civil Rights Mandates in the Low-Income Housing Tax Credit (LIHTC) Program.* Washington, DC: PRRAC.

Poverty & Race Research Action Council. 2008. *Building Opportunity: Civil Rights Best Practices in the Low-Income Housing Tax Credit Program*. Washington, DC: PRRAC.

Purcell, Mark. 2008. *Recapturing Democracy: Neoliberalization and the Struggle for Alternative Urban Futures*. New York, NY: Routledge.

Roisman, Florence Wagmen. 1998. "Mandates unsatisfied: The Low-Income Housing Tax Credit Program and the Civil Rights Laws." *University of Miami Law Review* 52: 1011–1050.

Saegert, Susan, Desiree Fields and Kimberly Libman. 2009. "Deflating the Dream: Radical Risk and the Neoliberalization of Homeownership." *Journal of Urban Affairs* 31(3): 297–317.

Schwartz, Alex F. 2006. *Housing Policy in the United States: An Introduction*. New York: Routledge.

Schwartz, Alex F. 2010. *Housing Policy in the United States: An Introduction, Second Edition*. New York: Routledge.

Schwartz, Alex and Edwin Melendez. 2008. "After year 15: Challenges to the Preservation of Housing Financed with Low-Income Housing Tax Credits." *Housing Policy Debate* 19(2): 261–294.

Shlay, Anne B. 1993. "Family Self-Sufficiency and Housing." *Housing Policy Debate* 4(3): 457–496.

Shlay, Anne B. 2006. "Low-Income Homeownership: American Dream or Delusion?" *Urban Studies* 43(3): 511–531.

Squires, Gregory, ed. 1992. *From Redlining to Reinvestment: Community Responses to Urban Disinvestment*. Philadelphia, PA: Temple University Press.

Swanstrom, Todd. 1999. "The Nonprofitization of United States Housing Policy: Dilemmas of Community Development." *Community Development Journal* 34: 28–37.

Thibault, Robert E. 2007. "Between Survival and Revolution: Another Community Development System is Possible." *Antipode* 39(5) 874–895.

U.S. General Accounting Office. 2004. *Fair Housing: Opportunities to Improve HUD's Oversight and Management of the Enforcement Process*. Washington, DC: US General Accounting Office.

Varady, David and Carole Walker. 2001. "Voucher Recipient Achievement of Improved Housing Conditions in the US: Do Moving Distance and Relocation Services Matter?" *Urban Studies* 38(8): 1273–1304.

Wallace, James E. 1998. "Evaluating the Low-Income Housing Tax Credit." *New Directions for Evaluation* 79: 43–62.

Yinger, John. 1999. "Sustaining the Fair Housing Act." *Cityscape: A Journal of Policy, Development and Research* 4(3): 93–106.

PART ONE

FAIR HOUSING, POLICY, AND PERCEPTIONS

# INTERGOVERNMENTAL ENFORCEMENT OF THE FAIR HOUSING ACT: THE FAIR HOUSING ASSISTANCE PROGRAM*

Eric M. Wilk, Charles M. Lamb, and Nicholas R. Seabrook

## Introduction

The United States has made progress in combating housing discrimination since the 1970s and 1980s (Turner et al. 2002, Turner et al. 1991, Wienk et al. 1979, Yinger 1995). However, effective and efficient enforcement of the nation's fair housing laws is imperative if additional progress is to be forthcoming. This chapter focuses on one major program in the fair housing enforcement effort—HUD's Fair Housing Assistance Program (FHAP)—with two specific objectives in mind. First, we provide an overview of the origins and evolution of the FHAP program since its inception in 1979. Second, relying on large, unique data sets obtained from HUD (U.S. Department of Housing and Urban Development 1991a, 2005), we explore the administrative implementation of the Fair Housing Acts of 1968 and 1988 (Title VIII) between 1980 and 2004 by comparing HUD's enforcement performance to that of state and local FHAP agencies.

We find that the number of state and local civil rights agencies participating in the FHAP program grew rapidly during the Reagan administration and continued to grow through George W. Bush's first term in the White House. Then, based on the HUD data sets, we show that Title VIII complaints processed by FHAP agencies increased markedly early in the Reagan administration, conciliations and closures by HUD and FHAP agencies fluctuated over time, and total monetary relief grew appreciably in the 1990s during the Clinton presidency. We conclude that, overall, the FHAP program is a valuable component in the federal fair housing enforcement effort. Yet the volume of Title VIII complaints processed, conciliated, and closed

* We thank the Baldy Center for Law and Social Policy, University at Buffalo, SUNY, for supporting this research and Donald B. Rosenthal for his valuable comments.

annually by HUD and FHAP agencies represent just a fraction of the instances of housing discrimination believed to occur each year.[1] Many instances of housing discrimination may not be reported, and even valid claims of discrimination that reach federal and state civil rights agencies or the courts do not necessarily result in a favorable outcome for complainants. Thus, while FHAP agencies have generally succeeded in providing needed enforcement assistance to HUD over the past three decades, a much broader, more concerted effort is essential if government is to eliminate or substantially reduce housing discrimination in America (Briggs 2005, Farley and Frey 1994, Lamb 2005, Massey and Denton 1993).

### Basic Elements of Title VIII Enforcement

Since the passage of the Fair Housing Act of 1968, as amended in 1988, HUD has been the lead agency in the federal fair housing enforcement effort (U.S. Commission on Civil Rights 1974, 1979, 1994). Under Title VIII, other federal agencies are responsible for promoting equal housing opportunity in their programs, where possible, including the Departments of Agriculture, Defense, and Veterans Affairs, the Federal Reserve Board, the Federal Deposit Insurance Corporation, and the Federal Home Loan Bank Board. More importantly, the Department of Justice (DOJ) plays the critical role of filing lawsuits in cases where there is reasonable cause to believe that Title VIII has been violated. Yet the Fair Housing Act designates HUD as the lead agency in Title VIII enforcement, indicating that it has special enforcement and coordination responsibilities (Kushner 1995, Schwemm 2009). The 1988 Fair Housing Amendments Act later expanded this role, vesting in HUD new powers to more effectively enforce federal anti-discrimination statutes in the housing arena.

HUD's complaint system has always been the centerpiece of its fair housing enforcement process (e.g., U.S. Department of Housing and Urban Development 1989, 1999, 2009). Specifically, HUD has carried out national housing discrimination policy since the late 1960s by investigating, conciliating, and closing administrative complaints filed under Title VIII by those who claim they are victims

---

[1] Compare our findings to the estimates of housing discrimination in Turner et al. 2002.

of discrimination.[2] After HUD's Office of Fair Housing and Equal Opportunity (FHEO) decides if it has jurisdiction to process a complaint, investigators conduct interviews and review relevant documents to determine whether there is reasonable cause to think that Title VIII has been violated or is about to be violated. If reasonable cause is found, HUD then attempts to work with complainants and respondents to resolve the dispute through conciliation. Conciliation occurs when a complaint is resolved by an agreement between a complainant and a respondent, or when a complaint is withdrawn. Agreements growing out of conciliation may include, among other things, monetary relief or the guarantee of a housing unit. Closure occurs with a successful conciliation attempt or when a Title VIII dispute is resolved in an appropriate judicial forum (U.S. Department of Housing and Urban Development 1996, 1999, U.S. General Accounting Office 2004).

However, problems have always plagued Title VIII enforcement (U.S. Commission on Civil Rights 1974, 1979, 1992, 1994), particularly in the years between the passage of the 1968 Fair Housing Act and its 1988 amendments. Perhaps the most serious problem over time has been that HUD's enforcement power was limited to the use of "informal methods of conference, conciliation, and persuasion." This enforcement approach, which grew out of political compromises struck during the passage of Title VIII, weakened federal fair housing enforcement from the outset (Graham 1990, 2000). It meant that HUD's enforcement power under the Fair Housing Act of 1968 depended almost entirely on the complaint process and attempts to conciliate disputes. If either party refused to conciliate, HUD could take no meaningful action because its enforcement powers were not backed up with any credible form of legal coercion. All the agency could do was to tell the complainant that he or she had the right to file a private lawsuit. Unlike the Equal Employment Opportunity Commission, for example, HUD could not file a lawsuit in federal court in instances where a legal violation seemed even apparent or blatant. Nor could HUD request that a court issue an injunction or restraining order to halt discrimination temporarily. Although the agency could refer cases of a pattern or

---

[2] HUD's process of investigating, conciliating, and closing Title VIII complaints is discussed in some detail in various agency publications. See, e.g., U.S. Department of Housing and Urban Development (2006:27–28; 2007:53–55; 2008:55). See also Figure 1.

practice of discrimination to the DOJ for a possible lawsuit, the Justice Department could decide not to pursue the matter, which was often the case (Schwemm 1989, 2009).[3] Alternatively, persons who felt they had experienced housing discrimination could file a private suit in federal court, but that procedure was time consuming and costly. HUD has therefore considered its complaint process to be "the most important strategy" for enforcing equal housing opportunity (U.S. Department of Housing and Urban Development 1980:21)—even though acknowledging that "all too often, this process did not work" (U.S. Department of Housing and Urban Development 1989:75).[4]

Title VIII enforcement changed significantly with the passage of the Fair Housing Amendments Act of 1988 (Kushner 1995, Schwemm 2009). That law gives HUD two options if conciliation fails. First, as before, HUD may refer a case to the DOJ if it has reasonable cause to believe that Title VIII has been violated. But under the 1988 law, the DOJ is authorized to sue in cases involving not only a pattern or practice of discrimination but, also, cases of 'general public importance,' cases dealing with exclusionary zoning, or in conciliated cases where HUD advises the DOJ that a respondent has violated a conciliation agreement. Second, HUD may instead refer the case to its own administrative law judges (ALJs). ALJs hear cases and reach decisions separate and apart from HUD's investigations into Title VIII complaints. When an ALJ finds a violation of Title VIII, remedies may include actual damages, injunctive relief, and attorney's fees (Seabrook and Lamb 2009). Monetary relief in Title VIII cases has increased over the years, as we shall see, especially during the second term of the Clinton administration. Major elements of the fair housing enforcement process at HUD are shown in Figure 1.

Despite the additional enforcement options set out in the 1988 Amendments Act, the complaint procedure remains the backbone of Title VIII enforcement (e.g., U.S. Department of Housing and Urban Development 2007, 2008, 2009). A key component of this procedure

---

[3] The Fair Housing Acts of 1968 and 1988 do not define what constitutes a pattern or practice of discrimination, but Title VIII complaints may be filed with federal, state, and local enforcement agencies alleging that discriminatory acts are part of a regular practice, instead of being sporadic or isolated.

[4] See U.S. Commission on Civil Rights (1974, 1979, 1992, 1994) for recommendations on how HUD could potentially go beyond its traditional reliance on complaints to enforce Title VIII more aggressively.

Intake: HUD staff ensures appropriate information is provided and that the inquiry falls under HUD's fair housing jurisdiction.

Discrimination alleged:

Aggrieved person believes discrimination occurred, knows of rules/prohibitions against it, knows how to file an inquiry, and does so.

(At any time during HUD's process, until the first day of an ALJ hearing, aggrieved person can file a civil action in federal court directly.)

Discrimination inquiry directed to...

20 days

**FHEO**

FHEO is not provided appropriate information to establish jurisdiction ⟶ **Process ends**

FHEO staff obtains appropriate information and establishes jurisdiction. FHEO will generally refer to FHAP if state/local law is substantially the same as the Fair Housing Act. For illustration, this figure shows HUD's basic process. FHAP agencies follow a similar process.

Investigation: Investigators determine whether reasonable cause exists to believe that a discriminatory housing practice has occurred, or is about to occur.

**HUD**

Administrative Closure (i.e. HUD loses contact with complainant, complainant does not cooperate, HUD is unable to locate the respondent, complainant withdraws complaint without resolution, or a trial begins in a private civil action brought by the complainant in a state or federal court.) ⟶ **Process ends**

Conciliation (FHEO is required to work with complainant and respondent to conciliate complaints to the extent feasible. HUD must approve and sign these agreements, reviewing them for protection of the public's interest, and may enforce compliance with any continuing obligations under such an agreement.) ⟶ **Process ends**

Withdrawal or Settlement (Parties may, independent of FHEO, agree to withdraw complaint.) ⟶ **Process ends**

100 days

No-cause determination (Hub director dismisses complaint after obtaining OGC concurrence.) ⟶ **Process ends**

Investigation Complete

Cause determination (With the concurrence of the Regional Counsel, FHEO will issue a determination of reasonable cause. The Regional Counsel will then issue a charge of discrimination, and file the charge with the Office of ALJs and notify the parties of the filing of the charge.)

Adjunction: For cause cases, independent fact finder determines whether respondent violated the Act. These decisions can be appealed.

| **ALJ** | **Federal District Court** |
|---|---|
| 20 days — Complainant or respondent can elect to have matter heard by federal district court, or | Federal civil action |
| 60 days — No determination of discrimination – charge dismissed. ⟶ **Process ends** | No determination of discrimination – charge dismissed. ⟶ **Process ends** |
| Discrimination determined – actual damages, injunctive or equitable relief, civil penalty. **Process ends** | Discrimination determined – actual and punitive damages can be awarded. **Process ends** |
| 120 days — ALJ hearings (Federal rules of evidence, parties can be represented by counsel, can call witnesses. | |

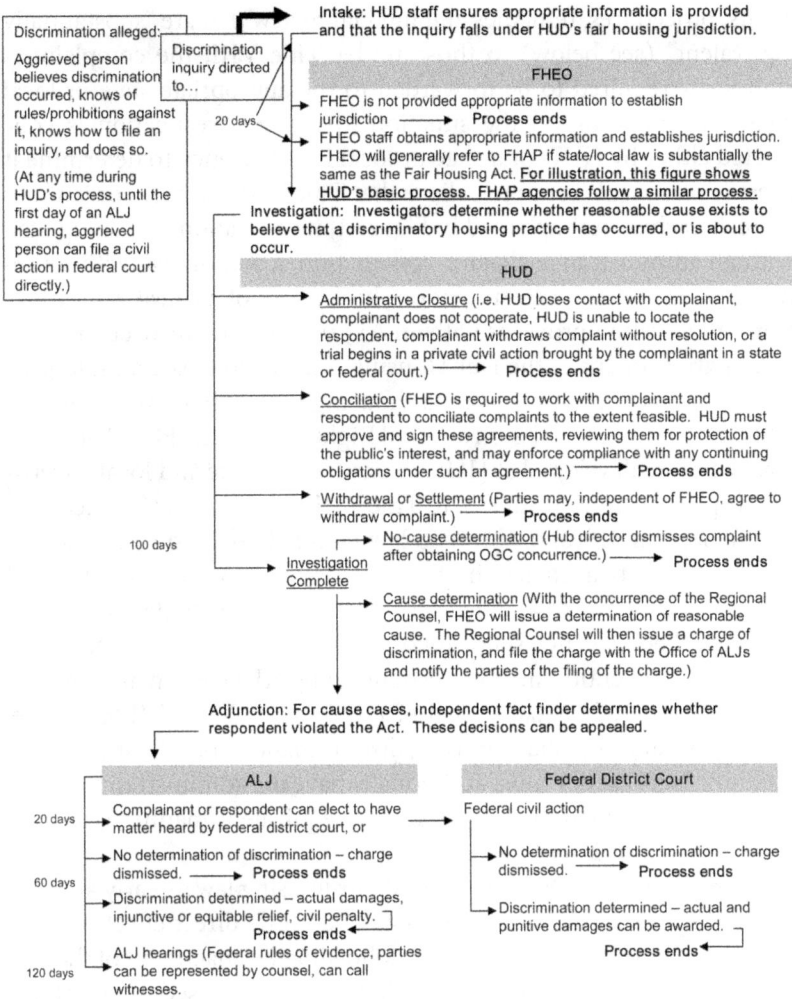

Figure 1. HUD's Fair Housing Enforcement Process
*Source:* Derived from U.S. General Accounting Office 2004–2010.

has been the involvement of state and local civil rights agencies in the enforcement of Title VIII through the FHAP program.

### FHAP's Origins and Evolution

Title VIII complaints are often processed in HUD's regional FHEO offices, but if a state or local housing discrimination law provides rights, procedures, remedies and judicial review that are "substantially equivalent" (see below) to those under Title VIII, the complaint is statutorily required to be forwarded to the appropriate state or local agency. Depending on the situation, then, an investigation is conducted either by HUD or a state or local FHAP agency to determine if there is reasonable cause to believe that Title VIII has been, or is about to be, breached. As explained in Figure 1, investigations are completed with an administrative closure, conciliation, a withdrawal with settlement, or a no-cause determination. In the case of a cause determination, adjudication proceeds with an ALJ or in federal district court.

Congress' intent in the Fair Housing Act was to create an intergovernmental partnership to combat housing discrimination (Lamb and Wilk 2010, U.S. Commission on Civil Rights 1992). The FHAP program was therefore developed at HUD to ensure that state and local governments played a significant role in Title VIII enforcement (Wallace et al. 1985). Section 810(c) of the 1968 law directed HUD to give state and local civil rights agencies the first opportunity to process Title VIII complaints if they had attained substantial equivalency status. Gaining substantial equivalency status involved two major requirements. First, a state or local entity must be recognized by HUD as having the legal authority generally equal to that of HUD under Title VIII to receive, investigate, and conciliate housing discrimination complaints. Second, a state or local agency must additionally have the administrative capacity to enforce its laws in a substantially equivalent manner (Kushner 1995, Schwemm 2009).

Despite being written into federal fair housing law as early as 1968, the concept of substantial equivalency had little direct effect on Title VIII enforcement for over a decade following the enactment of the Fair Housing Act because no state or local entities passed substantially equivalent housing discrimination laws during that period (Wallace et al. 1985). Consequently, the FHAP program was not created as a budget-line program by Congress until 1979, the final year of the Carter administration, when state and local governments first joined the national fair housing enforcement effort. Therefore, HUD apparently handled every Title VIII complaint filed nationwide between 1969 and 1979. During these years, the U.S. Commission on Civil Rights (1974:349, 1979:234) recommended on two different occasions that Congress create a program like FHAP to provide financial assistance to state and local agencies to assist with fair housing enforcement, but FHAP funds were not appropriated until fiscal year 1980.

Although the FHAP program was first funded by Congress at the end of the Carter presidency, it was during the Reagan administration's New Federalism (Conlon 1998, Eisinger and Gormley 1988) that the program quickly grew (Lamb and Twombly 1993, Lamb and Wilk 2009). Thus, in 1980, only 27 states and 11 localities were eligible for FHAP funding (38 jurisdictions), but these numbers soared to 36 states and 76 localities (112 jurisdictions) by 1988, Reagan's final year in office. After the passage of the Fair Housing Amendments Act of 1988, however, state and local governments were required to enact progressive new laws creating administrative law judges and protecting families with children and persons with disabilities. It naturally took several years for states and localities to meet these demanding standards. Figure 2 therefore depicts an enormous decline in the number of certified FHAP agencies between 1988 and 1992.

During the Clinton presidency, FHAP agencies were increasingly recertified under the new legal standards, and the number of certified state and local civil rights agencies continued to climb during the Bush II and Obama administrations. Thus, by 2005, 89 percent of the American population lived within the jurisdiction of a FHAP agency (U.S. Department of Housing and Urban Development 2006:43), and FHAP agencies closed 75 percent of all Title VIII complaints by 2007 (U.S. Department of Housing and Urban Development 2008:49 and 54). As of 2009, 108 jurisdictions had substantially equivalent status—39 states and 69 localities. The only states not to meet these standards by 2009 were Alabama, Alaska, Idaho, Mississippi, Montana, Nevada, New Hampshire, New Mexico, South Dakota, Wisconsin, and Wyoming (U.S. Department of Housing and Urban Development 2009).[5]

---

[5] HUD has long maintained a two-phase approach for deciding whether to certify a state or local civil rights agency as being substantially equivalent. First, an interim certification is made by the Assistant Secretary for FHEO, based on whether a state or local law provides rights, procedures, remedies, and judicial review that "on its face" are substantially equivalent to those under Title VIII. State and local FHAP agencies may receive an interim certification for three years. Then, in the second phase, the Assistant Secretary decides whether interim agencies "in operation" provide substantially equivalent rights, procedures, remedies, and judicial review. If a state or local agency is certified in this second phase, that certification is effective for five years, during which it is periodically assessed. If those evaluations are positive, the agency then may be recertified for another five years. If not, certification may be suspended or withdrawn (Schwemm 2009, U.S. Department of Housing and Urban Development, "Substantial Equivalence Certification," 2007).

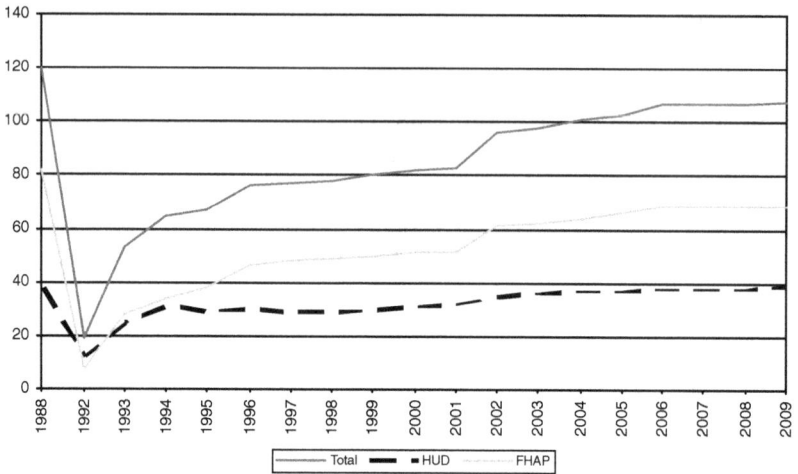

Figure 2. Number of Substantially Equivalent State and Local FHAP Agencies, 1988–2009

Source: Federal Register (various dates); Schwemm (various editions); U.S. Department of Housing and Urban Development (1990:11, 1991:4, 1992:3, 1996:23, 1997:A-3, 1999:4, 2005:43, 2006:147, 2007:41, 2008:45, 2009:31). Data for 1998 through 2000 are estimated given the number of each type of agency in 1997 and 2001.

The budget authority for the FHAP program has steadily mounted since 1980, as seen in Figure 3.[6] This growth in FHAP funding largely reflects the financial and technical assistance that HUD has provided to certified state and local agencies for processing Title VIII complaints. For example, the typical payment to state and local FHAP agencies for successfully processing individual Title VIII complaints increased from $500 in the mid-1980s to $2400 in recent years (Wallace et al. 1985, Office of Fair Housing and Equal Opportunity 2008).[7] Secondarily,

---

[6] A separate source of data on FHAP funding is found in various HUD reports. See, for example, U.S. Department of Housing and Urban Development (2006:19, 2007:15, 2008:17, 2009:45). Examining HUD reports over many years, however, suggests that the agency's definition of "FHAP funding" may have changed through time, casting some doubt on the accuracy of using that particular HUD data. We therefore rely on data published by the Office of Management and Budget (1976–2002) in Figure 3.

[7] Title VIII complaint-processing payments to FHAP agencies have critical consequences for intergovernmental enforcement of the Fair Housing Act, for without them many states and localities probably would not have passed progressive fair housing laws in the first place or significantly assisted the federal government in implementing its policy. Given their importance, we would emphasize that complaint-processing payments to state and local agencies have increased over time, with the amount of HUD payments being based on the "timeliness, complexity, and work involved" in handling complaints. During 2008, state and local FHAP agencies were

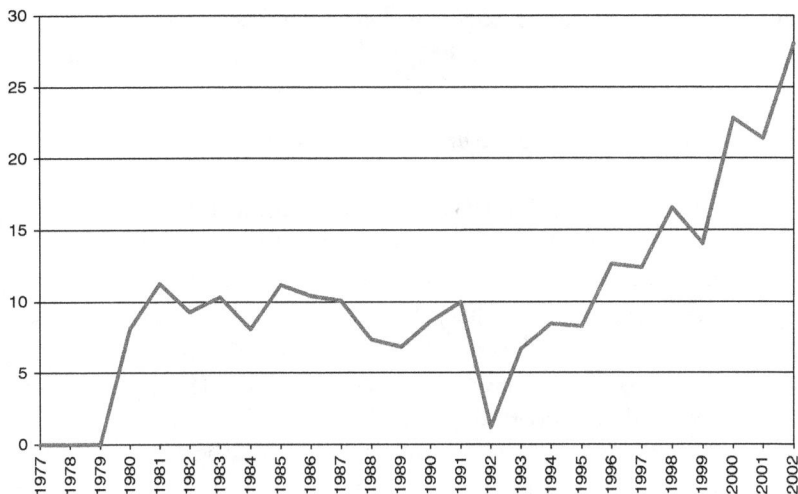

Figure 3. Budget Authority for FHAP Funding (in Millions of
Dollars), FY 1977–2002
Source: Office of Management and Budget (1976–2002).

these funds have been used for information systems, technical assistance, and personnel training to implement fair housing programs,
and for special projects at the state and local levels involving the elimination of housing discrimination and segregation (e.g., U.S. Department of Housing and Urban Development 1990, 2000, 2008, Wallace et
al. 1985). FHAP agencies are simply required to sign a memorandum
of understanding concerning how Title VIII complaints are to be processed to be eligible for these federal funds—funds important to many
state and local civil rights agencies, which have been historically
underfunded. Because FHAP agencies have typically received $2400
for each Title VIII complaint successfully processed in recent years, a

usually paid $2400 for each Title VIII complaint processed, plus an additional $500
"for cases that [were] resource intensive or that reach the adjudication phase" (Office
of Fair Housing and Equal Opportunity 2008:T-6). Importantly, HUD proposed that
payments in 2011 be increased to $2600 per complaint, with an additional $1000 possible "for complaints that reach the adjudication phase (i.e., a charge of discrimination
is issued or a determination of probable/reasonable cause is made)" (Office of Fair
Housing and Equal Opportunity 2010:P-11). Under this proposal, FHAP agencies
could receive a $700 increase for closing each complaint where there is a finding of
reasonable cause. As of this writing, it was too early to know whether that proposal
would become policy.

clear economic incentive exists for them to actively enforce Title VIII and continue to participate in FHAP's intergovernmental partnership.

*Intergovernmental Performance[8]*

On various occasions, HUD has praised the nation's intergovernmental system for enforcing Title VIII as working quite successfully (e.g., U.S. Department of Housing and Urban Development 2009:1). In this section we evaluate how well this intergovernmental partnership in fact performed between 1980 and 2004 (see also Schill 2007, Schill and Friedman 1999). Two data sets obtained from HUD (U.S. Department of Housing and Urban Development 1991a, 2005) through a Freedom of Information Act request permit us to examine various aspects of Title VIII enforcement by federal, state, and local civil rights agencies over this 28-year period.[9] The data consist only of Title VIII complaints, not housing discrimination complaints filed under other federal fair housing laws.[10] As a result, our conclusions pertain only to the enforcement of Title VIII and are not a comprehensive account of how federal housing discrimination law is implemented as a whole. Yet given the focus and scope of this chapter, the data do provide a complete picture of how well the three different levels of American government have enforced the Fair Housing Act of 1968, as amended in 1988.

Figure 4 depicts the total number of Title VIII complaints processed by each level of government from 1973 through 2004, which suggests several initial conclusions. First, the volume of Title VIII complaints

---

[8]  This section is an expanded and revised version of the analysis that appeared in Lamb and Wilk (2009:136–43).
[9]  These data sets are incomplete for 1988. As a result, we rely on HUD's 1989 annual fair housing report to Congress (U.S. Department of Housing and Urban Development 1990), where appropriate, to account for that year.
[10]  In addition to Title VIII, several other federal statutes are designed to combat housing discrimination. Federal legislation during the 1970s was especially directed at achieving this goal. The Equal Credit Opportunity Act of 1974, for example, outlawed discrimination by creditors on the basis of sex, marital status, race, color, religion, national origin, and age. The Home Mortgage Disclosure Act, passed by Congress the following year, provides data on the amount and location of home improvement and mortgage loans, to prevent lending institutions from discriminating against particular localities in providing loans. The Housing and Community Development Act of 1974 prohibits HUD and its funding recipients from discriminating. Various forms of age discrimination are outlawed as well by the Age Discrimination Act of 1975, the Americans with Disabilities Act of 1990, and the Housing for Older Persons Act of 1995. See Schwemm (2009).

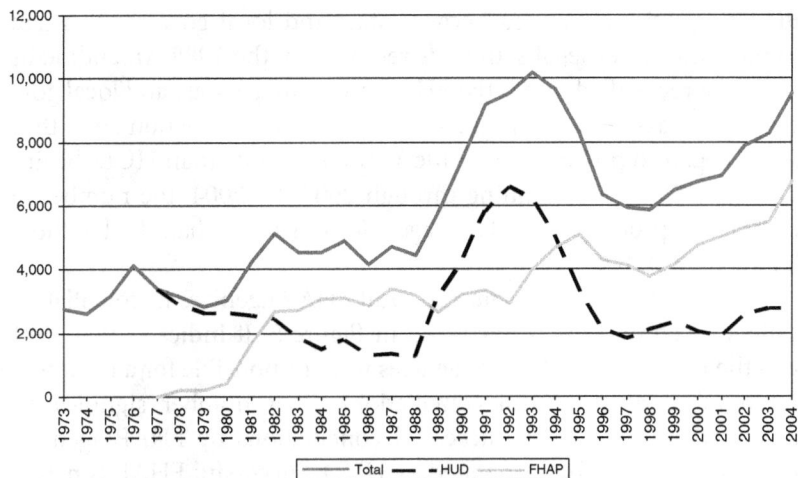

Figure 4. Total Title VIII Complaints Processed by HUD and FHAP
Agencies, FY 1973–2004
*Source:* Data for FY 1973–1987 taken from HUD's FHEO database (1991). Data for FY
1988 taken from U.S. Department of Housing and Urban Development (1990:13,
Exhibit 5–1). Data for FY 1989–2004 taken from HUD's FHEO database (2005).

filed between 1973 and 2004 has been far from constant over time, as
other research has indicated (Schill 2007, Schill and Friedman 1999).
Title VIII complaints peaked at more than 10,000 in 1993 after normally being less than half that number during earlier years. The volume of complaints continued to fluctuate from 1994 to 2000, decreasing
to less than 6,000 in 1998, but HUD has stated that complaints again
grew to more than 10,000 annually in recent years (U.S. Department of
Housing and Urban Development 2008:22). Second, HUD processed a
reasonably stable volume of complaints between 1973 and 1989, but
they more than doubled by 1994. The abrupt spike after 1988 is most
likely due to new Title VIII complaints based on family status or disability, which were added as protected classifications under the Fair
Housing Amendments Act. Third, major changes emerged in the level
of state and local involvement in Title VIII enforcement over time.
While our data indicate that no Title VIII complaints were referred to
FHAP agencies for a decade after the passage of the Fair Housing Act,
the percentage of Title VIII complaints processed by FHAP agencies
was actually greater than the percentage processed by HUD by the end
of 1982. That trend continued until 1989. However, from 1989 to 1995,
HUD once more processed a larger proportion of complaints than all

FHAP agencies combined because state and local governments had to meet the stiffer legal standards required by the 1988 Amendments Act to be recertified under the FHAP program. As state and local governments passed more progressive housing discrimination laws, they again began to process more Title VIII complaints than HUD, beginning in 1996 and continuing through 2004. By 2004, the number of complaints processed by FHAP agencies was more than double those handled by HUD.

The role of HUD and state and local FHAP agencies in conciliating Title VIII complaints is portrayed in Figure 5. It indicates that 1981 was the first year that FHAP agencies were responsible for a meaningful number of successful conciliations. That number significantly increased in 1982 when successful conciliations by FHAP agencies surpassed the number generated by HUD. Successful FHAP conciliations then grew throughout the Reagan administration. The patterns seen in Figure 5, showing total number of complaints processed, are also apparent in successful conciliations. Under President George H. W. Bush, the number of successful HUD conciliations exceeded those by FHAP agencies for the first time since 1981, but the proportion

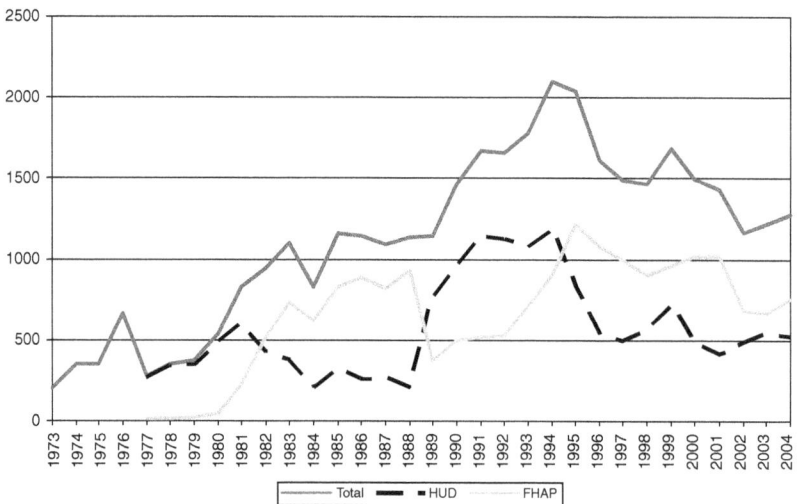

Figure 5.  Total Successful Title VIII Conciliations by HUD and FHAP Agencies, FY 1973–2004

*Source:* Data for FY 1973–1987 taken from HUD's FHEO database (1991). Data for FY 1988 taken from U.S. Department of Housing and Urban Development (1990:13, Exhibit 5-1). Data for FY 1989–2004 taken from HUD's FHEO database (2005).

of successful conciliations by HUD began to decline in the mid-1990s when FHAP agencies learned to conciliate discrimination complaints more successfully. It would therefore appear that New Federalism, as reflected in the FHAP conciliation process, also prospered during the Clinton administration. Then, between 2002 and 2004, the total number of conciliations increased again, largely because of the growing workload of FHAP agencies.

Figure 6 presents evidence on another important aspect of Title VIII enforcement: the volume of Title VIII complaints closed by federal, state, and local civil rights agencies. The data in Figure 6 show the same trends seen earlier in complaints processed and successful conciliations. Compared to HUD, closures by FHAP agencies are relatively insignificant until 1981, when they expanded dramatically. Indeed, FHAP closures eclipse those by HUD by 1983 but then level off after 1985. The differences between FHAP and HUD closures remain relatively stable through 1987 but in 1989 begin to follow the same fluctuating pattern apparent in Figures 4 and 5. (Note that the decrease in complaints closed in 2004 is due to missing data since many 2004 complaints were still being processed by HUD and FHAP agencies when the data set was received by the authors).

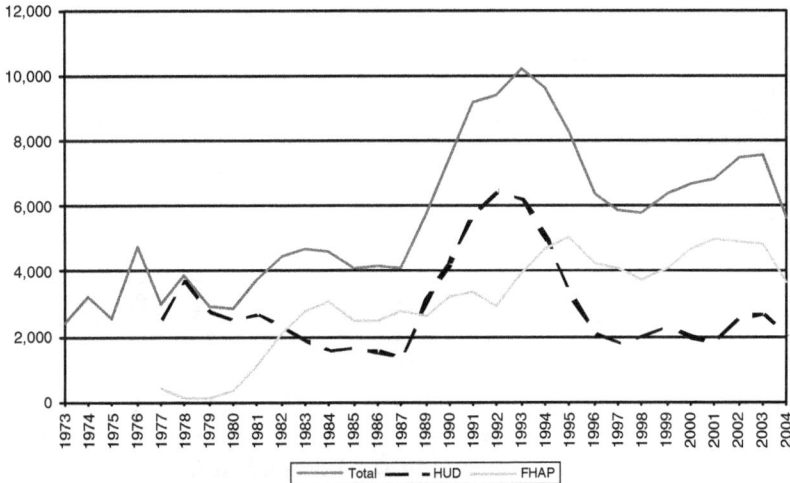

Figure 6. Total Title VIII Complaints Closed by HUD and FHAP Agencies, FY 1973–2004
Source: Data for FY 1973–1987 taken from HUD's FHEO database (1991). Data for FY 1989–2004 taken from HUD's FHEO database (2005).

Actual monetary relief provided to housing discrimination victims is another key indicator of intergovernmental Title VIII enforcement performance. Accordingly, Figure 7 shows the amount of monetary relief obtained by HUD and state and local FHAP agencies for Title VIII complainants from 1977 to 2004 (in constant 2004 dollars).[11] However, the trend seen in Figure 7 differs from the one evident in conciliations and closures because the slope of FHAP's monetary relief increases at a much slower rate than would be expected based on Figures 4 through 6. FHAP agencies equaled and then outpaced HUD in total conciliations attempted, total successful conciliations, and complaints closed in 1982, but did not match HUD in monetary relief until four years later.

The pattern in monetary relief seen in Figure 7 highlights the striking increase in monetary compensation for victims of housing discrimination during the Clinton administration. In fact, total monetary relief in 1997 was triple the relief provided in 1995. A huge spike in monetary relief awarded by HUD is also seen in 2000, but this figure is susceptible to an outlier since one HUD-processed case—received in September 1998 and closed in 2000—was awarded more than

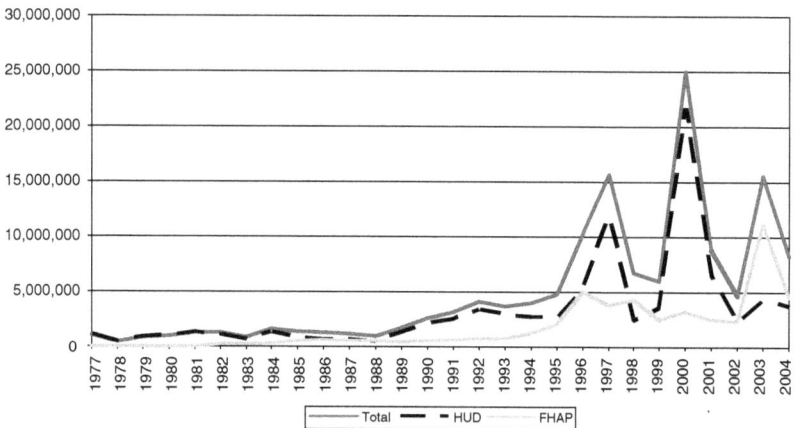

Figure 7. Monetary Relief Obtained by HUD and FHAP Agencies, 1977–2004 (in 2004 Dollars)

Source: Data for 1973–1987 taken from HUD's FHEO database (1991). Data for 1988 taken from U.S. Department of Housing and Urban Development (1990:13, Exhibit 5–1). Data for 1989-2004 taken from HUD's FHEO database (2005).

---

[11] This figure depicts the total amount of money awarded for all complaints closed during the calendar year, not the fiscal year.

$17 million (U.S. Department of Housing and Urban Development 2005). In addition, the HUD trendline is much more erratic than the FHAP trendline, although another outlying case caused a large spike in the monetary relief awarded by state and local civil rights agencies in 2003. The pattern becomes far more stable when the outlying cases are excluded. It is also noteworthy that the amount of monetary relief awarded by FHAP agencies exceeded the amount provided by HUD in 2002, 2003, and 2004. Prior to this, FHAP agencies only awarded more monetary relief than HUD in 1998.

A final indicator of the ability that federal, state, and local civil rights agencies have to aid victims of housing discrimination is reflected in the number of housing units obtained for complainants by different government agencies where a violation of Title VIII is found. These data are presented in Figure 8 for the period 1977 through 2004. Notice that the total number of units obtained steadily grew until 1981 and then skyrocketed to an all-time high in 1982, doubling the previous year's totals. Housing units obtained by HUD returned to previous levels in 1983 and slightly decreased until 1986, before another slight increase in 1987. While the number of housing units obtained by HUD jumped dramatically during the Bush I administration, they began to fall in 1992 and by 1997 were not significantly greater than in 1988. At the same time, housing units obtained by FHAP agencies surpassed those obtained by HUD between 1995 and 2004. This trend under-scores the importance of FHAP agencies, relative to HUD, in yet another aspect of Title VIII enforcement over time, even though the number of housing units obtained by fair housing agencies at all levels of government appears low given the volume of Title VIII complaints filed over time.

## Conclusion

The FHAP program, first funded by Congress in 1979, has become a mainstay in the enforcement of federal fair housing policy. Congress created an intergovernmental partnership in fair housing enforcement in 1968 by requiring HUD to refer Title VIII complaints to their geo-graphical place of origin if a substantially equivalent state or local civil rights agency had been certified by HUD in that location. Although this intergovernmental approach was essentially inoperative for a dec-ade after the passage of the Fair Housing Act, it blossomed under President Reagan's New Federalism, to the point that 112 state and

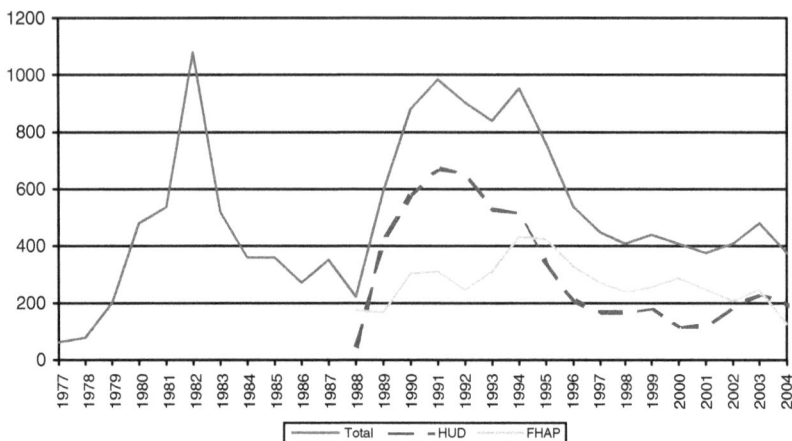

Figure 8. Housing Units Obtained by HUD and FHAP Agencies, FY 1977–2004

Source: Data for FY 1973–1987 taken from HUD's FHEO database (1991). Data for FY 1988 taken from U.S. Department of Housing and Urban Development (1990:13, Exhibit 5–1). Data for FY 1989-2004 taken from HUD's FHEO database (2005).

local FHAP agencies existed when Reagan left office. The program has continued to prosper since that time, serving as a solid example of cooperative federalism (see Elazar 1962, 1972, Grodzins 1966) from the early 1980s through today (Lamb and Wilk 2010).

Several conclusions concerning the intergovernmental enforcement of Title VIII are suggested by the data presented in this chapter. Most importantly, HUD's complaint procedures have resulted in a limited, passive enforcement of Title VIII. HUD processed relatively few Title VIII complaints from 1973 to 2000 compared to the amount of housing discrimination thought to have occurred during those years (Turner et al. 2002, Turner et al. 1991, Wienk et al. 1979, Yinger 1995). Beyond this, the percentage of complaints referred to FHAP agencies increased dramatically in the early 1980s, as state and local agencies did much of the work in enforcing Title VIII, instead of HUD. This chapter also shows that conciliations and closures by HUD and state and local governments fluctuated over time, and that total monetary relief increased markedly during the Clinton administration. Overall, our study indicates that HUD still plays an important role in the federal fair housing enforcement effort, but some of the data—particularly the rate of achieving success in conciliations—demonstrates a stronger enforcement performance by FHAP agencies than by HUD.

In the final analysis, Title VIII enforcement is and should be a shared responsibility between federal, state, and local governments, but states and localities have assumed a strong position in this federal-state-local partnership. In the early twenty-first century, state and local civil rights agencies combined were processing, conciliating and closing considerably more Title VIII complaints than HUD, supplying more housing units to persons claiming a Title VIII violation, and providing more monetary relief than HUD. Although HUD was the dominant figure in Title VIII enforcement for the first decade of the Fair Housing Act's operation, this is clearly no longer the case. In light of this, and the fact that FHAP agencies outperform HUD in several important ways (Lamb and Wilk 2010, Wilk and Lamb forthcoming), Congress should consider increasing funding for the FHAP program to entice other states and localities to pass stronger housing discrimination laws and join the nation's intergovernmental partnership in fair housing enforcement. Funding increases could be used, for example, to raise the amount of financial assistance received by state and local FHAP agencies for processing and closing Title VIII complaints. That, in turn, could improve the number of states and localities actually passing substantially equivalent fair housing laws in the future.

Congress should also exert greater pressure on HUD to enforce the Fair Housing Act more efficiently. For many years, HUD had "such a bad reputation for its delays in processing Fair Housing Act cases that many of the Department's constituents express reluctance to file complaints with the Department, out of the belief that nothing will come of it" (statement of Kenneth L. Marcus 2002:2). Over the past decade, HUD has reduced the percentage of Title VIII complaints that it has taken over 100 days to process, but further reductions are needed (U.S. Department of Housing and Urban Development 2009:19). Congress, therefore, might even consider reducing HUD appropriations unless the agency can significantly reduce its Title VIII backlog within a reasonable period of time.[12]

---

[12] HUD closed 2,516 Title VIII complaints in fiscal year 2008, for example, but failed to close an additional 817 complaints within 100 days of the date they were filed. Title VIII allows HUD to take over 100 days to close complaints where it is "impracticable" for the agency to do so (U.S. Department of Housing and Urban Development 2009:18–19). According to the U.S. Court of Appeals for the Sixth Circuit, Congress intended this "impracticable" exception to be used in "exceptional cases" only. *Kelly v. HUD* (1993).

## References

Briggs, Xavier de Souza, ed. 2005. *The Geography of Opportunity: Race and Housing Choice in Metropolitan America.* Washington, DC: Brookings Institution.

Conlon, Timothy. 1998. *New Federalism: Intergovernmental Reform from Nixon to Reagan.* Washington, DC: Brookings Institution.

Eisinger, Peter, and William T. Gormley, eds. 1988. *The Midwest Response to the New Federalism.* Madison: University of Wisconsin Press.

Elazar, Daniel J. 1962. *The American Partnership: Intergovernmental Co-operation in the Nineteenth-Century United States.* Chicago: University of Chicago Press.

Elazar, Daniel J. 1972. *American Federalism: A View from the States.* 2d ed. New York: Crowell.

Farley, Reynolds, and William H. Frey. 1994. "Changes in the Segregation of Whites from Blacks during the 1980s: Small Steps toward a More Integrated Society." *American Sociological Review* 59(1): 23–45.

Graham, Hugh Davis. 1990. *The Civil Rights Era: Origins and Development of National Policy.* New York: Oxford University Press.

Graham, Hugh Davis. 2000. "The Surprising Career of Federal Fair Housing Law." *Journal of Policy History* 12(2): 215–32.

Grodzins, Morton. 1966. *The American System: A New View of Government in the United States.* Edited by Daniel J. Elazar. Chicago: Rand McNally.

*Kelly v. HUD,* 3 F.3d 951 (6th Cir. 1993).

Kushner, James A. 1995. *Fair Housing: Discrimination in Real Estate, Community Development and Revitalization.* 2d ed. Colorado Springs, CO: Shepard's/McGraw-Hill.

Lamb, Charles M. 2005. *Housing Segregation in Suburban America since 1960: Presidential and Judicial Politics.* New York: Cambridge University Press.

Lamb, Charles M., and Jim Twombly. 1993. "Taking the Local: The Reagan Administration, New Federalism, and Fair Housing Implementation." *Policy Studies Journal* 21(3): 589–98.

Lamb, Charles M., and Eric M. Wilk. 2009. "Presidents, Bureaucracy, and Housing Discrimination Policy: The Fair Housing Acts of 1968 and 1988." *Politics and Policy* 37 (1): 127–49.

Lamb, Charles M., and Eric M. Wilk. 2010. "Civil Rights, Federalism, and the Administrative Process: Favorable Outcomes by Federal, State, and Local Agencies in Housing Discrimination Complaints." *Public Administration Review* 70(3): 412–21.

Massey, Douglas S., and Nancy A. Denton. 1993. *American Apartheid: Segregation and the Making of the Underclass.* Cambridge, MA: Harvard University Press.

Office of Fair Housing and Equal Opportunity. 2008. "Fair Housing Assistance Program: 2008 Summary Statement and Initiatives." http://www.hud.gov/offices/cfo/reports/2008/cjs/part2/fheo/fhap.pdf (accessed March 21, 2010).

Office of Fair Housing and Equal Opportunity. 2010. "Fair Housing Assistance Program: 2011 Summary Statement and Initiatives." http://www.hud.gov/offices/cfo/.../Fair_Housing_Assistance_Program_2011.pdf (accessed March 21, 2010).

Office of Management and Budget. 1970–2002. *Budget of the United States Government.* Washington, D.C.: Office of Management and Budget.

Schill, Michael H. 2007. "Implementing the Federal Fair Housing Act: The Adjudication of Complaints." Pp. 143–76 in *Fragile Rights within Cities: Government, Housing, and Fairness,* edited by John Goering. Lanham, MD: Rowman & Littlefield.

Schill, Michael H., and Samantha Friedman. 1999. "The Fair Housing Amendments Act of 1988: The First Decade." *Cityscape: A Journal of Policy Development and Research* 4(3): 57–78.

Schwemm, Robert G. 1989. "Federal Fair Housing Enforcement: A Critique of the Reagan Administration's Record and Recommendations for the Future."

Pp. 268–303 in *One Nation Indivisible: The Civil Rights Challenge for the 1990s*, edited by Reginald C. Govan and William L. Taylor. Washington, DC: Citizens' Commission on Civil Rights.

Schwemm, Robert G. 2009. *Housing Discrimination: Law and Litigation*. St. Paul, MN: Thomson West.

Seabrook, Nicholas R., and Charles M. Lamb. 2009. "Patterns of Behavior of Administrative Law Judges in Federal Fair Housing Enforcement." Paper presented at the annual meeting of the Northeastern Political Science Association, Philadelphia, PA, November 19.

Statement of Kenneth L. Marcus, General Deputy Assistant Secretary for Fair Housing and Equal Opportunity, U.S. Department of Housing and Urban Development. 2002. Before the House of Representatives Committee on Financial Services, Subcommittee on Housing and Community Opportunity and Subcommittee on Oversight and Investigations. http://www.hud.gov/offices/cir/test062502.cfm (accessed March 21, 2010).

Turner, Margery Austin, and Stephen L. Ross. 2003a. *Discrimination in Metropolitan Housing Markets: Phase 2—Asians and Pacific Islanders*. Washington, DC: U.S. Department of Housing and Urban Development.

Turner, Margery Austin, and Stephen L. Ross. 2003b. *Discrimination in Metropolitan Housing Markets: Phase 3—Native Americans*. Washington, DC: U.S. Department of Housing and Urban Development.

Turner, Margery Austin, and Stephen L. Ross. 2005. "How Racial Discrimination Affects the Search for Housing." Pp. 81–100 in *The Geography of Opportunity: Race and Housing Choice in Metropolitan America*, edited by Xavier de Souza Briggs. Washington, DC: Brookings Institution.

Turner, Margery Austin, Stephen L. Ross, George C. Galster, and John Yinger. 2002. *Discrimination in Metropolitan Housing Markets: National Results from Phase 1 HDS 2000*. Washington, DC: U.S. Department of Housing and Urban Development.

Turner, Margery Austin, Raymond J. Struyk, and John Yinger. 1991. *Housing Discrimination Study: Synthesis*. Washington, DC: U.S. Department of Housing and Urban Development.

U.S. Commission on Civil Rights. 1974. *The Federal Civil Rights Enforcement Effort—1974: To Provide … For Fair Housing*. Washington, DC: U.S. Commission on Civil Rights.

U.S. Commission on Civil Rights. 1979. *The Federal Fair Housing Enforcement Effort*. Washington, DC: U.S. Commission on Civil Rights.

U.S. Commission on Civil Rights. 1992. *Prospects and Impact of Losing State and Local Agencies from the Federal Fair Housing System*. Washington, DC: U.S. Commission on Civil Rights.

U.S. Commission on Civil Rights. 1994. *The Fair Housing Amendments Act of 1988: The Enforcement Report*. Washington, DC: U.S. Commission on Civil Rights.

U.S. Department of Housing and Urban Development. 1980. *Guide to Fair Housing Law Enforcement*. Washington, DC: U.S. Department of Housing and Urban Development.

U.S. Department of Housing and Urban Development. 1989. *New Directions in Housing and Urban Policy: 1981-1989*. Washington, DC: U.S. Department of Housing and Urban Development.

U.S. Department of Housing and Urban Development. 1990. *The State of Fair Housing: Report to the Congress Pursuant to Section 808(e)(2) of the Fair Housing Act*. Washington, DC: U.S. Department of Housing and Urban Development.

U.S. Department of Housing and Urban Development. 1991a. *Office of Fair Housing and Equal Opportunity Data Set*. Washington, DC: U.S. Department of Housing and Urban Development, obtained by the authors under a Freedom of Information Act request.

U.S. Department of Housing and Urban Development. 1991b. *The State of Fair Housing: Report to the Congress Pursuant to Section 808(e)(2) of the Fair Housing Act.* Washington, DC: U.S. Department of Housing and Urban Development.

U.S. Department of Housing and Urban Development. 1992. *The State of Fair Housing: Report to the Congress Pursuant to Section 808(e)(2) of the Fair Housing Act.* Washington, DC: U.S. Department of Housing and Urban Development.

U.S. Department of Housing and Urban Development. 1996. *1994 Annual Report to Congress on Fair Housing Programs.* Washington, DC: U.S. Department of Housing and Urban Development.

U.S. Department of Housing and Urban Development. 1997. *1995 Annual Report to Congress: [The State of Fair Housing in America].* Washington, DC: U.S. Department of Housing and Urban Development.

U.S. Department of Housing and Urban Development. 1999. *1996 Annual Report to Congress on the State of Fair Housing in America.* Washington, DC: U.S. Department of Housing and Urban Development.

U.S. Department of Housing and Urban Development. 2002. *The Housing Discrimination Study 2000.* Washington, DC: U.S. Department of Housing and Urban Development.

U.S. Department of Housing and Urban Development. 2005. *Office of Fair Housing and Equal Opportunity Data Set.* Washington, DC: U.S. Department of Housing and Urban Development, obtained by the authors under a Freedom of Information Act request.

U.S. Department of Housing and Urban Development. 2006. *The State of Fair Housing: FY 2005 Annual Report on Fair Housing.* Washington, DC: U.S. Department of Housing and Urban Development.

U.S. Department of Housing and Urban Development. 2007. "Substantial Equivalence Certification." http://www.hud.gov/offices/fheo/partners/FHAP/equivalency.cfm (accessed April 8, 2010).

U.S. Department of Housing and Urban Development. 2007. *The State of Fair Housing: FY 2006 Annual Report on Fair Housing.* Washington, DC: U.S. Department of Housing and Urban Development.

U.S. Department of Housing and Urban Development. 2008. *The State of Fair Housing: FY 2007 Annual Report on Fair Housing.* Washington: DC: U.S. Department of Housing and Urban Development.

U.S. Department of Housing and Urban Development. 2009. *The State of Fair Housing: FY 2008 Annual Report on Fair Housing.* Washington: DC: U.S. Department of Housing and Urban Development.

U.S. General Accounting Office. 2004. *Fair Housing: Opportunities to Improve HUD's Oversight and Management of the Enforcement Process.* Washington, DC: U.S. General Accounting Office.

Wallace, James E., William L. Holshouser, Terry Sanders Lane, and John Williams. 1985. *The Fair Housing Assistance Program Evaluation.* Washington, DC: U.S. Department of Housing and Urban Development.

Wienk, Ronald E., Clifford E. Reid, John C. Simonson, and Frederick J. Eggers. 1979. *Measuring Racial Discrimination in American Housing Markets: The Housing Market Practices Survey.* Washington, DC: U.S. Department of Housing and Urban Development.

Wilk Eric M., and Charles M. Lamb, 2011. "Federalism, Efficiency, and Civil Rights Enforcement." *Political Research Quarterly* 64(2): 392–404.

Yinger, John. 1995. *Closed Doors, Opportunities Lost: The Continuing Costs of Housing Discrimination.* New York: Russell Sage Foundation.

# THE FEDERAL COURTS AND FAIR HOUSING POLICY:
## A PRINCIPAL-AGENT INTERPRETATION*

Nicholas R. Seabrook, Charles M. Lamb, and Eric M. Wilk

## Introduction

Scholars have long been interested in civil rights policy making and enforcement through the federal courts (Halpern 1995, Lamb 2005, Wasby et al. 1977). The lion's share of this research highlights the Supreme Court and reflects the widely held view that it is the preeminent guardian of civil rights in America. After all, the Supreme Court boldly asserted leadership in civil rights, especially in the 1950s, when the other branches of government failed to protect the rights of racial minorities (Klarman 2004, Patterson 2001, Wilkinson 1979). An alternative view is presented in this study, however, based on principal-agent theory. We emphasize that the lower federal courts—the agents—actually assume the lead in safeguarding individual rights when new issues arise, because they determine what the law is when the Supreme Court—the principal—has not spoken (see Klein 2002, Songer et al. 2000). Indeed, we would generally expect that the lower courts would authoritatively resolve most legal questions in the federal judicial system since only a fraction of all lower court decisions are appealed to the Supreme Court, which in turn hears less than one percent of all cases appealed to it.[1]

Our argument may be simply stated. When the Supreme Court became progressively more conservative after the late 1960s, fair housing—more of a policy concern of liberal judges—gained little traction with the Court.[2] Moreover, the housing discrimination decisions that

* We thank the Baldy Center for Law and Social Policy, University at Buffalo, SUNY, for supporting this research and Donald B. Rosenthal for his valuable comments.
[1] Bowie and Songer (2009:396) estimate, for instance, that "less than one-tenth of 1 percent of [all] appeals court decisions are typically reviewed" by the Supreme Court.
[2] Between 1969 and 2008, twelve of fourteen new appointments to the Supreme Court were made by Republican presidents: Warren Burger, Harry Blackmun, Lewis Powell, and William Rehnquist (Richard Nixon); (Rehnquist was elevated from associate justice to chief justice by Reagan in 1986); John Paul Stevens (Gerald Ford);

the Court did announce were conservative. This left a power vacuum in the federal judicial system, allowing the courts of appeals and the district courts to play an expanded policy making role in both constitutional and statutory issues. Specifically, the lower federal courts have been able to affect fair housing policy by incrementally moving the law in a liberal direction, but avoiding the kind of sweeping decisions that might attract too much Supreme Court attention. Some more liberal decisions, especially those where a court of appeals has reversed a district court, have been overturned at the Supreme Court level, but many incrementally liberal decisions have been allowed to stand. We further suggest that the most liberal federal fair housing decisions since the early 1970s have come predominantly from the more liberal circuits that represent large northeastern and midwestern cities—precisely where the problems of housing discrimination and segregation are frequently most serious (Farley and Frey 1994, Massey and Denton 1989, 1993). These include the Second Circuit (New York City, Rochester, and Buffalo), the Third Circuit (Philadelphia, Pittsburgh, and New Jersey), the Sixth Circuit (Cleveland and Detroit), and the Seventh Circuit (Chicago and Indianapolis).

We focus on leading housing discrimination cases announced since 1970 because the federal courts did not make fair housing decisions on a regular basis before the passage of the Fair Housing Act of 1968 (Title VIII of the Civil Rights Act of 1968).[3] We examine five types of cases: exclusionary zoning, public housing segregation, intent and effect in housing discrimination, discrimination against persons with disabilities, and standing to sue. In the final analysis, we provide support for the view that lower federal courts have often filled the power vacuum

---

Sandra Day O'Connor, Antonin Scalia, and Anthony Kennedy (Ronald Reagan); David Souter and Clarence Thomas (George H. W. Bush); and John Roberts and Samuel Alito (George W. Bush). In nearly four decades, the only exceptions to this Republican-dominated trend were the appointments of Ruth Bader Ginsburg and Stephen Breyer by Bill Clinton. After 2008, Sonia Sotomayor and Elena Kagan were appointed to the Court during Barack Obama's first two years as president.

[3] It appears, for example, that the Supreme Court announced only eight decisions, on the merits, directly resolving housing discrimination issues prior to 1970: *Buchanan v. Warley* (1917); *Shelley v. Kraemer* (1948); *Hurd v. Hodge* (1948); *Barrows v. Jackson* (1953); *Reitman v. Mulkey* (1967); *Jones v. Alfred H. Mayer Co.* (1968); *Hunter v. Erickson* (1969); and *Sullivan v. Little Hunting Park, Inc.* (1969). However, the Court did accept cases before 1970 in which the justices ultimately failed to rule on the merits or failed to address the content of fair housing rights. See, e.g., *Corrigan v. Buckley* (1926) and *Hansberry v. Lee* (1940).

in fair housing law created by an increasingly conservative Supreme Court. Of the five fields, the one exception to this conclusion is found in standing cases, where Supreme Court decisions have established the major parameters of federal fair housing law.[4]

## Theory

The theoretical perspectives that form the basis of our argument are rooted in the literature on judicial behavior and decision making in the lower federal courts, and specifically in theories of strategic interaction within the federal court hierarchy.[5] Scholars have long since demonstrated that judges, like other political actors, make decisions based upon their own personal policy preferences (Pritchett 1948, Schubert 1965, 1974). Indeed, attitudinal theory, which posits that judges' ideological perspectives are the most important determinant of judicial behavior, albeit subject to certain constraints, has become the dominant model of judicial decision making in the literature on the U.S. Supreme Court (Bartels 2009, Segal and Spaeth 2002). Attitudinal theory also helps to explain lower federal court behavior, although lower court judges are significantly more constrained in their ability to make policy based on personal preferences because of institutional considerations dictated by the hierarchical structure of the federal court system and the norm of *stare decisis* (Howard 1981, Rowland and Carp 1996, Songer and Haire 1992, Songer et al. 1994). As a result, models of judicial behavior have turned to the rational-strategic approach to explain variation in lower court decision making that cannot be accounted for by attitudes alone (Bowie and Songer 2009, Cameron et al. 2000, Cross and Tiller 1998, Haire et al. 2003, Hettinger et al. 2004, Lindquist et al. 2007, Songer et al. 1994).

Studies of the federal judiciary have increasingly come to see the court system not as a pyramid but as a decentralized hierarchy, where

---

[4] See Kushner (1995) and Schwemm (2009) for detailed treatments of fair housing law in America, including many cases examined in this chapter.

[5] On the "strategic revolution" in the study of judicial politics generally, see Epstein and Knight (2000). They emphasize that rational choice theory, as applied to the courts, is anchored in three basic assumptions: "(1) social actors make choices in order to achieve certain goals; (2) social actors act strategically in the sense that their choices depend on their expectations about the choices of other actors; and (3) these choices are structured by the institutional setting in which they are made" (626). See also Maltzman, Spriggs, and Wahlbeck (2000).

"federal judicial power is widely diffused among lower court judges who are insulated by deep traditions of independence" (Howard 1981:3). Rather than the lower courts being dominated by the policy making power of the Supreme Court, which lacks the institutional capacity to control all aspects of judicial policy, there is in fact the potential for the lower federal courts to play a critical policy making role within this hierarchical framework where their preferences differ from those of a Supreme Court majority (Songer et al. 1994). This is especially true because of the flexible character of precedent that frequently affords lower court judges a certain amount of leeway in interpreting Supreme Court decisions (Johnson 1979, Songer and Sheehan 1990). In many other cases lower court judges simply decide questions "with no precise guidance from Supreme Court precedent" (Lindquist et al. 2007:607). We contend that the absence of directly relevant precedent at the Supreme Court level naturally leads to a power vacuum in the federal judiciary that can be easily filled by independent-minded lower court judges under the proper circumstances. The ability of the lower courts to make policy in particular issues, such as fair housing, is enhanced by the malleable nature of many Supreme Court decisions.

However, the policy making role of the lower courts is subject to the constraints imposed by Supreme Court oversight and supervision, because the decisions of the courts of appeals are influenced both by their level of ideological agreement with the Supreme Court and by the degree to which they have been scrutinized by the Supreme Court in past cases (Cameron et al. 2000, Haire et al. 2003). And while fear of reversal has not been shown to be a dominant explanation for lower court compliance (Bowie and Songer 2009, Klein 2002, Klein and Hume 2003), it can nevertheless act as a constraint on the behavior of lower federal court judges. Lower courts cannot hope to engage in policy making that departs in fundamental ways from the ideological preferences of their principal without risking appellate review, an outcome that becomes more likely as ideological divergence increases (Cameron et al. 2000, Songer et al. 1994). Furthermore, especially broad lower court decisions are more likely to involve dissent, en banc review, and major splits among the circuits, each of which act as signals that significantly increase the probability of Supreme Court review (Cameron et al. 2000, Perry 1991, Solimine 1988, Van Winkle 1997).

Finally, more liberal lower court decisions may partly be a function of region or locality. Some research suggests that judges' values may reflect things like their education and socialization (Carp and Wheeler

1972, Howard 1981). More liberal regional or local decisional environments may permit lower court judges to hand down decisions that
depart from precedent and tradition to a greater extent (King 1998).
There is a chance that most of the decisions identified in this study
originate in more liberal regions or localities of the country, including
more urbanized areas. As a consequence, these district and appeals
court judges may be more willing to make substantive fair housing
policy than judges in other regions or localities.

The implication of these studies is that the potential exists for the
lower federal courts to play an important policy making role in the
area of fair housing, subject to the constraints imposed by the federal
judicial hierarchy. We would expect more liberal circuit and district
courts, if they are acting strategically, to be able to advance the state of
fair housing law in a progressive direction, but to do so in an incremental fashion that avoids creating significant ideological divergence
from the Supreme Court, or otherwise provide a signal that might trigger higher court review (Cameron et al. 2000).

*Exclusionary Zoning*

For decades, local officials have contributed to racial segregation by
passing and enforcing exclusionary zoning laws (Danielson 1976, Haar
1996, Schuck 2002). The Supreme Court, as a rule, refrained from
dealing with challenges to these zoning ordinances before the 1970s,
but the Burger Court explicitly refused to strike down exclusionary
practices. In *Village of Belle Terre v. Boraas* (1974), for instance, the
Court upheld an ordinance that restricted Belle Terre, New York, to
single-family homes and defined a "family" to include any number of
related persons living together but only two unrelated people living at
the same residence. Three unrelated college students living in Belle
Terre filed suit in federal court, arguing the law denied them equal
protection as well as their rights to association, privacy, and travel.
Justice Douglas's opinion for the Court upheld the challenged zoning
ordinance, however, concluding that Belle Terre's exclusionary practices did not abridge any constitutional rights of the students. Belle
Terre did not involve racial minorities, but as we shall see later, especially in *Warth v. Seldin* (1975) and *Village of Arlington Heights v.
Metropolitan Housing Development Corp.* (1977), the Court exhibited
little concern over racial exclusion through local zoning practices.

Zoning referenda may have the same effect as exclusionary zoning laws, and the Supreme Court decided two referenda cases on the merits in the 1970s. One vital Burger Court case on the right to fair housing occurred in *James v. Valtierra* (1971). There, indigent California residents challenged an amendment to the California Constitution which required that a majority of citizens voting in a community referendum had to first approve of the development, construction, or acquisition of a low-rent housing project before such a project could be initiated. Under this provision, voters in a local referendum had prevented housing officials from applying for federal funds to build low-income housing, and the indigents in *Valtierra* argued that their equal protection rights had been violated.

Justice Black's majority opinion ruled, however, that the plaintiffs' right to equal protection had not been breached in *Valtierra*. Black dwelt on the fact that California had customarily reserved to its voters the power to initiate and reject laws by means of referenda. In this case the amendment had been added to the state constitution with the express purpose of permitting voters to veto the construction of new subsidized housing. This constitutional provision, to Black's way of thinking, upheld California's democratic tradition of permitting voters to participate in public policy making through the electoral process—a tradition that simply reflected the state's "devotion to democracy, not bias, discrimination, or prejudice" (402 U.S. at 141).

*Valtierra* clearly had negative implications for the right to fair housing. The ruling, though narrow, "disheartened advocates of open housing, particularly those who had pinned their hopes in the fight against suburban exclusion on a favorable ruling by the Supreme Court" (Danielson 1976: 181). Yet *Valtierra* was not the Burger Court's last word on zoning referenda. The Court ruled in favor of another restrictive referendum procedure to halt the construction of low-cost housing in *City of Eastlake v. Forest City Enterprises, Inc.* (1976). In this case, the Eastlake, Ohio, city charter stipulated that all proposed zoning changes must be submitted to a city-wide referendum, with a 55 percent favorable vote required for final approval. Forest City Enterprises, a real estate development company, had asked that a parcel of land be rezoned to build multi-family apartments. The city planning commission and the city council both endorsed the rezoning, but the 55 percent popular approval was not forthcoming at the polls. The Ohio Supreme Court then struck down the referendum requirement as "an unlawful delegation of legislative power ... denying appellant due process of law." The referendum procedure allowed the Tenth Amendment's police power to be used in a "standardless, hence arbitrary, and capricious manner," according to the state supreme court (41 Ohio St. at 747). Not surprisingly, the Burger Court overturned the Ohio Supreme Court, and Chief Justice Burger declared that a referendum cannot "be characterized as a delegation of legislative power" (426 U.S. at 672). More importantly, the Court again asserted that referenda reflect the very essence of democracy because all the citizens of the locality are afforded a mechanism for expressing their views on public policy, signaling to the lower courts that challenges to exclusionary zoning laws passed through direct legislation would be more likely to survive constitutional scrutiny than those enacted through local ordinances.

Compared to the High Court's record on exclusionary zoning, leading decisions from the 1980s demonstrated that lower federal court judges could make liberal contributions to combating exclusionary zoning and providing extensive relief without triggering a review on the merits by a more conservative Supreme Court majority. The common characteristics of these cases are that they focus on ordinances rather than referenda, and they strike down exclusionary zoning practices where the plaintiffs were able to demonstrate both discriminatory effect and discriminatory intent.

The best illustration is *United States v. City of Parma, Ohio* (1980). This case, from the suburbs of Cleveland, held that Parma had acted in violation of Title VIII by passing ordinances preventing multiple-family low-income dwellings from being built in this overwhelmingly white community. All told, Parma's actions reflected both discriminatory intent and discriminatory effect, the district court declared.[6] The Sixth Circuit upheld all but two of the injunctive orders laid out by the district court (*United States v. City of Parma, Ohio* [1981]). As a

---

[6] This case was followed by *United States v. City of Parma, Ohio* (504 F. Supp. 913 [1980]), dealing with relief. There, the district court announced an extremely comprehensive remedial plan that imposed seven affirmative requirements on Parma, including the building of at least 133 units of low- and moderate-income housing annually, and created a special master in the case who was given various powers designed to correct the legal violations that had occurred. Because of the sweeping nature of the district court's remedy, principal-agent theory suggests the increased likelihood of dissent on the three-judge court of appeals panel reviewing the district court. Indeed, the appeals court panel was divided. Judge Merritt's dissent argued that two district court requirements—that Parma's city council pass a resolution welcoming people of different races, creeds, and colors, and that Parma widely advertise that it was an equal

result, the lower courts took a bold step forward in the realm of housing discrimination, and the district court's order eventually affected low-income housing opportunities in what had been a virtually all-white town (Cooper 1988:79).

Other cases underscore the importance of the lower courts in combating exclusionary local referenda. In *United States v. City of Birmingham, Michigan* (1982), the district court held that Birmingham, which was almost completely white, breached Title VIII by agreeing to build housing for senior citizens but then refusing to do so for low-income families on grounds of race. The case arose when Birmingham was informed that if it was to build housing for senior citizens, it must construct one low-income unit for every two erected for seniors. Public opposition quickly grew to the idea of low-income housing, and an advisory referendum voted the construction down. The district court emphasized that an advisory referendum had never been previously used in Birmingham and that the city's interference with public housing was partially motivated by race, thereby making housing unavailable to minorities in violation of Title VIII.

Another lower court exclusionary zoning case announced that a local government must apply its zoning ordinances to low- and high-income housing units alike. *Hope, Inc. v. DuPage County, Illinois* (1983) arose when Hope, Inc., and ten other plaintiffs brought suit against DuPage County alleging that its exclusionary practices led to only high-income housing units being built, thus discriminating against African Americans and other poor people. Actions by county officials had, in fact, made it clear that low-income housing was not wanted. Finding an inconsistency in how the county applied its zoning ordinances, as well as discriminatory intent, the Seventh Circuit held that a lower court decree was valid because it forced DuPage to apply its zoning laws equally to all residents. In this case, as in *Parma* and *City of Birmingham*, the Burger Court denied a request that it review the lower court ruling. By working within the scope of the Supreme Court's existing constitutional standard, and focusing on the types of discrimination that were less likely to trigger appellate review, the lower federal courts were able to take important steps toward combating exclusionary zoning practices.

---

housing opportunity community—violated freedom of speech by forcing Parma to express a particular attitude on race (*United States v. City of Parma*, 661 F.2d at 580–81 [1981]).

## Segregated Public Housing

Chicago has long been one of the most residentially segregated cities in the United States (Bickford and Massey 1991, Hirsch 1998, Rubinowitz and Rosenbaum 2000). This segregation was compounded in the 1950s and 1960s by flagrant discrimination by the Chicago Housing Authority (CHA) against African Americans through site selection procedures for public housing and by assigning tenants to public housing projects according to race. In prolonged litigation, the lower federal courts found that HUD had facilitated CHA's policies and practices (see Polikoff 2006). The Court of Appeals for the Seventh Circuit concluded, in one key 1971 ruling, that HUD knowingly provided federal funds to CHA's discriminatory programs, thereby sanctioning CHA's illegal practices (*Hills v. Gautreaux*, 425 U.S. at 289). These HUD activities, the Court of Appeals said, breached both the due process clause of the Fifth Amendment and Title VI of the Civil Rights Act of 1964. The court remanded the case, and the district court subsequently declared that HUD must provide relief only in the City of Chicago, not in its suburbs. The Court of Appeals reversed the district court, calling for the use of a comprehensive metropolitan area plan.

Following these lower court rulings, the Supreme Court's only decision addressing segregated public housing came in *Hills v. Gautreaux* (1976), where the justices dealt with the remedies that could be legally imposed because of HUD's involvement in Chicago's hypersegregated public housing. Specifically, the Court faced the issue of whether a district court could require HUD to compensate for past discrimination in Chicago through a metropolitan-wide housing desegregation remedy where it was found to have violated the Fifth Amendment and Title VI. Affirming the Court of Appeals, Justice Stewart's majority opinion argued that, under the circumstances, an areawide remedy "was not impermissible as a matter of law" (425 U.S. at 306).

Justice Stewart spent a great deal of time distinguishing *Gautreaux* from *Milliken v. Bradley* (1974) in reaching his conclusion. *Milliken*, the famous busing decision, banned an area wide remedy for a *de jure* violation of the Fourteenth Amendment in Detroit's public schools because two conditions were not met: there was no proof of *de jure* segregation in the suburban school districts surrounding Detroit, and there was no proof that the *de jure* segregation in Detroit's public schools had a significant segregative effect on the suburban schools. Chief Justice Burger's majority opinion in *Milliken* emphasized that, under *Swann v. Charlotte-Mecklenberg Board of Education* (1971), "the nature of the violation determines the scope of the remedy" (402 U.S. at 16). In *Milliken*, though, the nature of the violation was insufficient to permit interdistrict busing because the above two conditions were not met.

In his *Gautreaux* opinion, Stewart carefully highlighted a key difference between *Milliken* and *Gautreaux*: the suburban school districts surrounding Detroit had not acted unconstitutionally, but HUD had violated the Fifth Amendment, as well as Title VI, in both the city and suburbs of Chicago. That is why the Court of Appeals had been correct to suggest the possibility of an area wide remedy in *Gautreaux*. Despite all of this, Stewart's decision in *Gautreaux* was by no means a ringing endorsement of using areawide HUD programs to integrate America's large, segregated urban centers. In fact, he did not rule that a metropolitan-wide remedy was required in this case of flagrant illegal behavior by HUD. He instead simply indicated that an areawide remedy "is not impermissible as a matter of law" and cautioned: "[o]ur determination that the District Court has the authority to direct HUD to engage in remedial efforts in the metropolitan area outside the city limits of Chicago should not be interpreted as requiring a metropolitan area order" (425 U.S. at 306). Whether a metropolitan-wide remedy was required in this case was, therefore, a matter for the district court to ponder in further proceedings.

The Supreme Court's jurisprudence in this area highlights its willingness to allow the lower courts to take the lead in defining the meaning of federal law in fair housing. *Gautreaux* announced very general guidelines for the lower courts, allowing them to decide the type and scope of the remedy called for where local housing authorities and HUD are responsible for racial segregation. Giving this power to the lower federal courts is significant because public housing in many American cities remains largely segregated, and in other prominent cases the lower courts took the lead against segregated public housing without triggering Supreme Court review. In *Young v. Pierce* (1985), HUD was sued by a class of applicants for, and residents of, HUD-assisted housing in thirty-six counties of East Texas. The class, all African Americans, alleged that HUD knowingly maintained segregated housing. The U.S. District Court for the Eastern District of Texas held that HUD had known of and supported racially segregated housing in the area and that financial assistance for such segregation was unconstitutional. The court further ruled that, even if HUD had not known about the discrimination, the agency still breached the Fifth Amendment "by willfully ignoring the facts necessary to fulfill its constitutional and statutory duties" (628 F.Supp. at 1055–56). *Young* is important, therefore, because it declared that HUD could no longer support segregated housing whether it knew of discrimination or not, giving HUD the constitutional obligation to examine housing that it financially supports to determine whether it is segregated.

Other lower courts have held that segregated public housing violates federal law,[7] and some address the use of quotas. A good example is *United States v. Starrett City Associates* (1988). Starrett City was a large housing development in Brooklyn, subsidized by HUD, that had agreed to be racially integrated. To achieve this objective, Starrett used quotas to maintain a specific racial balance and a tenant selection procedure in which racial information about applicants was used to determine who would reside in the complex. Because of this racially-oriented procedure and the racial mix of applicants, minorities were offered far fewer apartment opportunities than whites. A class of African American applicants brought suit in district court claiming that the tenanting procedures discriminated against them. Dissatisfied with the settlement in the case, the Department of Justice filed suit against Starrett City Associates.

The Second Circuit Court of Appeals declared in this case that Title VIII violations include both those involving discriminatory effect and discriminatory intent, emphasizing that any "action leading to discriminatory effects on availability of housing violates the [Fair Housing] Act" (840 F.2d at 1100). Because Starrett's procedures had an obvious racial impact, they abridged Title VIII. Still, the court ruled that not all quota plans are discriminatory and that temporary quotas that have "a defined goal as a termination point" may stand (840 F.2d at 1101). Because Starrett's integration goal had no foreseeable end in sight, the procedures offended Title VIII.

While the Supreme Court has yet to address tipping points in public housing and when quotas are justified to avoid them, lower court decisions prior to *Starrett City* had dealt with them. *Otero v. New York City Housing Authority* (1973) arose in response to a decision by the New York City Housing and Development Administration (HDA) not to

---

[7] See, e.g., *Cabrera v. Jakabovitz* (1994); *Jaimes v. Toledo Metropolitan Housing Authority* (1989); *NAACP, Boston Chapter v. HUD* (1987); *Shannon v. HUD* (1970); *Walker v. HUD* (1990).

honor a promise to give former residents of a housing project first choice in a newer project. When many new units were given to whites not formerly residing in the area, minority residents filed suit alleging that HDA had breached 42 U.S. Code Sections 1981, 1982, and 1983, the Civil Rights Act of 1964, and Title VIII. The Second Circuit held, however, that it was not necessary for HDA to give the former minority occupants priority. HDA must instead consider the impact of racial concentrations in the newer project in light of Congress's objective of racial integration in housing when it passed Title VIII.

## Intent and Effect

One of the most important housing discrimination rulings of the Burger-Rehnquist years came in *Village of Arlington Heights v. Metropolitan Housing Development Corp* (1977). It involved the refusal of Arlington Heights, a virtually all-white suburb of Chicago, to rezone a parcel of land to allow a nonprofit developer—the Metropolitan Housing Development Corporation—to build low- and moderate-income housing in a development to be known as Lincoln Green. After suit was filed, the U.S. District Court for the Northern District of Illinois, Eastern Division, ruled in favor of Arlington Heights, saying that its desire was to protect its zoning plan and property values, not to discriminate. The Court of Appeals for the Seventh Circuit reversed that decision, however, concluding the ultimate effect of the rezoning denial was racially discriminatory, thereby running afoul of the Fourteenth Amendment. Further, Judge Swygert, writing for a divided three-judge panel, chastised Arlington Heights. "This suburb," he observed, "has not sponsored nor participated in any low income housing developments, nor does the record reflect any such plans for the future. Realistically, Lincoln Green appears to be the only contemplated proposal for Arlington Heights that would be a step in the direction of easing the problem of de facto segregated housing." Rejecting the Lincoln Green project, then, "has the effect of perpetuating both this residential segregation and Arlington Heights' failure to accept any responsibility for helping to solve the problem" (*Metropolitan Housing Development Corporation v. Village of Arlington Heights*, 517 F.2d at 414 [1975]). Chief Judge Fairchild dissented, arguing that the ultimate effect of Arlington Heights' zoning decision was not to exclude low- and moderate-income housing from its borders because there were at least nine other undeveloped sites in Arlington Heights where it was "reasonably possible" that such housing could be built (517 F.2d at 416).

This lower court disagreement may have alerted the Supreme Court to the *Arlington Heights* case, and in this rare instance it reversed a liberal Court of Appeals decision. Indeed, the result of the Supreme Court's holding was apparent at the outset of Justice Powell's majority opinion. *Washington v. Davis* (1976) "made it clear that official action will not be held unconstitutional solely because it results in a racially disproportionate impact," Powell asserted. "Proof of racially discriminatory intent or purpose is required to show a violation of the Equal Protection Clause." While Powell acknowledged that the effect of Arlington Heights' refusal to rezone did "arguably bear more heavily on racial minorities," this alone did not invoke the prohibitions of the Fourteenth Amendment (429 U.S. at 269). The Burger Court said the plaintiffs must prove that Arlington Heights' refusal to rezone was motivated by a racially discriminatory intent in order to establish a constitutional violation. In this case the record showed no such willful intent, and the Court of Appeals' finding of discriminatory effect was deemed void.

The Court continued by explaining the factors that lower courts should consider in determining whether there was intent to discriminate that offended the Constitution. To begin with, disproportionate impact could provide an important "starting point" when attempting to prove discriminatory intent. Second, a zoning decision's historical background might be relevant to discovering intent, "particularly if it reveals a series of official actions taken for invidious purposes." Third, discriminatory intent might better be discerned by examining the "specific sequence of events" occurring prior to a zoning decision. Fourth, deviations from the standard sequence of procedures or normal substantive criteria could shed light on intent. Finally, the legislative and administrative history of the law might be pertinent, "especially where there are contemporary statements by members of the decision-making body, minutes of its meetings, or reports" (429 U.S. at 266–68). Yet none of these considerations came into play in *Arlington Heights*, according to the majority opinion.

While the Supreme Court's holding in *Arlington Heights* was clearly conservative, the lower courts have long been responsible for liberal decisions embracing the effect standard (see, e.g., *Smith v. Anchor Building Corporation* [1976]). The first of these decisions, *Kennedy*

*Park Homes Association v. City of Lackawanna, N.Y.* (1970) dealt with an attempt to build low-income housing for African Americans in Lackawanna, New York, outside the area in which they had always been concentrated. When local officials in this Buffalo suburb blocked the construction of the new low-income project, and the district court ruled in favor of minority litigants, the Second Circuit found that "the effect of Lackawanna's action was inescapably adverse" to the right to fair housing. In the words of retired U.S. Supreme Court Justice Tom Clark, then sitting on the Second Circuit, "even were we to accept the City's allegation that any discrimination here resulted from thought-lessness rather than a purposeful scheme, the city may not escape responsibility for placing its black citizens under a severe disadvantage which it cannot justify" (436 F.2d at 114). Plainly, then, *Kennedy Park Homes* stands in sharp contrast to *Arlington Heights*, with the district court and the Second Circuit enunciating an effects test favorable to fair housing advocates and the Supreme Court refusing to grant *certiorari*.

A few years later, another lower court decision on intent and effect gained national attention. *United States v. City of Black Jack, Missouri* (1974) arose when a newly incorporated town in St. Louis County passed an ordinance having the effect of halting the construction of HUD-sponsored low- and moderate-income housing for those resid-ing in poor areas of St. Louis. Black Jack, which was almost completely white, was then sued, and a three-judge panel for the Court of Appeals for the Eighth Circuit declared that Title VIII prohibited practices hav-ing a discriminatory effect. Rather than establishing intent, a plaintiff in a Title VIII case need merely show a discriminatory effect, and gov-ernment then bears the burden of proving the practices were followed pursuant to a compelling governmental interest, which they failed to meet in this case.

Again, the lower courts enunciated a liberal policy in *Black Jack* while the Supreme Court denied an appeal and remained silent on the matter of effect in housing discrimination. Moreover, even after the Supreme Court's holding in *Arlington Heights*, the lower courts contin-ued to recognize the relevance of discriminatory effect in fair housing litigation (see, e.g., *Resident Advisory Board v. Rizzo* [1977]). It happened in *Parma*, for instance, but the most prominent example is *Huntington Branch NAACP v. Town of Huntington* (1988). Huntington, New York, 95 percent white in 1980, had been unwilling to accept sub-sidized housing and was sued for denying affordable rental housing to low- and moderate-income families. The district court concluded that African Americans were much more affected by this housing shortage than whites, and the Second Circuit then held that only a discriminatory effect was necessary to establish a *prima facie* case of discrimination. Looking to Congress' intent in passing Title VIII, the court held that "the Act's stated purpose to end discrimination requires a discriminatory effect standard; an intent requirement would strip the statute of all impact on de facto segregation" (844 F.2d at 934). More liberal circuits, therefore, have occasionally continued to rely on the effects test in statutory cases despite the Supreme Court's policy statement in *Arlington Heights*. What distinguishes many of these cases from *Arlington Heights* is their reliance on statutory law, namely Title VIII, to strike down housing practices with obvious discriminatory effects, rather than constitutional law, where the Supreme Court had sent a clear signal that both discriminatory effect and discriminatory intent were required to prove a violation.

### Disability Discrimination

The law on disability discrimination provides a good illustration of the lower courts assuming the lead in fair housing rights. Since the Fair Housing Amendments Act—also known as Title VIII—prohibited housing discrimination against persons with disabilities in 1988, the Supreme Court has decided only one case to our knowledge that squarely addresses a broader issue, and even there it showed little willingness to boldly assert the individual rights involved.[8] It is in this area of fair housing law, therefore, where the opportunity has most presented itself for the lower federal courts to play a prominent policy making role. In the absence of clear signals or guidance from the Supreme Court, lower federal courts have been able to announce a number of liberal decisions that significantly expanded the housing rights of persons with disabilities without triggering a Supreme Court reversal.

In *City of Edmonds v. Oxford House, Inc.* (1995), Edmonds, Washington, had a single-family zoning law that defined "family" as

---

[8] The Supreme Court, however, has accepted fair housing cases based on other federal laws that prohibit disability discrimination, including the Americans with Disabilities Act of 1990. See Schwemm (2009).

"persons [without regard to number] related by genetics, adoption, or marriage, or a group of five or fewer [unrelated] persons" (514 U.S. at 728). The ordinance was challenged by Oxford House, Inc., which ran a group home for up to a dozen recovering alcoholics and drug addicts in an area zoned for single-family homes in Edmonds. In a technical majority opinion, Justice Ginsburg held that Section 3607(b)(1) of the Fair Housing Act "does not exempt prescriptions of the family-defining kind, *i.e.*, provisions designed to foster the family character of a neighborhood. Instead, Section 3607(b)(1)'s absolute exemption removes from the FHA's scope only total occupancy limits, *i.e.*, numerical ceilings that serve to prevent overcrowding in living quarters" (514 U.S. at 728). In short, the Edmonds ordinance was not exempt under the Fair Housing Act, and thus the Act does not permit towns to close their single-family zones to group homes.

While the Supreme Court has been reluctant to address major aspects of disability discrimination under the Fair Housing Amendments Act, the lower courts have announced decisions on disability rights each year since the Act became law. A number of these cases have dealt with the question of "reasonable accommodations" (Schwemm 2009). *Oxford House, Inc. v. Town of Babylon* (1993), for instance, addressed a zoning ordinance forbidding more than four unrelated persons from living in areas zoned for single families. Oxford House had obtained a contract and loan from New York State to create a group home for recovering alcoholics and drug addicts in one single-family area, which in turn generated local opposition. To keep from violating the ordinance, Oxford House requested reasonable accommodation pursuant to the Fair Housing Amendments Act, but Babylon initiated eviction litigation. The district court in *Babylon* ruled that a legal infraction is indicated if a disparate impact is proven or by showing a failure to make reasonable accommodations. In this case, although the local government's justification for keeping multiple family housing out of residential neighborhoods may be compelling, it is not furthered by the eviction of the tenants here and thus eviction would have constituted discrimination. Even granting the government's rationale, the court ruled that the discriminatory effect of the law far outweighed any governmental justification. The court consequently concluded it was a "reasonable justification" to redefine "family" so that the persons with disabilities in this case could live in the house in question, and that residing in this group home was beneficial to the recovery of the tenants.

In the 1990s, the case of *Hovsons, Inc. v. Township of Brick* (1996) involved whether the Township of Brick, New Jersey, made a reasonable accommodation under the Fair Housing Amendments Act when it refused to permit a variance to allow the construction of a nursing home in a residential area. The Third Circuit Court of Appeals concluded that Brick had in fact failed to reasonably accommodate disabled persons in this case, that the town would not suffer undue financial hardships or administrative burdens if it permitted the nursing home, and that the design of the home would not be incompatible with surrounding homes. In the final analysis, this case represents a liberal step for fair housing because it applied the Fair Housing Amendments Act in a way that prohibits the exclusion of nursing homes from the mainstream of American society.

Not all lower court decisions have benefitted persons with disabilities, however, and at times these cases have also been legally important. *Familystyle of St. Paul Inc. v. City of St. Paul* (1991) ruled, for instance, that the handicapped are not a suspect class. There, Familystyle operated group homes for mentally ill people in St. Paul and sought to expand its business. Regulations in both Minnesota and St. Paul, however, were geared toward keeping group homes from becoming "institutionalized." The Court of Appeals for the Eighth Circuit declared, in this case, that the regulations' goal of deinstitutionalization did not deny housing choices for persons with mental disabilities under the Fair Housing Amendments Act. Nor did they segregate them from the remainder of the populace. The regulations did not prevent the mentally ill from purchasing or renting property and, as a consequence, did not treat them as a suspect class. Yet by denying the handicapped classification as a suspect class, *Familystyle* made it difficult to prove illegal discrimination against those with mental illnesses. It is true, however, that the Supreme Court has often struck down lower federal court decisions that attempt to expand the definition of what constitutes a suspect classification (see, e.g., *San Antonio Independent School District v. Rodriguez* [1973]).

## Standing

A court must agree, of course, that a litigant has standing to sue for it to reach a decision on the merits. If standing is not granted, no decision on the merits is possible. This occurred in some housing discrimination appeals to the Supreme Court beginning in the early 1970s. Nevertheless, as we shall see, standing is the area in which the Supreme Court has made its most important contribution to fair housing law since the 1960s, and much greater Supreme Court involvement in questions of standing has meant significantly less opportunity for the lower federal courts to play an active policy making role.

A basic change in the law of standing occurred in *Flast v. Cohen* (1968), when the Warren Court liberalized the rules of standing, and this first had implications for fair housing litigation in *Trafficante v. Metropolitan Life Insurance Company* (1972). There, African American and white tenants in a San Francisco apartment complex claimed their landlord discriminated against minorities, thus injuring them by depriving them of the social benefits of integrated living and of business advantages that would have materialized. Their legal claims were anchored in the Fair Housing Act, and the Court held in favor of the tenants.

Justice Douglas's majority opinion emphasized that "person aggrieved" was broadly defined by Section 810(a) of the Fair Housing Act as "any person who claims to have been injured by a discriminatory housing practice." Congress intended a broad meaning for "person aggrieved," Douglas observed. In addition, one HUD assistant regional administrator viewed the petitioning tenants as aggrieved parties under Title VIII and that administrative interpretation was "entitled to great weight." The litigants had standing as aggrieved persons under the 1968 law because they experienced the claimed injuries due to discrimination (409 U.S. at 211–12).

*Trafficante* was an important liberal decision—one in which the Supreme Court formulated a policy that has promoted fair housing in the United States. The same was true of *Gladstone Realtors v. Village of Bellwood* (1979), where Bellwood, a Chicago suburb, and six individuals filed suit against Gladstone Realtors for steering testers to avoid housing integration in violation of the Fair Housing Act.[9] As in *Trafficante*, it was additionally claimed that the plaintiffs were denied the professional and social benefits of integrated housing because of

---

[9] Steering involves realtors directing homeseekers or renters toward or away from particular neighborhoods based on the race of the buyer or renter. Testers are "individuals who, without an intent to rent or purchase a home or apartment, pose as renters or purchasers for the purpose of collecting evidence of unlawful steering practices." *Havens Realty Corp. v. Coleman*, 455 U.S. at 363.

discrimination, but Gladstone Realtors alleged that the plaintiffs lacked standing. Justice Powell wrote on behalf of the majority in *Gladstone*. He first rejected arguments by Gladstone's attorneys that respondents must be "direct victims" to have standing under Section 812 of the Fair Housing Act. Instead, Powell determined that both Sections 810 and 812 of the Act were intentionally written broadly to cover "*all* victims—both direct and indirect—of housing discrimination by referring generally to those 'aggrieved'" (441 U.S. at 101). As a consequence, Bellwood, which argued that steering had affected its racial composition, and four Bellwood residents, testers who contended they lost professional and social benefits, each had standing.

Because of *Trafficante* and *Gladstone*, hope grew among fair housing proponents that the Court would relax conventional guidelines for standing in exclusionary zoning cases, but that hope was chilled in *Warth v. Seldin* (1975). *Warth* dealt with a zoning ordinance in Penfield, New York, an attractive white suburb of Rochester, that was challenged by four groups of plaintiffs, including low- and moderate-income nonresidents who said they were unable to find affordable housing in Penfield. The district court ruled that the plaintiffs lacked standing and did not establish a claim for which relief could be granted, and the Court of Appeals for the Second Circuit affirmed on the standing issue. Powell once more spoke for the majority, formulating a new test for causation: Did low- and moderate-income litigants "allege facts from which it reasonably could be inferred that, absent [Penfield's] restrictive zoning practices, there is a substantial probability that they would have been able to purchase or lease in Penfield"? Responding, Powell said that low- and moderate-income plaintiffs did not demonstrate a direct and concrete causal link between their own harm and Penfield's actions because they did not allege they had a "present interest in any Penfield property," that they were "subject to the ordinance's strictures," or that they had been "denied a variance or permit" by Penfield officials (422 U.S. at 504). In the final analysis, he reasoned, they were unable to find appropriate housing because they could not afford the existing housing in Penfield, not because of the Penfield ordinance or how it was implemented. Through other reasoning, he similarly denied standing to the other plaintiffs in the case.

The Burger Court handled the standing issue quite differently, several years later, in another steering case: *Havens Realty Corp. v. Coleman* (1982). There, an African American tester, Coleman, hired by a fair housing organization known as Housing Opportunities Made Equal

(HOME) in Richmond, Virginia, had been falsely told there were no vacancies in an apartment complex, yet a white tester had been informed that apartments were available in the same facility. The testers, together with HOME and others, alleged specific injuries resulting from steering, as prohibited by the Fair Housing Act, but the federal district court ruled that the testers lacked standing. The Supreme Court unanimously overturned the lower court, holding that Coleman had been denied accurate information on the availability of the property, in direct violation of the Fair Housing Act, and had standing even though he was not truly seeking to rent an apartment. The Court said, as well, that HOME had standing to challenge the steering in this case because these practices interfered with the organization's counseling and referral services to persons of low- and moderate-income, causing a drain on its limited resources.

*Havens* provided encouragement for fair housing groups in their efforts to gain standing in federal court to fight racial steering during the 1980s and 1990s. It stood for the proposition that testers may assist in both the resolution of fair housing complaints and the identification of illegal discrimination. After *Havens*, the Fair Housing Enforcement Demonstration at HUD financed private, local fair housing organizations to pursue the possibilities made possible by *Havens*, and the Demonstration determined that testing was "a highly productive device in identifying and developing hard evidence" on housing discrimination (U.S. Department of Housing and Urban Development 1989:79–80, see U.S. Department of Housing and Urban Development 1983).

Lower court standing decisions have not compared in importance to leading Supreme Court rulings like *Trafficante*, *Gladstone*, and *Havens*, and where worthy of note they often rely heavily on Supreme Court precedent. *Mayers v. Ridley* (1972), for example, announced that white property owners could advocate in court the rights of prospective African American buyers, where restrictive covenants were contained in deeds, because the pool of prospective buyers in those areas might be small and white owners could therefore suffer injuries. The D.C. Circuit's opinion hinged, however, on the Supreme Court's decision in *Sullivan v. Little Park, Inc.* (1969) in reaching its conclusions.[10] Likewise, in *Village of Bellwood v. Dwivedi* (1990), the Seventh Circuit

---

[10] Under different factual circumstances, *Sullivan* upheld the right of a white property owner to bring suit to advocate the rights of an African American lessee.

Court of Appeals announced that even testers may be granted standing in certain fair housing cases, but the court mainly relied on the Supreme Court's ruling in *Havens*.

In other cases, the lower courts have been unwilling to extend standing even to those directly affected by an action (e.g., *Debolt v. Espy* [1995]). In *Jaimes v. Toledo Metropolitan Housing Authority* (1985), a federal district court found that low-income blacks and Mexican Americans had been illegally segregated in Toledo's public housing projects. They had wanted to live in the suburbs but had been unable to find affordable suburban housing in the past. Given their legal injuries, they were entitled to live in the suburbs, the district court said, and subsidized low-income housing should be dispersed throughout the Toledo metropolitan area to facilitate that right. The Sixth Circuit reversed that decision on appeal. It ruled that minorities did not have standing because the absence of an opportunity to live in the suburbs did not constitute a direct personal injury. In *Warth v. Seldin*, the Supreme Court noted that the availability of low-income housing in the suburbs requires willing third parties to build such housing, and in *Hope, Inc. v. DuPage County, Illinois* (1984), the Seventh Circuit Court of Appeals stressed that plaintiffs in a similar case had not pointed to specific housing projects that they intended to live in or could afford. The low-income minority plaintiffs in *Warth* and *DuPage* never proved that suburban officials engaged in discriminatory housing practices, and these findings were analogous to the situation in *Jaimes*, according to the Sixth Circuit. Standing was denied. This illustrates how there was little opportunity for the lower federal courts to engage in policy making given the Supreme Court's particularly active role in standing cases. With clear directives from their principal in the form of established precedent, lower federal courts were unable to expand standing to sue in fair housing disputes, perhaps perceiving an increased likelihood of being overruled by the Supreme Court in litigation raising these questions.

## Conclusion

Rosenberg (2008:70) insists that the Supreme Court has had only a slight effect in the fight against housing discrimination and segregation in the United States. We believe that he is correct. The Court's fair housing decisions have, in Rosenberg's words, "resulted in no appreciable change" for several reasons: the Court has decided relatively few cases on the merits, it has addressed a small number of issues, it has often held against fair housing claims since the early 1970s, and it has required proof of intent before a constitutional violation can be proven. Most importantly, Supreme Court decisions have tended to be so narrow in scope that they have established no significant jurisprudence even when the fundamental notion of equal housing opportunity has been upheld. Except in a few standing cases, the Court has not stepped out to develop fair housing law in any truly important way. As a consequence, the federal courts of appeals and district courts, especially in the Northeast and Midwest, have filled the power vacuum. When new legal issues have arisen, the lower federal courts have largely defined the meaning of housing discrimination law because the Supreme Court has accepted relatively few of these cases on appeal. Avoiding sweeping rulings that would trigger Supreme Court review, the courts of appeals and district courts have slowly moved fair housing law along a more liberal path.

Future research should delve more deeply into this topic to determine the extent to which the rational-strategic model explains fair housing policy making in the federal courts. In particular, attention should be paid to examining how partisanship and ideology influence the behavior of lower court judges in this policy area, and whether those judges are constrained in their ability to make decisions based upon attitudinal considerations because of their position in the judicial hierarchy. Also, while this study has considered a subset of housing discrimination litigation, research should attempt to use existing data on the decisions of the courts of appeals and district courts to systematically examine the factors that affect judicial decision making in fair housing disputes, including the influence of case facts, ideological divergence between lower and higher federal courts, and the level of Supreme Court oversight.

## References

*Barrows v. Jackson*, 346 U.S. 249 (1953).

Bartels, Brandon L. 2009. "The Constraining Capacity of Legal Doctrine in the U.S. Supreme Court." *American Political Science Review* 103(3): 474–95.

Bickford, Adam, and Douglas S. Massey. 1991. "Segregation in the Second Ghetto: Racial and Ethnic Segregation in American Public Housing, 1977." *Social Forces* 69(4): 1011–36.

Bowie, Jennifer Barnes, and Donald R. Songer. 2009. "Assessing the Applicability of Strategic Theory to Explain Decision Making on the Courts of Appeals." *Political Research Quarterly* 62(2): 393–407.

*Buchanan v. Warley*, 245 U.S. 60 (1917).

*Cabrera v. Jakabovitz*, 24 F.3d 372 (2d Cir. 1994).

Cameron, Charles M., Jeffrey A. Segal, and Donald R. Songer. 2000. "Strategic Auditing in a Political Hierarchy: An Informational Model of the Supreme Court's Certiorari Decisions." *American Political Science Review* 94(1): 101–16.

Carp, Robert A., and Russell Wheeler. 1972. "Sink or Swim: The Socialization of a Federal District Judge." *Journal of Public Law* 21(2): 359–93.

*City of Eastlake v. Forest City Enterprises, Inc.*, 426 U.S. 668 (1976).

*City of Edmonds v. Oxford House*, 514 U.S. 725 (1995).

Cooper, Phillip J. 1988. *Hard Judicial Choices: Federal District Judges and State and Local Governments*. New York: Oxford University Press.

*Corrigan v. Buckley*, 271 U.S. 323 (1926).

Cross, Frank B, and Emerson H. Tiller. 1998. "Judicial Partisanship and Obedience to Legal Doctrine: Whistleblowing on the Federal Courts of Appeals." *Yale Law Journal* 107(7): 2155–76.

Danielson, Michael N. 1976. *The Politics of Exclusion*. New York: Columbia University Press.

*DeBolt v. Espy*, 832 F. Supp. 209 (S.D. Ohio 1993).

Epstein, Lee, and Jack Knight. 2000. "Toward a Strategic Revolution in Judicial Politics: A Look Back, A Look Ahead." *Political Research Quarterly* 53(3): 625–61.

*Familystyle of St. Paul, Inc. v. City of St. Paul*, 923 F.2d 91 (8th Cir. 1991).

Farley, Reynolds, and William H. Frey. 1994. "Changes in the Segregation of Whites from Blacks during the 1980s: Small Steps Toward a More Integrated Society." *American Sociological Review* 59(1): 23–45.

*Flast v. Cohen*, 392 U.S. 83 (1968).

*Gladstone Realtors v. Village of Bellwood*, 441 U.S. 91 (1979).

Haar, Charles M. 1996. *Suburbs under Siege: Race, Space, and Audacious Judges*. Princeton, NJ: Princeton University Press.

Haire, Susan B., Stefanie A. Linquist, and Donald R. Songer. 2003. "Appellate Court Supervision in the Federal Judiciary: A Hierarchical Perspective." *Law and Society Review* 37(1): 143–67.

Halpern, Stephen C. 1995. *On the Limits of the Law: The Ironic Legacy of Title VI of the 1964 Civil Rights Act*. Baltimore, MD: Johns Hopkins University Press.

*Hansberry v. Lee*, 311 U.S. 32 (1940).

*Havens Realty Corp. v. Coleman*, 455 U.S. 363 (1982).

Hettinger, Virginia A., Stefanie A. Lindquist, and Wendy L. Martinek. 2004. "Comparing Attitudinal and Strategic Accounts of Dissenting Behavior on the U.S. Courts of Appeals." *American Journal of Political Science* 48(1): 123–37.

*Hills v. Gautreaux*, 425 U.S. 284 (1976).

Hirsch, Arnold R. 1998. *Making the Second Ghetto: Race and Housing in Chicago, 1940-1960*. Chicago: University of Chicago Press.

*Hope, Inc. v. DuPage County, Illinois*, 717 F.2d 1061 (7th Cir. 1983).

*Hope, Inc. v. DuPage County, Illinois*, 738 F.2d 797 (7th Cir. 1984).

*Hovsons, Inc. v. Township of Brick*, 89 F.3d 1096 (3d Cir. 1996).

Howard, J. Woodford, Jr. 1981. *Courts of Appeals in the Federal Judicial System: A Study of the Second, Fifth, and District of Columbia Circuits*. Princeton, NJ: Princeton University Press.

*Hunter v. Erickson*, 393 U.S. 385 (1969).

*Huntington Branch NAACP v. Town of Huntington*, 844 F.2d 926 (2d Cir. 1988).

*Hurd v. Hodge*, 334 U.S. 24 (1948).

*Jaimes v. Toledo Metropolitan Housing Authority*, 758 F.2d 1086 (6th Cir. 1985).

*James v. Valtierra*, 402 U.S. 137 (1971).

Johnson, Charles A. 1979. "Lower Court Reactions to Supreme Court Decisions: A Quantitative Examination." *American Journal of Political Science* 23(4): 792–804.

*Jones v. Alfred H. Mayer Co.*, 392 U.S. 409 (1968).

*Kennedy Park Homes Association v. City of Lackawanna*, N.Y., 436 F.2d 108 (2d Cir. 1970).

King, Kimi Lynn. 1998. "Does Law Matter? Federal District Court Decision-Making in Fair Housing Cases, 1968–89." *Social Science Research* 27(4): 388–409.

Klarman, Michael J. 2004. *From Jim Crow to Civil Rights: The Supreme Court and the Struggle for Racial Equality*. New York: Oxford University Press.

Klein, David E. 2002. *Making Law in the United States Courts of Appeals*. New York: Cambridge University Press.

Klein, David E., and Robert J. Hume. 2003. "Fear of Reversal as an Explanation of Lower Court Compliance." *Law and Society Review* 37(3): 579–605.

Kushner, James A. 1995. *Fair Housing: Discrimination in Real Estate, Community Development, and Revitalization*. 2d ed. Colorado Springs, CO.: Shepard's/ McGraw-Hill.

Lamb, Charles M. 2005. *Housing Segregation in Suburban America since 1960: Presidential and Judicial Politics*. New York: Cambridge University Press.

Lindquist, Stefanie A., Susan B. Haire, and Donald R. Songer. 2007. "Supreme Court Auditing of the U.S. Courts of Appeals: An Organizational Perspective." *Journal of Public Administration Research & Theory* 17(4): 607–24.

Maltzman, Forrest, James F. Spriggs II, and Paul J. Wahlbeck. 2000. *Crafting Law on the Supreme Court: The Collegial Game*. New York: Cambridge University Press.

Massey, Douglas S., and Nancy A. Denton. 1989. "Hypersegregation in U.S. Metropolitan Areas: Black and Hispanic Segregation along Five Dimensions." *Demography* 26(2): 373–93.

Massey, Douglas S., and Nancy A. Denton. 1993. *American Apartheid: Segregation and the Making of the Underclass*. Cambridge, MA: Harvard University Press.

*Mayers v. Ridley*, 465 F.2d 630 (D.C. Cir. 1972).

*Metropolitan Housing Development Corporation v. Village of Arlington Heights*, 517 F.2d 409 (7th Cir. 1975).

*Milliken v. Bradley*, 418 U.S. 717 (1974).

*NAACP, Boston Chapter v. HUD*, 817 F.2d 149 (1st Cir. 1987).

*Otero v. New York City Housing Authority*, 484 F.2d 1122 (2d Cir. 1973).

*Oxford House, Inc. v. Town of Babylon*, 819 F. Supp. 1179 (E.D. N.Y. 1993).

Patterson, James T. 2001. *Brown v. Board of Education: A Civil Rights Milestone and Its Troubled Legacy*. New York: Oxford University Press.

Perry, H. W., Jr. 1991. *Deciding to Decide: Agenda Setting in the United States Supreme Court*. Cambridge, MA: Harvard University Press.

Polikoff, Alexander. 2006. *Waiting for Gautreaux: A Story of Segregation, Housing, and the Black Ghetto*. Evanston, IL: Northwestern University Press.

Pritchett, C. Herman. 1948. *The Roosevelt Court: A Study in Judicial Politics and Values 1937–1947*. New York: Macmillan.

*Reitman v. Mulkey*, 387 U.S. 369 (1967).

*Resident Advisory Board v. Rizzo*, 564 F.2d 126 (3d Cir. 1977).

Rosenberg, Gerald N. 2008. *Hollow Hope: Can Courts Bring About Social Change?* 2d ed. Chicago: University of Chicago Press.

Rowland, C. K., and Robert A. Carp. 1996. *Politics and Judgment in Federal District Courts*. Lawrence: University Press of Kansas.

Rubinowitz, Leonard S., and James E. Rosenbaum. 2000. *Crossing the Class and Color Lines: From Public Housing to White Suburbia*. Chicago: University of Chicago Press.

*San Antonio Independent School District v. Rodriguez*, 411 U.S. 1 (1973).

Schubert, Glendon. 1965. *The Judicial Mind: The Attitudes and Ideologies of Supreme Court Justices, 1946–1963*. Evanston, IL: Northwestern University Press.

Schubert, Glendon. 1974. *The Judicial Mind Revisited: A Psychometric Analysis of Supreme Court Ideology*. New York: Oxford University Press.

Schuck, Peter H. 2002. "Judging Remedies: Judicial Approaches to Housing Segregation." *Harvard Civil Rights-Civil Liberties Law Review* 37(2): 289–368.
Schwemm, Robert G. 2009. *Housing Discrimination: Law and Litigation*. St. Paul, MN.: Thomson West.
Segal, Jeffrey A., and Harold J. Spaeth. 2002. *The Supreme Court and the Attitudinal Model Revisited*. New York: Cambridge University Press.
*Shannon v. HUD*, 436 F.2d 809 (3rd Cir. 1970).
*Shelley v. Kraemer*, 334 U.S. 1 (1948).
*Smith v. Anchor Building Corporation*, 536 F.2d 231 (8th Cir. 1976).
Solimine, Michael E. 1988. "Ideology and En Banc Review." *North Carolina Law Review* 67(1): 29–76.
Songer, Donald R., and Susan Haire. 1992. "Integrating Alternative Approaches to the Study of Judicial Voting: Obscenity Cases in the U.S. Courts of Appeals." *American Journal of Political Science* 36(4): 963–82.
Songer, Donald R., Jeffrey A. Segal, and Charles M. Cameron. 1994. "The Hierarchy of Justice: Testing a Principal-Agent Model of Supreme Court-Circuit Court Interactions." *American Journal of Political Science* 38(3): 673–96.
Songer, Donald R., and Reginald Sheehan. 1990. "Supreme Court Impact on Compliance and Outcomes: Miranda and New York Times in the United States Courts of Appeals." *Western Political Quarterly* 43(2): 297–319.
Songer, Donald R., Reginald S. Sheehan, and Susan B. Haire. 2000. *Continuity and Change on the United States Courts of Appeals*. Ann Arbor: University of Michigan Press.
*Sullivan v. Little Hunting Park, Inc.*, 396 U.S. 229 (1969).
*Swann v. Charlotte-Mecklenburg Board of Education*, 402 U.S. 1 (1971).
*Trafficante v. Metropolitan Life Insurance Company*, 409 U.S. 205 (1972).
*United States v. City of Birmingham, Michigan*, 538 F. Supp. 819 (E.D. Michigan 1982).
*United States v. City of Black Jack, Missouri*, 508 F.2d 1179 (8th Cir. 1974).
*United States v. City of Parma, Ohio*, 494 F. Supp. 1049 (N.D. Ohio 1980).
*United States v. City of Parma, Ohio*, 504 F. Supp. 913 (N.D. Ohio 1980).
*United States v. City of Parma, Ohio*, 661 F.2d 562 (6th Cir. 1981).
*United States v. Starrett City Associates*, 840 F.2d 1096 (2d Cir. 1988).
U.S. Department of Housing and Urban Development. 1983. *Fair Housing Assistance Demonstration*. Washington, DC: U.S. Department of Housing and Urban Development.
U.S. Department of Housing and Urban Development. 1989. *New Directions in Housing Policy: 1981–1989*. Washington, DC: U.S. Department of Housing and Urban Development.
Van Winkle, Steven R. 1997. "Dissenting as a Signal: Evidence from the U.S. Courts of Appeals." Paper presented at the annual meeting of the American Political Science Association, Washington, DC, September 27.
*Village of Arlington Heights v. Metropolitan Housing Development Corporation*, 429 U.S. 252 (1977).
*Village of Belle Terre v. Boraas*, 416 U.S. 1 (1974).
*Village of Bellwood v. Dwivedi*, 895 F.2d 1521 (7th Cir. 1990).
*Walker v. HUD*, 912 F.2d 819 (5th Cir. 1990).
*Warth v. Seldin*, 422 U.S. 490 (1975).
Wasby, Stephen L., Anthony A. D'Amato, and Rosemary Metrailer. 1977. *Desegregation from Brown to Alexander: An Exploration of Supreme Court Strategies*. Carbondale: Southern Illinois University Press.
*Washington v. Davis*, 426 U.S. 229 (1976).
Wilkinson, J. Harvie. 1979. *From Brown to Bakke: The Supreme Court and School Integration, 1954–1978*. New York: Oxford University Press.
*Young v. Pierce*, 628 F. Supp. 1037 (E.D. Tex. 1985).

# FAIR HOUSING IN THE U.S. REAL ESTATE INDUSTRY: PERCEPTIONS OF BLACK REAL ESTATE PROFESSIONALS*

Robert Mark Silverman

## Fair Housing Policy and the U.S. Real Estate Industry

Housing discrimination is a persistent problem in the United States. It is estimated that African Americans, Latinos, and Asian Americans experience more than 3.7 million instances of discrimination, annually, when renting and purchasing housing (National Fair Housing Alliance 2008). This is a conservative estimate, since it does not include instances of housing discrimination experienced by individuals based on disability status, sex, familial status, and other characteristics. Housing discrimination is a reflection of historic residential segregation patterns in American society, and its continued occurrence functions to perpetuate these patterns (Massey and Denton 1998; Turner et al. 2007; Ellen 2008; Massey 2008; Roscigno et al. 2009).

Policy makers and scholars have offered a variety of explanations for the persistence of housing discrimination. Their work is based on studies of housing markets, demographic trends, discrimination complaints, general population surveys, and testing in the field. The findings from past research have prompted the enactment of fair housing law at the federal, state, and local levels. Despite these efforts, research and policy focused on ameliorating housing discrimination remains a work in progress. In this chapter I examine an understudied dimension of fair housing, real estate professionals' perceptions of housing discrimination. In particular, I focus on the manner in which fair housing and housing discrimination are perceived by black real estate professionals.

The analysis of real estate professionals' perceptions fills a critical gap in the literature on fair housing. Beyond anecdotal evidence, little is known about this group's perceptions of fair housing issues. Yet, real

* This research was supported in part by an annual research grant from the UB2020 Scholars Fund at the University at Buffalo. I would like to thank Gloria Kornowski for research assistance.

estate professionals are key providers of information and access to housing markets, and they subsequently facilitate housing transactions. It is important to understand the degree to which real estate professionals are sensitized to issues surrounding housing discrimination and cognizant of the scope of fair housing policy. Understanding the perceptions of real estate professionals adds to previous research on fair housing and informs the development of public policy.

*Federal, State, and Local Fair Housing Law*

Fair housing law exists at the federal, state, and local levels. The impetus for most anti-discrimination efforts related to housing was the Fair Housing Act of 1968 (amended in 1988). In its present form, the Act criminalizes discrimination in the sale and rental of housing based on: race, color, religion, sex, handicap, familial status, or national origin (Yinger 1999). Under the Act, it is illegal to discriminate at any point in housing transactions. The Act applies to advertising, sharing information about housing, lending, accessibility, and any other omission or decision that restricts housing choice to a group protected by law. Under the Act, the U.S. Department of Housing and Urban Development (HUD) is the federal agency that administers programs related to fair housing. HUD is authorized to *affirmatively* further fair housing in all of its programs and funded activities.

HUD's approach to fair housing entails public education and enforcement. Funding is made available to local governments and nonprofit agencies for both purposes. Historically, this funding has come from the community development block grant (CDBG) and other programs. Federal fair housing law also provides for monitoring. For instance, local governments receiving CDBG funding are required to report on the performance of housing programs, make progress toward meeting fair housing goals, and to prepare analysis of impediment reports approximately every six years. When the Act was originally passed in 1968, mechanisms for fair housing enforcement were weak. HUD had no enforcement powers when fair housing violations were identified. Instead, the agency filled a conciliation role and in extreme cases of discrimination could notify the US Attorney General's Office of violations. Also, individuals only had 180 days to file a lawsuit related to fair housing and punitive damages were capped at $1,000. The 1988 amendments to the Fair Housing Act addressed many of these shortcomings. HUD was empowered to hold administrative hearings and impose fines and damages for violations. HUD was required to address complaints within four months and individuals had up to two years to file civil lawsuits. In addition, caps on damages were significantly increased. The 1988 amendments were accompanied by the creation of the Fair Housing Initiatives Program (FHIP) and the Fair Housing Assistance Program (FHAP), which created a pool of funding for local public and nonprofit agencies engaged in fair housing monitoring, advocacy, and enforcement (Schill 2007; Lamb and Wilk 2009).

At the state and local levels additional fair housing protections are sometimes adopted to augment federal law. These protections are typically in four forms: the ability to file discrimination complaints with state and local agencies, the addition of resources for public education, the identification of protected groups not covered under federal law, and the adoption of state and local fair housing ordinances. The National Fair Housing Alliance's website (www.nationalfairhousing. org) references over 100 state and local fair housing laws that have extended fair housing protection to groups based on marital status, sources of income, sexual orientation, gender identification, political affiliation, Section 8 voucher status, and other characteristics. There is also increased emphasis placed on linking fair housing goals to land-use planning, zoning, and other regional development decisions (National Neighborhood Coalition 2001).

A number of other federal policies complement efforts to promote fair housing. For instance, data from the Home Mortgage Disclosure Act of 1975 (HMDA) (amended in 1989, 1992 and 2004) has been used to identify impediments to homeownership, and the Community Reinvestment Act of 1977 (CRA) has provided housing advocates with additional remedies to address discrimination in housing markets (Ross and Yinger 2002; Squires 2003; Friedman and Squires 2005). Of course, scholars like Sidney (2003; 2004) argue that the Fair Housing Act, HMDA, and CRA result in divergent strategies to address discrimination in housing markets and are not entirely compatible. Likewise, some federal policies aimed at promoting affordable housing have also been criticized for contributing to the geographic isolation of minorities and the poor. For example, some have argued that the Low-Income Housing Tax Credit program has been implemented in a manner that re-concentrates poverty (National Neighborhood Coalition 2001; National Fair Housing Alliance 2008; U.N. Committee on the Elimination of Racial Discrimination 2008).

On balance, fair housing policy in the US is highly fragmented across governmental agencies and nonprofit advocacy organizations. Connerly (2006) argues that over time a relatively robust policy has emerged in the US with strengthened enforcement mechanisms. However, this system is also hampered by a lack of coordination across agencies responsible for its implementation. Despite the relative merits of enforcement mechanisms in US fair housing policies, it is criticized for its limited focus on indirect forms of discrimination that continue to impact housing markets (Connerly 2006). Indirect discrimination presents an acute challenge to fair housing advocates in the contemporary period (Galster 1999; Connerly 2006). This type of discrimination is subtle, rooted in perceptions, and embedded in broader systems of inequality (Denton 1999; Kraus 2004a; Kraus 2004b; Squires and Kubrin 2005).

## Perceptions of Discrimination and Policy Implementation

Since the passage of the Fair Housing Act of 1968, there have been a number of efforts to measure discrimination in housing markets. Many of these efforts have used the paired testing method. In paired testing, minority and white individuals with equivalent income and employment profiles attempt to rent or purchase housing units. The results of testers' experiences in a housing market are compared in order to identify instances of differential treatment. Turner et al. (2002) used paired testing in a national study of discrimination in housing markets. This study found that although discrimination remained present in metropolitan housing markets, it had declined somewhat between 1989 and 2000. The largest decline in discrimination was found among paired testers attempting to purchase homes, where whites were favored over blacks in 29% of the tests in 1989 and 17% of the tests in 2000. In contrast, discrimination in rental markets saw the lowest change with whites favored over blacks in 26.4% of the tests in 1989 and 21.6% of the tests in 2000.

Paired tests represent one method for measuring the presence of discrimination in housing markets. Other studies have used surveys to detect the degree to which the general public is aware of fair housing law. Abravanel and Cunningham (2002) conducted a national survey measuring public awareness of fair housing laws and found that the public has a general awareness of existing policies. However, there was a discrepancy in the degree to which the public was aware of protections for various groups covered by fair housing laws. For instance, there was greater awareness of laws prohibiting discrimination based on race than on disability. The public has the lowest level of awareness of laws prohibiting discrimination based on family status (i.e., discrimination against families with children under 18 years of age). This was an important finding since discrimination based on family status sometimes disproportionately impacts minority home seekers in urban areas. In such instances, discrimination based on family status can also be a form of indirect discrimination based on race. Abravanel (2007) conducted a follow up survey in 2005 and found that knowledge of fair housing policy had not improved over time, although public support for fair housing had slightly increased.

Another telling result from Abravanel and Cunningham's (2002) survey was that 14% of the adult public believed that they had experienced some form of housing discrimination during the course of their lives. Yet, only 17% of individuals who reported that they experienced discrimination did anything about it. Of those who took action, most reported that they simply confronted the offending party without pursuing a formal complaint. Parallel to this result, Squires et al. (2002) surveyed Washington D.C. residents and found that over 25% of black respondents knew someone who had experienced housing discrimination in the previous three years.

The thrust of survey research on housing discrimination focuses on the experiences and perceptions of prospective renters, homebuyers, and the general public. Despite evidence of persistent discrimination, little is known about the perceptions of real estate professionals. Given this groups' position in the real estate industry, one might hypothesize that issues related to discrimination and fair housing would be highly salient. On the other hand, as members of the real estate industry, one might hypothesize that real estate professionals would downplay these issues in order to protect their industry. This exploratory research provides evidence supporting aspects of both hypotheses. The findings suggest that the perceptions of minority real estate professionals are shaped by a complex set of relationships embedded in housing markets and professional networks.

## The Role of the Real Estate Industry

In the absence of survey data measuring real estate professionals' perceptions of discrimination and fair housing, past research on the real estate industry serves as a starting point for inquiry. Historically, three issues have been associated with discrimination and fair housing in the real estate industry. The first has involved concerns related to open housing. At its core, this issue focuses on the degree to which minorities have access to housing in all communities. Debates about open housing have centered on whether landlords and sellers of real estate have the right to refuse to rent or sell property to minorities. Fair housing laws have been one of the primary tools used to establish open housing as an underlying principle for contemporary housing markets. Since the adoption of such legislation, surveys of the general population have indicated that growing support exists for open housing (Goering 2007).

Complementary judicial rulings and legislative initiative have been enacted since the passage of fair housing laws which have expanded the concept of open housing. Fair share housing and inclusionary zoning policies are two examples (Lerman 2006; Schuetz et al. 2009). Under fair share rulings and legislation, the distribution of affordable housing is managed at the regional or statewide level. As a result, local communities are mandated to provide access to affordable housing and produce their fair share of a region's affordable units. Inclusionary zoning is a related land use tool designed to ensure that a set proportion of housing units in new developments are affordable.

The second issue associated with discrimination and fair housing in the real estate industry is the practice of steering (Turner et al. 2002; Turner et al. 2007; Ellen 2008; Squires 2008). Steering refers to the practice in which real estate brokers or agents guide prospective homebuyers toward or away from certain neighborhoods, based on race or some other characteristic. The practice of steering by real estate professionals has helped to produce and reinforce patterns of segregation across the United States. During the early and mid-1900s steering was widespread. It became illegal with the passage of civic rights and fair housing laws. However, steering still happens, evidenced from individual discrimination complaints and through the use of paired testing in local housing markets.

The third issue associated with discrimination and fair housing in the real estate industry is the practice of blockbusting (Orser 1997; Gotham 2002; Squires 2008). Blockbusting is a practice used by real estate brokers and agents to encourage white property owners to sell their homes by giving the impression that increased numbers of minorities are moving into their neighborhood. Blockbusting is one of the more insidious practices used by real estate agents because it relies on racism as a mechanism to augment property sales. This practice allows unscrupulous real estate agents to pressure homeowners into selling their properties to minority buyers. As a result, real estate agents profit from artificially enhanced sales. Like steering, blockbusting is prohibited under fair housing and other laws. Nevertheless, suspected blockbusting is periodically still reported.

In large part, the real estate industry is self regulating with respect to open housing, steering, blockbusting and other areas related to fair housing. One of the primary mechanisms for self regulation has been professional education and training programs. Real estate professionals are required to undergo fair housing training prior to licensing at the state level and continuing education is required for re-licensing. Today, education and training is endorsed by the National Association of Realtors (NAR), its local affiliates, and other professional associations. Nonprofit housing organizations and other local agencies support education and training of real estate professionals. These organizations and agencies also monitor real estate practices and enforce fair housing laws. In spite of these efforts, discrimination continues to exist in housing markets.

The contemporary milieu represents the culmination of a number of changes in fair housing law, public perceptions, and real estate practices. Most of these changes are relatively new and can be traced back to the late-1960s. Prior to that period, there were no fair housing laws at the federal level, public attitudes were less supportive of open housing, and organizations like the NAR openly discriminated against minority clients and realtors. Within the real estate profession, many of the reforms that have occurred contemporaneously were the result of changes in law, public attitudes, and advocacy from black realtors.

## Methods and Data

This research is based on a national survey of black real estate professionals. The survey included 31 questions measuring the perceptions of black real estate professionals. Questions measured perceptions of: the effectiveness of fair housing law, the prevalence of discriminatory practices in the real estate profession, and the experiences of minority real estate professionals in the real estate industry. The survey was administered between July 2009 and December 2009. It entailed an initial mailing and a follow-up postcard sent to survey recipients.

A total of 1,595 real estate professionals in the United States were mailed surveys. At the end of that period a 9.4% (n=151) response rate was reached. This response rate was consistent with past mail surveys involving minority respondents, potentially sensitive questions, and sampling in a non-institutional setting (Schuman and Presser 1996; Nardi 2003; Sue and Ritter 2007). Pearson (2010) indicates that mail surveys of this nature typically invoke a 5% response rate, and this can be enhanced with follow-up contacts and other techniques. He also notes that the degree to which low response rates are problematic is predicated by differences between respondents and non respondents. The respondents were identified on the membership roster of the National Association of Real Estate Brokers (NAREB). The NAREB is the largest association of minority real estate professionals and the oldest minority trade association in America. Its membership is predominantly composed of black real estate professionals.[1]

The NAREB was formed in 1947 in order to advocate for open housing and the rights of black professionals in the real estate industry. At the time that the organization was formed, blacks were not permitted to join the NAR. Consequently, blacks were not permitted to identify themselves as 'realtors,' since the term was trademarked by the NAR and only applicable to its members. In response, the NAREB coined the term 'realtist' to refer to its members. Although barriers to NAR members were lifted in response to the civil rights movement, many black professionals remained members in the NAREB only and continued to identify as 'realtists' (Smith 2006). Several respondents referenced the relationship between the NAR and NAREB in open-ended responses that were incorporated in the survey. One respondent provided this comment which was representative of the sentiment expressed by others:

> I have remained an active member of a local board of the National Association of Real Estate Brokers, the nation's oldest and largest minority trade association. The NAREB, as we are known, was organized more than 70 years ago when local brokers were denied membership in the local trade association. Membership in the REALTORS® was not open to minorities in our area until 25 years later. We attend an annual

---

[1] The respondents are identified as "black" instead of "African-American" in this chapter because some of them are African Immigrants and others are non-U.S. citizens.

convention each year, very educational and informative of real estate as it affects minorities in many areas of our country. Locally we meet monthly throughout the year with a similar goal. I am active now and hold a life membership in my local housing concerns board. I joined in [the early 1970s]. I serve [on] our local board. We have local boards in most of the States and Regions of our country. Our national office is in the Washington Metro Area. Our motto is "Democracy in Housing."

The survey focused on the perceptions of black real estate professionals in order to achieve two research goals. At the macro-level, data were collected on industry-wide issues related to fair housing implementation. At the micro-level, data were collected on the experiences and perceptions of minority professionals within the real estate industry. Combining these two levels of data illuminates a unique perspective on fair housing by examining the degree to which a nexus exists between housing opportunities for the population at large and experiences of minority group members. An underlying assumption of the survey was that black real estate professionals would be more sensitized to the nuances and dynamics of discrimination and fair housing. As a result, a purposive sample was drawn for this exploratory analysis.

Table 1 summarizes characteristics of the survey respondents. The respondents to the survey represented the population surveyed along several dimensions. Regionally, 12.6% of the respondents were located in the Northeast, 13.9% were located in the Midwest, 58.3% were located in the South, and 15.2% were located in the West. This mirrored the population at large, where 12.9% were located in the Northeast, 13.6% were located in the Midwest, 54.2% were located in the South, and 16.3% were located in the West. Likewise, 94.7% of the survey respondents were black, with another 3.3% identifying as "other race" and specifying that they were multi-racial with some black ancestry. Immigrants made up 2.0% of the respondents. Men and women were almost equally represented among respondents. The majority (75.4%) of the respondents were 50 years of age or more. The average respondent had 20.5 years of experience in the real estate profession. The typical respondent worked in a firm with eight other real estate professionals. On average, 63.7% of those other real estate professionals were minority group members and 51.3% were women. Finally, 78.0% of the clientele of the typical respondent were minority group members.

Table 1. Summary of Survey Respondents' Characteristics (n=151)

| | |
|---|---:|
| *Region* | |
| Percent Northeast | 12.6 |
| Percent Midwest | 13.9 |
| Percent South | 58.3 |
| Percent West | 15.2 |
| *Race* | |
| Percent Black | 94.7 |
| Percent Native American | 0.7 |
| Percent White | 1.3 |
| Percent Other | 3.3 |
| *Immigration Status* | |
| Percent immigrant | 2.0 |
| *Gender* | |
| Percent female | 48.7 |
| *Age* | |
| Percent 30–39 years | 8.0 |
| Percent 40–49 years | 16.7 |
| Percent 50–59 years | 31.7 |
| Percent 60 years and above | 44.6 |
| *Professional Experience* | |
| Average number of years in the real estate profession | 20.5 |
| Average number of years at current firm | 13.2 |
| Median number of real estate professionals in current firm | 8 |
| Percent of real estate professionals in current firm that are minority group members | 63.7 |
| Percent real estate professionals in current firm that are female | 51.3 |
| Percent of clientele that are minority group members | 78.0 |
| *Fair Housing Training* | |
| Percent required to complete training at time of licensing | 70.9 |
| Average hours of training currently required in metropolitan area | 3.1 |

In terms of exposure to fair housing training, 70.9% of the respondents completed fair housing training prior to receiving their real estate license and each respondent was required to have approximately three hours of continuing education, annually, in this area. Despite broad access to fair housing training and continuing education, there was a perception that the scope of fair housing training provided to real estate professionals was deficient. For example, 37.7% of respondents indicated that real estate professionals received a low level of fair housing training and 42.4% indicated that they received a moderate level. In contrast, only 19.2% of respondents indicated that all real estate professionals received a high level of fair housing training in the United States. The general perception was that fair housing received cursory treatment in the typical continuing education programs that real estate professionals were exposed to.

As a baseline measure, the respondents were also asked about their perceptions of trends in housing discrimination, nationally, and in their metropolitan area during the past 10 years. In terms of national trends, 57.5% of respondents perceived that discrimination had declined during the past decade. An additional 24.1% felt that discrimination had remained about the same and 18.4% said it had increased. Considering their metropolitan areas, 50.0% of respondents perceived that housing discrimination had declined during the same time period. Another 25.3% felt that discrimination had remained about the same and 24.7% said it had increased. One respondent's open-ended comment captures the essence of this distinction:

> I live in St. Louis. Of course, we have had major issues in the present and past. There are still people in our area that do not want a black/African-American realtor. We have issues here that are not just fair housing issues, but major black/white issues that have not been addressed for many years. It was as late as 1965 when the first black person was allowed to join the Board of Realtors here.

Although many legislative and public policy milestones have been achieved at the national level, the perception remains that they have not fully penetrated at the local level. This distinction is of interest, since some respondents perceived less progress toward ameliorating discrimination in their local communities. Given this distinction, it could be assumed that a similar pattern would emerge in responses to other questions about fair housing when comparing national and local perceptions.

## Fair Housing, Discrimination, and Institutional Responses

### Perceptions of Fair Housing and Discrimination

In general, respondents' perceptions of housing discrimination indicated that there was a trend toward less discrimination, however it was more pronounced at the national level. National policy may have tempered general attitudes about fair housing and discrimination, but this has not permeated to metropolitan areas at the same rate. Ironically, the reverse relationship was expressed when real estate professionals were asked about specific forms of discrimination nationally and locally. Respondents were asked to rate the intensity of barriers to fair housing for a number of groups at the national and local levels. The ratings were done on a scale of 1 to 10, where 1 indicated that a group was perceived to face "no barriers to fair housing" and 10 indicated that a group was perceived to face "many barriers to fair housing." The results of these ratings are found in Table 2. For each group rated in Table 2, a paired sample t-test was conducted.

Table 2 reveals a number of nuances related to the perceptions of black real estate professionals in relation to barriers to fair housing. The groups perceived to face the greatest number of barriers to fair housing at both the national and local level were households receiving welfare and Section 8 voucher holders. These groups were followed by the mentally disabled. In essence, poor people receiving public assistance and the indigent were perceived as the most disadvantaged in national and local housing markets. The next three highest ranked groups were blacks, Native Americans, and Hispanics. Respondents perceived historically disenfranchised minorities as the third most disadvantaged groups in national and local housing markets. Following these groups, the magnitude of barriers faced by specific groups tended to moderate at both the national and local levels. At the national level, perceptions of barriers to fair housing only fell below the midpoint of the scale for two groups: Asians and veterans. At the local level, perceptions of barriers to fair housing fell below the midpoint of the scale for one additional group: lesbians and gays.

It is also noteworthy that for each group, barriers to fair housing were rated lower at the local level. The differences between national and local ratings were statistically significant at the .05 level or above for all of the groups rated with the exception of: single parent households, households receiving welfare, Section 8 voucher holders, and

Table 2. Paired Samples T-Test for Perceived Barriers to Fair Housing Nationally and in Respondents' Metropolitan Areas (n=151)

| Group facing barriers | Mean for nation | Mean for metropolitan area | T-value |
|---|---|---|---|
| Black/ African-American | 6.80 | 6.33 | 3.544*** |
| Native American | 6.27 | 5.73 | 3.412** |
| Asian/Asian-American | 4.63 | 4.04 | 3.964*** |
| Hispanic/ Hispanic-American | 6.36 | 5.80 | 3.739*** |
| Physically Disabled | 6.17 | 5.47 | 4.791*** |
| Mentally Disabled | 6.99 | 6.65 | 1.271 |
| Elderly | 5.49 | 5.04 | 3.210** |
| Single Parent Households | 5.46 | 5.28 | 1.118 |
| Households Receiving Welfare | 7.27 | 6.94 | 1.849+ |
| Section 8 Voucher Holders | 7.21 | 6.89 | 1.841+ |
| Veterans | 4.50 | 4.06 | 2.494* |
| Immigrants | 6.11 | 5.49 | 3.306*** |
| Lesbians and Gays | 5.32 | 4.91 | 2.558* |

Note: means are based on a scale of 1–10 where 1= "no barriers to fair housing" and 10= "many barriers to fair housing".
+ $p<.10$, * $p<.05$, ** $p<.01$, *** $p<.001$.

the mentally disabled. Despite general perceptions that discrimination was subsiding more rapidly nationally than locally, respondents perceived significantly fewer barriers to fair housing at the local level. This could be interpreted a number of ways. For instance, respondents may have perceived historic levels of discrimination as being higher nationally. Therefore, the more rapidly declining discrimination at the national level represented a convergence of national and local levels. On the other hand, respondents may perceive discrimination in the aggregate differently than for individual groups. As a result, advocacy and legislation at the national level could be seen as reducing overall levels of discrimination more rapidly at the national level than the local level. In contrast, individuals may perceive a greater locus of control when dealing with discrimination faced by specific groups at the local level. A similar dilemma presents itself when examining perceptions of discrimination in subsectors of the housing market.

Respondents were asked to rate levels of discrimination in different subsectors of housing markets at the national and local levels. The ratings were done on a scale of 1 to 10, where 1 indicated "no discrimination" and 10 indicated "extremely high levels of discrimination." The results of these ratings are found in Table 3. For each subsector rated in Table 3, a paired sample t-test was conducted.

Table 3 adds to our understanding of the perceptions of black real estate professionals. The subsector of national and local housing markets where the highest levels of discrimination were perceived was the mortgage lending market. Real estate professionals perceived banks and financial institutions as the greatest sources of discrimination in housing markets at the national and local levels. Two other subsectors on the owner-occupied side of the real estate industry were perceived as having relatively high levels of discrimination. These were the insurance and home appraisal subsectors. The other subsector where an above average level of discrimination was perceived was the rental housing market where discrimination is typically attributed to actions of individual landlords. In contrast, perceptions of discrimination moderated in the residential real estate sales subsector. It is not

Table 3. Paired Samples T-Test for Perceived Level of Discrimination Nationally and in Respondents' Metropolitan Areas (n=151)

| Area of the housing market | Mean for nation | Mean for metropolitan area | T-value |
|---|---|---|---|
| Rental housing market | 6.48 | 6.09 | 2.516* |
| Residential real estate sales | 5.78 | 5.50 | 1.995* |
| Mortgage lending | 6.85 | 6.42 | 3.074** |
| Home appraisals | 6.30 | 5.86 | 2.917** |
| Home insurance | 6.50 | 6.11 | 2.888* |
| Rental insurance | 6.13 | 5.73 | 2.537* |

*Note:* means are based on a scale of 1–10 where 1= "no discrimination" and 10= "extremely high level of discrimination".
+ $p<.10$, * $p<.05$, ** $p<.01$, *** $p<.001$.

surprising that real estate professionals perceived less discrimination on their side of the business. Importantly, this adds credence to the argument that an individual's locus of control over specific aspects of real estate transactions moderates perceptions of discrimination. Support for this argument is also found when comparing national and local perceptions of discrimination by subsector.

At the national level, perceptions of discrimination began to moderate for the residential real estate sales subsector. At the local level, perceptions of discrimination moderated for two other subsectors: home appraisals and rental insurance. Real estate professionals may have perceived greater accessibility to these two subsectors at the local level, and subsequently perceived lower levels of discrimination. It should also be noted that for each subsector, perceptions of discrimination were rated lower at the local level. The differences between national and local ratings were statistically significant at the .05 level or above for all of the subsectors rated with the exception of residential real estate sales. It should be noted that although perceptions of discrimination in residential real estate sales were relatively moderate, black real estate professionals maintained suspicions about unscrupulous practices such as steering and blockbusting.

*They're Still Steering, But There Are Fewer Blocks to Bust*

Black real estate professionals were asked two questions about steering and blockbusting. Each question asked respondents to rate the level of steering and blockbusting in their metropolitan area as: high, moderate, low, or not present. Despite legislative efforts to curb steering, it remained a salient issue at the local level. Almost 60% of black real estate professionals indicated that there was a high (15.9%) or moderate (43.7%) degree of steering in their metropolitan areas. Some of the respondents provided open-ended comments that referred to steering as a local problem. One respondent elaborated on the issue, pointing out that steering occurred in his metropolitan area when "... non-minority realtors refused to show [properties], or if the customer insisted to see the property, [the realtor] talked it down." Another respondent added that before the local chapter of the NAR in his area allowed blacks to become members, "... [the local NAR chapter] was responsible for a lot of steering and covenants that were very restrictive, [today] our real estate association has very few, if any blacks, teaching or holding positions."

Steering was perceived as a persistent problem in respondents' metropolitan areas. It was attributed to individual acts of discrimination on the part of unscrupulous real estate professionals, as well as a lack of access to professional networks for blacks. In contrast, blockbusting was perceived as less problematic in respondents' metropolitan areas. The majority of black real estate professionals indicated that there was a low degree (47.3%) or no (20.9%) blockbusting in their metropolitan areas. Only 6.1% of the respondents indicated that there was a high degree of blockbusting, while 25.7% perceived a moderate degree. In part, this finding was a reflection of the extent to which most metropolitan areas in the United States remain segregated. One respondent's open-ended comment captured this fact about American cities when he pointed out that there was "… not much blockbusting, as white property owners have moved already." This issue's lack of salience seems to be an artifact of an historic process that had already run its course. Steering seems to have remained a primary mechanism for perpetuating residential segregation, while blockbusting was less pronounced in already segregated metropolitan environments.

### Sources of Fair Housing Training and Advocacy

There continues to be a need for increased professional training and advocacy due to the persistence of barriers to fair housing, discrimination in subsectors of housing markets, and unethical practices like steering. Information provided by respondents related to questions about sources of fair housing training and advocacy enhances our understanding of this dimension of public policy aimed at ameliorating discrimination in housing markets. Respondents were asked to identify organizations offering fair housing training in their metropolitan areas. These data are presented in Table 4. These data identify local real estate associations as the primary source of fair housing training, followed by local nonprofit housing organizations, government agencies, and educational institutions.

The role of local real estate associations in fair housing training has developed after several decades of conflict between the NAR and the NAREB. In the past, the NAREB functioned as the primary source of advocacy for fair housing in the real estate industry. Consequently, its local chapters were among the first to develop fair housing training programs for real estate agents and brokers. In addition to continuing education, NAREB chapters provide mentoring and educate the

Table 4.  Organizations Offering Fair Housing Training in
Respondents' Metropolitan Areas (n=151)

| Type of organization | Percent identified by respondents |
| --- | --- |
| Local real estate association | 90.00 |
| Local nonprofit housing organizations | 54.44 |
| Local educational institutions | 37.58 |
| Government agencies | 42.28 |
| Private consulting firms | 12.84 |
| Other organizations | 18.12 |

general public about fair housing. For example, one respondent who
was affiliated with his local chapter of the NAREB provided this reply
to an open-ended question, "… we host a lot of educational events for
[our] realtor mentors to help them excel and better their careers, as
well as events for the public." In the contemporary period, NAR affiliates have also expanded the scope of their fair housing educational
opportunities. One respondent from a large metropolitan area in the
South, described activities of her local NAR chapter related to fair
housing education:

> I serve on the Fair and Affordable Housing Committee of our Realtor
> Association. We have a model [for fair housing education and certifica-
> tion]. It provides in-depth training on Affordable and Fair Housing. We
> have eight realtors in the city that are certified. I am one of them. Fair
> housing is important in all areas and [discrimination] should not be tol-
> erated. More education is needed.

Sustained advocacy by organizations like the NAREB and the lowering
of racial barriers in the real estate industry have facilitated the development of fair housing training initiatives across the industry. However,
blacks only gained access to NAR membership and other subsectors of
the real estate industry in recent history. The penetration of fair housing principles is also a relatively new phenomenon for nonprofit advocacy organizations, government agencies, and educational institutions.
Its emergence can be traced back to the1988 amendments to the Fair
Housing Act, which created a pool of funding for local public and
nonprofit agencies engaged in fair housing monitoring, advocacy and
enforcement.

In many respects, fair housing policy is in its infancy. This is particularly true with respect to education and advocacy activities. Respondents were asked a series of questions about institutional sources of advocacy in order to understand their perceptions of support for expanded fair housing policy. These data are summarized in table 5.

These data indicate that the strongest sources of advocacy for expanding housing opportunities in respondents' metropolitan areas were local real estate associations and local nonprofit housing organizations. This is not surprising since the two key constituencies for fair housing reform have been associations representing minority realtors and nonprofit housing organizations that advocate for individuals facing discrimination in housing markets.

Sustaining federal support for programs like FHIP and FHAP represents one critical component of continued support for the development of fair housing policy. However, constituencies of fair housing policy initiatives are not simply involved in their implementation. These constituencies are also a source of information about emerging

Table 5. Perceptions of the Degree to Which Organizations Advocated for Expanding Housing Opportunities in Respondents' Metropolitan Areas (n=151), Reported as Percentages by Type of Organization

| Type of organization | High degree of advocacy | Moderate degree of advocacy | Low degree of advocacy | No advocacy |
|---|---|---|---|---|
| Local real estate association | 33.3 | 41.7 | 17.4 | 7.6 |
| Local nonprofit housing organizations | 44.5 | 35.9 | 10.9 | 8.6 |
| Local educational institutions | 15.6 | 29.4 | 24.8 | 30.3 |
| Government agencies | 24.4 | 43.9 | 18.7 | 13.0 |
| Elected officials | 10.2 | 37.3 | 29.4 | 22.9 |
| Grassroots organizations | 29.7 | 30.5 | 24.6 | 15.3 |

issues related to fair housing. They are central to the policy development process. For instance, the most frequently identified issue in open-ended comments involved unfair lending and foreclosed properties. One respondent raised the issue of unfair lending practices in the following comment:

> I counsel individuals and families regarding their current housing situation. The majority of families requesting assistance are minorities. Their loan types, interest rate and terms are higher and considered predatory compared to majority races. These loans should have never been offered and/or closed to these borrowers. The current lending programs are preventing many of these disadvantaged families from refinancing and/or disposing of toxic assets.

The nexus between fair housing policy and unfair lending practices is illustrated in this comment. Other respondents identified the unique problems that foreclosures entailed for black real estate professionals. One respondent described how foreclosed properties in her metropolitan area were, "being given 80% to non-minority brokers, 80% of the time a listing broker's office is over 25 miles away, or more." On one end of the spectrum, black real estate professionals were witnessing a disproportionate number of minority homeowners experiencing foreclosure. At the other end of the spectrum, non-minority realtors were the listing agents for a disproportionate number of foreclosed properties at a discount, while, as one respondent put it, "minority businesses are closing." These examples illustrate how black real estate professionals are one of the primary sources of contextual evidence that helps to identify emerging issues related to fair housing. They are also a primary source of advocacy for these issues in broader public policy venues.

## A Vision for Reform

Black real estate professionals occupy a unique position in the real estate industry. Historically, they were excluded from membership in organizations like the NAR and forced into the periphery of real estate markets. Out of this experience, a tradition of advocacy for fair and affordable housing has developed among this group of professionals and through associations like the NAREB. Because of their unique position in the real estate industry, their perceptions provide a deeper understanding of the scope of fair housing issues in the industry and emerging trends.

The survey results reveal that although general perceptions of discrimination have declined in the past decade, concerns about specific forms of discrimination remain salient both nationally and locally. The survey results also reveal that perceptions of progress toward ameliorating various forms of discrimination in housing markets are closely associated with an individual's locus of control. Barriers to fair housing and levels of discrimination were perceived to be lower in relation to dimensions of housing markets that individuals had access to. As a result, barriers to fair housing were perceived to be lower at the local versus the national level, likely since people felt they had greater control over their local environments. Likewise, subsectors of real estate markets that were most accessible to respondents were perceived as entailing less discrimination.

These results suggest that individuals affected by unfair housing practices and discrimination need greater access and representation in some key areas of the real estate industry and housing markets. Despite progress in the real estate industry, there is still a need for broader representation of minorities. In particular, efforts to expand the scope of fair housing education requires sustained advocacy. There is also a need for sustained advocacy within the industry for greater minority penetration into areas of trade such as commercial real estate and luxury housing. In subsectors of housing markets, minorities need to makes gains in areas such as banking, finance, insurance, and real estate appraisal.

Additionally, there is a need for advocates and policy makers to pay more attention to rental housing markets. The groups perceived as facing the most barriers to fair housing, the poor and disabled, tend to concentrate in rental markets. Concomitantly, rental housing markets were perceived among the most discriminatory subsectors by respondents. This signals a need for added emphasis on landlord training efforts, as well as strategies to promote minority entrepreneurship in areas such as property management. Reasserting rental housing as a fair and affordable housing issue is a critical enterprise for the future.

Quintessentially, efforts to address fair housing and discrimination in housing markets center on increasing the scope of access that consumers and minority professionals have to key aspects of subsectors in housing markets. A movement toward improved disclosure and the dissemination of information about housing choices is a component of such reforms. These reforms would entail enhanced enforcement efforts and an expansion in the scope of housing rights. Additional opportunities for minority employment and enterprise across housing subsectors would also be part of reforms. On a broader scale, local communities need to develop their own housing bills of rights to augment state and federal law. Experimentation with expanded housing rights at the local level would incubate new policy at the state and national levels.

## References

Abravanel, Martin D. and Mark K. Conningham. 2002. *How Much Do We Know?: Public Awareness of the Nation's Fair Housing Laws.* Washington, D.C.: The Urban Institute.

Abravanel, Martin D. 2007. "Paradoxes in the Fair Housing Attitudes of the American Public, 2001–2005." Pp. 81–105 in *Fragile Rights within Cities: Government, Housing and Fairness*, edited by John Goering. New York, NY: Rowman and Littlefield.

Connerly, Charles E. 2006. "Fair Housing in the US and the UK." *Housing Studies* 21(3): 343–360.

Denton, Nancy. 1999. "Half Empty or Half Full: Segregation and Segregated Neighborhoods 30 Years After the Fair Housing Act." *Cityscape* 4(3): 107–122.

Ellen, Ingrid Gould. 2008. "Continuing Isolation: Segregation in America Today." Pp. 261–277 in *Segregation: The Rising Costs for America*, edited by James H. Carr and Nandinee K. Kutty. New York, NY: Routledge.

Friedman, Samantha and Gregory D. Squires. 2005. "Does the Community Reinvestment Act Help Minorities Access Traditionally Inaccessible Neighborhoods?" *Social Problems* 52(2): 209–231.

Galster, George C. 1999. "The Evolving Challenges of Fair Housing Since 1968: Open Housing, Integration, and the Reduction of Ghettoization." *Cityscape: A Journal of Policy, Development and Research* 4(3): 123–138.

Goring, John. 2007. "An Overview of Key Issues in the Field of Fair Housing Research." Pp. 19–38 in *Fragile Rights within Cities: Government, Housing and Fairness*, edited by John Goering. New York, NY: Rowman and Littlefield.

Gotham, Kevin Fox. 2002. *Race, Real Estate and Uneven Development: The Kansas City Experience, 1900–2000.* Albany, NY: State University of New York Press.

Kraus, Neil. 2004a. "Local Policymaking and Concentrated Poverty: The Case of Buffalo, New York." *Cities* 21(6): 481–490.

Kraus, Neil. 2004b. "The Significance of Race in Urban Politics: The Limitations of Regime Theory." *Race & Society* 7: 95–111.

Lamb, Charles M. and Eric M. Wilk. 2009. "Presidents, Bureaucracy, and Housing Discrimination Policy: The Fair Housing Act 1968 and 1988." *Politics and Policy* 37(1): 127–149.

Lerman, Brian R. 2006. "Mandatory Inclusionary Zoning: The Answer to the Affordable Housing Problem." *Environmental Affairs* 33: 383–416.

Massey, Douglas and Nancy Denton. 1998. *American Apartheid: Segregation and the Making of the Underclass.* Cambridge, MA: Harvard University Press.

Massey, Douglas S. 2008. "Origins of Economic Disparities: The Historic Role of Housing Segregation." Pp. 39–80 in *Segregation: The Rising Costs for America*, edited by James H. Carr and Nandinee K. Kutty. New York, NY: Routledge.

Nardi, Peter M. 2003. *Doing Survey Research: A Guide to Quantitative Methods.* New York, NY: Allyn and Bacon.

National Fair Housing Alliance. 2008. *Dr. King's Dream Denied: Forty Years of Failed Federal Enforcement*. Washington, DC: National Fair Housing Alliance.

National Neighborhood Coalition. 2001. *Affordable Housing and Smart Growth: Making the Connection*. Washington, DC: National Neighborhood Coalition.

Orser, W. Edward. 1997. *Blockbusting in Baltimore: The Edmonson Village Story*. Lexington, KY: The University Press of Kentucky.

Pearson, Robert W. 2010. *Statistical Persuasion: How to Collect, Analyze, and Present Data... Accurately Honestly, and Persuasively*. Thousand Oaks, CA: Sage Publications.

Roscigno, Vincent J., Diana L. Karafin and Griff Tester. 2009. "The Complexities and Processes of Racial Housing Discrimination." *Social Problems* 56(1): 49–69.

Ross, Stephen L. and John Yinger. 2002. *The Color of Credit: Mortgage Discrimination, Research Methodology, and Fair Lending Enforcement*. Cambridge, MA: MIT Press.

Schill, Michael H. 2007. "Implementing the Federal Fair Housing Act: The Adjudication of Complaints." Pp. 143–176 in *Fragile Rights within Cities: Government, Housing and Fairness*, edited by John Goering. New York, NY: Rowman and Littlefield.

Schuetz, Jenny, Rachel Meltzer, and Vicki Been. 2009. "31 Flavors of Inclusionary Zoning: Comparing Policies From San Francisco, Washington D.C., and Suburban Boston." *Journal of The American Planning Association* 75(4): 441–456.

Schuman, Howard and Stanley Presser. 1996. *Questions & Answers in Attitude Surveys*. Thousand Oaks, CA: Sage Publications.

Sidney, Mara S. 2003. *Unfair Housing: How National Policy Shapes Community Action*. Lawrence, KS: University of Kansas Press.

Sidney, Mara S. 2004. "The Struggle for Housing Equality: Impact of Fair Housing and Community Reinvestment Laws on Local Advocacy." *Cityscape: A Journal of Policy Development and Research* 7(1): 135–163.

Smith, Jessie Carney, ed. 2006. *Encyclopedia of African American Business*. Westport, CT: Greenwood Press.

Squires, Gregory D., Samantha Friedman and Catherine E. Saidat. 2002. "Experiencing Residential Segregation: A Contemporary Study of Washington D.C." *Urban Affairs Review* 38(2): 155–183.

Squires, Gregory D. 2003. *Organizing Access to Capital: Advocacy and the Democratization of Financial Institutions*. Philadelphia, PA: Temple University Press.

Squires, Gregory D. and Charis E. Kubrin. 2005. "Privileged Places: Race, Uneven Development and the Geography of Opportunity in Urban America." *Urban Studies* 42(1): 47–68.

Squires, Gregory D. 2008. "Prospects and Pitfalls of Fair Housing Enforcement Efforts." Pp. 305–323 in *Segregation: The Rising Costs for America*, edited by James H. Carr and Nandinee K. Kutty. New York, NY: Routledge.

Sue, Valorie M. and Lois A. Ritter. 2007. *Conducting Online Surveys*. Thousand Oaks, CA: Sage Publications.

Turner, Margery Austin, Stephen L. Ross, George C. Galster, and John Yinger. 2002. *Discrimination in Metropolitan Housing Markets: National Results from Phase I HDS 2000*. Wasington, D.C.: The Urban Institute.

Turner, Margery Austin, Todd M. Richardson, and Stephen L. Ross. 2007. "Housing Discrimination in Metropolitan America: Unequal Treatment of African Americans, Hispanics, Asians and Native Americans." Pp. 39–60 in *Fragile Rights within Cities: Government, Housing and Fairness*, edited by John Goering. New York, NY: Rowman and Littlefield.

U.N. Committee on the Elimination of Racial Discrimination. 2008. *Residential Segregation and Housing Discrimination in the United States*. New York, NY: United Nations.

Yinger, John. 1999. "Sustaining the Fair Housing Act." *Cityscape: A Journal of Policy, Development and Research* 4(3): 93–106.

PART TWO

AFFORDABLE HOUSING, FINANCE, AND LAND USE ISSUES

# BARRIERS TO FAIR HOUSING POLICY IMPLEMENTATION: FINANCE, REGULATION, AND PUBLIC OPINION

## J. Rosie Tighe

Housing policy in the United States currently emphasizes deconcentrating poverty to encourage equal access to opportunity (Imbroscio 2008). The equitable distribution of affordable housing across regions, otherwise known as 'fair housing,' represents a key factor in encouraging equity and opportunity (Briggs 2005; Galster and Killen 1995; Rosenbaum 1995). Developing this housing, however, is not a simple process. The necessity to compile complicated and delicate financing structures, to navigate local, regional, and state regulatory systems, and to appease a skeptical public, has thwarted the success of public policies designed to alleviate poor and unaffordable housing conditions. This chapter analyzes how each of these barriers can prevent advocates, developers, and policymakers from achieving affordability and access to opportunity through the production of federally subsidized housing. Understanding these barriers to implementation is an essential component of producing successful fair housing policies in the future.

A steady decline in federal funding for housing over the past thirty years resulted in a shift in fiscal responsibility and policy-making authority to municipal governments (Dreier and Keating 1990). The withdrawal from direct provision of housing for low-income households in favor of devolution to state and local jurisdictions resulted in fragmented and often contradictory housing programs. As a result, the goals of improving housing for the poor, increasing opportunity for poor and minority households, and eliminating discrimination in the housing market remain unfulfilled. While funding and policy guidance for affordable housing originates at the federal level, siting and development decision-making occurs locally. Individual cities and towns bear the responsibility to respond effectively to the housing needs of their various populations. However, local governments seldom build affordable housing themselves – private and nonprofit developers construct the vast majority of the units. Thus, in the current policy context, 'Affordable Housing' is most often privately built and publicly subsidized. While this system achieves results without direct provision of housing by the federal government, it does not operate without challenges.

## Financial Challenges and Local Capacity Constraints

For decades, the federal government was the primary provider of very low-income rental housing via public housing (Wallace 1995). Today, nonprofit and private developers are the principle providers of federally subsidized housing. Nonprofit housing agencies currently provide nearly 1.5 million households with affordable housing – nearly 25% more than the current stock of public housing (Bratt 2009). Research also demonstrates that nonprofit developers are much more likely than for-profit entities to provide housing to low and very-low income households (those earning less than 50% of Area Median Income (AMI) and 30% of AMI, respectively) (Bratt 2008). Nonprofit housing agencies also tend to develop larger units that can be made available to families (Bratt 2008), and are more apt to redevelop distressed areas and develop housing with little to no profit potential (Herbert and Wallace 1998; Keyes et al. 1996; Koebel 1998).

However, the challenges of housing finance often limit smaller non-profits' ability to obtain funding for such projects (Bockmeyer 2003; Cummings and DiPasquale 1999). Instead, for-profit developers obtain the vast majority of the public and private funding available for housing construction (Bratt 2009) and these entities typically produce smaller, more expensive units in areas with strong or healthy housing markets. In other words, nonprofit housing agencies target households and neighborhoods with the greatest need for affordable housing, yet they are at a disadvantage when competing for funding and are extremely vulnerable to delays or loss of financing mechanisms that might sink a project.

The lack of a coherent vision for housing policy at the federal level adversely affects municipalities' ability to determine adequate administrative processes for program implementation (Mueller and Schwartz 2008). Furthermore, federal policy rules and funding mechanisms produce outcomes that often run counter to the stated goals of policymakers. Finally, the shift in housing provision from the public to private sector places the responsibility for the implementation of housing policy on the private sector, which seeks profit maximization – and

nonprofit housing agencies, which have limited financial and organizational capacity (Bratt 2009; Herbert and Wallace 1998; Keyes et al.
1996; Koschinsky 1998). Each of these challenges inhibits the production of enough affordable housing to meet the needs of low and very-
low income households, and shapes its siting in a way that undermines
fair housing goals.

## Federal Funding Rules and Impediments

The current policy emphasis on developing housing outside of poor
areas means higher land and construction costs. Thus, implementing
federal policies means lower profit margins and added difficulties during the development process. Further complicating matters is the fact
that rules and regulations in federal housing programs – particularly
the two main funding streams, the Low Income Housing Tax Credit
(LIHTC) and HOME block grant – often run counter to fair housing
goals. Even when developers are motivated to build affordable housing
in non-poor neighborhoods, efforts can be undermined by higher land
costs and program regulations.

The LIHTC is the principle financing mechanism for the development of affordable housing (Cummings and DiPasquale 1999; McClure
2000), contributing to the development of over 1.5 million units since
its inception in 1986 (Williamson et al. 2009). Yet the LIHTC program
provides added incentive for developers to build in 'qualified census
tracts' (QCT). A qualifying tract must consist of at least 50 percent
households with an income less than 60 percent of the area median
household income (AMI). As a result of this preference, 54 percent of
LIHTC developments are located in central cities (McClure 2000).
Furthermore, research concludes that "the program has been used
most often to provide better housing in poor neighborhoods rather
than housing opportunities for poor households in higher-income
neighborhoods" (Cummings and DiPasquale 1999:303). One survey
found that in 2005, only seven percent of tax credit units served
those earning below 30 percent of area median income, and only
12 percent served those earning under 40 percent of AMI (Guggenheim
2007). While improving housing in poor neighborhoods is valuable,
tax credits have not directly succeeded in deconcentrating poverty or
in providing opportunities for the poor in more affluent areas; these
federal funding mechanisms have not successfully furthered fair housing goals.

The HOME block grant program provides federal funding to afford-able housing projects as well, but HOME funds typically make up a significantly lower proportion of total funding for any given project than LIHTC. This program has aided in the development of over 860,000 units since its inception in 1993, yet this program also includes provisions that can prove challenging for developers. While the HOME program does not contain explicit language regarding the location of projects using its financing, as LIHTC does, HOME rules stipulate that projects obtain local approval and that municipalities proactively involve the community in decisions regarding distribution of HOME funds (Nyden et al. 2003). This requirement for community support increases the potential for neighborhood opposition to projects sited in more affluent neighborhoods. As Hamilton (in Nyden 2003) states, "local level decision-making can be impacted by activists or advocacy groups who may be pursuing their own narrow interests. This adds a dimension to public policy decision making as the agendas of these activists and neighborhood groups may be contrary to the broader needs of the area" (p. 37). Thus, utilizing HOME funds to locate fair housing in non-poor areas could be severely limited by rules empha-sizing public input.

Further complicating matters is the current economic recession stemming from a massive crisis in housing finance. Between 2006 and 2008, the foreclosure rate increased by 225 percent. These foreclosures are largely a result of defaults in the subprime sector (RealtyTrac.com 2009). The subprime market originated loans to households who did not fit the criteria required by standard mortgage lenders. Spurred on by a mortgage system that diluted the risk of lending to marginally qualified applicants, the subprime market grew by 900 percent during the 1990s. By 2008, subprime loans comprised a substantial portion of the housing market, making up nearly 15 percent of all loans in 2008 – increasing from only seven percent in 1989 (Bond and Williams 2007). While these changes resulted in greater access to capital for low-income and minority borrowers, many of the lenders took advantage of their clients by pushing them into mortgages they had little ability to pay back. As a result, a disproportionate number of foreclosures occur in low income and minority communities (Haurin et al. 2007; Immergluck and Smith 2006). As banks across the country close and the federal government institutes bailouts, national debate once again centers on housing policy.

While such scrutiny has primarily centered on the private lending sector, the high rate of foreclosures and uncertainness in the development community severely affects public financing as well. The recent economic downturn has severely affected the value of LIHTC credits. Instability in the housing market has lessened the appeal of housing credits as an investment opportunity. According to one report, "many experts estimate that the size of the market for LIHTCs in 2009 will be less than half the size it was in 2007, dropping from around $9 billion to less than $4.5 billion" (Kaplan and Lambert 2009). Due to this decline in investor interest, the value of credits has fallen from the standard $.85 per dollar to around $.65 (West 2009). Thus, every dollar of federal investment has lost 20% of its value in terms of units developed. Such reductions in the value of the most effective financial tool used to develop affordable housing will have lasting ramifications on the supply of low-income units for years to come.

Households at the extreme end of the income scale (those earning less than 30% of area median income) are those with the fewest affordable housing options, and neither LIHTC nor HOME funds target these households. Nationwide, there are 9 million extremely low-income households, but only 6.2 million units available that are affordable to them, resulting in a gap of 2.8 million units. The National Housing Trust Fund (NHTF), created as part of the Housing and Economic Recovery Act of 2008, represents a significant leap forward in providing necessary gap funding directed at extremely low income households. The trust is funded through revenue generated by government-sponsored enterprises such as Fannie Mae and Freddie Mac, generating an estimated $500 million per year (Community Change 2008). According to the NLIHC, at least 90% of fund dollars must be dedicated to rental housing, and at least 75% of those funds must benefit extremely low-income households (at or below 30% of AMI).

While the NHTF represents significant progress toward the provision of funds dedicated to the poorest Americans, the extent to which it can and has been used to improve fair housing outcomes for those populations has not yet been established (National Low Income Housing 2010). Furthermore, such measures do not address the problem that the main sources of affordable housing finance are not targeting very low-income households. As long as LIHTC and HOME continue to target moderate-income households earning from 50–80%

of AMI, the needs of the most vulnerable populations will continue to go unmet.

### "Creative Finance" and Challenges for Nonprofit Developers

While tax credit, block grants, and the Affordable Housing Trust Fund bring needed resources to the financing of affordable housing, federal funds alone are not sufficient to develop housing affordable to low income renters. Programmatic regulations, high land costs, and limited profit margins force developers to utilize numerous funding streams in order to finance affordable housing (Wallace 1995). In order to provide adequate financing, developers of affordable housing need to combine – on average – between six and eight funding sources from private, state, local, and federal grants and loans (Koebel 1998; Koschinsky 1998). This system of layering or 'creative finance' is an extremely inefficient way to produce affordable housing, and puts immense pressure on nonprofit agencies whose organizational capacity is already stretched due to budgetary and personnel constraints.

Nonprofit organizations play an increasingly prominent role in the development of affordable housing; yet they face significant capacity constraints. As the government removes itself from direct production, the difficulties in layering financing puts immense pressure on these agencies. As a result, nonprofits are pressed, "To focus their creative energies on financial packaging rather than on ensuring that the families who will occupy their housing receive the services they need to be more productive, self-sufficient members of the community" (Stegman 1989:358). Since it is primarily small nonprofit organizations that provide housing for the neediest populations, the lack of capacity coupled with extremely difficult development circumstances, means that housing for very low-income populations is most vulnerable to financial failure. The need for multiple financing mechanisms makes affordable housing development extremely vulnerable to cost overruns, delays, and other financial woes (Bockmeyer 2003; Herbert and Wallace 1998; Koschinsky 1998). For-profit developers have a greater capacity to manage these complex financial structures and absorb losses associated with the development process (Bratt 2008).

Despite the efforts of nonprofit and community development agencies to make up for the decline in direct government provision, the lack of simple or clear financing mechanisms impedes their ability to provide housing for low and moderate-income households.

While numerous organizations (many of which are federally-funded) exist to aid community development corporations (CDCs) and other nonprofit housing agencies, including NeighborWorks America, Local Initiatives Support Coalition (LISC), and the Enterprise Foundation, they cannot always help small community enterprises address issues inherently local in nature. This is particularly problematic when developing housing in middle-income or affluent neighborhoods where, by definition, the land costs are higher than in lower-rent areas and limit the effectiveness of fair housing policies designed to improve access to opportunity by building affordable housing in suburban or affluent communities.

## Local Government Capacity and Resource Constraints

While municipalities possess significant discretion over federal funds, they receive intense pressure from many sides including the development community, local interest groups, and voters. Cities and towns must balance demand for affordable housing with investment in economic development, as well as negotiate debates over land use and growth management (Basolo 2000; Mueller and Schwartz 2008). Such conflicts create a difficult political environment for developing affordable housing and each proposed project invites scrutiny from neighbors, local businesses, and other interest groups. Mueller and Schwartz (2008) found that local government programs are those least likely to produce housing for the poor, due in large part to "the difficulty of raising substantial funds for redistributive purposes at the local level, and the opposition of middle-class residents to siting affordable rental housing in their neighborhoods" (p. 133). The lack of innovation in local policies, coupled with increased reliance on private and nonprofit developers highly dependent upon traditional financing, limits developers' ability to target their projects to very low-income households or to build units suitable for poor families (Bratt 2009; Stoecker 1997).

A lack of state action further compounds this problem, leaving municipalities on their own to develop housing plans and policies in line with their needs (Downs et al. 1990; Katz et al. 2003). Studies show that, "states are not using their discretion to target income groups below those specified at the federal level" (Mueller and Schwartz 2008:131). In short, devolution has resulted in "less money for lower-income housing; less targeting for lower-income people and lower-income communities, and more political clout for interests inimical to both"

(Davis 2006:385). Thus, devolution of power to cities and states results in opportunities for local interest groups to have a larger influence on funding, siting, design, and income- targeting decisions than when policy rules were made at the federal level.

The shift from federal to state and local control over affordable housing production was intended to inspire innovative programs that could respond to local and regional needs better than federal policies (Orlebeke 2000). However, when devolution pairs with retrenchment and considerable cuts in funding, as it did during the 1980s, it eliminates the resources necessary for municipalities to develop innovative programs (Davis 2006; Goetz 1995; Mueller and Schwartz 2008). Thus, rather than increased flexibility resulting in more housing targeted to the neediest populations, the outcomes of devolution include housing policies plagued by inadequate production, cost overruns, and poor planning (Buki 2002).

*Overcoming Financial and Capacity Challenges*

Devolution placed the onus for affordable housing construction on municipalities; retrenchment removed many of the resources formerly at their disposal (Davis 2006; Mueller and Schwartz 2008). Providing affordable housing and other social services does not directly aid the municipal coffers – rather, it is perceived as a burden on precarious city finances. Cities therefore often feel pressed to choose between affordable housing and economic development mechanisms, with affordable housing seldom claiming victory (Basolo 2000; Goetz 1995). Financially strapped cities must choose between affordable housing goals, economic development, job creation, and other social service needs. Absent significant increases in federal funding mechanisms and streamlined program requirements, development of affordable housing for low-income Americans will likely remain a low priority for most municipalities. However, efforts to increase Federal funding and improve nonprofit competitiveness could increase housing targeted to very low-income households and improve access to opportunity for these populations.

*Increasing Federal Funding and Streamlining Existing Programs*
In 2002, the Millennial Housing Coalition (MHC) – a bipartisan commission of housing experts – delivered a report to HUD and Congress outlining the state of housing affordability in America and suggested a

number of important changes to existing programs designed to facilitate and streamline housing development (Bipartisan Millennial Housing 2002). The recommendations of the MHC included eliminating barriers to combining HOME and other financing mechanisms with LIHTC; extending tax credit financing to preservation efforts and rehabilitation programs; allowing and encouraging additional tax credit funds for properties in 'high-poverty, high-cost areas;' and allowing the use of Temporary Assistance to Needy Families (TANF) funds as gap funding for existing properties (Bipartisan Millennial Housing 2002). The commission also recommended increased funding to the HOME program. However, few of these suggestions were implemented before the 2007 economic crisis spurred renewed government attention on housing issues.

The 2008 Economic Recovery Act legislation provided a number of incentives and changes to federal rules that had been recommended six years earlier by the BMHC, including increasing tax credit allocations to states (Goldstein and Miller 2008). However, few of the other recommendations submitted by the MHC were put into practice, and it is not clear the extent to which such changes will improve the housing situation for extremely and very-low income households. Furthermore, existing funding streams have declined in recent years. According to the National Low Income Housing Coalition (NLIHC), the HOME program budget has declined from $1.9 billion in 2005 to $1.8 billion in 2010, and the president's 2011 request is $1.65 billion, which is certainly not the increase recommended by the Millennial Housing Coalition (National Low Income Housing 2010).

While the current economic crisis places great pressure on municipalities struggling with cuts in service provision and layoffs, it may also represent a great opportunity for the use of public funds to preserve affordable housing. The Neighborhood Stabilization Program (NSP), also funded through the 2008 ERA, provides nearly $2 billion in public funds to prevent foreclosures and aid cities and towns in land-banking efforts to lock foreclosed units into long-term affordability. However, such programs may meet the same fate as current financing efforts, including lack of both municipal and nonprofit capacity to administer the program, and failure to target those with the greatest need (Ellen and Been 2009). Furthermore, even with NSP funds, gaining control of foreclosed units poses some significant challenges – particularly the issue that municipalities must compete with private sector investors. There is no provision granting municipal planning agencies or nonprofit land banks priority when attempting to purchase foreclosed homes, and the massive opportunities for private investment and property "flipping" presents a serious barrier to the successful implementation of this program. Future authorizations of this funding stream should provide some method for pressuring banks holding foreclosed loans to prioritize public and nonprofit organizations using NSF dollars to prevent such competition and allow for better long-term planning. Such methods would ensure long-term preservation of affordable housing targeted to low-income households.

An additional measure that would further deconcentrate poverty and better align federal funding policies and fair housing goals would be the elimination of the QCT provision in the LIHTC program rules. Removing the preference for development in already poor communities may provide enough incentive for housing developers to steer projects toward more affluent communities. Clarifying the public process rules in the HOME program could also ensure a more transparent and fair development process. Local leaders should provide opportunities for public involvement that include the beneficiaries of affordable housing, rather than simply the existing community members. Such outreach techniques would enhance the ability of local decision-makers to provide housing for a diverse population while maintaining open communication with the community. Streamlining these programs would allow for deeper income targeting as well as greater opportunities for the development of affordable housing outside of poor areas. However, as long as nonprofit housing providers are the only agencies developing housing for very low income households, their own capacity constraints may continue to limit the development of these units.

*Improving Nonprofit Capacity*
As the primary developers of housing for low-income populations, CDCs are under immense pressure to respond to the current and future residents of their projects, while also maintaining a presence in the community by serving other needs – including job training, education, and health service provision. This diversification can be problematic for organizations already stretched in terms of finances and personnel, but such services provide a necessary connection with the community, ensuring continued support for all the activities of the organization. In order to overcome such challenges, nonprofit housing developers must make a number of difficult choices regarding their mission.

As Bratt and Rohe (2007) state, "[CDCs] should pay considerable attention to the question of how much it should diversify the types of services offered, the geographic area served, the sources of funding utilized, and the clientele of the housing units developed" (p. 8). Maintaining strong ties with their host communities is essential to the continued success of CDCs' housing efforts (Bratt and Rohe 2007). It is especially important for CDCs to maintain a positive reputation in the community. As Silverman (2008) finds, the higher the reputation the CDC enjoys among city administrators, the better the funding the CDC receives. Ensuring that each project is a success is essential to maintaining a good reputation among policymakers; providing essential services to the community is essential to maintaining a good reputation. However, CDCs are often forced to choose between committing resources to community-based services or fair housing projects.

Additional resources would allow CDCs to continue to function as community services providers and successful affordable housing developers. Yet few funding sources allow their dollars to be utilized to provide additional operating funds for nonprofit organizations, which is one of the primary challenges to fulfilling their diverse missions. The low wages and long hours expected of most CDC employees creates an overworked and underpaid labor force, which often results in a failure to plan strategically and long-term (Bratt and Rohe 2007). Furthermore, such challenges limit the ability of CDCs to successfully navigate other obstacles to housing development, including local land use regulations and opposition from neighbors and communities. If current federal funding mechanisms, including the NHTF, allowed funds to be used for both programming and operating costs, CDCs may be able to increase salary, provide better benefits, and thus attract and retain quality employees. This stability would allow the organizations to be more competitive and flexible when planning and developing affordable housing.

### Regulatory Challenges

While capacity constraints and financial difficulties seriously limit the production of affordable housing, regulatory barriers compound these challenges – particularly when fair housing is proposed in stable, middle-class neighborhoods. Property rights and homeownership are protected through numerous legal mechanisms – including zoning, subdivision regulations, and private covenants – that present obstacles to the development of affordable housing in nonpoor areas (Ihlanfeldt 2004; Pendall 2000). Zoning and land use regulations, which receive very little guidance from state or federal governments, comprise some of the most effective legal mechanisms to separate the poor from other parts of society. Such regulatory mechanisms historically deepened segregation by both race and class, and continue to do so, albeit in a less obvious and explicit manner than the overt policies of the pre-Civil Rights Act era (Orfield 2006; Seitles 1998). While such regulations are designed to protect the property of all Americans, they limit the ability of minorities and the poor to move out of inner-city neighborhoods and into suburban areas (Pendall 2000).

*Zoning*

Land use and zoning ordinances lie at the heart of the protection of the public's health, safety, and welfare. Zoning has been the dominant form of local land control since it was first applied in the early 20th century (Valente et al. 2001). Before zoning laws, only nuisance laws – a strictly reactive measure that dealt with noise, safety, or health complaints from neighbors – regulated use of private property. Zoning, in contrast, is inherently proactive and preventative in that it identifies and codifies allowable uses for private property. While zoning fulfills the task of protecting residential areas from environmental and noise hazards, it is important to note that, "all local zoning ordinances affect the cost and supply of housing" (Valente et al. 2001:370). Local zoning regulations influence the location and type of jobs available in a community as well as the type and location of housing available in the community.

    Before 1950, zoning regulations explicitly prevented minority households from moving into white neighborhoods (Fischel 2004; Pendall 2000). However, due to the legal changes mandated by Brown v. Board of Education and the Civil Rights and Fair Housing Acts, "anything that looked like racial zoning was almost never tolerated by the courts. Zoning could, however, be used to reduce potential contact between races, or between high- and low-income people, by the facially neutral expedient of insisting on large lots and single family homes in residential districts" (Fischel 2004:330). While some states limit large lot zoning, most cities and towns may zone however they wish, so long as the language does not include any overt references to exclusion of any protected classes, including members of any specific races, genders, or religions.

Towns widely employ zoning to ensure that residential areas stay separate from industrial and commercial developments in order to avoid undue exposure to the potentially harmful health, safety, and environmental externalities associated with many commercial or industrial uses (Fischel 2004; Pogodzinski 1991). However, restrictive zoning measures can effectively exclude lower income residents from moving into a community by limiting residential development at a scale affordable to them (Cowan 2006; Ihlanfeldt 2004). Since zoning regulations commonly group multi-family residences together with commercial and industrial uses, multi-family developments are typically severely restricted in primarily residential areas (Ihlanfeldt 2004). Furthermore, multi-family housing does not enjoy the same status and protection from any deleterious effects associated with proximity to industrial or commercial facilities accorded single-family homes. For the most part, multi-family housing is much more affordable than its single-family counterparts (Cowan 2006), and also commonly includes a greater percentage of renters than single-family housing (Pendall 2000). Therefore, zoning multi-family residential separate from single-family residential not only separates renters from homeowners, but also serves to restrict the amount of affordable housing that can be developed in suburban and rural areas in which a very small percentage of the land is zoned for commercial development (Ihlanfeldt 2004).

*Growth Patterns and Management Policies*

The early years of suburban growth reflected increased opportunities for homeownership and upward mobility. Over the last few decades, however, urban sprawl has exacerbated economic separation in metropolitan areas. Unchecked growth during the middle part of the 20th century and reactions from the burgeoning environmental movement in the 1970s contributed to widespread public attitudes favoring growth management (Fischel 2004). Growth management encourages the implementation of regulations to limit or stop growth outside of the city centers thereby limiting sprawl and protecting the environment as well as agricultural uses and open space (Buki 2002; Downs 2004). While such techniques limit sprawl, checks on development "will not always benefit low-income of minority residents. It may instead promote gentrification" (Pendall 2000:125–6). The 'smart growth' regulations that seek to protect low-density land and limit sprawl include growth boundaries, building permit caps, utility district lines, and zoning restrictions on multifamily housing (Downs 2004). While these measures ensure environmental protection and limit the ability for cities to grow unsustainably, they also can increase the cost of living substantially (Arigoni 2001; Danielson et al. 1999; Downs 2004).

While growth management mechanisms can be, and have been, designed to accommodate housing for all income levels, more often, "the mottos of no-growth, slow growth, managed growth and (currently) smart growth are all facially neutral watchwords which nonetheless are effective substitutes for more selective means of keeping the poor out of the suburbs" (Fischel 2004: 332). By adopting 'smart growth' techniques and mechanisms, local governments can effectively, whether intentionally or not, restrict entire regions from access by the lower classes.

*Racial Segregation and the Politics of Exclusion*

The groundwork for the segregation of U.S. cities and suburbs was established decades ago through numerous mechanisms, including the public housing program and FHA lending policies (Briggs 2005; Collins and Margo 2000; Squires and Kubrin 2005). Various structures and institutions, exacerbated by public policy, kept the poor and minorities from moving outward and upward, and caused stagnation and disinvestment in low-income neighborhoods (Jargowsky 2006; Squires and Kubrin 2005). Those same policies enabled working and middle class whites to obtain housing in communities far superior to those they left behind in the inner cities. According to Orfield, "this isolation is perpetuated not only by the concentration of existing affordable housing in central cities and older suburbs, but by the barriers to developing affordable housing in most outlying suburbs" (2006: 102). The preservation of racially segregated communities has long been recognized as one of the motives behind exclusionary land use ordinances (Massey and Denton 1993; Pendall 2000). Exclusionary zoning practices and poorly designed smart growth plans often serve to maintain and even to deepen race- and class-based divisions. Despite civil rights and fair housing laws designed to prevent *de jure* segregation, research shows that exclusionary land use regulations continue to contribute to *de facto* racial segregation.

Furthermore, since the advent of smart growth and anti-growth regulations, spatial segregation actually increased. Until the mid-1970s, spatial isolation was declining – Americans were increasingly likely to live in mixed-income as well as mixed-race neighborhoods. However, since the mid-1970s, this trend reversed – at least in terms of income, creating by 1990, "a social environment that was far more homogeneously privileged than at any other time in the previous 20 years" (Massey 1996: 395). While class (or income-based) segregation technically is legal, racial discrimination and exclusion is not, and it has been shown that, "Low-density only zoning has historic and current connections with racial exclusion" (Pendall 2000: 140). Thus, income – or class-based – segregation often correlates strongly to racial exclusion and isolation. Such barriers limit contact between classes and races, resulting in increased mistrust and reducing the ability for people in different neighborhoods to recognize and address common goals (Young 1999).

Further complicating the goals of those seeking residential integration through the development of affordable housing are the limited legal tools available to promote inclusionary policies. Over the past thirty years, the courts steadily reversed many of the desegregation and civil rights advances of the 1950s and 1960s (Anderson 2002; Orfield 1995; 2004) and in the 1990s the Supreme Court handed down three major decisions (School Board of Oklahoma City v. Dowell, Freeman v. Pitts, and Missouri v. Jenkins) that authorized the reversal of schools' desegregation plans (Orfield 1995). As the courts back away from desegregating schools, residential integration remains the most promising method of promoting equality of opportunity (Cashin 2004; Ellen 2000; Rivkin 1994).

However, residential integration also faces considerable legal obstacles. According to Pendall, "federal constitutional case law suggests that even if a land use control system has racially exclusionary effects, it will survive challenges unless plaintiffs can prove that the local government in question explicitly intended to exclude suspect classes when it adopted the regulations" (2000: 126). Therefore, segregation does not qualify as explicitly illegal unless it can be demonstrated that it results directly from a discriminatory act. These changes in tone and content indicate that, "the courts have turned away from racial integration as a positive ideal for civil society, narrowing their focus merely to remedying discrimination. This narrowing of vision ignores the ways segregation operates as an independent race-based barrier to equality

of opportunity that is properly addressed by state intervention"
(Anderson 2002: 1198). As a result, racial segregation remains a barrier to equal opportunity and the mechanisms available for disman-
tling it are steadily disappearing.

*Overcoming Regulatory Challenges*

Ensuring equitable distribution of affordable housing, rather than concentration in poor and minority neighborhoods, embodies an important component of successful housing policy. Doing so promotes racial
and economic desegregation, deconcentration of poverty and overall
equality of access to opportunity. Despite housing policy's emphasis on
siting projects in a geographically equitable manner, implementation
challenges and market forces thwart efforts to develop housing outside
of poor areas. As a result, subsidized housing continues to be located
primarily in central cities and low-income communities (Anderson
et al. 2003; Briggs 2005; Cowan 2006; Turner 2003).

*Prioritizing Fair Housing in Municipal and Regional Land Use
Regulations*
Many municipalities, counties, and states are embarking upon growth
management policies, yet they vary greatly by type, as well as impact
on the area housing market. One study published by the Brookings
Institution distinguishes between growth 'control' and growth 'management,' emphasizing that the former has greater effects on area housing prices, and encouraging governments to enact more comprehensive
growth 'management' policies (Nelson et al. 2002). Numerous studies
have researched the effects of growth control policies on housing
prices, and they largely conclude that the size and intensity of the price
effects depends primarily on how the growth controls are crafted and
implemented (Arigoni 2001; Buki 2002; Downs 2004; Nelson et al.
2002; Phillips and Goodstein 2000). Therefore it is imperative that
regional and municipal growth control measures are designed not to
'control' growth, but to 'manage' growth and incorporate affordable
housing into their policies.

Portland, Oregon's growth boundary is one example of a successful
policy. Like most growth management or growth control measures,
Portland limits sprawl-type development outside of the growth boundary. It places severe restrictions on subdivision of farmland, pre-
serves open space, and discourages all growth outside the boundary.

However, it also allows for dramatically higher density inside the growth boundary. By increasing density, and thus, multifamily development, Portland's growth boundary has had minimal effects on housing prices (Phillips and Goodstein 2000). This balance between preservation and density is vital to prevent housing prices from skyrocketing in areas governed by growth control measures.

However, most land use regulations, particularly 'smart growth' or 'growth management' regulations, do not sufficiently incorporate affordable and fair housing into their policies (Buki 2002; Downs 2004; Nelson et al. 2002; Pendall 2000). Nelson et al., find that many other growth boundaries have been crafted in a way that housing prices have experienced a dramatic rise – particularly those in California and Colorado. Yet they conclude that, "When crafted properly, growth management programs break the chain of exclusion by incorporating policies that increase housing densities, mandating a mix of housing types, and promoting regional fair share housing or other inclusionary housing elements" (Nelson et al. 2002:7).

In order to counter the price effects of limiting development, well-designed local growth management policies must increase density in appropriate areas, not only limit development. This emphasis on density is essentially what differentiates 'smart growth' from 'no growth' policies. Such policies that limit land supply must counter the resultant price effects by providing sufficient alternative land for development as well as provide the opportunity to develop housing at a range of prices and with a mix of types. Particularly important is the inclusion of multi-family and rental housing, which is typically more affordable as well as more sustainable than its single-family counterpart. Such growth management policies, which are designed to be inclusive, rather than exclusive, can successfully mitigate sprawl while also providing options to further fair and affordable housing in the area.

*Re-Asserting Federal Control*
While crafting more comprehensive local growth policies that include fair housing is an important step, it would still leave us with piecemeal fair housing policies with few overarching standards or guidelines. A more comprehensive federal approach to housing could ensure that fair housing goals are included in local land use regulations, and would likely achieve the goal of dramatically increasing the number of families living in quality, affordable housing. It also would likely require a strong federal hand to induce municipalities to implement fair

housing goals. Inclusionary or 'fair share' housing could provide such a framework. The principle objective of such policies is to increase the supply of affordable housing in a manner that fosters greater economic integration yet prevents any neighborhood or community from bearing an excessive burden.

A number of states already have mechanisms in place to encourage the equal distribution of affordable housing across municipalities, including California, Massachusetts, and New Jersey. These programs fall into two categories – voluntary and mandatory, with programs implemented either through legislative or judicial action. The leading example of a voluntary mechanism is California, while both Massachusetts and New Jersey have pursued mandatory regulations. The Massachusetts program was passed through the state legislature, and limits the regulatory power of municipalities, while a Supreme Court case (Southern Burlington County N.A.A.C.P. v. Mount Laurel Township) is the basis for New Jersey's statewide initiative. In each case, the inclusionary housing ordinance has become the single-most effective mechanism for the development of affordable housing in the state. In New Jersey, over 60,000 units were constructed; in Massachusetts – 56,000; and in California, 34,000 (Calavita 1997; Citizens Housing and Planning 2009; Council on Affordable Housing 2010). These programs can serve as a model for other states, but in order to be most effective, federal housing policy should require, or at least promote, the adoption of such measures nationwide.

While a voluntary measure similar to California's would be more politically feasible than a mandatory approach, leaving the choice of whether to implement inclusionary zoning of housing policies to states or municipalities would likely result in a continuation of the status quo. One study stated that while voluntary inclusionary zoning programs "can generate upper-range moderate income housing (with a significant number of developer incentives), they generally fail to produce affordable housing for low- and very-low- income households in the absence of subsidies" (Brunick et al. 2003:3). The mandatory models also have their problems – New Jersey's was hotly contested and won only through a court case; Massachusetts continues to struggle with developer opposition, and the results have not been as substantial as the other models.

A successful national inclusionary housing ordinance should be both mandatory and regional – so that fair-share calculations are instituted to combat regional disparities, yet maintain the individual character of each community. The most important aspect of any successful inclusionary housing ordinance is identifying which income levels should be targeted. In Massachusetts and California, 'affordable' is considered anything affordable to a household earning at or below 80% of area median income – which may be a reflection of the extremely high housing costs in those states. New Jersey's target of at or below 50% of AMI seems much more reasonable at a national level.

Because implementation of inclusionary housing ordinances would be at the state and/or local level, federal involvement is restricted to limited oversight and possibly funding, which is in line with current policy goals and federal initiatives. It simply implements a regulatory system that requires the private – or nonprofit – sector to produce affordable housing. Thus, the scope of government involvement – as well as government finance – remains limited, ensuring the primacy of the private market. Inclusionary housing also fosters equity. Such programs encourage or require the fair distribution of affordable housing throughout a state or region, thus avoiding the concentration of such housing in particular areas. It can also be argued that inclusionary housing fosters self-reliance by increasing opportunities for low-income families. To some extent, any housing policy can face opposition with the argument that it fosters dependency, but by deconcentrating poverty, inclusionary housing provides significant opportunities for low-income families to find better work opportunities, attend better schools, and have access to community amenities such as improved transportation, public parks, and neighborhood programs.

*Public Opposition*

Even when developers or policymakers overcome the financial and regulatory barriers created by the present system of affordable housing development, public opposition can sink a project before it even begins (Dear 1991; Koebel 2004; Stein 1992). This neighborhood opposition, often referred to as 'Not in My Backyard' or 'NIMBY' opposition, can cause delays, force changes to the residential make-up of projects, and make untenable demands that can serve to undermine the successful development of affordable housing (Galster 2003; Gibson 2005). When such opposition succeeds, it limits the effectiveness of public policies driving the development of affordable housing, hindering access to opportunity for moderate- and low-income families (Advisory Committee on Regulatory Barriers to Affordable Housing 1991; Pendall 1999).

Restrictive local land use regulations and zoning rules often make it very difficult to site affordable housing without obtaining zoning variances (Euchner 2003; Field 1997; Koebel 2004). Such variances often require public approval, and the process of obtaining a variance through public hearings can be quite contentious (Cowan 2006). Public opposition tends to be more sophisticated in middle and upper class neighborhoods, where community engagement and agency are stronger (Gibson 2005; Advisory Committee on Regulatory Barriers to Affordable Housing 1991; Nyden et al. 2003; Pendall 1999). Because affordable housing development involves such a delicate process, even a slight delay can sink a project. As a result, neighborhood opposition can be a significant factor in preventing the implementation of fair housing policies – particularly in more affluent areas (Iglesias 2002; Wilton 2002; Wolsink 1994).

Public opinion surveys show that Americans overwhelmingly value equal access to opportunity and racial integration at the neighborhood level (Alesina et al. 2001; Erikson and Tedin 2003; Krysan 2000). However, they seldom show as much support for the specific policies designed to achieve those goals, a trend known as the 'principle-implementation gap' (Schneider and Ingram 1993). This is particularly true when the means to that end is the development of affordable housing in suburban or middle-class neighborhoods (Dear 1992; Schaffer and Saraf 2003; Stein 1992). Americans take action when their property is threatened, and subsidized housing is almost always perceived as a threat (Koebel 2004; Stover 1994). As Pendall concludes, "new housing developments, both market rate and subsidized, sometimes also look harmful. Every community has and needs housing, but the effects of a new residential development can spill over its borders to be borne by the entire community. Consequently, established residents have long been vigilant about and even opposed new houses" (Pendall 1999:113). This opposition is particularly strong when the housing is set aside for those earning little money.

*NIMBY and Non-Housing Facilities*

The term NIMBY, was originally coined to describe struggles over the siting of contentious environmental and energy facilities, namely waste disposal and energy facilities (Dear 1992; Lake 1993). The term applies to debates over the siting of land uses that are typically viewed as societal necessities, yet produce local costs and therefore elicit concern when they are placed nearby (Galster 2002; Pendall 1999). As outlined in Dear (1992), the main areas of concern for NIMBYs include threats to property values, decline in public safety, and burdens on neighborhood amenities. When proposals include energy facilities (Dear 1992) or waste management sites (Lober and Green 1994), such concerns are primarily voiced in terms of health or safety, thus the conflict often revolves around the potential environmental or health impacts of the facility. Yet when human services facilities – including mental health facilities (Piat 2000), housing for AIDS patients (Takahashi 1997), or housing for the homeless (Somerman 1993) are proposed, the environmental argument is replaced by concerns regarding the values or behavior or prospective residents or clients of the facility.

Dear (1992) also finds that siting unwanted land uses in more homogenous communities elicits a stronger NIMBY response than in more diverse areas. This typically means that suburban areas with more homogeneous populations and land uses are more likely to notice a different proposed land use, and are more likely to oppose it (Dear 1992). Studies also find that larger facilities, facilities catering to a less-desirable clientele (e.g., the poor or homeless) or clients seen as culpable for their situations (e.g., drug users or AIDS patients) will elicit a stronger NIMBY response.

## NIMBY and Housing

Stemming from such studies is additional research regarding the underlying reasons for NIMBY response that involve ideological or value-driven attitude determinants. Such research approaches are particularly prevalent in the field of human services facility siting (Somerman 1993; Wilton 2002) but also have appeared in studies relating to hazardous waste facilities (Lober and Green 1994). This body of research concludes that, in general, NIMBY responses are complex, and dependent on respondents' trust in government, ideology, and their views about the need for the proposed facilities (Pendall 1999). In the case of human services siting, one of the most important influences on NIMBY attitudes is the perception of the character or anticipated behavior of the residents or clients of proposed facilities (Dear 1992; Takahashi 1997; Wilton 2002).

Declining property values is the most oft-stated concern of those living nearby a proposed affordable housing project. For the most part, research on the potential negative effects of affordable housing on neighborhoods has shown that there are few demonstrable negative outcomes that result from the construction of affordable housing, and that it often can improve, rather than depress, the value of neighboring properties (Freeman 2002; Galster 2002; Nguyen 2005). One review of the connection between affordable housing and property values finds that any adverse impacts on property values depend on, "design and management of affordable housing, compatibility between affordable housing and host neighborhood, and concentration of affordable housing" (Nguyen 2005:1). Despite the evidence that affordable housing does not typically result in lower property values, crime, increased traffic, or overcrowded schools, these assurances do little to placate opposition that is concerned with the potential effects of the proposed housing.

Public opinion research has suggested that, despite being a race-neutral policy, the public associates affordable housing with the race of its potential residents (Hartman 2008; Pendall 1999; Tighe 2009). This association of affordable housing with minorities correlates to lower support for affordable housing, and greater concern about negative outcomes emanating from the development of such housing nearby. Such research corresponds with studies suggesting that middle and upper class America continues to regard the poor and minorities with suspicion, and that they do not wish to share their neighborhoods with such populations (Anderson et al. 2003; Belden et al. 2004; Berinsky 2002; Bobo and Zubrinsky 1996). Americans continue to believe that minorities and the poor lack motivation, take advantage of government programs, and do not care for their personal property (Cashin 2004; Goetz 2008). When land use conflicts over the construction of affordable housing arise, the concerns voiced by neighborhood residents reflect these stereotypes and perceptions. Thus, Americans associate 'Affordable Housing' with minority and poor populations. When these populations are viewed as lazy, not invested in the community, and predisposed to crime, it is no wonder that Americans do not wish to have them as neighbors.

*Overcoming Public Opinion Challenges*

When confronted with neighborhood opposition, it is common for planners, developers, and policymakers to present a case for affordable housing that demonstrates its value to the community as a whole, and share evidence demonstrating the lack of negative externalities (Dear 1991; Field 1997; Stover 1994). However, such outreach efforts seldom calm neighbors' fears, and local opposition to affordable housing continues to hinder the successful implementation of fair housing goals. A number of studies provide guidance for municipalities, advocates, and developers to manage NIMBY opposition (Dear 1992; Katz et al. 2003; Koebel 2004; Pendall 1999; Stover 1994). Others present examples of cases where these techniques have been applied (Dear 1991; Field 1997; Stover 1994). Advocates, planners, and developers have utilized various techniques to attempt to overcome this opposition – primarily education, negotiation, and litigation.

*Education*
Numerous states and cities have pursued educational campaigns to garner support for affordable housing. In Fort Collins, Colorado, posters and flyers were distributed showing the 'faces of affordable housing' – including teachers, firefighters, and auto mechanics – and the 'places of affordable housing' – portraying attractive single and multi-family affordable homes (Koebel 2004:3). Advocacy groups in Chicago, Minnesota and elsewhere, have applied similar strategies (Belden and Russonello 2003). By highlighting working people who are essential components of communities, these strategies seek to overcome the negative stereotypes typically voiced toward affordable housing. These education and advocacy campaigns portray affordable housing and its residents as average working Americans, not as dependent, jobless vagrants. Including pay rates for these types of workers as well as the amount needed to rent or own a home in the community, presents evidence that affordable housing is targeted to the 'submerged middle class' – people who simply need a leg up to succeed, not those who might abuse government subsidy (Belden and Russonello 2003; Dear 1991; Goetz 2008; Koebel 2004).

While education might be effective as a proactive measure, there is little evidence to show that it effectively counters an already established opposition. As Pendall (1999) points out, the opposition has little reason to trust those advocating for a particular development. Furthermore, some cases show that the opponents agreed with the basic premise that affordable housing was necessary in the area, but argued with the siting (Koebel 2004:71). Some research suggests that using terminology other than 'affordable' or 'low income' may increase support (Goetz 2008), but regardless of the terminology applied, any description remains subject to each individuals' own perception and understanding of that term. Thus, education about the community need for affordable housing would do little to mitigate this type of opposition. Consequently, a more typical first step is negotiation.

*Negotiation*
Numerous articles and studies have described negotiation strategies (Dear 1991; Field 1997; Koebel 2004; Stover 1994), yet not all provide cases where these techniques overcame opposition or explain how well they worked. Examination of these works reveals a number of general techniques applicable to overcoming or managing opposition. These include proactive and early meetings with citizens, education and media outreach methods; partnerships with local supporters and advocates of affordable housing; gaining support from political leaders where possible; and open and honest dialogue (Stein 1992).

Many advocates and developers respond to opposition by making aesthetic changes, or otherwise altering the project to make it more acceptable to neighbors, with varying degrees of success (Dear 1991; 1992; Iglesias 2002; Koebel 2004; Stein 1992; Stover 1994). In many cases, these changes increase the cost of development, reduce the number of units, and generally decrease affordability – undermining public policy and planning initiatives (Heudorfer 2002; Stover 1994). Constant opposition or fear of opposition can also result in developers preemptively proposing more 'acceptable' types of housing perceived to have fewer negative impacts, such as single family homes, housing for elderly populations, or housing for higher income residents (Field 1997; Galster 2003; Koebel 2004; Stover 1994). Developers may also choose to site affordable housing in neighborhoods that offer less resistance – either in more peripheral areas with lower populations or in neighborhoods that lack the political and social capital to present a coordinated resistance (Buki 2002; Estes 2007). However, such strategies placate opposition that is concerned primarily with the *residents*, not the appearance or size, of the project. Furthermore, avoiding development of affordable housing in upper and middle class neighborhoods undermines the dispersal goals of fair housing policies.

*Litigation*
The courts have a long history of involvement in housing battles, from discriminatory sales or rental practices (Shelley v. Kraemer; Jones v.

Mayer Co.) to the overturning of exclusionary zoning (Mt. Laurel). Less well known, however, is the role of litigation – or the threat of litigation – in particular siting conflicts. In many cases, the race of the residents or other unconstitutional discrimination underlies opposition to affordable housing. One such example of this is a NIMBY battle that occurred in Yuba City, California, over proposed farm worker housing. According to one study, "opponents, who had initially raised objections running from property value decline to the inappropriateness of spending federal funds on assisted housing, eventually focused their arguments on school overcrowding" (Stover 1994:52). This argument proved successful in blocking the permitting required for the development, despite the fact that the project met all the criteria set up by the city council. Because the rejection was based on the argument that the minority residents tend to have more school age children than their white counterparts, the nonprofit developer sued based on discrimination and won.

Litigation is typically considered a last-resort for developers of affordable housing, but in some cases, it has been used in excess, even "including preemptory threats of litigation to silence opposition" (Koebel 2004:46). While threats of lawsuits may quell some opposition, many perceive it to be an overly aggressive and unfair tactic. Successful outcomes like those in California are extremely rare. Furthermore, suits filed requesting monetary damages due to NIMBY delays have largely failed (Koebel 2004), suggesting that land use battles should be resolved at the project, municipal, or even state level rather than in the courtroom. The legal basis for many suits is that opposition thwarts the fair housing goal of racial integration. However, seldom is overt racial discrimination displayed in land use conflicts, despite suspicions that opposition to affordable housing is at least partially based on racial prejudice (Pendall 1999; Tighe 2009). Absent evidence of direct racial discrimination, the Fair Housing Act cannot successfully be applied in such cases, which limits the extent to which litigation can be used as a tool to combat opposition to affordable housing.

## Confronting Development Challenges

Providing fair housing options for low and moderate-income families in every region is vital to our nation's communities (Shlay 1995; Squires and Kubrin 2005). On an individual level, an unstable housing situation has a negative impact on family well-being, child development, stress, economic achievement, and self-sufficiency (Acevedo-Garcia and Osypuk 2004; Braconi 2001; Bratt 2002; Evans et al. 2000; Shlay 1993). On a broader level, ensuring affordable options for all income strata creates healthier communities – economically, socially, and environmentally (Davis 2006; Iglesias 2007; Katz et al. 2003). Yet significant challenges prevent the construction of affordable housing in a fair and equitable manner.

Local planners are those most often tasked with dealing with the siting challenges faced by affordable housing developers, yet their loyalties are torn. As public employees, planners have little political power, and are expected to serve the public good. However, when there are multiple publics, it is not always clear which 'good' should be served. The American Planning Association describes in its American Institute of Certified Planners (AICP) code of ethics two main tenets that are evoked by the content of this volume. The first states that planners should "give people the opportunity to have a meaningful impact on the development of plans and programs that may affect them. Participation should be broad enough to include those who lack formal organization or influence" (American Planning Association 2005). The second states, "We shall seek social justice by working to expand choice and opportunity for all persons, recognizing a special responsibility to plan for the needs of the disadvantaged and to promote racial and economic integration. We shall urge the alteration of policies, institutions, and decisions that oppose such needs" (American Planning Association 2005). The inability to implement housing policy in a fair and equitable manner presents a conflict between these two professed goals.

While it is important to incorporate the first goal of community participation into development plans, it is imperative that this participation does not impede the second goal of racial and economic integration. As Susan Fainstein states, "the appropriate criterion for evaluating a group's claims should not be procedural rules alone; evaluation must comprise an analysis of whether realization of the group's goals is possible and, if so, whether such realization leaves intact the principle of social justice. Democracy is desirable, but not always" (Fainstein 2000:469). Planners must strike a balance between democratic participation and advocacy on behalf of those who cannot participate. Undertaking such action promotes the achievement of racial and economic integration through the development of affordable housing, and ensures that deference to community or neighborhood preferences does not become an excuse for exclusionary attitudes and practices.

Planners should also heed the AICP admonition to alter such policies, institutions, and decisions that undermine the needs of the disadvantaged or the promotion of racial and economic integration. Many of the recommendations proposed in this chapter focus on streamlining federal, state and local policies to achieve fair housing goals, as well as emphasizing housing needs when crafting smart and sustainable growth policies. However, planners need to also take the lead in mitigating or overcoming community opposition to fair housing. As Anthony Downs states, "as long as full power over what housing can be built in a community resides with its local government, we are not going to see much additional affordable housing created in the suburbs. Yet that is where most growth of jobs and population is occurring. So that is where society most needs additional affordable units" (Downs 2003:2). As long as planners and policymakers cede control to local whims, it is doubtful that much affordable housing will be developed in the areas where it is most needed.

Dealing with local land use conflicts requires addressing regional and public needs. The very purpose of urban planning is to mediate between the private market and the public sector in order to promote policies and programs that enhance the livability, affordability, and economic viability of cities and regions. Neighborhood-level land use decisions can thwart policies and plans designed to improve entire metropolitan areas and undermine federal policy initiatives. Piecing together numerous funding sources is a difficult job. Finding areas that have appropriate zoning in place, or gaining zoning variances for affordable housing can be nearly impossible in many locations. If a developer succeeds in these endeavors only to be met with neighborhood opposition, it can not only sink the entire project, but also erode the will to try again in the future. Such barriers to implementation threaten the success of fair housing laws, policies, and projects, no matter how well-conceived they may be.

## References

Acevedo-Garcia, Dolores, and Theresa Osypuk. 2004. Racial Disparities in Housing and Health. *Poverty & Race* July/August.

Advisory Commission on Regulatory Barriers to Affordable Housing. 1991. *"Not In My Back Yard": Removing Barriers to Affordable Housing.* Washington, D.C.: U.S. Department of Housing and Urban Development, July 1991.

Alesina, Alberto, Edward Glaeser, and Bruce Sacerdote. 2001. "Why Doesn't The US Have A European-Style Welfare State?" In *The Brookings Panel On Economic Activity*.

American Planning Association, APA. 2008. *American Institute of Certified Planners Code of Ethics and Professional Conduct* 2005 [cited 08/29/08 2008]. Available from http://www.planning.org/ethics/conduct.html.

Anderson, Elizabeth S. 2002. "Integration, Affirmative Action, and Strict Scrutiny." *New York University Law Review* 77(13:46): 1195–1271.

Anderson, Laurie M., Joseph St. Charles, Mindy T. Fullilove, Susan C. Scrimshaw, Jonathan E. Fielding, and Jacques Normand. 2003. "Providing Affordable Family Housing and Reducing Residential Segregation by Income: A Systematic Review." *American Journal of Preventive Medicine* 24(3, Supplement 1):47–67.

Arigoni, Danielle. 2001. *Affordable Housing and Smart Growth: Making the Connection*. Washington DC: Smart Growth Network.

Basolo, Victoria. 2000. "City Spending on Economic Development Versus Affordable Housing: Does Inter-City Competition or Local Politics Drive Decisions?" *Journal of Urban Affairs* 22(3): 317–332.

Belden, Nancy, John Russonello, Tresa Undem and David Vaina. 2003. *Valuing Housing: Public Perception of Affordable Housing in the Chicago Region*. Chicago: Housing Illinois.

Belden, Nancy, Andrew Shashaty, and John Zipperer. 2004. "What We Know About Public Attitudes on Affordable Housing: A Review of Existing Public Opinion Research." In *NeighborWorks Symposium on Multifamily Excellence*. The Campaign for Affordable Housing.

Berinsky, Adam J. 2002. "Silent Voices: Social Welfare Policy Opinions and Political Equality in America." *American Journal of Political Science* 46(2): 276–287.

Bipartisan Millennial Housing, Commission. 2002. *Meeting Our Nation's Housing Challenges*. Washington, DC: United States Congress.

Bobo, Lawrence, and Camille L. Zubrinsky. 1996. "Attitudes on Residential Integration: Perceived Status Differences, Mere In-Group Preference, or Racial Prejudice?" *Social Forces* 74(3): 883–909.

Bockmeyer, Janice. 2003. "Devolution and the Transformation of Community Housing Activism." *The Social Science Journal* 40:175–188.

Bond, Carolyn, and Richard Williams. 2007. "Residential Segregation and the Transformation of Home Mortgage Lending." *Social Forces* 86(2): 671–698.

Braconi, Frank. 2001. "Housing And Schooling." *The Urban Prospect* March/April, 1–4.

Bratt, Rachel G. 2002. "Housing and Family Well-Being." *Housing Studies* 17(1):13–26.

Bratt, Rachel G. 2008. "Nonprofit and For-Profit Developers of Subsidized Rental Housing: Comparative Attributes and Collaborative Opportunities." *Housing Policy Debate* 19 (2):323–365.

Bratt, Rachel G. 2009. "Challenges For Nonprofit Housing Organizations Created by the Private Housing Market." *Journal of Urban Affairs* 31(1): 67–96.

Bratt, Rachel G., and William M. Rohe. 2007. "Challenges and Dilemmas Facing Community Development Corporations in the United States." *Community Development Journal* 42 (1):63–78.

Briggs, Xavier de Souza, ed. 2005. *The Geography of Opportunity*, James A Johnson Metro Series. Washington, DC: Brookings Institution Press.

Brunick, Nick, Lauren Goldberg, and Susannah Levine. 2003. *Voluntary or Mandatory Inclusionary Housing? Production, Predictability, and Enforcement*. Washington, DC: Business and Professional People for the Public Interest.

Buki, Charles. 2002. *Affordable Housing and Growth Management and Sprawl*. Washington, DC: Millennial Housing Commission.

Calavita, Nico. 1997. "Inclusionary Housing in California and New Jersey: A Comparative Analysis." *Housing Policy Debate* 8(1): 109–142.

Cashin, Sheryll. 2004. *The Failures of Integration: How Race and Class are Undermining the American Dream*. 1st ed. New York.

Citizens Housing and Planning, Association. *40B Fact Sheet* 2009. Available from http://www.chapa.org/pdf/40BFactSheetOctober2009.pdf.

Collins, William J., and Robert A. Margo. 2000. "Residential Segregation and Socioeconomic Outcomes: When Did Ghettos Go Bad?" *Economics Letters* 69(2): 239.

Council on Affordable Housing, NJ. 2010. *Proposed and Completed Affordable Units*. State of New Jersey 2010 [cited February 25, 2010 2010]. Available from http://www.state.nj.us/dca/affiliates/coah/reports/units.pdf.

Cowan, Spencer M. 2006. "Anti-Snob Land Use Laws, Suburban Exclusion, and Housing Opportunity." *Journal of Urban Affairs* 28(3): 295–313.

Cummings, Jean, and Denise DiPasquale. 1999. "The Low-Income Housing Tax Credit: An Analysis of the First Ten Years." *Housing Policy Debate* 10(2):251–306.

Danielson, Karen, Robert Lang, and William Fulton. 1999. "Retracting Suburbia: Smart Growth and the Future of Housing." *Housing Policy Debate* 10(3):513–540.

Davis, John Emmeaus. 2006. "Between Devolution and the Deep Blue Sea: What's a City or State to Do?" In *A Right to Housing: Foundation for a New Social Agenda*, edited by R. Bratt, C. Hartman and M. Stone. Philadelphia, PA: Temple University Press.

Dear, Michael. 1991. Gaining Community Acceptance. Princeton, NJ: The Robert Wood Johnson Foundation.

Dear, Michael. 1992. "Understanding and Overcoming the NIMBY Syndrome." *Journal of the American Planning Association* 58(3):288–300.

Downs, Anthony. 2004. *Growth Management and Affordable Housing: Do They Conflict?* Washington, DC: Brookings Institution Press.

Downs, Anthony, Denise DiPasquale, and Langley C. Keyes. 1990. A Strategy for Designing a Fully Comprehensive National Housing Policy for the Federal Government of the United States. In *Building foundations : Housing and Federal Policy*. Philadelphia: University of Pennsylvania Press.

Dreier, Peter, and W. Dennis Keating. 1990. "The Limits of Localism: Progressive Housing Policies in Boston, 1984–1989." *Urban Affairs Quarterly* 26(2): 191–216.

Ellen, Ingrid Gould. 2000. *Sharing America's Neighborhoods: The Prospects for Stable Racial Integration*. Cambridge, MA: Harvard University Press.

Ellen, Ingrid Gould, and Vicki Been. 2009. "In the Wake of the Foreclosure Crisis: Targeting Neighborhood Stabilization Funds." In *Housing After the Fall: Reassessing the Future of the American Dream*. New York, NY: Center for Real Estate, Paul Merage School of Business.

Erikson, Robert S., and Kent L. Tedin. 2003. *American Public Opinion: Its Origins Content and Impact*. 6th ed. New York: Addison Wesley Longman.

Estes, Chris. 2007. NCHC Housing Communication Manual. North Carolina Housing Coalition.

Euchner, Charles. 2003. *Getting Home: Overcoming Barriers to Housing in Greater Boston*. Boston, MA: Pioneer Institute for Public Policy Research.

Evans, Gary W., Hoi-Yan Erica Chan, Nancy M. Wells, and Heidi Saltzman. 2000. "Housing Quality and Mental Health." *Journal of Consulting and Clinical psychology* 68(3): 526–30.

Fainstein, Susan S. 2000. "New Directions in Planning Theory." *Urban Affairs Review* 35(4): 451–478.

Field, Charles G. 1997. Building Consensus for Affordable Housing. *Housing policy debate* 8(4): 801–832.

Fischel, William A. 2004. "An Economic History of Zoning and a Cure for its Exclusionary Effects." *Urban Studies* 41(2): 371–340.

Freeman, Lance. 2002. "Subsidized Housing and Neighborhood Impacts: A Theoretical Discussion and Review of the Evidence." *Journal of Planning Literature* 16(3): 359–378.

Galster, George. 2002. *A Review of Existing Research on the Effects of Federally Assisted Housing Programs on Neighboring Residential Property Values*. National Association of Realtors.

Galster, George, Peter Tatian, Anna M. Santiago, Kathryn L.S. Petit, Robin E. Smith. 2003. *Why Not in My Backyard?* New Brunswick, NJ: Center for Urban Policy Research, Rutgers University.

Gibson, Timothy A. 2005. "NIMBY and the Civic Good." *City and Community* 4(4): 381–401.

Goetz, Edward G. 1995. "Political Effects of Federal Policy Devolution on Local Housing Expenditures." *Publius* 25(3): 99–116.

Goetz, Edward G. 2008. "Words Matter: The Importance of Issue Framing and the Case of Affordable Housing." *Journal of the American Planning Association* 74(2): 222–229.

Goldstein, Richard S., and Forrest D. Miller. 2010. *Housing Tax Credit and Multifamily Bond Provisions of HR 3221—The Housing and Economic Recovery Act of 2008*. Nixon Peabody LLP 2008 [cited 2/11/2010 2010].

Guggenheim, Jow. 2007. *Survey Data Shows Small Share of LIHTC Units Receiving 2005 Allocations Were Intended to Serve Poor Households*. Available from http://www.housingtaxcredits.net/id44.html.

Hartman, Chester. 2008. "Comment on 'The New Politics of Affordable Housing'". *Housing Policy Debate* 19(2): 255–259.

Haurin, Donald R, Christopher Herbert, and Stuart Rosenthal. 2007. "Homeownership Gaps Among Low-Income and Minority Households." *Cityscape* 9(2):5–52.

Herbert, Scott, and James Wallace. 1998. "Nonprofit Housing: A Study of Costs and Funding." In *Shelter and Society: Theory, Research, and Policy for Nonprofit Housing*, edited by C. T. Koebel. Albany, NY: State University of New York Press.

Heudorfer, Bonnie. 2002. *Taking the Initiative: a Guidebook on Creating Local Affordable Housing Strategies*. Boston, MA: Citizens Housing and Planning Association with The Massachusetts Housing Partnership.

Iglesias, Tim. 2002. "Managing Local Opposition to Affordable Housing: A New Approach to NIMBY." *Journal of Affordable Housing* 12(1):78–122.

Iglesias, Tim. 2007. "A Place to Call Home? Our Pluralist Housing Ethics and the Struggle for Affordability." *Wake Forest Law Review* 42(2):511–593.

Ihlanfeldt, Keith R. 2004. "Exclusionary Land-use Regulations within Suburban Communities: A Review of the Evidence and Policy Prescriptions." *Urban Studies* 41(2): 261–283.

Imbroscio, David. 2008. "'United and Actuated by Some Common Impulse of Passion': Challenging the Dispersal Consensus in American Housing Policy Research." *Journal of Urban Affairs* 30(2): 111–130.

Immergluck, Dan, and Geoff Smith. 2006. "The External Costs of Foreclosure: The Impact of Single-Family Mortgage Foreclosures on Property Values." *Housing Policy Debate* 17(1):57–79.

Jargowsky, Paul A. 2006. *Concentration of Poverty and Metropolitan Development*. Atlanta, GA: U.S. Federal Reserve Bank, Annual Community Affairs Officers Conference, May 9, 2008.

Kaplan, Heidi, and Matt Lambert. 2009. "Forward: Innovative Ideas for Revitalizing the LIHTC Market." In *Innovative Ideas for Revitalizing the LIHTC Market*. Washington, DC: Federal Reserve Bank.

Katz, Bruce, Margery Austin Turner, Karen Destorel Brown, Mary Cunningham, and Noah Sawyer. 2003. *Rethinking Local Affordable Housing Strategies*. Brookings Institution.

Keyes, Langley C., Alex Schwartz, Avis Vidal, and Rachel Bratt. 1996. "Networks and Nonprofits: Opportunities and Challenges in an Era of Federal Devolution." *Housing Policy Debate* 7(2): 201–231.

Koebel, C. Theodore, ed. 1998. *Shelter and Society: Theory, Research, and Policy for Nonprofit Housing*. Edited by J. Bohland and P. Edwards, *SUNY Series in Urban Public Policy*. Albany, NY: State University of New York Press.

Koebel, C. Theodore, Robert E. Lang, Karen A. Danielsen. 2004. *Community Acceptance Of Affordable Housing*. Washington, DC: Center For Housing Research and Metropolitan Institute: Virginia Tech.

Koschinsky, Julia. 1998. "Challenging the Third Sector Housing Approach: The Impact of Federal Policies (1980–1996)." *Journal of Urban Affairs* 20(2): 117–135.

Krysan, Maria. 2000. "Prejudice, Politics, and Public Opinion: Understanding the Sources of Racial Policy Attitudes." *Annual Review of Sociology* 26:135–168.

Lake, Robert W. 1993. "Planners' Alchemy Transforming NIMBY to YIMBY: Rethinking NIMBY." *Journal of the American Planning Association* 59(1):87–93.

Massey, Douglas S., and Nancy A. Denton. 1993. *American Apartheid: Segregation and the Making of the Underclass*. Harvard University Press.

McClure, Kirk. 2000. "The Low Income Housing Tax Credit as an Aid to Finance: How Well Has it Worked?" *Housing Policy Debate* 11(1):91–114.

Mueller, Elizabeth J., and Alex Schwartz. 2008. "Reversing the Tide: Will State and Local Governments House the Poor as Federal Direct Subsidies Decline?" *Journal of the American Planning Association* 74(1): 122–135.

National Low Income Housing Coalition. 2010. *FY11 Budget Chart for Selected HUD Programs*. [cited 2/24/10] Available from http://www.nlihc.org/doc/FY11-Budget-Chart-HUD-Programs.pdf.

National Low Income Housing Coalition. 2010. *National Housing Trust Fund* 2010 [cited 2/24/10]. Available from http://www.nlihc.org/template/page.cfm?id=40.

Nelson, Arthur C., Rolf Pendall, Casey J. Dawkins, and Gerrit J. Knapp. 2002. *The Link Between Growth Management and Housing Affordability: The Academic Evidence*. Washington, DC: Brookings Institution.

Nguyen, Mai Thi. 2005. "Does Affordable Housing Detrimentally Affect Property Values? A Review of the Literature." *Journal of Planning Literature* 20(1): 15–26.

Nyden, Phil, James Lewis, Kale Williams, and Nathan Benefield. 2003. *Affordable Housing in the Chicago Region: Perspectives and Strategies*. Chicago: Housing Affordability Research Consortium.

Orfield, Gary. 1995. "Metropolitan School Desegregation: Impacts on Metropolitan Society." *Minnesota Law Review* 80:825–900.

Orfield, Gary. 2004. "Why Segregation Is Inherently Unequal: The Abandonment of Brown and the Continuing Failure of Plessy." *New York Law School Law Review* 49: 1041–1052.

Orfield, Myron. 2006. "Land Use and Housing Policies to Reduce Concentrated Poverty and Racial Segregation." *Fordham Urban Law Journal* 33(877): 101–159.

Orfield, Myron. 2006. *Minority Suburbanization, Stable Integration, and Economic Opportunity in Fifteen Metropolitan Regions*. Institute on Race and Poverty.

Orlebeke, Charles. 2000. "The Evolution of Low-Income Housing Policy, 1949–1999." *Housing Policy Debate* 11(2) 489–520.

Pendall, Rolf. 1999. "Opposition To Housing: Nimby And Beyond." *Urban Affairs Review* 35(1): 112–136.

Pendall, Rolf. 2000. "Local Land Use Regulation and the Chain of Exclusion." *Journal of the American Planning Association* 66(2): 125–142.

Phillips, Justin, and Eban Goodstein. 2000. "Growth Management and Housing Prices: The Case of Portland, Oregon." *Contemporary Economic Policy* 18(3):334–344.

Pogodzinski, J.M. 1991. "The Effects of Fiscal and Exclusionary Zoning on Household Location: A Critical Review." *Journal of Housing Research* 2(2):145–160.

RealtyTrac.com. 2009. *Last Updated Foreclosure Rates* 2009 [cited February 5, 2009 2009]. Available from http://www.realtytrac.com/foreclosure/foreclosure-rates.html.

Rivkin, Steven G. 1994. "Residential Segregation and School Integration." *Sociology of Education* 67(4):279–292.

Schaffer, Kim, and Irene Basloe Saraf. 2003. "The Numbers Say Yes." *The NIMBY Report.* Available at http://www.nlihc.org/nimby/2003–1.pdf.

Schneider, Anne, and Helen Ingram. 1993. Social Construction of Target Populations: Implications for Politics and Policy. *The American Political Science Review* 87(2): 334–347.

Seitles, Marc. 1998. "The Perpetuation of Residential Racial Segregation in America: Historical Discrimination, Modern Forms of Exclusion, and Inclusionary Remedies." *Journal of Land Use & Environmental Law* 14(1):89–123.

Shlay, Anne. 1993. "Family Self-Sufficiency and Housing." *Housing Policy Debate* 4(1): 457–495.

Silverman, Robert Mark. 2008. "The Influence of Nonprofit Networks on Local Affordable Housing Funding: Findings from a National Survey of Local Public Administrators." *Urban Affairs Review* 44(1): 126–141.

Somerman, Frances B. 1993. "Value, Attitude, and Belief Determinants of Willingness to Accept a Facility for the Homeless." *Journal of Social Distress and the Homeless* 2(3):177–192.

Squires, Gregory, and Charis Kubrin. 2005. "Privileged Places: Race, Uneven Development and the Geography of Opportunity in Urban America." *Urban Studies* 42(1): 47–68.

Stegman, Michael. 1989. "The Excessive Costs of Creative Finance: Growing Inefficiencies in the Production of Low-Income Housing." *Housing Policy Debate* 2(2):357–373.

Stein, Debra. 1992. *Winning Community Support for Land Use Projects.* Urban Land Institute.

Stoecker, Randy. 1997. "The CDC Model of Urban Redevelopment: A Critique and an Alternative." *Journal of Urban Affairs* 19(1): 1–22.

Stover, Mary, Valerie Cloud, Jenny Garner, Sue Phillips and Leslie Strauss. 1994. *Overcoming Exclusion In Rural Communities: Nimby Case Studies.* Housing Assistance Council.

Takahashi, Lois M. 1997. "The Socio-Spatial Stigmatization of Homelessness and HIV/AIDS: Toward an Explanation of the NIMBY Syndrome." *Social Science & Medicine* 45(6): 903–914.

Tighe, J. Rosie. 2009. *Public Perceptions of Affordable Housing: How Race and Class Stereotyping Influence Views.* Ph.D. Dissertation, University of Texas, Austin.

Turner, Margery Austin. 2003. *Strengths and Weaknesses of the Housing Voucher Program.* Testimony for the Committee on Financial Services, Subcommittee on Housing and Community Opportunity, United States House of Representatives, June 17, 2003. Washington, DC: The Urban Institute.

Valente, William D., David McCarthy Jr., Richard Briffault, and Laurie Reynolds. 2001. *Cases and Materials on State and Local Government Law.* 5th ed. St. Paul, MN: West Group.

Wallace, James. 1995. "Financing Affordable Housing in the United States." *Housing Policy Debate* 6(4): 785–814.

West, John J. 2009. "The St. Louis Equity Fund and LIHTCs: Past and Future." In *Innovative Ideas for Revitalizing the LIHTC Market.* Washington DC: Federal Reserve Bank of the United States.

Williamson, Anne R., Marc T. Smith, and Marta Strambi-Kramer. 2009. "Housing Choice Vouchers, the Low-Income Housing Tax Credit, and the Federal Poverty Deconcentration Goal." *Urban Affairs Review* 45(1): 119–132.

Wilton, Robert D. 2002. "Colouring Special Needs: Locating Whiteness in NIMBY Conflicts." *Social & Cultural Geography* 3(3):303–321.

Wolsink, Maarten. 1994. "Entanglement of Interests and Motives: Assumptions behind the NIMBY-theory on Facility Siting." *Urban Studies* 31(6): 851–866.

Young, I.M. 1999. "Residential Segregation and Differentiated Citizenship." *Citizenship Studies* 3(2): 237–52.

# THE LOW-INCOME HOUSING TAX CREDIT

Alex Schwartz

*Introduction*

The Low-Income Housing Tax Credit (LIHTC) is the nation's largest rental housing subsidy program. Established by the Tax Reform Act of 1986, the program has helped finance nearly two million housing units, accounting for more than 25% of all subsidized rental housing in the United States. The program accounts for about half of all multi-family rental housing constructed in recent years, and it is frequently combined with other federal and state subsidies. Unlike all other major housing programs, the LIHTC is overseen not by the US Department of Housing and Urban Development but by the Internal Revenue Service. Also, unlike all other rental housing subsidy programs, the LIHTC does not provide direct federal subsidies to housing developers, owners, or renters. As a tax credit, it provides incentives for private investors to provide funds for the acquisition, rehabilitation, or construction of affordable rental housing. The program enables investors to reduce their federal income taxes by acquiring an ownership stake in low-income rental housing.

This chapter assesses the strengths and weaknesses of the LIHTC over its history of nearly 25 years. After a brief summary of how the credit works, the chapter assesses the program's performance. This assessment focuses on three criticisms that scholars and policy analysts have made over the years. These criticisms concern:

(a) The program's complexity and inefficiency;
(b) The program's potential to exacerbate problems of concentrated poverty and racial segregation; and
(c) The long-term sustainability and viability of tax-credit housing and of the program itself.

## Program Mechanics[1]

The LIHTC provides investors with ten years of tax credits. In exchange, the housing must remain affordable to the targeted low-income population for at least 15 years. The amount of the tax credit is based on the total cost of the property (excluding the cost of land and certain financing and transaction costs) and the proportion of the property occupied by low-income renters. The total eligible costs ('qualified basis') is multiplied by a federally-determined percentage to yield the annual tax credit. Projects involving construction or substantial rehabilitation are entitled to a 9% annual credit; projects financed with tax-exempt bonds or that involve acquisition only, or minor amounts of renovation, receive a credit of about 4%.[2] Properties located in neighborhoods with high rates of poverty or in areas with exceptionally high development costs are eligible for additional tax credits.[3]

Unlike other tax incentives associated with real estate, the LIHTC is not awarded automatically. Developers must submit applications for tax credits to designated state agencies (usually state housing finance agencies, or HFAs). Properties financed with tax-exempt bonds are automatically eligible for 4% tax credits, but the availability of these credits is rationed by the fact that developers must apply for tax-exempt bonds, and the availability of these bonds is capped by a federal formula. These agencies allocate tax credits to housing developments on the basis of criteria developed by each state. The total dollar amount of

---

[1]  This section is based on Schwartz 2010.

[2]  The amount of the larger credit is based on 70% of the present value of a project's qualified basis; the smaller credit is based on 30%. Until 2008, the amount of the tax credit was determined each month as the weighted average cost to the US Treasury of long-term debt, with maturities comparable with those for tax-credit projects. Although the tax credit based on 70% of the present vale of the qualified basis is often referred to as the '9% credit,' and that based on 30% of the present value as the '4% credit,' in actuality the larger credit fluctuated around 8% from the late 1990s to 2008 and the smaller credit hovered around 3%. However, the Housing and Economic Recovery Act of 2008 temporarily set the larger credit at no less than 9%. Developments placed in service from July 31, 2008, through December 31, 2013, must receive annual credits of at least 9%. The legislation applies only to projects with 9% credits; the credit rate for the smaller credit continues to be set each month— although legislation was pending as of April, 2010 to set that rate at a minimum of 4%.

[3]  Properties located in 'Qualified Census Tracts' and 'Difficult Development Areas' are eligible for a "basis boost" of 30%. Qualified Census Tracts are places where at least half of all households have incomes below 60% of the area's median family income, or where the poverty rate is at least 25%. In Difficult Development Areas the cost of housing is high relative to income (Schwartz 2010).

credits is determined by state population. In 2010, states could allocate $2.00 per capita per year in tax credits, with the amount adjusted for inflation thereafter. [4] At least 10% of a state's tax credit allocations must go to housing developed by nonprofit organizations.

Rental housing developments are eligible for the tax credit if at least 20% of their units are affordable to households earning up to 50% of the area's median family income, or if at least 40% of the units are affordable to households earning up to 60% of the area median. Most developers designate most if not all of the units in their tax-credit properties for low-income occupancy, both to maximize the amount of credit they can receive and to have the option of marketing the units to households with somewhat higher incomes.

The maximum allowable rent is set at 30% of either 50 or 60% of median family income, depending on the proportion of tax-credit units within the development. Unlike other federal housing programs, in which renters pay no more than 30% of their adjusted income on rent and the government makes up the difference, residents of tax-credit housing with incomes below the program's maximum limit can face a rent burden well above 30% of their family income.

Housing developers seldom use the LIHTC themselves. Instead, they 'sell' the credit to private investors and use the proceeds to help cover acquisition, construction, and other development costs. More precisely, they sell interests in the development to private investors, with the investors receiving the tax credit, other tax benefits (depreciation allowances), and perhaps some cash flow from operations and a portion of the capital gains if the property is sold. Developers either sell their interests directly to outside investors or, more frequently, turn to syndicators for this purpose. Syndicators, which include for-profit and nonprofit organizations, sell interests in assemblages of tax-credit developments to corporations and other investors. They establish limited partnerships, in which the investors act as limited partners with no managerial authority over the tax-credit properties. Syndicators distribute the syndication proceeds, after taking out fees and other transaction costs, to the developers. Syndicators also oversee the

---

[4] Allocations to states were originally set at $1.25 per capita. In 2002, the government increased it to $1.75 per capita and pegged the amount to inflation for each year afterwards. The Housing and Economy Recovery Act of 2008 temporarily increased the allocation for 2009 to $2.20 per capita. The legislation calls for the cap to revert to $2.00 in 2010.

management of their tax-credit properties, in part to reduce the risk of the properties violating the program rent and income restrictions, which could subject investors to major financial penalties.

The amount of equity generated by the tax credit depends on two factors: the amount of money investors are willing to pay for each dollar of tax credit, and the various transaction costs connected to the sale or syndication of tax credits. As I will explain below, the 'price' investors were willing to pay for tax credits increased markedly over time, and transaction costs decreased. As a result, housing developers received increasing amounts of equity per tax-credit dollar—or did so until 2008 when the financial crisis eviscerated the market for tax credits.

*Assessment*

Scholars and policy analysts have levelled three main criticisms against the LIHTC over the years. These concern (a) its complexity and inefficiency; (b) its tendency to reinforce patterns of concentrated poverty and racial segregation; and (c) its long term viability and sustainability. In the remainder of this chapter I assess the program in light of these concerns.

*Complexity and Inefficiency*

In the early years of the program, policy analysts viewed it as a very inefficient and convoluted way of financing low-income housing. In 1990, for example, Patrick Clancy, chief executive of one of the nation's largest nonprofit housing developers, wrote that the LIHTC combines the worse aspects of tax incentives and direct federal housing subsidy programs. According to Clancy, it is inefficient like other tax incentives in that a substantial proportion of the subsidy does not go into housing but goes into transaction costs and investor profit. Like other federal subsidy programs for privately owned rental housing, the program is extremely bureaucratic, with complicated procedures for obtaining the credit and extensive reporting requirements to document compliance with the program's regulations (Clancy 1990). Two years later, Michael Stegman criticized the program for making the underwriting of low-income housing unduly complicated and cumbersome: "It simply doesn't make sense to have a national housing policy in which the deeper the targeting and the lower the income group served, the more costly and complicated it is to arrange the financing" (Stegman 1992:363).

The LIHTC was inefficient during its first years of existence. Investors purchased tax credits at a steep discount, typically paying less than 50 cents for each tax-credit dollar. Accounting, legal, and other transaction costs absorbed as much as 10 to 15 cents of every dollar paid by tax-credit investors. As a result of the low prices paid by investors, and high transaction costs, developers usually received about 40 cents for every dollar in tax credits allocated to the property. Developers therefore required additional sources of funding besides the tax-credit equity. They seldom could take out a market-rate mortgage for the rest of the property's development costs, since that would cause rents to be unaffordably high, and exceed the program's limits. Instead, developers had to supplement the tax credit equity and a mortgage with additional grants and low-interest loans, known as 'gap financing,' from state and local governments, foundations, and other sources. During the first 10 or so years of the program's existence it was not unusual for LIHTC properties to receive funding from five to ten separate sources (Hebert et al. 1993). Producing affordable housing with the LIHTC required developers to put together a wide assortment of subsidies, making the development process time consuming and costly. The program was indeed inefficient.

Over time, however, the LIHTC became significantly more efficient. Investors paid increasing amounts for each tax-credit dollar and transaction costs declined. As the program became more familiar to investors and after Congress made the program 'permanent' in 1993, investors saw less risk in investing in tax-credit properties and therefore accepted a lower rate of return. Whereas investors might have demanded an annual return of 30% in the program's early years, they accepted 7.5% or less by 2001 and as little as 5% by 2006. As a result, the price investors paid per tax credit dollar increased. While tax-credit prices vary by region, project type, and other factors, by 2001 developers on average received upwards of 80 cents for each tax-credit dollar (Ernst & Young 2003; Smith 2002), and by 2006 developers frequently received $1.00 or more per credit (Ernst & Young 2007). This increase reflected lower returns demanded by investors and a decrease in the cost of syndication (Roberts 2001).

With investors willing to pay higher prices for tax credits and downward pressure on syndication and other transaction costs, developments received more equity from the sale of tax credits. This reduced the need for additional sources of subsidy (gap financing) and made it possible to target lower income renters. Thirty-nine percent of all LIHTC projects put into service between 2003 and 2007 received no other subsidy besides the LIHTC and 48% received just one additional subsidy (usually tax-exempt bonds or HOME block grants). Eleven percent received two additional subsidies and less than 2% received three or more (HUD 2010b: Table 7). The need for multiple funding sources had not disappeared, especially if projects were to house families with incomes well below 60% of median family income, but it certainly abated. However, as I discuss later in the chapter, the market for tax credits was severely impaired by the financial crisis that began in 2007. To the extent that investors were interested in acquiring any tax credits, they demanded significantly higher yields than before, thus driving down the amount of equity available to developers.

## *The LIHTC, Concentrated Poverty, and Racial Segregation*

Several scholars and fair-housing advocates contend that the LIHTC reinforces prevailing concentrated poverty and racial segregation (Bookbinder et al. 2008; Newirth 2004; Freeman 2004; Van Zandt and Mhatre 2009). They point out that LIHTC properties are disproportionately located in neighborhoods with high rates of poverty and/or with predominantly minority populations. Indeed, the program's very design would seem to promote poverty concentration. As discussed above, properties located in "Qualified Census Tracts" (QCT), where at least half of all households have incomes below 60% of the area median, or where the poverty rate is at least 35%, are eligible for a 'basis boost' of 30%, effectively increasing the property's tax credit allocation by that amount. About 17% of all LIHTC properties put in service through 2007, accounting for 20% of all LIHTC units, received a basis boost for being in a QCT. An additional 12% of LIHTCs units, representing 10% of all units, were also located in QCT but did not receive a basis boost. In total, about 29% of all LIHTC properties and units are situated in QCTs (HUD 2010a). In addition, the LIHTC program provides little incentive for developers to include higher income households within tax-credit developments. Since the tax credit applies only to low-income units, developers choose to maximize the credit they can receive by allocating all, or almost all, of the units for low-income occupancy.

In the aggregate, a disproportionate share of tax-credit housing is located in census tracts with substantial concentrations of poverty and with large minority populations. Table 1 shows that more than 20% of all LIHTC units put in service from 1995 through 2007 are in tracts with poverty rates of 30% or higher, and 44% are in tracts with a minority population of 50% or higher. These figures are much higher than for all rental housing. However, compared to the geography of public housing, households in tax-credit units are far less likely to reside in high poverty or high-minority tracts. For example, 38% of all public housing in 2008 was located in census tracts with poverty rates of 30% or higher—nearly twice the percentage for LIHTC housing (Schwartz 2010).

The geography of LIHTC housing is also quite varied. LIHTC housing in suburban and nonmetropolitan locations is less likely, than such housing in central cities, to be located in census tracts with high levels of poverty or with predominantly minority populations. This distinction is especially important since cities account for only half of all LIHTC housing (HUD 2010a). Whereas more than one-third of all LIHTC housing in central cities is located in census tracts with a poverty rate of at least 30%, the same is true for just 6.2% of all suburban LIHTC housing. More than 61% of all central-city LIHTC housing is located in census tracts with a minority population of 50% or higher, compared to 31% of all suburban LIHTC housing (see Table 1).

Table 1. Percentage of LIHTC Units Put in Service 1995–2007 and All Rental Housing Units in Census Tracts with High Rates of Poverty and Predominantly Minority Populations

| | Total | | Central city | | Suburb | | Non-Metropolitan area | |
|---|---|---|---|---|---|---|---|---|
| | LIHTC units | All rental units | LIHTC units | All rental units | LIHTC units | All rental units | LIHTC units | All rental units |
| Over 30% of population in poverty | 21.7 | 12.3 | 35.5 | 20.8 | 6.2 | 3.5 | 11.4 | 8.1 |
| Over 50% minority population | 44.6 | 31.5 | 61.5 | 44.9 | 31.1 | 23.3 | 16 | 11.3 |

Source: HUD 2010b.

Table 2. Percent Distribution of LIHTC Housing, Voucher Holders, and Public Housing, by Tract Poverty Rate and Percent Minority

|  | LIHTC housing (in 2004) | Voucher holders (in 2000) | Public housing (in 2008) |
|---|---|---|---|
| *Census tract poverty rate* | | | |
| Less than 10% | 29.0 | 24.8 | 11.8 |
| 10 to 20% | 31.0 | 36.0 | 26.6 |
| 20 to 30% | 18.0 | 22.0 | 23.4 |
| 30 to 40% | 13.0 | 11.4 | 16.2 |
| 40% or more | 9.1 | 5.8 | 22.1 |
| *Percent minority in tract* | | | |
| 0 to 10% | 16.5 | 17.7 | 22.1 |
| 10 to 29% | 24.8 | 22.2 | 19.7 |
| 30 to 49% | 15.9 | 15.6 | 12.3 |
| 50 to 79% | 19.3 | 21.0 | 17.5 |
| 80% or more | 23.5 | 23.5 | 28.4 |

*Source:* Schwartz 2010: Tables 6.5 and 8.9.

Moreover, McClure (2006) shows that the average poverty rate for suburban LIHTC housing is 12.5% (in 2002) compared to 10.7% for all suburban renters and 26% for all renters overall. He also found that half of all suburban LIHTC housing is located in census tracts with poverty rates of less than 10%.

On balance, the geographic distribution of LIHTC housing compares favorably with that of the federal Housing Choice Voucher program, and far better than the public housing program. Table 2 compares the percentage of housing units in the three programs in census tracts with varying degrees of poverty and minority concentration. It shows that LIHTC has the largest proportion of units located in census tracts with poverty rates less than 10% and its proportion of households in tracts with minority population of less than 10% is only one percentage point below that of the voucher program. In sum, the geography of tax-credit housing is very diverse, with sizeable concentrations in areas with high and low levels of poverty and minority concentration.

Finally, although a substantial portion of LIHTC is located in areas of concentrated poverty, especially in central cities, this does not necessarily mean that this housing contributes to or exacerbates poverty concentration. Notwithstanding the program's name, most tenants in LIHTC housing have incomes that are above the poverty line. Unless they also have federal rental vouchers, residents' income is usually around 50 to 60% of the area's family income, while the poverty line is usually around 30% of median. As a result, the provision of tax-credit housing in census tracts with relatively high rates of poverty may actually reduce the poverty rate (McClure 2006; Schwartz 2010). Unfortunately, no information is available on the racial or ethnic composition of the residents of tax-credit housing, so it is not possible to determine the extent to which the program perpetuates or reduces patterns of racial segregation.

In summary, a sizable portion of LIHTC housing is situated in neighborhoods with high levels of poverty and/or predominantly minority populations. However, a substantial potion is also located in neighborhoods with much lower concentrations of poverty and of minority populations. Compared to other housing subsidy programs, including tenant based vouchers, the LIHTC is more effective in helping low-income families and individuals access housing in a wide range of neighborhoods, including what may be called 'neighborhoods of opportunity;—low poverty, racially diverse or predominantly white populations, with access to employment, recreation, shopping, and good public schools (Briggs 2005; McClure 2006). The varied geography of LIHTC housing also reflects a tension between the goals of community development and of fair housing. On one hand, the LIHTC has been vital to the physical renovation of many inner city neighborhoods, channelling capital for the renovation of dilapidated buildings and the construction of new ones. In many instances, LIHTC housing constitutes the only new development in years, and in some instances led the way to new private investment. On the other hand, the program includes incentives (basis boost) to locate housing in impoverished neighborhoods, neighborhoods that are often also predominantly minority. These incentives may run counter to the Fair Housing Act and subsequent judicial decisions that mandate that subsidized housing should "affirmatively further fair housing" (Bookbinder et al. 2008; Orfield 2005).

*Sustainability*

Until the advent of the financial crisis, the dominant concern about the LIHTC program revolved around the affordability and viability of tax-credit units after the program's income and rent restrictions expire, after a property's first 15 years of operation. When the program was first established, the federal government required that all tax-credit-funded units remain affordable to low-income tenants for a minimum of 15 years: the 10 years in which investors receive tax credit and five years thereafter. Failure to meet income and/or rent restrictions during this period would subject investors to 'credit recapture'—repayment of tax credits, plus interest and other penalties.

After 15 years of occupancy, the owners of tax-credit properties were allowed to charge any rent, and house tenants of any income, unless the property was subject to additional affordability restrictions besides those imposed by the tax-credit program. For example, approximately one third of all LIHTC properties put into service through 1989, containing more than one quarter of all tax-credit units, also received financing through the Federal Farmers Home Administrations (later renamed Rural housing Services), which required 50 years of affordability (Collignon 1999). Local and state governments and other funders of tax-credit properties have also imposed additional affordability restrictions that extended beyond year 15.

Congress passed legislation in 1989 and 1990 to help preserve the affordability of tax-credit housing. The Revenue Reconciliation Act of 1989 requires properties completed after 1989 to maintain their original affordability requirements for an additional 15 years after the expiration of the initial compliance period. The Omnibus Budget Reconciliation Act of 1990 further strengthened the prospects for long-term affordability by granting qualified nonprofit groups, tenant organizations, and public agencies, rights of first refusal to acquire tax-credit units at below-market prices.

These two laws significantly improved the prospects for continued affordability of tax-credit housing beyond year 15. In addition to extending the minimum affordability period, these laws made it easier for LIHTC properties to be acquired by organizations with an interest in maintaining their long-term affordability. However, although these laws made it far more difficult for owners to convert tax-credit properties to market-rate occupancy, they do not guarantee the long-term viability of this housing. In some circumstances, the extended affordability period can be waived if the current owner wishes to sell the property and neither the owner nor the state housing finance agency is able to find a buyer willing to pay the requisite price. In such instances, rents can be increased to market rates, and limits on resident income waived. Existing low-income residents are protected from increased rents for a minimum of three years (Schwartz and Melendez 2008). The only tax-credit property not subject to the legislative reforms of 1989 and 1990 are developments put into service before 1990. They comprise about 17% of all LIHTC properties completed through 2006, but only 9% of all units, reflecting the small average size of early tax-credit projects (Schwartz and Melendez 2008; Smith 2002).

Few properties that have reached year 15 have converted to higher income occupancy. Ernst & Young found that 6% had been converted to market-rate rents as of 2007. In contrast, 42% had been resyndicated with tax credits and 25% had been refinanced and maintained as affordable housing without additional tax credits (Ernst & Young 2007: 35; Melendez and Schwartz 2008). A national survey of owners of LIHTC properties that had reached or were facing the end of their 15-year compliance period also found that few were at serious risk of converting to market rate occupancy (Melendez and Schwartz 2008). One reason for the apparently low incidence of LIHTC properties converting to market rents is that increased competition for tax credits among developers enabled many state housing finance agencies to discourage or even prohibit them from exercising their right to have the property converted to market rents if they were unable to find a buyer (Christensen 2004: 51). In evaluating applications for low-income housing tax credits, some state housing finance agencies give extra weight to proposals that waive this right. Others explicitly reject from consideration proposals that do not waive this option. Another reason may simply be that most owners and their partners are interested in providing affordable rental housing for low-income households.

The expiration of affordability restrictions poses one challenge to the preservation for tax-credit housing for low-income renters; more daunting is the need to finance the acquisition and physical improvement of LIHTC properties after year 15. Affordability restrictions of even the longest duration mean little if resources are not available to purchase the property from the original owners and to invest in the property's continued physical viability. After 15 years, virtually any building will need upgrading and replacement of major elements, such as heating and air conditioning systems, roofs, windows, and appliances.

Properties financed in the first years of the program are especially likely to need capital improvements. Because the tax credit generated more equity later on, these early projects tended to involve modest amounts of renovation as opposed to the new construction and gut rehabilitation that was to characterize most LIHTC projects from the mid 1990s onwards. As a result, they will generally require more rehabilitation by year 15 than later LIHTC projects. Making matters worse the earliest LIHTC developments are less likely to have reserve funds available by year 15 to help pay for essential capital improvements. The earliest projects tended to be underwritten with smaller reserve funds than those for later projects, and these reserves have often been exhausted well before year 15 (Schwartz and Melendez 2008).

Capital improvements for LIHTC housing are most often funded by refinancing the property's mortgage. The proceeds of the new mortgage are used to pay for necessary renovation and sometimes to finance the purchase of the property from its limited partners. Mortgage refinancing, however, is not always, feasible. Of particular concern are properties whose rent rolls are too small to support a mortgage large enough to finance the cost of acquisition and capital improvements. Most vulnerable are early projects that underwent only moderate amounts of rehabilitation and are located in weak housing markets as well as properties with large mortgages that are due as a balloon payment (Schwartz and Melendez 2008).

*LIHTC and the Financial Crisis*
Until the onset of the mortgage crisis and the broader financial crisis it precipitated, concerns about the sustainability of the LIHTC revolved around the prospects for long-term affordability and physical viability of housing financed with tax credits. The crisis raises questions about the sustainability and viability of the program itself.

Investor demand for the LIHTC peaked in 2006. It declined modestly in 2007, largely because Fannie Mae and Freddie Mac curtailed their tax-credit investments for tax reasons. Demand for tax credits plummeted the following two years in the wake of the crisis. The market for tax credits had become dominated by large financial institutions since the late 1990s, in particular the two federally sponsored secondary mortgage institutions Fannie Mae and Freddie Mac and the nation's largest banks. In 2008, the federal government effectively nationalized Fannie Mae and Freddie Mac, which together accounted for about 40% of all tax-credit investment in recent years. Moreover, several of the largest financial institutions, collapsed or were forced to merge with other firms. Those that survived racked up billions of dollars in losses. With little if any taxable income, and the prospects for future profits uncertain at best, banks and other financial institutions decreased their investments in the LIHTC (Joint Center for Housing Studies 2009; Schwartz 2010).

With the market for tax credits greatly diminished, the syndication of tax credits generated significantly less equity for housing developers. They, therefore, needed unexpectedly large amounts of gap financing. Worse still, a growing number of projects were unable to attract any tax-credit investors at all. In May 2009, it was reported that tax-credit equity investment was likely to total $4 billion to $4.5 billion, down from about $9 billion in 2007 (Pristin 2009). While projects in the strongest housing markets continue to attract investors, albeit at a lower price per tax credit dollar, projects in weaker markets are languishing. The market is especially moribund for the 4% tax credit (Joint Center for Housing Studies 2009).

The federal government, as part of a broader effort to revive the economy, passed legislation in 2008 and 2009 to strengthen the LIHTC program. The Housing and Economic Recovery Act of 2008 (HERA) temporarily increased the amount of tax credits that state housing finance agencies could distribute to eligible properties. It increased the amount of tax credits that could be allocated to each state from $2.00 to $2.20 per capita and it set the larger of the two tax credits at a minimum of 9%, effectively increasing the amount of tax credits available to investors by about one percent of a project's qualified basis.

Although these measures increased the amount of tax credits that could be allocated to low-income housing developments, they failed to whet investor demand for tax credits. The American Recovery and Reinvestment Act of 2009, President Obama's economic stimulus bill, sought to strengthen the LIHTC in a different way. The legislation created the Low Income Housing Tax Credit Assistance Program (TCAP) and the Low Income Housing Exchange Program (TCEP). TCAP allocated $2.25 billion to state housing finance agencies to provide gap financing for LIHTC projects that did not receive sufficient equity from the syndication of tax credits. LIHTC projects that had received tax credit allocations from fiscal years 2007 through 2009 were eligible for the program (Hahn and Kimm 2010; Joint Center for Housing Studies 2009). The TCEP program allows state housing finance agencies to exchange their 9% tax credits from fiscal 2008 and 2009 for cash grants. Instead of allocating tax credits to housing developers, TCEP gave state housing finance agencies the option of providing cash instead (Hahn and Kimm 2010; Joint Center for Housing Studies 2009). In effect, the program gives states the option of replacing tax credits with block grants (at 85 cents per dollar of tax credit). Unlike tax credits, block grants enable states to provide equity directly to eligible housing developments (Schwartz 2010).

In 2010, Congress extended the TCEP program for another year. As of June 2010, Congress was also considering legislation aimed to further strengthen the market for tax credits. In order to increase investor demand for the LIHTC, one bill would allow the credit to be applied against federal income taxes from the five previous years prior to the purchase of the credits; at present, investors can only apply the credit for one year retroactively. By enabling investors to apply the credit against past as well as future taxes, Congress hoped that the LIHTC would become more appealing to financial institutions and other potential investors. In addition, the legislation would enable other types of corporations to be able to use the credit.[5] Finally, other legislation would set the smaller of the two tax credits at 4% annually, just as HERA set the larger credit at 9%. At present, the credit rate for the small credit is set monthly, and has hovered around 3%.

It remains to be seen if federal legislation will resuscitate the market for the LIHTC. In any event it is highly unlikely that housing developers will receive upwards of 95 cents in equity for each tax-credit dollar allocated to their developments. They will probably be lucky to garner 80 or even 75 cents. At present, if LIHTC properties attract any funds from investors, they are fortunate to receive 60 cents per tax credit dollar. The market for the LIHTC, in other words, has reverted back to the pricing that was prevalent in the early 1990s. As a result, developers of tax-credit housing will require far more gap financing than they needed in recent years, and it will become much more difficult to underwrite tax-credit developments with rents that are affordable to households earning less than the maximum allowed (60% of area median family income).

*Conclusions*

The LIHTC, at least until the onset of the mortgage crisis, was widely viewed as among the most successful subsidy programs in the United

---

[5] Federal tax law effectively limits the LIHTC to corporations; passive loss restrictions severely limit the extent to which individuals, partnerships, and closely held corporations can use the LIHTC to reduce their income taxes (Schwartz 2010). The proposed legislation would waive passive loss restrictions against partnerships, S-corporations, and closely held C-Corporations, which pass their income and expenses to individual owners (Joint Center for Housing Studies 2009:19).

States for low-income rental housing, probably the most successful. It has produced more housing than public housing and all other federal housing programs. And unlike these other programs, the LIHTC program has seen very little scandal or corruption. The housing is largely in good physical and financial shape, is well integrated within the surrounding community, and has not been stigmatized by extreme poverty, crime, or neglect (Ernst and Young 2007; Schwartz and Melendez 2008; Joint Center for Housing Studies 2009). Moreover, the long-term preservation of LIHTC housing has, at least so far, been less problematic than for previous federal programs. Whereas the vast majority of LIHTC housing has remained affordable to low-income households beyond the expiration of the initial 15-year period of restricted rents and tenant income, the nation has lost hundreds of thousands of subsidized housing units built under Section 236 and Section 8 through mortgage prepayment and the refusal of owners to renew their Section 8 subsidy contracts (Schwartz 2010).

Until around 2007, the LIHTC would have been considered an unequivocal success. Today, an assessment of the program's performance would be far more mixed. The financial crisis revealed fundamental limitations. It shows that the program's increased efficiency since the late 1990s, as measured by decreasing investment yields and rising prices, were not based entirely on financial fundamentals. Much of the rise in tax credit prices was driven by a small number of financial institutions who were as interested in regulatory and political benefits as in financial return. Banks were motivated to invest in tax credits in large part for its effect on their Community Reinvestment Act ratings. Fannie Mae and Freddie Mac were motivated by similar reasons.[6] In bidding up the price of tax credits, these institutions eventually drove out other corporate investors from the LIHTC market; yields had become too low. The new reality, with the GSEs under government conservatorship, and the surviving banks reluctant to commit themselves to acquire tax credits that must be taken over the course of 10 years, has caused the price of tax credits to drop, and in some cases has made tax credits unsellable at any price. As noted above, it is highly unlikely that they will bounce back to where they were in the years

---

[6] The Community Reinvestment Act (CRA) requires banks to serve all areas from which they draw deposits. Part of a bank's CRA rating derives from its investments in community development—which include LIHTC investments. Fannie Mae and Freddie Mac were subject to the Congressionally mandated affordable housing goals, which could be met in part through LIHTC investments.

before the crisis to 95 cents or more per tax credit dollar. In other words, the credit will likely be significantly less efficient in the years to come.

Congress is currently considering legislation designed to make the LIHTC more appealing to potential investors. As noted above, proposed legislation would allow investors to claim the credit against income taxes from up to five previous years—thereby increasing the likelihood that investors would be able to use the credits if their taxable income in the future is insufficient. It would also expand the pool of potential investors by lifting restrictions on passive losses for partnerships and closely held corporations. Other legislation would broaden the Tax Credit Exchange Program to cover 4% tax credits as well as 9% credits. Additional options, which have not been incorporated into legislation would make tax credits refundable (i.e., enable investors to use them whether or not they have any income tax obligations); would accelerate the use of tax credits (more credits would be taken earlier on during the property's operation, fewer later on); and would waive passive loss restrictions for individual investors (Ernst and Young 2009; Joint Center for Housing Studies 2009; Schwartz 2010).

Most fundamentally, the downturn in tax-credit prices and the resulting decrease in equity generated by the sale of tax credits reflects the risk of relying on the tax incentives to subsidize low-income housing. Sudden changes in the investment marketplace can lead to sharp swings in the availability of funds to support new housing development. Perhaps the Obama Administration's decision to allow state housing finance agencies to exchange their tax credit allocations for cash represents a superior alternative to the tax credit. If the government provides funds directly to housing developers, it would avoid much of the uncertainty and complexity that currently surrounds the tax credit program. While direct appropriations would register as an expense in the federal budget, tax credits also cost the government in the form of foregone tax revenue. The difference is that tax expenditures are treated differently from an accounting perspective. In effect, the LIHTC is a block grant, with states having wide discretion in deciding how tax credits may be allocated and used.

A potential disadvantage of replacing the LIHTC with direct subsidies is that the nation could lose the benefit of private oversight of subsidized properties. Syndicators of the LIHTC oversee the management of their properties to protect the interests of their investors. They check to ensure that the properties comply with the program's rent and tenant income requirements, and that the properties are properly maintained. A direct subsidy program would most likely rely entirely on government oversight. Another disadvantage of direct subsidy programs is that their funding is always vulnerable to reduced appropriations. Whereas the LIHTC produced a steady increase in affordable rental housing every year to 2008, Congress has repeatedly cut funding for other federal low-income housing subsidy programs (after inflation, if not before) (Schwartz 2010). As a result, the total stock of rental housing with direct federal subsidies has declined since the mid 1990s (Schwartz 2010). Choosing between direct subsidy programs and tax expenditure programs depends in large part on whether one has more confidence in the vicissitudes of governmental appropriation process or in the investment marketplace. In the end, it probably makes most sense to have a more balanced system that does not rely overwhelmingly on either tax expenditures or direct subsidies.

## Reference

Bookbinder, S., A. Buchanan, T. Daniel, J. Hooks, S. Parker, and P. Tegeler. 2008. "Building Opportunity: Civil Rights Best Practices in the Low Income Housing Tax Credit Program." Report prepared for Poverty & Race Research Action Council and Lawyers' Committee for Rights Under Law. (Dec.). http://www.prrac.org/pdf/2008-Best-Practices-final.pdf.

Briggs, X. editor. 2005. The Geography of Opportunity. Washington, D.C.: Brookings Institution Press.

Christensen, S. L. 2004. "Year 15 Exit Strategies." Journal of Affordable Housing and Community Development Law 14(1): 46–62.

Clancy, P. E. 1990. "Tax Incentives and Federal Housing Programs: Proposed Principles for the 1990s." In D. DiPasquale and L. Keyes, eds., Building Foundations: Housing and Federal Policy (Chapter 11). Philadelphia: University of Pennsylvania Press.

Collignon, K. 1999. "Expiring Affordability of Low-Income Housing Tax Credit Properties: Next Era in Preservation." Cambridge, MA: Harvard Joint Center for Housing Studies.

Ernst & Young. 2007. Understanding the Dynamics IV: Housing Tax Credit Investment Performance (June). Washington, DC.

Ernst & Young. 2009. "Low-Income Housing Tax Credit Survey." Prepared for Enterprise Community Partners, Inc. and Local Initiatives Support Corporation. www.enterprisecommunity.org/public_policy/documents/lihtc_legislative_study.pdf.

Hahn, J. and T. Kimm. 2010. "Beware of TCAP, Exchange Pitfalls." Affordable Housing Finance (Jan./Feb.). www.housingfinance.com/ahf/articles/2010/march/0310-specialfocus-Beware-of-TCAP-Exchange-Pitfalls.htm.

Hebert, S., K. Heintz, C. Baron, N. Kay, and J. E. Wallace. 1993. "Nonprofit Housing Costs and Benefits: Final Report." Abt Associates, Inc., with Aspen Systems for U.S. Department of Housing and Urban Development, Office of Policy Development and Research.

Joint Center for Housing Studies of Harvard University. 2009. "The Disruption of the Low-income Housing Tax Credit Program: Causes, Consequences, Responses, and Proposed Correctives." (December). www.rentalhousingaction.org/files/JCHS _Disruption_of_the_lihtc_program_2009.pdf.

McClure, K. 2006. "The Low Income Housing Tax Credit Goes Mainstream and Moves to the Suburbs." *Housing Policy Debate* 17(3): 419–446.

Melendez, E. and A. Schwartz. 2008. "Year 15 and the Preservation of Tax-Credit Housing for Low-Income Households: An Assessment of Risk." *Housing Studies* 23(1): 67–87.

Neuwirth, R. 2004. "Renovation or Ruin?" *Shelterforce Online* 137 (September/ October). www.nhi.org/online/issues/137/LIHTC.html.

Orfield, Myron. 2005. "Racial Integration and Community Revitalization: Applying the Fair Housing Act to the Low Income housing Tax Credit." *Vanderbilt Law Review* 58(6): 1749–1804.

Poverty and Race Research Action Council. No date.

Pristin, T. "Shovel Ready But Investor Deprived." *New York Times* (May 5). www .nytimes.com/2009/05/06/realestate/commercial/06housing.html?_r=1&partner =rss&emc=rss.

Roberts, B. 2001. "Tax Deduction Incentives for Individual Investors in Housing." Memo prepared for the Millennial Housing Commission (April 16).

Schwartz, A. 2010. *Housing Policy in the United States* (Second Edition). New York: Routledge.

Schwartz, A. and E. Melendez. 2008. "After Year 15: Challenges to the Preservation of Housing Financed with Low Income Housing Tax Credits." *Housing Policy Debate* 19(2): 261–294.

Smith, D. A. 2002. "The Low Income Housing Tax Credit's Effectiveness and Efficiency: A Presentation of the Issues." Boston, MA: Recapitalization Advisors, Inc.

Stegman, M. 1990. "The Role of Housing in a Revitalized National Housing policy." In D. DiPasquale and L. Keyes, eds., *Building Foundations: Housing and Federal Policy* (Chapter 13). Philadelphia: University of Pennsylvania Press.

U.S. Department of Housing and Urban Development. 2010a. Low Income Housing Tax Credit Data Base.

U.S. Department of Housing and Urban Development. 2010b. "Updating the Low Income Housing Tax Credit Data Base: Projects Placed in Service Through 2007." www.huduser.org/datasets/lihtc.tables9507.pdf.

Van Zandt S. and P. Mhatre. 2009. "Growing Pains: Perpetuating Inequality Through the Production of Low-Income Housing in the Dallas Metroplex." *Urban Geography* 30(5): 490–513.

# INCLUSIONARY HOUSING AND FAIR HOUSING

Dennis Keating

## Exclusionary Housing in the Suburbs

American suburbs have long been characterized as 'exclusionary.' Suburbs differ considerably in their composition and character. Through a combination of factors, like high land and housing prices and practices like zoning, many have excluded not only unwanted land uses like heavy industry or high density development but also unwanted people. Middle and upper class suburbs have not wanted lower-income residents who could not pay their way, i.e., whose homes would not generate enough local property taxes to cover the public services that they would require such as police and fire and schools. In addition, many predominantly white suburbs have long excluded racial and ethnic minority group members. The NIMBY (not in my backyard) phenomenon has often led to resident opposition to any attempted introduction of publicly-subsidized, low-income housing. After reviewing this history and efforts to counter suburban exclusion in housing, my chapter will then focus on suburban inclusionary zoning and housing programs and their relationship to fair housing.

In its 1968 report on civil disorders in American cities, the Kerner Commission warned of affluent white suburbs segregated from impoverished cities with disproportionately large numbers of racial and ethnic minority residents living in blighted neighborhoods and argued for opening up the suburbs to them. While racially discriminatory practices violate the Fourteenth Amendment of the United States constitution and federal, state and local fair housing laws, they are difficult to prove and expensive to challenge. Nevertheless, beginning in the late 1960s, civil rights organizations and their lawyers began to sue suburbs selectively in the hope of ending the pattern of exclusionary housing and neighborhoods. Paul Davidoff and his Suburban Action Institute played a leading role in this litigation (Davidoff and Davidoff 1970–1971). In part, this movement was intended to allow low-income and minority residents living in poor urban neighborhoods an opportunity to move to better neighborhoods in the suburbs with better prospects for employment, education, and housing in safer and healthier surroundings. These lawsuits were often triggered by the actions of suburban governments rejecting efforts to build subsidized housing for lower-income occupants, many of whom would be racial and ethnic minorities. Contrary to the civil rights movement's previous fight to desegregate the Jim Crow South, this campaign often focused on northern suburbs, following the violent resistance of the Chicago suburb of Cicero to a march organized by Martin Luther King in the summer of 1966. The national fair housing movement's efforts to change federal policy won the passage of the federal fair housing law in April, 1968, following the assassination of Martin Luther King. It quickly came to a head in the summer of 1971 when the administration of President Richard Nixon undercut the attempt of George Romney, his Secretary of Housing and Urban Development (HUD), to force suburban communities to enact and enforce "open housing" policies as a condition of receiving federal housing and community development funding (Lamb 2005). Largely white suburbs, particularly 'blue collar' suburbs like Warren, outside Detroit in Romney's home state of Michigan, were particularly resistant to calls for racial integration in housing and schools. In a 1976 U.S. Supreme Court decision, Detroit's suburban schools were successful in resisting being made part of a regional judicial remedy to racial segregation in the metropolitan area's public schools.[1]

Nevertheless, in a handful of cases, especially where there was egregious and provable racial segregation in housing, federal courts found violations of the federal fair housing laws and, like court-ordered desegregation of the public schools, imposed remedies intended to force suburbs to permit the construction of lower-income housing with minority residents in previously all or predominantly white communities. This occurred, for example, in the affluent Chicago suburb of Arlington Heights after a 1977 decision of the U.S. Supreme Court led to a finding that rejection of a subsidized housing project had a "disparate impact" on racial minorities otherwise unable to afford to live there, even though a deliberate intent to discriminate racially by public officials could not be proven.[2] A court-ordered approval of the project

[1] *Milliken v. Bradley,* 418 U.S. 717 (1976).
[2] *Village of Arlington Heights Vv. Metropolitan Housing Development Corp.,* 429 U.S. 252 (1977).

eventually led to its being built (contrary to other lawsuits where courts ruled against fair housing advocates making similar claims about discriminatory treatment of proposals to build federally-subsidized housing). In 1980 in a suit brought by the U.S. Department of Justice, a federal judge ruled that the working class Cleveland suburb of Parma had long deliberately excluded African-Americans and imposed a mandate to force it to promote desegregation. This order lasted for almost two decades (Keating 1997).

Perhaps the best known example of court-ordered housing desegregation in an American suburb came in 1985 in Yonkers, a large Westchester County suburb of New York City. After a federal judge found the city guilty of deliberately racially segregating its public housing (and schools), when the city council defied his order to build new racially-mixed public housing in previously all-white neighborhoods, he fined the city on an escalating basis that threatened its bankruptcy. After a tense stand-off, eventually the city capitulated and agreed to fund new subsidized housing to be located in those neighborhoods (Belkin 1999). In 2009, affluent Westchester County was found to be in violation of its obligation to use its Community Development Block Grant (CDBG) funding from HUD to "affirmatively further fair housing" and it settled the case by agreeing to fund additional subsidized housing to be built in those communities with the smallest minority populations. Its attempted defense that funding affordable housing met its fair housing obligation was not accepted by the federal judge.[3] This was a case brought by a civil rights organization, which was later joined by the U.S. Department of Justice.

These few examples illustrate the difficulty of challenging suburban exclusionary practices by suing individual cities when litigation, even if successful, takes a long time, involves extensive remedial orders, and is very expensive. The involvement of the U.S. Department of Justice (DOJ) on the side of the plaintiff is almost a requirement for success in the face of persistent municipal opposition. However, the DOJ has rarely invoked the 1968 federal Fair Housing Act to sue individual suburban cities.

Perhaps the most glaring example of the obstacles in seeking an effective and timely judicial remedy to racial discrimination in

---

[3] Peter Applebome. "Integration Faces a New Test in the Suburbs," New York Times, 2009 (Aug. 23) at 3 (Sunday News of the Week).

housing was the lawsuit by the nonprofit Business and Professional People for the Public Interest against the Chicago Housing Authority (CHA) in 1966. Public housing in Chicago had been racially segregated from its birth. After many twists and turns and against the obdurate resistance of Chicago's powerful mayor Richard J. Daley, the lawsuit (heard by a black federal judge previously allied with the mayor) finally prevailed. Nevertheless, the resistance of white neighborhoods, the mayor, and the city council made it virtually impossible to implement the remedy of building new public projects housing black residents previously denied access to these neighborhoods. Therefore, the court-ordered remedy eventually created what became known as the Gautreaux demonstration program. This allowed CHA minority residents to be subsidized in apartments in predominantly white neighborhoods in numerous suburbs surrounding Chicago (Polikoff 2006). The results of this experiment have been much studied and led to a similar HUD demonstration program in five cities called Moving to Opportunity (MTO).

The MTO experiment was designed to promote an economic rather than a racial mix, with participants required to move from poor inner city neighborhoods to suburban locations with low poverty rates (Goering 2005). The evaluations of these two programs have concluded the impact on the minority participants has been mixed. The former showed improvements in employment and the education of children with most remaining in their new neighborhoods over time. The results of the latter were more mixed (Rosenbaum et al. 2005). Since both experimental programs involved the introduction of minority residents in subsidized housing in selected suburbs on a very small scale, they did not have a major impact. The federal government has not adopted such a national policy. Instead, the policy has been to enforce the laws outlawing racial discrimination in housing rather than affirmatively promoting racial integration and diversity throughout metropolitan areas.

Nevertheless, many of the low-income holders of HUD's Housing Choice Vouchers (HCVs), previously called the Section 8 program, have used their rent subsidy certificates to rent units outside the central cities, where most 'conventional' public housing projects have previously been located. While one hope for this development was a greater integration of the poor, including minorities, in previously racially and economically segregated suburbs, this has not usually been the case. Since it is up to private landlords to accept federally-subsidized tenants at regulated and capped rents, tenants' choices are limited. As a result, poor tenants using HCVs in the suburbs often end up in concentrated areas of minority race and lower income residents, as have their urban counterparts previously (Varady 2007). Suburbs have not been welcome to this program but they have no control over tenants' choices of where to locate.

## State Approaches to Inclusionary Zoning

The two best examples of policies aimed at ending suburban exclusionary practices and promoting widespread mixed-income suburban housing have occurred in the states of Massachusetts and New Jersey. In 1969, Massachusetts adopted what became known as the "anti-snob" zoning law (Chapter 40B). An unusual policy that emerged amidst the bitter battle over public school desegregation in Boston and passed over the opposition of suburban legislators, this law overrode municipal 'home rule.' If developers of housing with at least 25 percent below market 'affordable' units are denied approval, they can appeal to a state board which is empowered to order issuance of a building permit if it finds that a municipality's reasons for the denial are not justified (Citizens Housing and Planning Association 2009). Most of the cases brought to this board have resulted in decisions favoring the developer. If a city meets the threshold standard of having at least ten percent of its housing stock affordable, it is no longer subject to the threat of a developer complaint. Of course, it can deny approval for legitimate reasons such as environmental problems or lack of necessary infrastructure. Otherwise, while all localities are supposed to meet this state standard, there are no penalties for non-compliance and no mandate to adopt inclusionary zoning. After more than four decades, this policy remains in effect despite periodic attempts by suburban and rural communities to have the state legislature either repeal or significantly weaken the law. As of 2009, it had produced 56,000 units of affordable units (39,000 rental, 17,000 owner-occupied). Yet a majority of the state's 351 cities and towns have not yet met the threshold standard (only 51 had complied, with another 117 close, needing only 100 or fewer units to comply). Connecticut and Rhode Island have both adopted similar laws, although with less impact to date.

In 1971, the town of Mt. Laurel, New Jersey, located on the fringe of the metropolitan area around the impoverished city of Camden, formerly a manufacturing center, became the target of a lawsuit aimed at its 'fiscal' zoning. This was a policy employed by many of its suburban counterparts in New Jersey. By limiting housing almost entirely to single-family houses on large lots, these suburbs kept out renters and low-income housing. In the case of Mt. Laurel, which became a rapidly growing suburb, access to its housing by lower-income African-Americans and other minorities was very limited. The lawsuit was intended to end this pattern of exclusionary zoning. In two extraordinary rulings in 1975 and 1983, the New Jersey Supreme Court ruled constitutionally that most of New Jersey's 566 localities had to take into account the regional welfare in zoning, despite home rule (Haar 1996). The court indicated that inclusionary housing programs offered one way for localities to meet their affordable housing obligation. After a firestorm of suburban opposition to these rulings, in 1985 a state agency (the Council on Affordable Housing [COAH]) was created to determine affordable housing needs throughout the state and to assign a 'fair share' of the regional needs to each affected municipality. Certain areas of the state were not subject to the reach of the court's rulings and COAH. And the legislature allowed municipalities to sell off up to half of their fair share obligation to communities in need of affordable housing (thereby allowing more affluent suburbs to shift much of this to cities like Camden). After the 1975 decision, builders filed numerous lawsuits against localities accused of non-compliance with the court's decision. COAH is empowered to certify that New Jersey municipalities are in compliance by meeting their affordable housing obligation, thereby immunizing them from developer lawsuits. As of 2007, approximately 60,000 new and rehabilitated housing units had been produced. Like Massachusetts, a majority of New Jersey's affected localities have not yet been certified as being in compliance with the Mt. Laurel decisions.[4]

Massachusetts and New Jersey can be said to have adopted what might be called 'inclusionary housing' policies. These are aimed at having mixed-income housing. Aside from these two unusual statewide examples, inclusionary housing is a policy that became popular in some cities beginning in the 1970s, largely due to very high housing costs that priced many out, including public employees and commuting workers. This was a bi-coastal pattern. California has had the most localities adopt inclusionary housing, given its high housing costs and the problem created by the 1978 adoption by constitutional initiative

---

4  New Jersey Council on Affordable Housing: www.state.nj.us/dca/affiliates/coah.

of a cap on property taxes in response to a rapid inflation in housing values. Cities and counties, which are supposed to address affordable housing needs in their master plans, were then limited in what, if anything, they could spend on reducing housing costs. In addition to requiring housing developers to provide infrastructure and facilities like roads, schools, parks, and police and fire stations as a condition of approval of their developments, about one-third of California's cities and counties had adopted inclusionary housing policies as of 2007.[5]

While inclusionary housing programs can be voluntary, to be effective they usually have to be mandatory (Lerman 2006). Developers are required to devote a percentage (typically between 10 to 25 percent) of housing in larger housing developments to below market housing. The income limits of eligible occupants are usually those set by the federal government for low and moderate income households. To offset any loss of income by developers, localities usually offer offsetting incentives such as a 'density bonus' (additional units beyond normal density limits), 'fast track' review of applications, and waivers of building requirements such as parking. Since some developers are reluctant to incorporate below market housing onsite in their projects for fear of buyer resistance, many inclusionary housing programs offer them the option of paying 'in-lieu' fees which will finance offsite affordable housing or 'dedicating' land for offsite affordable housing development. However, this defeats a goal of inclusionary, mixed-income housing to promote social interaction among different income groups.

While there have been legal challenges to inclusionary housing requirements by some developers and real estate representatives, inclusionary housing has generally been upheld by the state and federal courts. In addition to suburban communities, it has been adopted on a citywide basis by many large cities: Baltimore, Boston, Denver, Sacramento, San Diego, San Francisco, Seattle, and Washington, D.C. Chicago and New York City have more limited inclusionary housing policies.

One of the earliest and most successful inclusionary housing programs was adopted in 1973 by Montgomery County, Maryland. Montgomery County, outside Washington, D.C., is one of the wealthiest counties in the United States. Its Moderately Priced Dwelling Unit

---

[5] See the California Inclusionary Housing Policy Database: www.calruralhousing.org/inclusionary-housing-database.

(MPDU) program was adopted over the veto of the Council Executive, overridden by the County Council, and despite the threat of a lawsuit by homebuilders (Rusk 1999). Initially, it imposed a mandatory requirement of the dedication of 15 percent (later changed to 12.5–15 percent) of the units in all new residential subdivisions of 50 or more units (later reduced to a threshold of 35 units and currently 20 units or more) with density bonuses of 20 percent (later increased to 22 percent). Initially, price controls lasted only for five years but were later extended to 10 and then 20 years for rental units and 30 years for owner-occupied units. Upon the expiration of the required affordability period, the Montgomery County Housing Opportunities Commission (HOC) was given the first right of refusal to purchase up to one-third of the MPDU units, which it then rented to low-income households. The MPDU program allowed developers to provide affordable housing offsite and to make in-lieu payments to make units affordable, including condominiums. As of 2007, Montgomery County cumulatively had produced a total of 12,500 MPDUs (71 percent owner-occupied, 29 percent rental). At that date, only 2,260 units were still under affordability controls. The HOC controlled another 1,700 units that it had purchased.[6]

### Inclusionary Housing and Increased Diversity

While inclusionary programs have created more affordable housing in many suburbs where low- and moderate-income households would otherwise have been either deliberately excluded or would have been unable to afford prevailing housing prices, have they led to greater racial and ethnic integration? Unfortunately, there is little data on the profiles of those who occupy inclusionary units. In the Montgomery County program, as of 1997, the profile of the occupants of its MPDUs was: 41 percent White, 28 percent Asian, 22 percent Black, and 7 percent Hispanic (which equals 57 percent minority) (Rusk 1999:191). This, compared to the 2000 U.S. Census profile of the county's residents which reports a 37.5 percent minority (15 percent Black, 11.5 percent Hispanic/Latino, 11 percent Asian). About the same time, a limited survey of suburban occupants of housing produced under

---

[6] Montgomery County, Maryland.

the Mt. Laurel rulings and the COAH-assigned fair share quotas in New Jersey, found that disproportionately few were African-American (or other minorities) (Bailin and Eisdorfer 1997). This is ironic because the lead plaintiff in the Mt. Laurel lawsuit was an African-American, although the basis of the lawsuit was economic, not racial, discrimination (Kirp et al. 1995). According to the 2000 Census, three decades after it was sued, only seven percent of Mt. Laurel's population was African-American. There are no racial data on the occupants of the affordable housing produced under the Massachusetts Chapter 40B program or under the many California inclusionary housing programs.

It is hardly surprising inclusionary housing is not linked to greater racial diversity. Those localities that have adopted inclusionary housing programs have not been motivated by the issue of racial segregation in housing. Instead, it has been the shortage of affordable housing. Likewise, the other source of support has been affordable housing advocates. Using the examples of Denver and Minneapolis-St. Paul, Mara Sidney concludes:

> When affordable housing advocates with a regional perspective enter the fair housing arena, as they did in Minneapolis-St. Paul, they tend to use fair housing tools to secure more affordable housing, often stopping short of advocating for guarantees that racial minorities will have access to such housing or promoting the value of diverse communities. Indeed, they may consciously avoid such advocacy, since their efforts to win affordable housing are difficult enough without facing implicit or explicit racial prejudice as part of the opposition. (Sidney 2005:284)

### The Limits of Exclusionary Zoning

The era of advocacy for greater racial integration of the predominantly white suburbs seems to have faded (Cashin 2004). Since inclusionary housing programs have mostly been adopted voluntarily by localities, it would be politically risky and legally-suspect if inclusionary housing programs had racial and ethnic quotas, in addition to income limits to benefit lower income recipients.[7] There would probably be a backlash

---

[7] In *United States v. Starrett City Associates*, 840 F. 2d 1096 (2d Cir.) cert. denied, 488 U.S. 946 (1988), the federal Court of Appeals ruled that "rigid racial quotas of indefinite duration to maintain a fixed level of [racial] integration" violated the

in many predominantly white suburban communities against promoting inclusionary housing under the fair housing banner rather than as mixed-income and affordable housing. So, it is unlikely that this will occur unless there is proof of past racial discrimination in housing and a court-ordered remedy that includes inclusionary housing. It must be remembered that inclusionary housing is tied to the development of new housing. Therefore, usually the number of new inclusionary housing units and their occupants will be very small compared to existing housing stock and number of residents. While inclusionary housing programs may increase the number of minority residents in some communities, this will not necessarily make a major impact on existing racial patterns in most predominantly white suburbs that adopt inclusionary housing.

## References

Belkin, Lisa. 1999. *Show Me a Hero: A Tale of Murder, Suicide, Race and Redemption.* New York: Little, Brown and Company.
Cashin, Sheryll. 2004. *The Failures of Integration: How Race and Class are Undermining the American Dream.* New York: Public Affairs.
Citizens Housing and Planning Association. 2009 (October). *Fact Sheet on Chapter 40B: The State's Affordable Housing Law.* Boston: www.chapa.org.
Davidoff, Paul and Linda. 1970–1971. "Opening the Suburbs: Toward Inclusionary Land Use Controls." *Syracuse Law Review* 22:509–536.
Goering, John. 2005. "Expanding Housing Choice and Integrating Neighborhoods: The MTO Experiment", in Xavier de Souza Briggs, ed., *The Geography of Opportunity: Race and Housing Choice in Metropolitan America.* Washington, D.C.: Brookings Institution Press.
Haar, Charles M. 1996. *Suburbs under Siege: Race, Space, and Audacious Judges.* Princeton, NJ: Princeton University Press.
Keating, W. Dennis. 1997. "The Parma Housing Racial Discrimination Remedy Revisited." *Cleveland State Law Review* 45: 235–250.
(Kerner) National Commission on Civil Disorders. 1968. *Report.* New York: Bantam Books.
Kirp, David L., John P. Dwyer, and Larry A. Rosenthal. 1995. *Our Town: Race, Housing, and The Soul of Suburbia.* New Brunswick, NJ: Rutgers University Press.
Lamb, Charles M. 2005. *Housing Segregation in Suburban America since 1960: Presidential and Judicial Politics.* Cambridge: Cambridge University Press.
Lerman, Brian R. 2006. "Mandatory Inclusionary Zoning: The Answer to the Affordable Housing Problem." *Environmental Affairs* 33: 383–416.
Polikoff, Alexander. 2006. *Waiting for Gautreaux: A Story of Segregation, Housing, and the Black Ghetto.* Evanston, IL: Northwestern University Press.

---

federal fair housing law. Whether to minimize or maximize racial participation in inclusionary housing programs, it is unlikely that similar racial quotas would withstand a legal challenge.

Rosenbaum, James, Stefanie DeLuca, and Tammy Tuck. 2005. "New Capabilities in New Places: Low-Income Black Families in Suburbia", in Xavier de Souza Briggs, ed., *The Geography of Opportunity: Race and Housing Choice in Metropolitan America.* Washington, D.C.: Brookings Institution Press.

Rusk, David. 1999. *Inside Game, Outside Game: Winning Strategies for Saving Urban America.* Washington, D.C.: Brookings Institution Press.

Sidney, Mara S. "Fair Housing and Affordable Housing Advocacy: Reconciling the Dual Agenda", in Xavier de Souza Briggs, ed., *The Geography of Opportunity: Race and Housing In Metropolitan America.* Washington, D.C.: Brookings Institution Press.

Varady, David P. and Carole C. Walker. 2007. *Neighborhood Choices: Section 8 housing vouchers and residential mobility.* New Brunswick, NJ: Center for Urban Policy Research Press.

PART THREE

RENT VOUCHERS, A TOOL TO DECONCENTRATE POVERTY

# WHAT SHOULD HOUSING VOUCHERS ACCOMPLISH?[1]

## David Varady

### Introduction

Beginning around 1980, U.S. low-income housing policy shifted from subsidies to buildings, to tenant subsidies (also called housing vouchers). Thirty years into the implementation of this new strategy it is appropriate to ask: What should the housing voucher program do? Should it primarily deal with severe rent burdens and poor housing conditions or should it assign equal priority to poverty and minority deconcentration as well as to family self sufficiency?

At present, under the U.S. Department of Housing and Urban Development's Housing Choice Voucher Program (HCVP), eligible families pay 30 percent of their income for rental costs and the federal government pays the rest up to a payment standard for the metropolitan area. The program is administered by the local public housing authority (PHA) whose staff insures that housing units utilized meet housing quality standards. For a more detailed discussion of how the housing voucher program has evolved see Varady and Walker (2007).

Policymakers believe that vouchers not only offer a more cost-effective way to provide decent and affordable housing than supply programs (Deng 2005), but that they also encourage low-income people to move into better neighborhoods with less crime, better schools, and better access to good jobs.

This chapter builds upon my review of the housing voucher literature published in the *Journal of Planning Literature* in 2003 and later revised for my book, *Neighborhood Choices* (2007), co-authored with Carole Walker. Consequently, it will focus primarily on research published since 2002.

I will begin with a discussion of the recent work dealing with the HCVP, America's 'regular' voucher program focusing on what has been learned about housing search and neighborhood outcomes,

---

[1] An earlier version appeared in the *Journal of Housing and the Built Environment*.

impacts on self-sufficiency, and clustering controversies. I then switch attention to recent literature concerning two special mobility programs (the Gautreaux Program and Moving to Opportunity). The third part examines the American and European literature on the neighborhood effects of mixed income developments and mixed income neighborhoods. Taken together, the three parts show that without special geographical requirements and intensive counselling, voucher recipients generally do not move to low-poverty suburban neighborhoods. Furthermore, there is little evidence that those who do make such moves benefit from exposure to middle-class role models and take advantage of middle-class social networks.

## The Housing Choice Voucher Program (HCVP)

HCVP, the US Department of Housing and Urban Development's (HUD) largest program, does not require recipients to live in low-poverty neighborhoods, but implicitly assumes that voucher holders will exercise their mobility option to find housing in lower-poverty, higher-quality neighborhoods. As I show below, current research does not strongly support this assumption.

### Housing Search and Residential Outcomes

#### National Studies
Feins and Patterson's 2005 study, which examined the geographic mobility of families with children that entered the HCV Program between 1995 and 2002, showed little improvement in neighborhood conditions. The pre-program neighborhoods and the areas where families leased their initial units through the voucher program were very similar in terms of neighborhood characteristics as measured by census data.

A study of the Welfare to Work Voucher Program (WTWVP) produced more positive results. Participants using these vouchers experienced better neighborhoods, as measured by poverty and unemployment rates than the control groups that did not receive vouchers. Moreover, the study reveals that positive impacts were stronger for one racial/ethnic subgroup, non-Hispanic blacks (Patterson et al. 2004; Abt Associates et al. 2006). Climaco et al.'s 2008 article on HCVP portability also provides welcome news for voucher advocates. The data "show reductions in census tract poverty rates and other neighborhood indicators for households that completed portability moves" (p. 5).

National studies like these assume that census variables – especially the poverty rate – can serve as valid proxies for residents' assessments of neighborhood conditions. Buron and Patrabansh (2008) question this assumption noting that the correlation between the poverty rate and neighborhood satisfaction was not very strong. One reason for this seemingly surprising result is that the individual recipient's neighborhood may not coincide with a census tract. The 'real' neighborhood may be smaller or larger or be an area that crosses census tract boundaries. Second, census variables like the poverty rate may not be the factors that drive voucher holders' ratings. Crime rates and measures based on home loan applications may be more sensitive indicators of neighborhood conditions.

*Local Studies*
These studies help us to better understand how voucher recipients conduct housing searches and the extent to which these searches lead to improvements in housing and neighborhood conditions. Varady and Walker (2007) in their four-city comparative case study of families forced to move from severely distressed, subsidized private developments in Baltimore, Newport News, Kansas City, and San Francisco, show that "although many of the displaced residents chose to remain in the same area, most improved their situation by moving. The overwhelming majority were satisfied with their new homes and neighborhoods, and most said that they were more satisfied with their new homes and neighborhoods than they had been with their former ones. However most of the families continued to live in racially segregated areas" (p. 160).

Chicago HOPE VI studies show that many who used vouchers to move into the private market are living in better housing in safer neighborhoods. However, many tenants awaiting relocation have physical and mental health problems and other serious personal challenges that make them unappealing to landlords. Furthermore, the transformed public housing and the private housing market have few spaces for the most 'hard to house' families, particularly multi-problem families with one or more of the following problems: substance abuse, domestic abuse, domestic violence, criminal records, and poor mental and physical health (Popkin et al. 2003; Popkin et al. 2004; Popkin et al. 2005).

In Chicago HOPE VI children were moving from bad schools and unsafe conditions; however, many of these children had behavioral problems and hence, posed a challenge for destination neighborhoods:

"About two-thirds of older children (aged 6 to 14) have one or more reported behaviour problems; about half have two or more" (Popkin et al. 2004:405). The behavior problems index includes six specific measures: having trouble getting along with teachers; being disobedient in school; hanging around with kids who get in trouble; bullying; being restless or hyperactive; and being unhappy or clinically depressed.

Clampet-Lundquist's 2004 study of relocation from the DuBois HOPE VI project in Philadelphia helps us to understand why many HOPE VI relocatees remain in the city.

In the first place, of the three housing agencies the Philadelphia Housing Authority contracted with to help DuBois tenants as they looked for a Section 8 unit, none specialized in middle-class neighborhoods or the suburbs. Secondly, relocatees were constrained in their housing search because they lacked knowledge about suburban housing opportunities or perceived that suburban housing opportunities were too far away. Furthermore, many did not have a car or believed that suburban access to public transportation was extremely poor and quite expensive. Finally, many preferred nearby known amenities. Although DuBois relocatees remained within Philadelphia city boundaries, they were able to move to more racially mixed, more affluent and more residentially stable areas than those where public housing units were located.

In their Santa Ana, California (Orange County) study, Basolo and Nguyen (2005) investigated the level and impact of mobility on the neighborhood quality of voucher holders, their neighborhood conditions by race and ethnicity, and perceived obstacles to mobility. Santa Ana is one of the poorest areas of the county and is three-fourths Hispanic. About one-third of the sample moved during the study, and moving resulted in improved neighborhoods only for whites. Minorities were shown to live in more impoverished, overcrowded neighborhoods than non-minorities, even when controlling for mobility status, contract rent and other factors. Khadduri (2005) criticizes the authors' main conclusion, that "minority deconcentration may not be accomplished through the voucher program because minorities who use vouchers live in worse neighborhoods than their non-Hispanic white neighbours" (p. 303). I agree with Khadduri (2005) who argues that Basolo and Nguyen have unrealistic expectations about housing vouchers; mobility is not a primary program goal. Furthermore, Santa Ana HCVP minority recipients generally did not live in bad neighborhoods or high poverty ones whether they moved or not. Thus, they were not badly hurt by their inability to move to white areas and newer ones. Finally, housing officials should not be blamed for the lack of minority deconcentration because they have little control over patterns of racial discrimination.

The preceding results suggest that in tight housing markets like Orange County it is necessary to (1) offer housing search assistance, (2) expand the supply of affordable rental housing, and (3) pass and then enforce anti-discrimination legislation based on source of income. However, McClure (2005a:357) thinks that anti-discrimination legislation is not a productive route to take:

> It is already illegal in several areas for landlords to refuse to rent to a household on the basis of income or the use of housing assistance, but these legal sanctions have not improved success rates for households with vouchers ... This lack of improvement suggests that little will be gained by compelling landlords to participate in the program. It seems that deconcentration would be better served by using carrots rather than sticks; program administrators must be able to offer incentives in the form of higher rents if necessary.

Kleit and Manzo's 2006 article on Seattle's High Point HOPE VI project emphasizes the value of high quality relocation counselling. According to Kleit and Manzo, "bilingual relocation counsellors from the Seattle Housing Authority spent the summer of 2001 travelling to residents' homes to interview every household head and family member to assess their needs and tell them about their rights and the relocation process" (2006:279). As a result, most of the residents were able to carry out their desired choices. Sixty-four percent of those who wanted to return to the High Point HOPE VI project were able to do so; 68 percent who wanted to participate in the voucher program were able to do so.

It is widely believed that opposition to the Section 8 program is fuelled by NIMBYism and stereotypes that have made it more difficult for low-income families to move to middle-income neighborhoods (Bratt 2005). However, Marr's 2005 Los Angeles research suggests that stereotypes about irresponsible tenants are based on more than just a kernel of truth: "[L]ow incomes, poor credit, previous evictions, a history of substance abuse and/or homelessness, a lack of knowledge of appropriate renter behaviour, and the presence of teenage children, who are often thought to cause trouble, can make landlords apprehensive about renting units to voucher holders" (p. 92).

Katz and Turner (2001; 2008) argue that the current fragmented system of administering housing assistance by multiple local housing

authorities hinders the ability of families to move from the jurisdiction
of one housing authority to that of another. They contend that Housing
Choice vouchers need to be administered regionally with the agency
chosen as a result of a competitive process. Their proposal may be relevant for the Los Angeles region where, according to Marr (2005)
voucher agencies compete with one another. However, housing authorities in Alameda County, California (Varady and Walker 2003; 2007)
and Orange County, California (Basolo 2003) have been able to work
cooperatively in order to promote housing voucher portability, that is,
to be able to move with a voucher from one voucher issuing jurisdiction to another. A 'one size fits all strategy' of regional housing authorities does not seem appropriate for all U.S. metropolitan areas.

The preceding results can be summarized by saying that while "a
great deal of research finds that the [HCV] program fails to move
households into demonstrably better neighborhoods" (McClure
2005a:350) and that while it is true that housing vouchers do better
than public housing in avoiding high-poverty areas, few voucher holders as part of HCVP move to low-poverty areas (Briggs et al. 2007).

*Self-Sufficiency*

The Housing Choice Voucher Program has succeeded in reducing the
severe rent burdens of low income families and individuals. According
to McClure, "about 38 percent of all households in the program paid
more than 31 percent of income on housing in 2002, down from 47
percent just 2 years earlier" (2005b:2). In addition, because all HCVP
occupied housing units have to meet minimum quality standards, the
program does succeed in providing decent and safe housing and in
reducing overcrowding (Khadduri 2005; McClure 2005b). However,
policymakers want to know whether assisted housing, including housing vouchers, promotes long-term, full-time independence from economic assistance programs such as welfare.

Previous scholarly writings offer two contradictory hypotheses.
On the one hand, some argue that housing assistance provides an
important basis of support and stability for families attempting to raise
themselves out of poverty. Housing assistance might enable a mother
to move away from a high-crime area and reduce the time spent monitoring her children, thereby enabling her to find and keep a job. On the
other hand, a prolonged presence in assisted housing (or receiving a
housing voucher) might reduce the motivation to work thereby
increasing the likelihood of long-term dependency. If a recipient earns

more, her rent payment will increase. Furthermore, she may be unwilling to leave behind housing assistance for a job fearing that if she loses her job she might be unable to get a voucher again because of the long waiting lists.

In fact, research shows that, at best, HCVP has no impact on self-sufficiency; in some demographic groups and in some places the program actually promotes dependency.

- HOPE VI tracking studies indicate that even when voucher recipients moved to 'better neighbourhoods' based on census indicators this did not cause them to become self-sufficient (Popkin and Cunningham 2000; Popkin et al. 2004; Popkin et al. 2005).
- Feins and Patterson's 2005 study of mobility of families with children who entered the HCVP program between 1995 and 2002 showed that "the number of times a household moved appeared to be associated with very slight *decreases* [italics in original] in total household income and in the percentage of income from earnings" (p. 42).
- Experimental research on the Welfare to Work Voucher program showed that the program reduced employment and increased welfare receipt (Abt Associates et al. 2006; Patterson et al. 2004).
- Olsen et al. (2005) found participation in each of the three broad types of housing assistance (public housing, subsidized private housing developments, and housing vouchers) had a similarly negative impact on labour earnings; however, participation in HUD's Family Self Sufficiency program (see below) significantly increased labour earnings.
- Susin (2005), using a 1996–1999 panel, found that, compared to unsubsidized households, participation in any of the three subsidy programs had a similar negative impact on individual earnings.
- Tatian and Snow (2005) looked at economic trends for those who lived in HUD-supported housing for a minimum of eight years. The steepest increase in income was for households in project-based Section 8 units and the odds of being employed were about the same for residents of Section 8 site-based, tenant-based, and public housing programs.

Howard Husock (2000) calls for a time limit on receipt of housing vouchers noting that America's welfare program, Temporary Assistance for Needy Families, (TANF) already has a time limit. Presumably a time limit on HCV would encourage recipients near the cut-off point to seek employment, or if employed, to seek a better paying job. Furthermore, HCVP recipient turnover would make openings available for other eligible rental households.

There is, however, no empirical evidence available indicating that such a time limit would spur employment activity. Freeman (2005) argues that time limits are unlikely to promote self-sufficiency unless administered in conjunction with both human capital programs (including but not limited to job training) and expanded housing opportunities (meaning subsidized housing) for moderate income families who have achieved some mobility. The need for subsidized housing would be especially great in tight housing markets like New York City's.

It is possible to assume that if public housing authorities expanded their Family Self-Sufficiency Programs (FSS) and additional PHAs initiated them, more families could be assisted in becoming and remaining employed and obtaining higher-paying jobs by improving their skills. The FSS program is an employment and savings incentive program for low-income families that have HCVP vouchers or live in public housing. Enacted in 1990, FSS includes both case management services that help participants pursue employment and escrow accounts into which the PHA deposits the increased rental charges that a family pays as its earnings rise. Families that complete the program may withdraw funds from these accounts for any reason after five years. As Sard (2004) observes, FSS is currently underutilized. Fewer than five percent of families with children in the public housing and HCVP currently participate in FSS.

Research into the Jobs-Plus Community Revitalization Initiative for Public Housing Families (Jobs-Plus) suggests that this model might work for voucher families as well. The model combines on-site employment-related services with new rent rules that allow residents to keep more of their earnings as well as a neighbour-to-neighbour outreach strategy to share information about employment opportunities (Verma et al. 2005). Both a sophisticated national evaluation and studies at four specific sites have shown that this strategy has substantially improved earnings (Riccio 2008).

*HCVP Clustering*

Devine et al.'s (2003) widely quoted national study implies that housing voucher recipients are not concentrated spatially. In 90 percent of all tracts with any voucher recipients, the program accounts for less than five percent of all households. But where vouchers are clustered, the clustering is in high-poverty, mostly minority central-city neighborhoods. Enough of these clusters exist in American cities to present major challenges to governmental officials, especially in this period of economic downturn.

Census analyses understate clustering because the concentrations are often confined to parts of census tracts and it is at this smaller geographical scale –the voucher recipient's actual neighborhood—that the concentration of voucher holders and other assisted families is likely to affect a recipient's attitudes and behavior. For example, as Churchill et al.'s 2001 case study of Patterson Park (Baltimore) makes clear, HOPE VI relocatees clustered in only one part of the community, the part where poverty rates were highest and ownership rates lowest. Voucher recipients comprised less than the 10 percent of households in all of Patterson Park. Anyone using the arbitrary 10 percent threshold for a high density cluster would miss the clustering at the subcommunity level in Patterson Park.

Wang and Varady's 2005 hot spot analysis of voucher clustering in Hamilton County (Cincinnati) also responds to this need for research on Section 8 clustering at a lower geographical scale. Hot spot analysis, a density-based spatial clustering technique can provide specific additional information on the spatial patterning of housing voucher recipients that goes beyond that provided by traditional dot mapping and census analysis techniques. Hot spot analysis is widely used in criminological and epidemiological research.

Wang and Varady highlighted three types of hot spots in Hamilton County: ones in the traditional black ghetto, in racially changing areas, and in Low Income Housing Tax Credit developments.[2] In a more recent study, Wang et al. (2008) examined changes between 2000 and 2005 in HCVP clustering in eight U.S. metropolitan areas—New York, Baltimore, Miami, Houston, Chicago, Cincinnati, Phoenix, and Los Angeles. The study provides evidence that the HCVP is not shifting to the suburbs, that the HCVP is not promoting poverty or minority

---

[2] The LIHTC is a credit or reduction in tax liability each year for ten years for owners and investors in low-income rental housing that is based on the costs of developments and the number of qualified low-income units. LIHTC is administered by the U.S. Department of the Treasury, not HUD.

deconcentration, and that the incidence of HCVP clustering is either stable or increasing in particular metropolitan areas.

The spatial arrangements of voucher housing stemming from public housing transformation have come under media scrutiny in terms of perceived impacts of voucher concentration on neighborhoods (Briggs and Dreir 2008; Eckholm 2008; Moore 2008; Rosin 2008; Venkatesh 2008). Across the country, politicians and civic leaders are expressing their concern that the restructuring of public housing and the vouchering out of many residents is leading to a shift of crime and other social problems into their neighborhoods.

Churchill et al.'s 2001 qualitative study of Section 8 controversies at eight sites provides additional evidence of perceived harms to destination neighborhoods. The meaning of the term 'Section 8 concentration' varies among the sites: a single development (in Camden County, New Jersey), a neighborhood (in Baltimore, Maryland; Lynn, Massachusetts; San Antonio, Texas and Syracuse, New York), a city (Norristown, Pennsylvania in Montgomery County), or a part of a county (the Route 1 corridor in Fairfax County, Virginia and the southern suburban part of Cook County, Illinois). At all sites, problems like crime, falling test scores and anti-social tenants, created community conflict. The weak administration of the Section 8 program was a major cause as well. This included "(1) failure to monitor housing market change and locations of Section 8 housing, (2) insufficient attention to assisting families to move to a broad range of neighborhoods, (3) inadequate attention to rent reasonableness[3] and housing quality standards, (4) insufficient attention to Section 8 household behaviour, and (5) unresponsiveness to community complaints" (p. ii). Housing authorities that want to improve acceptance of the Section 8 program in their communities must be willing to embark on long-term efforts to remedy all five weaknesses. Listening to residents' concerns is a necessary first step.

Although there have been a number of sophisticated empirical studies of the impacts of subsidized housing developments on housing prices Galster et al.'s (1999) Baltimore County study is the only one

---

[3] If housing officials use data for the metropolitan area in setting the payment standard, then it is possible that the rents landlords can charge to HCVP recipients will be higher than those paid by market-rate tenants. When this happens landlords sometimes seek out HCVP participants; this encourages the creation of ever larger HCVP hotspots.

that looks at the impact of voucher recipient concentrations on housing prices.[4] Galster shows that in low-valued or moderately valued
census tracts experiencing real declines in values since 1990, Section 8
sites and units located in high densities had a considerable negative
impact on prices within 2,000 feet. When the number of Section 8
households in any neighborhood reached a certain tipping-point (six
or more within 500 feet), there was a decline in housing values. Thus,
the adverse influences on property values are more likely to occur
when affordable housing is clustered and located in disadvantaged and
declining neighborhoods.

Two more recent articles by Galster examine the non-linear relationship between the rate of poverty and neighborhood social decline.
A 2005 article states that "poverty concentrations start to create
negative external effects when they exceed 15 percent to 20 percent"
(p. 123). In a 2008 book chapter, Galster and colleagues show that
"marginal increases in poverty when neighborhood poverty rates are
in the range of 10–20 percent result in dramatic declines in values and
rent [more so than for the under 10 percent category], strongly suggesting a threshold ..." (p. 127).

Galster's research over the past decade suggests the need to keep
disadvantaged households below a threshold of 20 percent in any one
neighborhood, and that advantaged households should be kept in a
majority. Kingsley and Pettit (2005:131) argue, however, that limiting
residents of high poverty neighborhoods from moving to vulnerable
moderate poverty ones "... is a non-starter. We have no mechanisms in
place for controlling mobility in this way because doing so would be
inconsistent with basic freedoms."

### Special Mobility Programs

Mobility is a feature of HCVP; recipients can presumably use their
vouchers anywhere in the U.S. However, HCVP is a passive mobility
program that relies on the recipients to make locational choices.
Because of its reliance on individual choice and the tendency of recipients to make short distance moves to stay close to friends and relatives,
HCVP cannot serve well as a poverty and minority deconcentration

---

[4] For a review of these studies see Nguyen's 2005 article.

mechanism (Basolo and Nguyen 2005). In contrast to HCVP, both the Gautreaux and Moving to Opportunity programs explicitly promote poverty or racial concentration. Although both the Gautreaux program and the Moving to Opportunity program are small in size, together they provide the impetus for a large and influential scholarly literature.

*The Gautreaux Program*

The Gautreaux Assisted Housing Program was created as a result of a series of class-action lawsuits filed against the Chicago Housing Authority (CHA) and the U.S. Department of Housing and Urban Development (HUD), beginning in 1966. The suits alleged that the housing authority deliberately segregated black families through its tenant selection and site selection policies while HUD continued to fund such civil rights violations. Administered by the nonprofit Leadership Council for Metropolitan Open Communities in Chicago, the program provided access to private sector apartments either in mostly white suburbs or within the city of Chicago. Suburbs that were more than 30 percent black were excluded by the consent decree. Participants were assigned to city or suburban locations in a quasi-random manner. Although in theory the voucher recipients had the choice of whether to accept or to reject a unit, in actuality, they were placed wherever the program happened to have housing openings at the time.

In the fall of 1988, a random sample of demographically similar Gautreaux participants – 224 in the suburbs and 108 in the city—were interviewed. Among those who were employed before the move, the suburbanites fared 14 percent better than the city residents in obtaining employment. Among the previously unemployed, the suburban residents fared 53 percent better than the city residents in finding jobs. These results led the principal researchers to conclude that Gautreaux-type programs are a cost-effective way to promote social mobility (Popkin et. al 1993; Rosenbaum and Popkin 1991; Rubinowitz and Rosenbaum 2000)

However, the preceding results tell only half of the story. Neither those who moved to the suburbs nor those who moved within the city improved their employment status with respect to hourly wages or hours worked per week. City movers actually had a slightly lower rate of employment after they moved while those who relocated to the suburbs experienced no change. Consequently, while a move to the suburbs was relatively more beneficial than a move within the city from an employment v. unemployment perspective, the move produced few benefits in terms of moving toward self-sufficiency.[5]

Gautreaux Two, introduced in 2002, added poverty dispersion to Gautreaux One's focus on racial dispersion. Gautreaux Two vouchers could only be used in "opportunity areas," i.e., ones where no more than 23.49 percent lived in poverty and no more than 30 percent were black residents. Additionally, only leaseholders in good standing with the Chicago Housing Authority were eligible to sign up for a HCV through Gautreaux Two (i.e., if they were not behind in their rent, had not damaged their unit, and had no misdemeanour convictions in the past two years).

Three research projects on Gautreaux Two that have relied on qualitative data have highlighted program weaknesses. Firstly, about 18 months after orientation sessions began, only about one-third of all Gautreaux Two participants had leased-up, that is, had moved to an 'opportunity area' (Pashup et al. 2005). Non-movers cited both external and internal hurdles. The former included a tight rental market, discrimination, and bureaucratic delays. The latter included minimal housing search experience and program understanding, large household size, health problems, or a busy work or school schedule that made it difficult to look for a suitable home and move.

Landlord discrimination was not simply a result of prejudice but it also resulted from concerns that landlords had about the administration of the program. Discrimination against voucher holders resulted in part from landlords' past experiences with voucher programs including delays in receiving security deposits and rent payments.

Secondly, about one-half of the Gautreaux Two participants made secondary moves and within this group the vast majority (81 percent) moved to non-opportunity areas (Boyd 2008). Secondary moves typically resulted from a feeling of isolation from friends and kin as well as transportation difficulties. However, there were also fundamental differences between movers and stayers. These results indicate the need for both pre-and post-placement counselling to help families adjust to their new locations.

---

[5] See Welfeld (1998) for a fairly pessimistic interpretation of the Gautreaux findings.

Thirdly, moving low-income women and their families out of segregated, high-poverty neighborhoods into more affluent ones had little or no impact on their employment situation (Reed et al. 2005). Many of the women moved in and out of jobs when they had children or were not able to get adequate child care or were laid off from temporary jobs. To achieve optimal results, Gautreaux-type housing mobility programs need to coordinate with family planning agencies.

None of the three articles answers the obvious question: Why was Gautreaux One far more successful than Gautreaux Two in producing positive employment and educational outcomes? There is no simple answer.

*Moving to Opportunity*

In the Moving to Opportunity Demonstration (MTO) begun in 1994 in Baltimore, Boston, Chicago, Los Angeles, and New York City public housing families were randomly assigned to one of three groups: (1) an experimental group where members received a voucher and search assistance but were required to find a housing unit in a low-poverty neighborhood, (2) a comparison group where members received a regular housing voucher with no restrictions on where it could be used, and (3) a control group where members remained in public housing. Because MTO employed a random sample, superior to the quasi-random sample employed by the Gautreaux Demonstration, consequently the MTO results are more robust and more appropriate for use in policy development.

MTO has failed to live up to expectations. Firstly, many people in the MTO Demonstration were unable to use a combination of a voucher and search assistance to find and 'lease up' housing in a lower-poverty neighborhood (Briggs and Turner 2006; Clampet-Lundquist 2004; Orr et al. 2003). Many who wanted to move were unable to do so due to physical or mental health problems. Others were unable to do so because of (1) racial discrimination or discrimination based on Section 8 voucher status, (2) family level constraints (lack of knowledge of housing choices, limited search capacity), and (3) administrative weaknesses (including fragmented local housing systems that discourage families from porting, that is, using their voucher to move across jurisdictional lines) (Briggs and Turner 2006).

Secondly, by the time of the interim MTO evaluation two-thirds of those in the experimental complier group (i.e., those who had originally leased-up), had already moved at least once and among those in this group a majority (56 percent) had moved back to high-poverty areas (Briggs and Turner 2006). Many of them did so because of an involuntary move (e.g., the landlord had sold the house, rents had been raised, or the tenant had to leave because of a tenant-landlord dispute). And when this occurred many who faced inadequate options in 'good neighborhoods' chose adequate housing even though it was located in dangerous neighborhoods. Post-move counselling might have helped such families from making poorly judged decisions.

Thirdly, while there is some proof that those in the experimental group moved to safer neighborhoods, there is no evidence that the program led to better employment or educational outcomes (Kling et al. 2004; Popkin et al. 2004). Orr et al. (2003) found evidence that the program enabled movers to live in better housing in safer neighborhoods. However, there is no indication as yet of the kinds of employment or educational effects seen in Gautreaux.

Fourthly, while MTO has been successful in raising adults' satisfaction with their neighborhoods, this is not necessarily true for their children, especially the boys:

> Neighborhoods that are "peaceful" to parents are often "boring" for teenagers, offering the latter little to do (according to them) and, in some cases, posing strains of acculturating to a different class culture, with its largely unwritten rules of appropriate speech, dress, and conduct. Adolescents with strong kin ties to inner-city neighborhoods were more likely to visit those neighborhoods often, maintain peer relationships there, and seek out some of the very risks their parents feared. MTO parents were often sensitive to these desires while trying to buffer their children from the most serious risks. (Briggs et al. 2007: 3; see also Briggs and Turner 2006)

Because mobility strategies like MTO are, by themselves, unlikely to produce effects on work outcomes for low-income residents, Briggs and Turner (2006) recommend "mobility plus," which links "rental housing subsidies and counselling to workforce development, reliable transportation, health care, informed school choice, and other *family-strengthening supports*" (italics added) (see also Riccio 2008). Given the fact that black single women head virtually all MTO households, what can be done to strengthen these households? A comprehensive approach would combine governmental job creation and training programs to promote work among black men and efforts from within the black community to encourage black fathers to take more responsibility for their children.

Daniel Patrick Moynihan's 1965 report that highlighted weakening black family structure was sharply criticized at the time by black activists and as a result social scientists have continued to shy away from studying it. There now appears to be a growing willingness among black politicians and communal leaders to discuss this subject. In a July 14, 2008 speech to the National Association of Colored People (NAACP) conference, then presidential candidate, Barack Obama, called for black men to assume greater responsibility for their children. The speech was warmly received by the mostly black audience (Blow 2008).

## Neighborhood Effects from Mixed-Income Neighborhoods and Developments

In the United States there is growing consensus among policymakers and researchers that inner city conditions (e.g., high crime, high levels of welfare dependency) have adverse effects on adults and children over and beyond the impacts of debilitating individual characteristics. The flip side of the problem is the widely held belief that if public housing is restructured so as to allow poor and non-poor families to live side-by-side or if low-income families use vouchers to relocate to middle-income communities, the change in residential environment will help them to achieve social mobility, but, is there evidence to support this assumption?

Mixed-income developments and mixed-income neighborhoods could promote social mobility in four ways (Andersson et al. 2007; Bramley and Karley 2007; Galster 2007; Galster et al. 2008; Joseph 2006; Kearns and Mason 2007). Firstly, improved social networks could help people with low income learn about jobs. Secondly, the presence of middle- income families could lead to more informal social controls resulting in a greater degree of safety. Thirdly, living in a mixed-income community could cause low-income people to drop destructive, antisocial habits that are part of the culture of poverty and to adopt middle-class norms needed to attain social mobility. Fourthly, a high number of middle-income families could generate both market and political pressure for high quality shopping and high quality government public services.

European, as well as American research supports the second and fourth arguments only (Andersson et al. 2007; Bramley and Karley 2007; Galster 2007; Galster et al. 2008; Joseph 2006; Kearns and Mason

2007). While mixed-income areas may possibly provide a safer, more stable environment for families, there is little evidence that living in such a community in and of itself can help lower-income families move out of poverty. Mixed-tenure communities generally enjoy better reputations and are less stigmatized than traditional social housing, but social interaction between owners and renters remains limited. Furthermore, cooperation between owners and renters usually takes place in relation to residential issues like community control, rather than personal ones like employment (Berube 2006).

The foregoing indicates the need to lower expectations about what mixed-income developments and communities can accomplish. According to Joseph (2006:223): "Promoting sustainable changes in the lives of low-income residents who move from neighborhoods with concentrated poverty to mixed income developments [or to middle-class suburban neighborhoods, *wording added*] will generally require combining housing with investments in social services, education, job readiness, training and placement, and transportation."

## Conclusion

Through a review of the recent social science literature I have sought to critically evaluate housing vouchers as a strategy for helping low-income families move to better neighborhoods and to move toward self-sufficiency. The question I initially asked was: What should housing vouchers do? Should they primarily focus on affordability problems and housing conditions or should the strategy also promote poverty deconcentration and family self-sufficiency? I have also attempted to determine whether voucher recipients cluster in particular neighborhoods thereby contributing to declining property values, higher crime rates and other problems.

The answers in the research evidence are mixed concerning the ability of voucher holders to move to better neighborhoods. America's main housing voucher program (HCVP) has not led to either poverty or minority deconcentration. The good news from the two 'special' mobility programs—Gautreaux and Moving to Opportunity—is that intensive counselling enabled many to move to low-poverty neighborhoods. The bad news however, is that many of these families who initially moved to low-poverty neighborhoods subsequently moved back to the same or similar poor inner city areas.

Econometric studies suggest that participation in the regular voucher program reduces labour earnings as a result of the built-in tax feature of the program (higher earnings lead to less subsidy). Contrary to what had been hoped, Moving to Opportunity has not led to higher employment rates or reduced participation in welfare. MTO's disappointing results undoubtedly reflect the fact that vouchers do not address the underlying causes of poverty (including weak and unstable families and women who move in and out of the workforce). Finally, there is growing scepticism among both American and European researchers about the presumed social benefits of mixed communities (i.e., positive role models from working families, social networks yielding job information).

The preceding suggests that HCVP should focus primarily on providing additional decent and affordable housing opportunities. Other social goals like poverty/minority deconcentration and family self-sufficiency should have a much lower priority.

Hot spot analysis shows that Section 8 recipients often *do* cluster in higher poverty, high minority neighborhoods, and in ones that are already vulnerable to economic and racial change. Churchill et al.'s (2001) Abt Inc. study showed that politicians, government officials and civic leaders in a wide range of communities across the U.S. believe that clustering is linked to crime, drug dealing, falling test scores and other social problems. Unfortunately, with the exception of Galster et al.'s (1999) Baltimore County study dealing with housing prices, there has been very little sophisticated empirical research on the impacts of HCVP clustering. Nevertheless, policymakers need to act based on the evidence available to them. Turner et al. (2009) find the available evidence robust enough to conclude that "the overconcentration of subsidized households can threaten the economic stability of fragile middle-income communities and place large demands on city and local services, taxing the resources of the community" (p. 89). In order to improve the image of the program and to defuse controversies, program officials need to better monitor the number of voucher recipients in particular communities and changes in the quality of life (e.g., the crime rate, public school test scores) and share this information with community residents. Strengthening the way the HCVP is carried out could modestly reduce the extent of clustering (Turner et al. 2009).

Housing vouchers have been successful in providing decent and affordable housing but, unfortunately, virtually all local housing authorities have a long waiting list for rental subsidies. Would it be possible to convert HCVP into an entitlement program and make them similar in this respect to the housing benefit programs in the Netherlands and the United Kingdom (Priemus et al. 2005)?

There is no shortage of innovative proposals for shifting to an entitlement program or for fundamentally restructuring HCVP.

- Polikoff (2006) and McClure (2005a) call for allocating 50,000 vouchers per year to a Gautreaux-type voucher program that would require blacks to move into predominantly white suburban neighborhoods. This strategy would enable blacks to skip over income-mixed, but declining, inner-suburban communities to locate in more stable white areas with high performing public schools. The program would be strongly fought by white suburbanites, but in addition, blacks might object strongly to being told where to move.
- Grigsby and Bourassa (2004) suggest making housing vouchers an entitlement program while integrating vouchers with other elements of the federal safety net.
- Quigley (2008) proposes replacing HCVP with a tax credit system. The individual tax payer could apply for the credit through the federal tax form. The tax credit could be mailed in monthly instalments to the taxpayer, the landlord or the housing authority.
- Katz and Turner (2008) propose a comprehensive demand side strategy aimed at insuring that all households have adequate income (or a housing voucher) to make minimally decent housing affordable. They recommend combining a modest increase in the federal minimum wage with a substantial expansion of the Earned Income Tax Credit (EITC) along with three targeted pools of vouchers for those not working: one for the elderly and disabled, a second self-sufficiency voucher for those not working, and a third one for families with children living in distressed neighborhoods who would be willing to relocate to communities with good schools.

While these recommendations may help stimulate policy debate, it is unlikely, with America's current financial crisis, that any one of these policies will be adopted. In recent years, housing advocates have had to work hard to maintain current HCVP funding levels. According to Briggs and Turner (2006:57), "Congress has several times overturned HUD proposals to cut voucher funds, impose stricter rent limits, and turn local programs into state-run block grant programs."

A more realistic scenario might be to expand the program by capitalizing on the success of HCVP in providing decent affordable housing while at the same time implement incremental improvements aimed at broadening neighborhood choices. HUD needs to provide funding for housing placement assistance for tight markets. States need to encourage localities to implement inclusionary zoning in the suburbs in order to increase the availability of affordable rental housing. Inclusionary zoning (IZ) requires developers to make a percentage of housing units in new residential developments available to low- and moderate-income households. Finally, local housing authorities need to require landlords to strictly screen applicants to prevent anti-social householders from entering. Though this might be considered a form of discrimination, a landlord or housing manager needs some ways to create a stable, sustainable housing unit. This scenario could lead to an improved image for the HCVP and more rental opportunities in advantaged communities.

## References

Abt Associates, Gregory Mills, Daniel Gubits, Larry Orr, David Long, Judie Feins, Bulbul Kaul, Michelle Wood, Amy Jones & Associates, and The QED Group. 2006. *Effects of Housing Vouchers on Welfare Families, Prepared for the U.S. Department of Housing and Urban Development, Office of Policy Development and Research.* Washington DC: HUD.

Andersson, Roger, Sako Musterd, George Galster, and Timo N.M. Kauppinen. 2007. "What mix matters? Exploring the relationships between individuals' income and different measures of their neighborhood context." *Housing Studies* 22: 637–60.

Basolo, V. 2003. "Local response to federal changes in the housing voucher program: A case study of intraregional cooperation." *Housing Policy Debate* 14: 143–68.

Basolo, Victoria, and Mai Thi Nguyen. 2005. "Does mobility matter? The neighborhood conditions of housing voucher holders by race and ethnicity." *Housing Policy Debate* 16 (3/4): 297–324.

Berube, Alan. 2006. "Comment on Mark Joseph's 'Is mixed-income development an antidote to urban poverty?'" *Housing Policy Debate* 17(2): 235–47.

Blow, Charles. M. 2008. "Talking down and stepping up." *New York Times*, July 12, A27.

Boyd, Melody L. 2008. "The role of social relations in making housing choices: The experience of the Gautreaux Two Residential Mobility Program." *Cityscape: A Journal of Policy Development and Research* 10(1): 41–68.

Bramley, Glen, and Noah Kofi Karley. 2007. "Homeownership, poverty and educational achievement: School effects as neighborhood effects." *Housing Studies* 22(5): (September): 693–721.

Bratt, Rachel. 2005. "Comment on Victoria Basolo and Mai Thi Nguyen's 'Does mobility matter? The neighborhood conditions of housing voucher holders by race and ethnicity.'" *Housing Policy Debate* 16(3/4): 335–45.

Briggs, Xavier de Souza, Jennifer Coney, and Gretchen Weisman. 2007. "Little room to maneuver: Housing choice and neighborhood outcomes in the MTO experiment, 1994–2004." Unpublished paper, Cambridge, MA, MIT.

Briggs, Xavier de Souza and Peter Dreir. 2008. "Memphis murder mystery? No, just mistaken identity." *Shelterforce.* <http://www.shelterforce.org/article/special/1043/>.

Briggs, Xavier de Souza and Margery Austin Turner. 2006. "Assisted housing mobility and the success of low-income minority families: Lessons for policy, practice, and future research." *Journal of Law and Social Policy* 1(1)(Summer): 25–61.

Buron, Larry, and Satyendra Patrabansh. 2008. "Are census variables highly correlated with housing choice voucher holders' perception of the quality of their neighborhoods?" *Cityscape: A Journal of Policy Development and Research* 10 (1): 157–83.

Churchill, Sarah, Mary Joel Holin, Jill Khadduri, and Jennifer Turnham. 2001. *Strategies that Enhance Community Relations in Tenant-based Section 8 Programs*, Contract C-OPC-18571, Task Order 4, prepared for the U.S. Department of Housing and Urban Development. Washington DC: HUD.

Clampet-Lundquist, Susan. 2004. "HOPE VI relocation: Moving to new neighborhoods and building new ties." *Housing Policy Debate* 15(2): 415–47.

Climaco, Carissa G., Christopher N. Rodger, Judith D. Feins, and Ken Lam. 2008. "Portability moves in the Housing Choice Voucher Program, 1998–2005." *Cityscape: A Journal of Policy Development and Research* 10(1): 5–40.

Deng, Lan. 2005. "The cost-effectiveness of the Low-Income Housing Tax Credit relative to vouchers: Evidence from six metropolitan areas." *Housing Policy Debate* 16(3/4):469–511.

Devine, Deborah J., Robert W. Gray, Lester Rubin, and Lydia B. Taghavi. 2003. *Housing Choice Voucher Location Patterns: Implications for Participants and Neighborhood Welfare*. Washington, DC: HUD.

Eckholm, Erik. 2008. "Washington's grand experiment to rehouse the poor." *New York Times*, March 21, A12.

Feins, Judith D., and Rhiannon Patterson. 2005. "Geographical mobility in the Housing Choice Voucher Program: A study of families entering the program, 1995–2002." *Cityscape: A Journal of Policy Development and Research* 8(2): 21–47.

Freeman, Lance. 2005. "Does housing assistance lead to dependency? Evidence from HUD administrative data." *Cityscape: A Journal of Policy Development and Research* 8(2): 115–33.

Galster, George C. 2005. "Consequences from the redistribution of urban poverty during the 1990s: A cautionary tale." *Economic Development Quarterly* 19(2): 119–25.

Galster, George C. 2007. "Should policy makers strive for neighborhood social mix? An analysis of the Western European evidence base." *Housing Studies* 22(4): 523–45.

Galster, George C., Jackie M. Cutsinger, and Ron Malega. 2008. "The costs of concentrated poverty: Neighborhood property markets and the dynamics of decline," in Nicholas Retsinas and Eric S. Belsky, eds., *Revisiting Rental Housing: Policies, Programs and Priorties*. Washington DC: Brookings Institution, pp. 93–143.

Galster, George C., Peter Tatian, and Robin Smith. 1999. "The impact of neighbors who use Section 8 Certificates on property values." *Housing Policy Debate* 10(4): 879–917.

Grigsby, William G., and Steven C. Bourassa. 2004. "Section 8: The time for fundamental program change?" *Housing Policy Debate* 15(4): 805–34.

Husock, Howard. 2000. "Let's end housing vouchers." *City Journal* 10(4)(Autumn): 84–91.

Joseph, Mark L. 2006. "Is mixed-income development an antidote to urban poverty?" *Housing Policy Debate* 17(2): 209–34.

Katz, Bruce, and Margery Austin Turner. 2001. "Who should run the housing voucher program? A reform proposal." *Housing Policy Debate* 12(2): 239–62.

Katz, Bruce, and Margery Austin Turner. 2008. "Rethinking U.S. rental housing policy: A new blueprint for federal, state, and local action," in Nicholas Retsinas and Eric S. Belsky, eds., *Revisiting Rental Housing: Policies, Programs and Priorities*. Washington DC: Brookings Institution, pp. 319–58.

Kearns, Ade, and Phil Mason. 2007. "Mixed tenure communities and neighborhood quality." *Housing Studies* 22(5)(September): 661–91.

Khadduri, Jill. 2005. "Comment on Victoria Basolo and Mai Thi Nguyen's :'Does mobility matter? The neighborhood conditions of housing voucher holders by race and ethnicity.'" *Housing Policy Debate* 15(3/4): 325–34.

Kingsley, G. Thomas, and Kathryn L. S. Pettit. 2005. "Comment on George C. Galster's 'Consequences from the redistribution of urban poverty during the 1990s: A cautionary tale.'" *Economic Development Quarterly* 19(2)(May): 126–32.

Kleit, Rachel Garshick, and Lynne C. Manzo. 2006. "To move or not to move: Relationships to place and relocation in HOPE VI." *Housing Policy Debate* 17 (2): 271–308.

Kling, Jeffrey R, Jeffrey Liebman, Lawrence F. Katz, and Lisa Sanbonmatsu. 2004. *Moving to Opportunity and Tranquility: Neighborhood Effects on Adult Economic Self-Sufficiency and Health from a Randomized Housing Voucher Experiment*, Princeton University, Department of Economics, Industrial Relations Section, Working Paper no. 5. Princeton, NJ. <http://ideas.repec.org/p/pri/indrel/860.html>.

Marr, Matthew D. 2005. "Mitigating apprehension about Section 8 vouchers: The positive role of housing specialists in search and placement." *Housing Policy Debate* 16(1): 85–112.

McClure, Kirk. 2005a. "Comment on Victoria Basolo and Mai Thi Nguyen's : 'Does mobility matter? The neighborhood conditions of housing voucher holders by race and ethnicity." *Housing Policy Debate* 16(3/4): 347–59.

McClure, Kirk. 2005b. "Rent burden in the housing choice voucher program." *Cityscape: A Journal of Policy Development and Research* 8(2): 5–20.

Moore, Solomon. 2008. "As housing program moves poor to the suburbs, tensions follow." *New York Times*. August 9 <http://www.nytimes.com/2008/08/09/us/09housing .html?_r=1&hp&oref=slogin>.

Moynihan, Daniel P. 1965. *The Negro Family: The Case for National Action*. Washington DC: Office of Policy Planning and Research, U.S. Department of Labor.

Nguyen, Mai Thi. 2005. "Does affordable housing detrimentally affect property values? A review of the literature." *Journal of Planning Literature* 20(1)(August): 15–26.

Olsen, Edgar O., Catherine A. Tyler, Jonathan W. King, and Paul E. Carrillo. 2005. "The Effects of Different Types of Housing Assistance on Earnings and Employment." *Cityscape: A Journal of Policy Development and Research* 8(2): 163–87.

Orr, Larry, Judith D. Feins, Robin Jacob, Erik Beecroft, Lisa Sanbonmatsu, Lawrence F. Katz, Jeffrey B. Liebman, and Jeffrey R. Kling. 2003. *Moving to Opportunity Interim Impacts Evaluation*. Prepared by Abt Associates Inc. and the National Bureau of Economic Research for the U.S. Department of Housing and Urban Development. Washington, D.C.: HUD.

Pashup, Jennifer, Kathryn Edin, Greg J. Duncan, and Karen Burke. 2005. "Participation in a residential mobility program from the client's perspective: Findings from Gautreaux Two." *Housing Policy Debate* 16(3/4): 361–92.

Patterson, Rhiannon, Michelle Wood, Ken Lam, Satyendra Patrabansh, Gregory Mills, Steven Sullivan, Hiwotte Amare, and Lily Zandniapour. 2004. *Evaluation of the Welfare to Work Voucher Program: Report to Congress*. Washington, DC: U.S. Department of Housing and Urban Development.

Polikoff, Alexander. 2006. *Waiting for Gautreaux: A Story of Segregation, Housing and the Black Ghetto*. Evanston, IL: Northwestern University Press.

Popkin, Susan J., and Mary K. Cunningham. 2000. *Searching for Rental Housing with Section 8 in the Chicago Region*. Washington, DC: Urban Institute. <http://www .urban.org/UploadedPDF/410314.pdf>.

Popkin, Susan J., Mary K. Cunningham, and Martha Burt. 2005. "Public housing transformation and the hard-to-house." *Housing Policy Debate* 16(1): 3–24.

Popkin, Susan J., Mary K. Cunningham, and William T. Woodley. 2003. *Residents at Risk: A Profile of Ida B. Wells and Madden Park*. Prepared for the Ford Foundation. Washington, DC: The Urban Institute. <http:/www.urban.org/uploaded PDF/310824_residents_at_risk.pdf>.

Popkin, Susan J., Victoria E. Gwiasda, Lynn M. Olson, Dennis P. Rosenbaum, and Larry Buron. 2004. *A Decade of HOPE VI: Research Findings and Policy Changes.* Washington D.C.: The Urban Institute. May 18 <http://www.urban.org/url.cfm?ID=411002>.

Priemus, Hugo, Peter A. Kemp, and David P. Varady. 2005. "Housing vouchers in the United States, Great Britain, and the Netherlands: Current issues and future perspectives." *Housing Policy Debate* 16(3/4): 575–609.

Quigley, John M. 2008. "Just suppose: housing subsidies for low-income renters," in Nicholas Retsinas and Eric S. Belsky, eds. *Revisiting Rental Housing: Policies, Programs and Priorities.* Washington DC: Brookings Institution, pp. 300–18.

Reed, Joanna M., Jennifer Pashup, and Emily Snell. 2005. "Voucher use, labor force participation, and life priorities: Findings from the Gautreaux Two housing mobility study." *Cityscape: A Journal of Policy Development and Research* 8(2): 232–39.

Riccio, James A. 2008. "Subsidized housing and employment: Building evidence of what works," in Nicholas Retsinas and Eric S. Belsky, eds., *Revisiting Rental Housing: Policies, Programs and Priorities.* Washington DC: Brookings Institution, pp. 191–224.

Rosenbaum, James. E. and Susan J. Popkin. "Employment and earnings of low-income blacks," in Christopher. Jencks & Paul E. Peterson, eds., *The Urban Underclass.* Washington DC: The Brookings Institution. pp. 342–356.

Rosin, Hannah. 2008. "American murder mystery." *Atlantic Monthly,* July/August: 40–54.

Rubinowitz, Leonard and James E. Rosenbaum. 2000. *Crossing the Class and Color Line: From Public Housing to White Suburbs.* Chicago: University of Chicago Press.

Sard, Barbara. 2004. "'Family Self-Sufficiency' Program imperiled by HUD's fiscal year 2005 budget request." Center on Budget and Policy Priorities, March 23 <http://www.cbpp.org/3-23-04hous.htm>.

Susin, Scott. 2005. "Longitudinal outcomes of subsidized housing recipients in matched survey and administrative data." *Cityscape: A Journal of Policy Development and Research* 8(2): 189–218.

Tatian, Peter A., and Christopher Snow. 2005. "The effects of housing assistance on income, earnings, and employment." *Cityscape: A Journal of Policy Development and Research* 8(2): 135–61.

Turner, M. A., Popkin, S. J., Rawlings, L. 2009. *Public Housing and the Legacy of Segregation.* Washington, DC: Urban Institute Press.

Varady, David P. 2003. "Using housing vouchers to move to the suburbs." *Journal of Planning Literature* 18(1): 17–30.

Varady, David P. and Carole C. Walker. 2007. *Neighborhood Choices: Section 8 Housing Vouchers and Residential Mobility.* New Brunswick, NJ: Center for Urban Policy Research.

Venkatesh, Sudhir Alladi. 2008. "To fight poverty, tear down HUD." *New York Times,* A19.

Verma, Nandita, James A. Riccio, Howard S. Bloom, and Johanna Walter. 2005. "Raising Hope with Jobs-Plus." MDRC <http://www.mdrc.org/publications/416/overview.html>.

Wang, Xinhao, and David P. Varady. 2005. "Using hot-spot analysis to study the clustering of Section 8 housing voucher families." *Housing Studies* 20(1) (January): 29–48.

Wang, Xinhao, David P. Varady, and Yimei Wang. 2008. "Measuring the deconcentration of Housing Choice Voucher Program Recipients in eight U.S. metropolitan areas using hot spot analysis." *Cityscape: A Journal of Policy Development and Research* 10(1): 65–90.

Welfeld, Irving. 1998. "Gautreaux: Baby steps to opportunity," in David. P. Varady, Wolfgang. F. E. Preiser, and Francis P. Russell, eds. *New Directions in Urban Public Housing.* New Brunswick, NJ: Center for Urban Policy Research, pp. 226–234.

# STUCK IN BUFFALO, *BUT WHY?*: RESIDENTIAL SPATIAL PATTERNS OF HOUSING CHOICE VOUCHER HOLDERS IN A RUST BELT CITY[1]

## Kelly L. Patterson

### *Housing Policy As Tool to Address Structural Discrimination*

Residential segregation and concentrated poverty remain two of the most intractable social problems of this era. For poor African Americans, especially those living in declining rust belt cities in the Northeast and Midwest, these problems are exacerbated and create a plethora of spatially defined disadvantages. Poor blacks segregated in impoverished neighborhoods lack access to good services, quality schools, and healthy and nutritious food. They also experience higher crime rates, school dropout rates, teen pregnancy rates and a host of other social pathologies. In essence, the neighborhoods where they live possess elements which limit the life chances of those who reside in them (Wilson 1987, Massey et al. 1991, Massey and Denton 1993, Jargowsky 1997, Goering et al. 2002). Moreover, many residents in these neighborhoods lack the resources to escape thereby creating an environment of racial and class isolation which requires structural interventions.

U.S. housing policies and the programs that grow out of them attempt to be those interventions. For years, the federal government played a significant role in the creation of poor, racially segregated neighborhoods through the development of public housing projects which were geographically concentrated in urban areas with high poverty rates (Varady and Walker 2003). By the late 1960s, with the release of the Moynihan report on the black family and the Kerner Commission report on civil disorders, there was growing concern about the effects of poverty and racial segregation on African Americans and society as a whole. Housing policy was seen as a mechanism for dealing with these problems. In the 1970s, legislation was enacted which began to

---

[1] I would like to thank Barbara Rittner for her comments on an earlier version of this chapter.

change the emphasis of housing programs from public project based housing to certificate based assistance in the private market (Mitchell 1985; Feins et al. 1997, Varady and Walker 2003).

The Section 8 Housing Certificate Program was the result of the Housing and Community Development Act of 1974. This legislation allowed participants to find and rent privately owned housing within the jurisdiction of the public housing authority (PHA)[2] which provided the assistance (Varady and Walker 2003). When a family moved the subsidy followed the family. In addition, under the rental certificate program, the PHA made subsidy payments directly to the owners on behalf of the family rather than making payments to the family. The certificate program grew rapidly and was popular with Congress, local governments, owners, and low income families. One of the reasons it was so popular was that it dispersed families throughout the community and did not create new housing projects or associated site selection problems (U.S. Department of Housing and Urban Development 2001).

Expanding on the certificate program, the rental voucher program was formally authorized as a program in the Housing and Community Development Act of 1987. It was similar to the certificate program, but it allowed families more options in housing selection by providing assistance to families based on a pre-determined calculation of assistance amount. Thus, depending on the cost of the housing they actually rented, families could pay more or less than 30 percent of adjusted income toward rent. Another key difference between the rental certificate and rental voucher programs was that the rental voucher program did not have a fair market rent (FMR)[3] limitation. This meant that there could be exceptions to the FMR in areas where rents were higher which served to expand the neighborhood choices of voucher recipients mainly outside of poor areas. The 1987 Act signaled a further shift in federal housing policy away from public housing to private rental

---

[2] Historically, when public housing was the sole and then largest subsidized housing program, PHA stood for public housing authority since public authorities managed public housing. Over time, as the HCV program grew into the largest subsidized housing program, PHA has come to stand for public housing agency because, in most jurisdictions, nonprofit agencies administer the voucher program.

[3] FMRs are gross rent estimates that are primarily used to determine payment standard amounts for the HCV Program. HUD sets FMRs to assure that a sufficient supply of rental housing is available to program participants.

housing. It also highlighted how integral tackling the issues of poverty and minority concentration had become in federal housing policy.

These foci were crystallized in 1999 when the U.S. Department of Housing and Urban Development (HUD) made two significant changes to the Section 8 program. It merged and changed the name of the Section 8 Voucher and Certificate Programs to the Housing Choice Voucher Program (HCV) as a way to consolidate the two programs and emphasize the 'choice' aspect of the federal housing program (U.S. Department of Housing and Urban Development 2001). The primary goal of giving low income residents a reduction in housing costs so that they could afford decent living accommodations in neighborhoods of their choice, remained the same (Khadduri 2005). However, providing opportunities for very low-income families to obtain rental housing outside areas of poverty and/or minority concentration was even more entrenched in this program.

The other important change that HUD initiated was the Section 8 Management Assessment Program (SEMAP). It is a tool designed by HUD to measure the performance of PHAs administering the HCV program. SEMAP measures the performance of PHAs on 14 key indicators, and one bonus indicator. Two of the performance indicators deal specifically with deconcentration and are limited to those PHAs operating in metropolitan fair market rent (FMR) areas. The 'expanding fair housing' indicator covers three areas. First, it shows whether the PHA has adopted and implemented a written policy to encourage participation by owners of units located outside areas of poverty or minority concentration. Second, it informs rental voucher holders of the full range of areas where they may lease units both inside and outside the PHA's jurisdiction. Finally, it supplies a list of landlords or other parties who are willing to lease units or help families find units, including units outside areas of poverty or minority concentration (U.S. Department of Housing and Urban Development 2001). The 'deconcentration bonus' indicator allots bonus points to PHAs for their achievements in encouraging assisted families to choose housing in low poverty areas. A low poverty census tract is defined as a census tract where the poverty rate of the tract is at or below 10 percent, or at or below the overall poverty rate for the principal operating area of the PHA, whichever is greater. The PHA determines the overall poverty rate for its principal operating area using the most recent available decennial Census data (U.S. Department of Housing and Urban Development 2001). Measuring the performance of PHAs with the

SEMAP tool was another important step in formalizing the goals of deconcentration of poverty and racial and ethnic integration since high performing PHAs receive national recognition from HUD and may be given a competitive advantage in funding decisions.

In addition to the policy changes which, over time, have increasingly addressed deconcentration, there have been a succession of judicial interventions which have had an impact on several jurisdictions administering the certificate and voucher programs (Popkin et al. 2000). The twin problems of minority and poverty concentration are being addressed through a series of consent decrees which were the result of lawsuits brought by residents. These lawsuits claimed that PHAs were discriminating in their management of public housing and/or administration of the certificate and voucher programs. One of the remedies of the public housing discrimination cases was the allocation of Section 8 certificates or vouchers (Popkin et al. 2000, Rubinowitz and Rosenbaum 2000). For cases involving the certificate and voucher programs, the majority consisted of black or Latino plaintiffs complaining of having less access to, and long waits for, Section 8 assistance in comparison to their white peers. They would also assert that whites were given more affordable housing opportunities (Popkin et al. 2000).

In those cases where the discrimination lawsuit was settled through a consent decree in favor of the plaintiffs, the consent decree usually led to the creation of a housing discrimination remediation program. The goal of these programs was to reduce plaintiffs' exposure to racially and income isolated neighborhoods. This would be achieved by providing additional special Section 8 vouchers to help address obstacles that had conventionally impeded free choice. Typically, the additional vouchers came with restrictions such as the recipients had to be part of a minority group, and had to use the voucher to rent a unit in a low poverty, low minority area (Popkin et al. 2000).

In addition to the vouchers, under many consent decrees, mobility counseling was required in order to use the vouchers. Mobility counseling was seen as another way to address segregation brought on by racial discrimination since one of the primary goals of mobility counseling is to give the renter knowledge about different potential neighborhoods and to provide them with a basic understanding of renters' rights and fair housing laws (Trudeau 2006). This facilitates more moves outside of concentrated areas because it served to lessen some of the fears and misconceptions that renters have of more affluent areas especially those where few minorities reside. Thus, the potential

significance of tenant-based assistance goes beyond the goals of providing decent, affordable housing. In addition to these goals, the
Housing Choice Voucher program can be used as a means to deconcentrate poverty (Turner 1998, Goering et al. 1999, Khadduri 2001,
Varady and Walker 2003) and to address the problem of racial residential segregation (Popkin et al. 2000).

*Addressing Structural Discrimination in Buffalo, New York*

The following analysis assesses whether the Housing Choice Voucher
program is effective in Buffalo, NY and Erie County, NY at addressing
the problem of poverty concentration and racial segregation. It is based
on an examination of the residential spatial patterns of 8,742 voucher
holders in this metropolitan region in 2008. For several reasons,
Buffalo and Erie County, which surrounds the city, are ideally suited
locations for an examination of the effectiveness of the HCV program's
goals. In 2008, Buffalo was listed as the third poorest city in the U.S.
with a 30.3% poverty rate. Erie County had a low 13.6% rate of poverty
(ACS 2008). This is clearly seen in Figure 1. With the exception of six
small census tracts, the largest of which is an Indian reservation with
1,997 people, Erie County is basically free from poverty.

In addition to being a highly impoverished city, Buffalo is also a
hyper-segregated city. According to Yin (2009), the Buffalo metropolitan area was ranked the nation's 12th most segregated SMA between
blacks and whites in 1980, 10th in 1990, and 8th in 2000 (US Census
Bureau 1980, 1990, 2000), demonstrating persistent patterns of residential segregation from 1980 to 2000. Indices of dissimilarity[4] and
isolation[5] which highlight the degree of segregation in an area, show
that segregation in the Buffalo metropolitan area is considerably high
with a dissimilarity index of .70 and an isolation index of .74 in the
year 2000 (Trudeau 2006). Any area with an index higher than .5 is
considered highly segregated according to Massey and Denton (1988).
By contrast, the black isolation index of .18 in the suburbs is much

---

[4] The dissimilarity index score is the percentage of the two groups included in the
calculation that would have to move to different geographic areas in order to produce
a distribution that matches that of the other group. In this case, 70% of blacks would
have to move.
[5] The isolation index measures the concentration or isolation of one group. The
maximum value is 100 and the minimum value is 0.

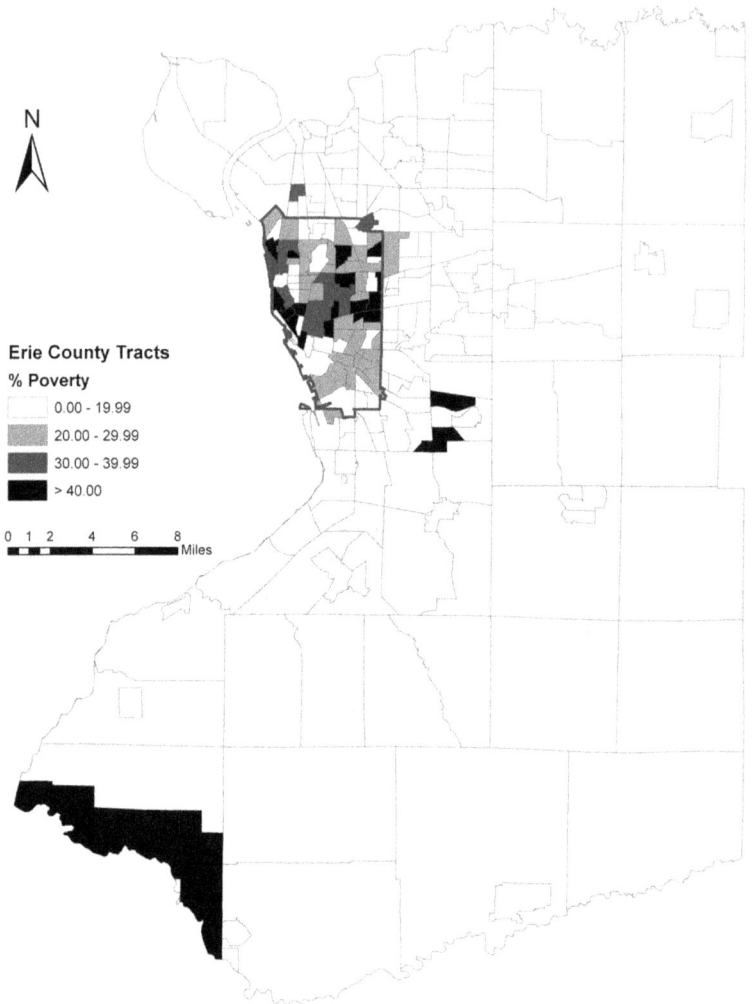

Figure 1.  Poverty Rates in Erie County, NY in 2000
*Source:* 2000 U.S. Census.

lower in 2000. This low number is characteristic of jurisdictions where the population of the minority group is very small compared to the dominant group (Lieberson 1981, Trudeau 2006).

The racial composition of Buffalo and Erie County also reveals the highly segregated spatial pattern of the area. According to the 2000 U.S. Census, African Americans represent 13% of the population of Erie County. However, only .02% lives outside of Buffalo. Whites make up 95% of those living outside of Buffalo in Erie County. These percentages only marginally change in 2008 according to the American Community Survey. In 2008, blacks represented 13.5% of the population of Erie County but only .03% lived outside of Buffalo. In the impoverished city of Buffalo, African Americans are the largest minority group. They represented 37% and 38% of the population in 2000 and 2008 respectively. Whites represented 55% of the population in both 2000 and 2008. These statistics alone do not reveal the nature of racial concentration patterns in Buffalo.

The historical patterns of racial segregation run deep with blacks persistently concentrated east of Main Street on the east side of Buffalo and in many cases making up more than 90% of a neighborhood's population.[6] As you can see in Figure 2, the city of Buffalo represents is highly segregated with blacks primarily concentrated east of Main Street. The surrounding county of Erie is predominately white. The consequence of this type of spatial patterning is that poor blacks are concentrated in distressed neighborhoods inside Buffalo with limited opportunities for social or economic mobility and higher probabilities for various types of social maladies such as dropping out of high school, teenage pregnancy, and joblessness (Wilson 1987, Massey et al. 1991).

There are three other characteristics of the Buffalo area that make it rather ideal for a study on the effectiveness of the voucher program. Most prior research that focused on the mobility experiences of voucher holders was conducted in tight housing markets where there was limited affordable housing available (Hartung and Henig 1997, Katz et al. 2001, Rosenbaum and Harris 2001, Goetz 2002). In these markets landlords resist renting to voucher holders since they know they can charge higher rents to those without vouchers. This literally leaves low-income renters holding a voucher with nowhere to go. In Washington D.C. alone, 40% of those with vouchers fail to find and lease a privately owned rental property before the vouchers expire. As a result, although most jurisdictions generally offer 60-day extensions, Washington, D.C. extends vouchers for 180 days because of the tight real estate market (Kunkle 2001). Nationally, 31% of those holding Section 8 vouchers in 2001 were unable to find homes before the vouchers expired (Varady and Walker 2003).

---

[6] Main Street is a historic dividing line in Buffalo.

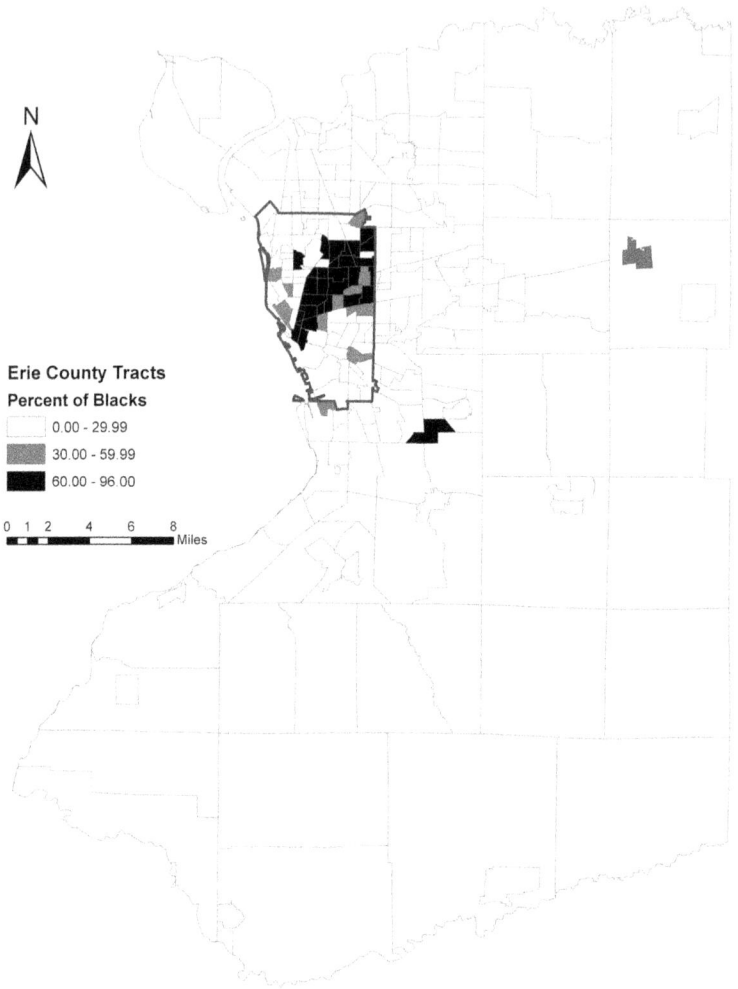

Figure 2. Percent of Blacks in Erie County, NY in 2000
*Source:* 2000 U.S. Census.

Buffalo and Erie County do not have housing availability issues and it becomes even more evident when you compare this area with the Northeast region and the U.S. Based on the 2000 U.S. Census, Buffalo and Erie County have significantly higher rental availability than other regions and the country as a whole. The city of Buffalo had 38% of its vacant housing for rent. That is out of a total of 22,854 vacant units. After subtracting the number of Buffalo vacancies, Erie County had

12,141 vacant units. Out of those, 36% were for rent. In the Northeast region of the country 22% of vacancies were for rent out of 1,894,818 vacant units in 2000. Nationally, there were 10,424,540 total vacant units and 26% were vacant for rent. In Buffalo, the percentage of vacancies for rent was more than 16% higher than the Northeast region and 12% higher than the national average. In Erie County the numbers were similar. The percentage of vacancies for rent was more than 14% higher than the Northeast region and 10% higher than the national average. Though supply is a primary barrier for low income voucher holders in tight housing markets, that was not the case in Western New York. Voucher holders in Buffalo did not have the same obstacles when it came to available rentals. The suburbs of Erie County also had a high percentage of units available for rent.

The question then becomes, are the available rental units affordable? This is a persistent problem for renters, but low-income renters face an even greater burden. According to Harvard's Joint Center for Housing Studies (2008), the median gross rent rose 2.7 percent in real terms from 2001 to 2006 while the median renter income fell by 8.4 percent (from over $31,600 to $29,000). As a result, nearly half of all renters paid more than 30 percent of their incomes for housing in 2006 and about a quarter, nearly 9 million households, spent more than 50%. Fully 52 percent of the lowest-income renters (with annual incomes of $24,200 or less in 2006) spent more than half their incomes on housing in 2006, up from 47 percent in 2001. In absolute terms, the number of lowest-income renters with severe cost burdens increased by more than one million between 2001 and 2006 to surpass the eight-million mark (Joint Center for Housing Studies 2008). In a report from HUD on trends in housing costs from 1985–2000, Eggers and Moumen (2008) found that monthly housing costs for renters increased from $424 in 1985 to $830 in 2005 and that between those same years renter household income declined by seven percent.

Nationally, it is clear that there is an increasing burden on low-income renters to be able to afford decent housing; however, when discussing housing markets it is important to focus regionally and locally because of the variations in markets across the country or even across states. New York State is a great example of vastly different housing markets. In New York City, according to the National Low Income Housing Coalition's "Out of Reach" 2007–2008 report, the FMR for a two bedroom apartment was $1,198. In order for a low income, hourly minimum wage worker earning $7.15 to afford a unit at that price

without paying more than 30% of income on housing, he or she must
work 129 hours a week for 52 weeks a year. Or, there must be 3.2 minimum wage workers who work 40 hours a week year round. On the
other hand, the Buffalo metropolitan area had the third lowest FMR in
the state. The FMR for the Buffalo region was $704. That means that
the hourly wage needed to afford a two bedroom apartment without
paying more than 30% of income on housing is $13.54 and the number
of full time jobs at minimum wage needed to afford the apartment is
1.9. So within the state of New York there is a great range of fair market
rental prices.

Comparing median gross rents[7] across the region and nation also
gives a clear picture of the affordability of Buffalo's rental housing (See
Table 1). For this assessment, I compared Buffalo and Erie County to
the state of New York, the Northeast region, and the U.S. so that the
inflated rental prices of New York City would not skew the picture.
Based on the 2008 American Community Survey, the median gross
rent for the city of Buffalo was $646 and for Erie County the median
gross rent was $677. In comparison, the median gross rent in the state
of New York was $953, in the Northeast it was $915, and in the nation
it was $824. This is more revealing when comparing the median gross
rent as a percentage of household income for these different geographies. The percentage addresses the fact that while the Buffalo region
does have low rents the people of Buffalo also have lower household
incomes. Thus, the comparison will show what proportion of their
incomes renters are spending on housing which gives a more complete
picture of the affordability of the rental market in the region. As you
can see, the residents of Buffalo paid 37% of their income for housing
which is 7% over the recommended limit of 30% by HUD.[8] In the more
affluent Erie County, residents paid 31% of their income in rent.
In New York State, the Northeast region and the U.S., residents paid the
recommended 30% of their income for housing. The renters in Buffalo
do pay lower rents, but they also pay a higher proportion of their
incomes for rent leaving them more vulnerable to structural changes
in the economy which at any time could render them cash poor.

It is clear that rental housing is both available and affordable in
Buffalo and Erie County. Therefore, HCV holders have more choices

---

[7] Gross rent is the cost of rent and utilities.
[8] However, the HCV program will allow voucher holders to pay up to 40% of their
income on housing.

Table 1.  Rent Characteristics for Various Geographies in 2008

| Rent variables | Buffalo | Erie county | New York state | Northeast region | U.S. |
|---|---|---|---|---|---|
| Median contract rent (occupied units) | $453 | $507 | $837 | $788 | $687 |
| Median gross rent (occupied units) | $646 | $677 | $953 | $915 | $824 |
| Median gross rent as % of income | 37 | 31 | 30 | 30 | 30 |

*Source:* American Community Survey, 2008.

for rentals all over the county in areas without poverty and minority concentration especially those suburban neighborhoods outside of Buffalo. Since the barriers that are often seen in other metropolitan areas across the country are not at play here, voucher holders should locate in more dispersed patterns than other places. In addition, race, which is so salient when analyzing mobility patterns of different groups in other places, may not have as great an impact in places where there are more options for housing.[9]

## Data and Methods

The data utilized in this study come from two PHAs that are contracted to administer the Housing Choice Voucher Program in the city of Buffalo and its surrounding metropolitan area. Together these two PHAs distribute 98% of the total vouchers in the area. The Buffalo Municipal Housing Authority controls the remaining vouchers (approximately 200) which are mainly attached to the housing units they manage in the city of Buffalo. Since those vouchers are attached to specific housing, thereby not constituting a free choice, they are not included in the analysis.

---

[9] Another factor that may have a positive impact on mobility patterns in Buffalo and Erie County is the 1997 *Comer vs. Cisneros* consent decree which mandated the creation of the Greater Buffalo Community Housing Center. The Center provides housing search assistance and other services to participants of Erie County's HCV programs. The reason this was not stated as a major characteristic that would facilitate mobility was that utilization of the Center's services has not been a requirement of voucher holders since 2002.

As of 2008, 8,879 total vouchers had been distributed by the two PHAs. There were 8,835 voucher holders living in the target area. The other 44 voucher recipients took their vouchers and moved out of state to other jurisdictions that participate in the HCV program. Those voucher holders are not included in this analysis. In addition, the data-set is limited to African-American and white voucher recipients. These voucher holders constitute 99% of the HCV population. The other 1% or 89 voucher holders are comprised of Asians, Native Americans, and Native Hawaiians. These recipients are excluded because they are too few in number to support a separate analysis. Thus, the final dataset utilized for this study includes 8,742 HCV holders.

This dataset is both unique and rich in that it consists of more than the residential address and race of the voucher recipients (See Table 2). It includes socio-demographic information as well as information about choice of housing, the price of rent and utilities, and the subsidy attached to each voucher. The socio-demographic data is comprised of age, gender, race, ethnicity, income, single parent status, number of children under six years of age, and number of years on the program. The data also include information on whether the household is 'hard to house.' 'Hard to house' is a category created by the PHAs to alert them as to whether the voucher holder is disabled, other household member/s are disabled, or whether there are three or more children in the household. Therefore, this variable measures hardship both from the perspective of the PHA to house this household, and hard-ship on the voucher recipient in terms of the process of acquiring an acceptable housing unit.

In addition to socio-demographics, this dataset includes informa-tion on the actual rental unit and measures associated with the voucher subsidy attached to the unit. Information about the rental unit consists of rental type, such as a high-rise, single detached home, row house, duplex or three unit. The number of bedrooms, whether or not utilities and appliances are included in the rent, and the year the unit was con-structed are also part of this dataset.

Data concerning actual rent of the unit is comprised of several vari-ables. They include: tenant rent or the amount of rent that the voucher holder must pay out of pocket for the unit, the voucher subsidy or the amount the PHA pays directly to the landlord, and the contract rent which is the amount the landlord actually charges for rent. Finally, the voucher gross rent is the contract rent plus the utility allowance for a specific unit if a voucher holder qualifies for a utility allowance.

Table 2.  Socio-Demographic and Housing Characteristics for Voucher Holders, 2008

| Variables | All voucher holders (N=8742) | Black voucher holders (N=5376 or 61.5%) | White voucher holders (N=3366 or 38.5%) |
|---|---|---|---|
| *Socio-demographic* | | | |
| Mean age | 46 | 44 | 51 |
| Gender | | | |
| %Female | 83 | 85 | 80 |
| %Male | 17 | 15 | 20 |
| %Hispanic | 8 | 2 | 17 |
| Median income | $9,576 | $9,505 | $9,641 |
| %Single parent | 38 | 46 | 25 |
| %Households w/children under 6 | 21 | 26 | 14 |
| %Hard to house | 40 | 43 | 35 |
| *Housing* | | | |
| Mean years in program | 7 | 6.6 | 7.3 |
| Mean tenant rent | $162.46 | $157.44 | $169.82 |
| Mean PHA payment | $348.65 | $357.65 | $334.29 |
| Mean contract rent | $508.39 | $512.34 | $502.58 |
| Mean number of bedrooms | 2.37 | 2.53 | 2.13 |
| Residence | | | |
| %Buffalo | 76 | 90 | 53 |
| %Erie County | 24 | 10 | 47 |
| %Residence in impacted area* | 63 | 78 | 38 |

*Source:* Buffalo and Erie County PHA dataset, 2008.
*Impacted area is a 20% or higher poverty rate.

The PHA also records the census tract where the rental unit is located in order to evaluate whether the unit is in an impacted or non-impacted area. An impacted area in their estimation (based on HUD standards) is any census tract with a 20% or higher poverty rate. The inclusion of census tract data was valuable for linking additional census information to this already rich dataset. This enabled a more comprehensive analysis of neighborhood-specific socio-demographic characteristics. The additional census variables include: a ratio of vacancies for rent, median contract rent, and median gross rent as a percentage of income.

The HCV dataset is particularly well suited to the study of residential location patterns across different types of neighborhoods since each recipient's address was also geo-coded using ARCGIS software then matched to the corresponding census tracts. This procedure allowed the tracking of voucher holders, through the process of mapping, between poor and non poor neighborhoods utilizing identifiers which incorporate information on the different neighborhoods. Subsequently, the residential location is first analyzed visually through a series of maps which present housing patterns for various groups at various measurement levels. While census tracts are an administrative delineation, as is common in housing research, they are used here to geographically approximate neighborhoods.

*Dependent Variable*

The variable Buffalo is a dummy variable measuring where the recipient lives either in the city of Buffalo or in the surrounding suburbs in Erie county (0 = outside Buffalo or Erie county; 1 = Buffalo). This variable is highly correlated to poverty because, as you can see in Figure 1, only six tracts outside of Buffalo are poor based on HUD's standard of a 20% or higher poverty rate. These types of neighborhoods are considered impacted and are found to suffer from the deleterious effects of concentrated poverty described by Wilson (1987, 1993).

*Explanatory Variables*

The explanatory variables utilized in the analyses include socio-demographic characteristics of the individual HCV holders and their families, as well as features of their neighborhoods and the metropolitan area. Descriptive statistics of these variables appear in Table 1. The operationalizations are straightforward. For the individual voucher holders, demographic variables such as age and a series of dummy variables are included. These include the recipient's gender (0 = male; 1 = female), race (0 = white; 1 = black), ethnicity (0 = non-Hispanic; 1 = Hispanic), single parent (0 = not a single parent status; 1 = single parent), presence of children under 6 (0 = no child under 6; 1 = has child or children under 6), and hard to house (0 = not hard to house; 1 = hard to house). Even though this dataset is skewed toward poor people since individuals would not qualify for a voucher if they did not meet specified income limits, income is still used to determine if even slight differences in income will be significant in whether or not a household chooses to reside inside or outside of Buffalo. Income is the voucher recipient's total personal income in the calendar year preceding their entry into the program. Unfortunately, education, a seemingly important socio-economic variable which impacts life choices, is absent here since neither HUD nor the local PHAs use it or require it in making the determination of whether a person is eligible for a voucher.

The housing and program characteristics are measured by a series of variables that are related to the HCV program or connected to the actual rental unit. Years in program measures the number of years that the recipient has held a voucher. This does not include the number of years that individuals were in the system, qualified and waiting for a voucher. Tenant rent is what the voucher holder pays for their rental unit. This amount should not go above 30% of their monthly income. Number of bedrooms is simply a count of the number of bedrooms in a unit.

The census tract variables included in the analyses are median contract rent and median gross rent as a percentage of income. According to the U.S. Census, contract rent is total rent paid per rental unit and gross rent is the total rent plus the utilities for each rental unit. In addition, one standardized variable was included. It represents the ratio of vacancies for rent in each census tract to average vacancies for rent in all census tracts. These data are from the 2000 U.S. Census SF 3 data files and were used in order to obtain a better picture of the voucher recipients' neighborhoods.

Two other tract-level characteristics are used for the purposes of mapping to visually highlight the types of neighborhoods and the degree of poverty concentration and segregation in which voucher holders live. Poverty is a census variable which is broken up into four levels of poverty (0–19.99%, 20–29.99%, 30–39.99%, 40% and above). Forty percent and higher represents an extreme poverty neighborhood and is characterized by the trending downward of several neighborhood indicators which represent quality of life. In these neighborhoods there are several spatially defined disadvantages. Black measures the proportion of blacks that live in a census tract. It is broken down into three categories (0–29.99%, 30–59.99%, 60–96%).

*Analytic Strategy*

The analysis is done in four stages. First, geo-coding of the voucher holders' addresses was done and an ArcGIS shapefile was created in order to develop a database that could be utilized for the mapping process. Then, maps of the HCV addresses in Buffalo and Erie County were created to visualize the location of those households. Next, census tract data were joined with the GIS shapefile so that census data could be overlaid on the maps to examine the type of neighborhoods where voucher holders lived. Mapping was used in this study to visually observe the residential spatial patterns and spread of HCV holders throughout Buffalo and its surrounding county. It enhances and confirms subsequent statistical analyses because we can observe the patterns prior to running statistical tests and this is more effective than viewing the patterns in tabular form. Finally, binary logistic regression is used to estimate the impact of the explanatory variables on the log-odds of whether a voucher holder will live in an impacted area in the city of Buffalo or outside of it in a non-impacted area and whether this differs by race.

*Results*

Figure 3 reveals the housing locations of the 8,742 recipients in the HCV program in Erie County. As you can see, the voucher holders are mainly concentrated in the city of Buffalo. Since Buffalo is a poor city, many of its census tracts are impacted with at least a 20% poverty rate. Thus, we can surmise then that many HCV holders live in impacted areas in the city. This research examines whether this differs by race and how much race impacts location patterns as previous research has shown (Hartung and Henig 1997, Pendall 2000, Khadduri 2001, Rosenbaum and Harris 2001, Goering et al. 2002, Devine et al. 2003, Wang and Varady 2005).

Figures 4 and 5 reveal the location patterns by race overlaid on a census tract poverty map for Buffalo and Erie County. Visually you can

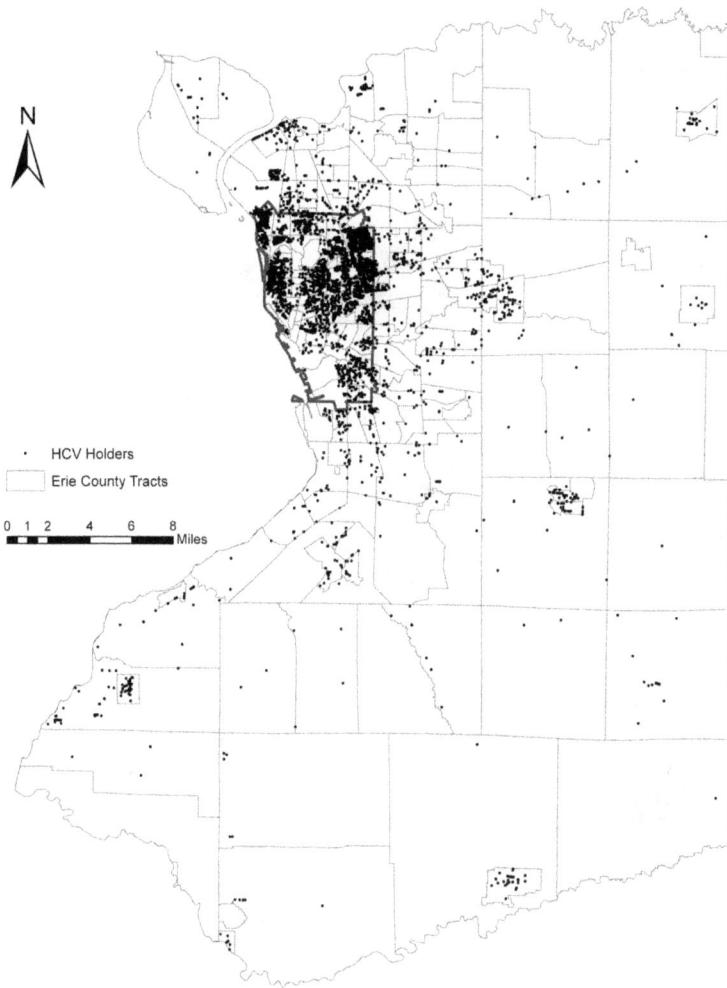

Figure 3. Location of Housing Choice Voucher Holders, 2008
*Source:* PHA data set, 2008.

see the concentration of blacks and the spread of whites in Erie County.
Blacks are concentrated in a northeast southwest pattern that is framed
by Main Street which delineates the east side and west side of Buffalo.
The east side of Buffalo contains some of the poorest tracts in Erie
County (Taylor 1990, Kraus 2000). It appears that blacks with HCVs
who have the option to move throughout the metropolis choose to
remain in Buffalo's poorest neighborhoods and may not be gaining the
full benefits from the voucher program (see also New York State

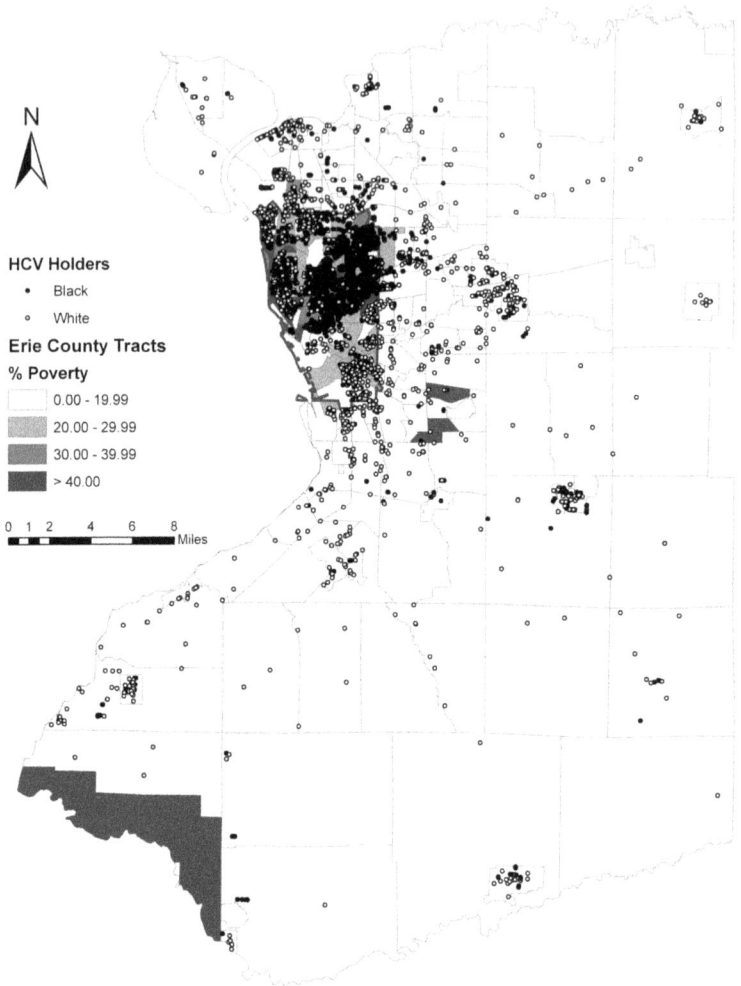

Figure 4. Location of Voucher Holders by Race Overlaid on Percent Poverty in Erie County, 2008
*Source:* 2000 U.S. Census and PHA data set, 2008.

Advisory Committee 1999). Whites' mobility patterns are much more spread and are not concentrated in the poorest tracts of Buffalo. As a result, they are living in a sparser pattern outside of Buffalo and outside of poor tracts. The tendency for whites to locate outside of Buffalo and outside of impoverished tracts in Buffalo suggests that they are experiencing the housing choice program in the way it was intended.

This pattern is even more pronounced in Buffalo (See Figure 5). Whites are located more heavily on the north and south sides of Buffalo. These areas contain more stable and less poor tracts. It should be noted that the far west side of Buffalo, where you see whites more densely located in an impoverished area, is the historic Hispanic community and is heavily populated with residents of Puerto Rican descent.

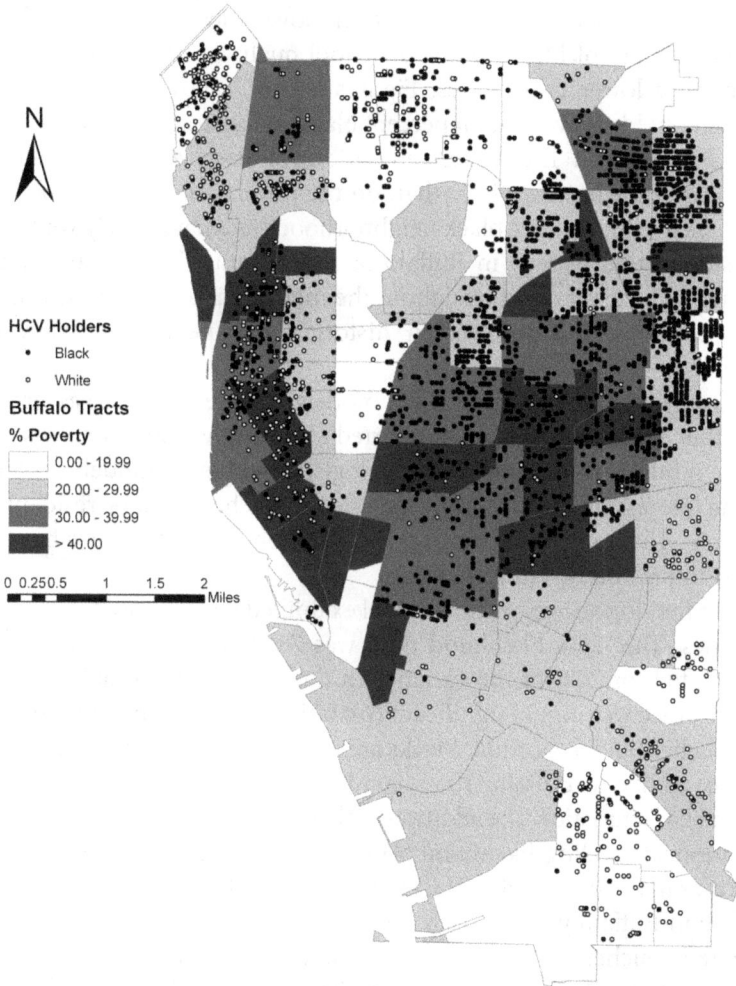

Figure 5. Location of Voucher Holders by Race Overlaid on Percent Poverty in Buffalo, 2008
*Source:* 2000 U.S. Census and PHA data set, 2008.

Of the 688 Hispanic voucher holders, 84% identify as white and 16% identify as black. Taken together these poverty maps show clearly that black voucher holders live in concentrated poverty and that the mobility and choice option which vouchers provide is not being effectively utilized by this population.

Segregation is another trend that housing policy was designed to address. The goal was to give segregated populations, and blacks in particular, the opportunity to live in more racially diverse neighborhoods. These neighborhoods, if not impoverished, are said to offer a higher quality of life in terms of school quality, better access to services, and lower crime rates. Figures 6 and 7 show the location of voucher holders overlaid on percent black census tract maps of Buffalo and Erie County. The segregated pattern of black voucher holders is even more clearly seen here than on the poverty map. Black voucher holders live in majority black neighborhoods and have barely ventured outside of that pattern in Buffalo or Erie County. Whites, again, are shown to be dispersed throughout the metropolis and only show limited concentration patterns in historically white areas outside of Buffalo.

Three binary logistic regression models were developed to ascertain whether these patterns are supported statistically. Table 3 shows the three models. The results from the logistic regression models provide some interesting insight into what affects voucher holders' residential choices. The models also answer the question of whether race has the most impact on housing choices.

The first logistic regression model examined voucher holder characteristics. The -2log-likelihood ratio was 7558.470 and the pseudo $R^2$ accounted for 22% of the variance in the dependent variable. In this model, race was highly significant (p<.001) and the strongest predictor of voucher holder location. Blacks are almost 10 times more likely than whites to live in Buffalo. The second model added housing and program characteristics. The addition of these variables improved the fit of the model to a -2log-likelihood of 6487.392 and increased the $R^2$ to .25. Here, as in the first model, Blacks are significantly (P<.001) more likely to live in Buffalo with an odds ratio of 11.042. The final model incorporated voucher holder characteristics, housing and program characteristics, and neighborhood characteristics. This model had the best fit with a −2log-likelihood of 4219.374 which was an improvement of 3339.096 over the first model. This model also explained the most variance with an $R^2$ of .44.

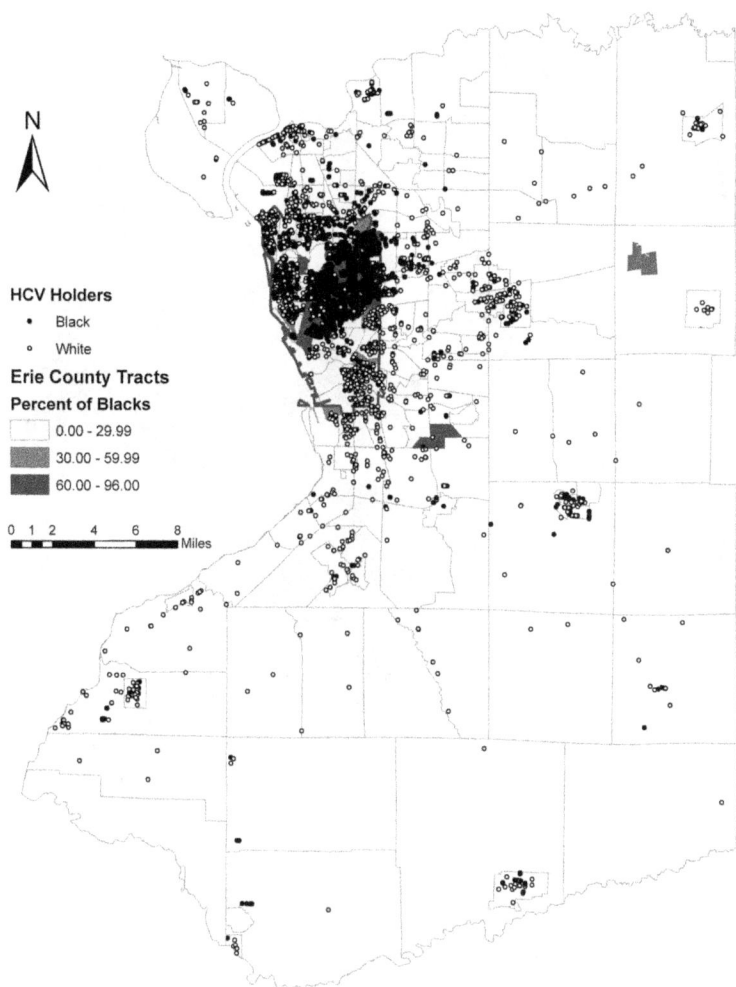

Figure 6. Location of Voucher Holders by Race Overlaid on Percent Black in Erie County, 2008
*Source:* 2000 U.S. Census and PHA data set, 2008.

The final inclusive model reveals several significant findings which give a picture of how effective the HCV program is at minority and poverty deconcentration in the Western New York area. As is the case in the first two models, race is both highly significant and has the highest probability for predicting where a voucher holder will reside. Blacks are 5.5 (p<.001) times as likely to live in Buffalo as whites despite not having to endure some of the major obstacles that blacks in other

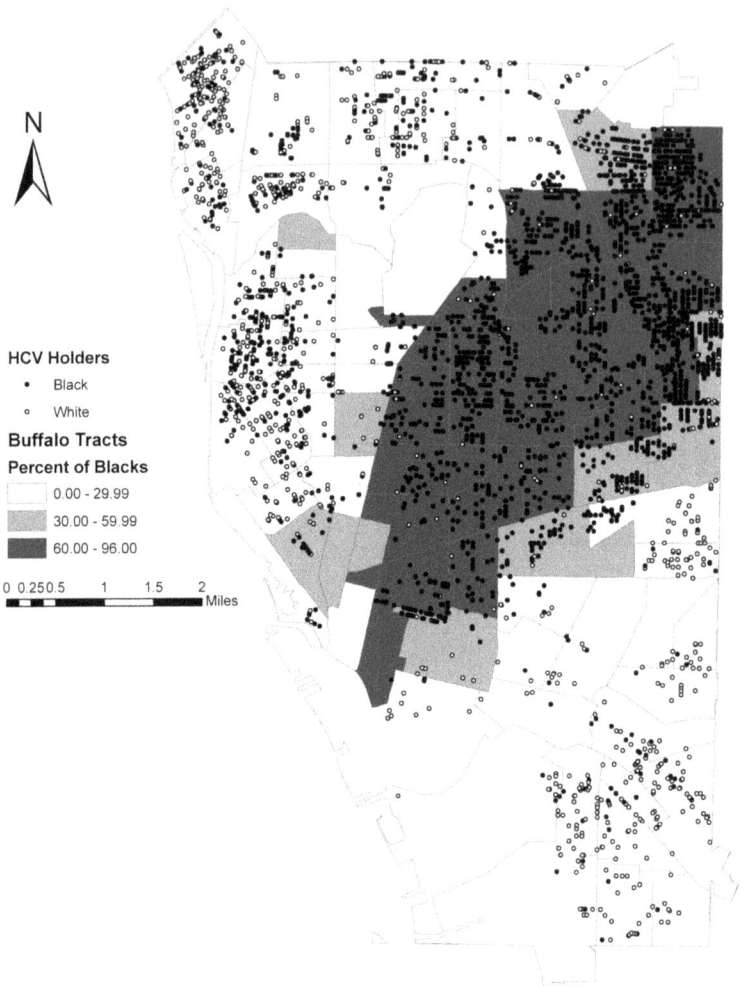

Figure 7.  Location of Voucher Holders by Race Overlaid on Percent
Black in Buffalo, 2008
*Source:* 2000 U.S. Census and PHA data set, 2008.

metropolitan areas face such as availability of affordable housing. The
same holds true for Hispanics who, like blacks, tend to concentrate in
impoverished areas especially in older cities of the Northeast and
Midwest. In the Buffalo area, the odds ratio for Hispanics was 2.881
(p<.001) and is the second largest odds ratio after race. Hispanics are
almost three times more likely to live in Buffalo than non-Hispanics.

Table 3. Binary Logistic Regression Models Predicting the Likelihood of Living in Buffalo

| Explanatory variables | Model 1 | | Model 2 | | Model 3 | |
|---|---|---|---|---|---|---|
| | β | Exp(β) | β | Exp(β) | β | Exp(β) |
| *Voucher holder characteristics* | | | | | | |
| Age | .000 | 1.000 | .006 | 1.006* | .006 | 1.006 |
| Gender | −.201 | .818** | −.362 | .696*** | −.543 | .581*** |
| Race | 2.284 | 9.819*** | 2.402 | 11.042*** | 1.699 | 5.469*** |
| Ethnicity | 1.730 | 5.641*** | 1.624 | 5.071*** | 1.058 | 2.881*** |
| Income | −.267 | .766*** | .084 | 1.088 | −.341 | .711*** |
| Single parent | .214 | 1.239** | .076 | 1.079 | .139 | 1.149 |
| Child under 6 | .139 | 1.150 | −.031 | .760 | .151 | 1.163 |
| Hard to house | .830 | 2.294*** | .861 | 2.365*** | .824 | 2.279*** |
| *Housing and program characteristics* | | | | | | |
| Number of bedrooms | | | .216 | 1.241*** | .088 | 1.092 |
| Tenant rent | | | −.003 | .997*** | .001 | 1.001 |
| Years on program | | | −.017 | .983** | −.014 | .986* |
| *Neighborhood characteristics* | | | | | | |
| Ratio of vacant for rent | | | | | −.094 | .910 |
| Median contract rent | | | | | −.015 | .985*** |
| Median gross rent as % of income | | | | | .233 | 1.262*** |
| Intercept | −.004 | | −.428** | | .491 | |
| -2 log-likelihood ratio | 7558.470 | | 6387.392 | | 4219.374 | |
| Pseudo *R²* (N = 8,742) | .22 | | .25 | | .44 | |

*Source:* Buffalo and Erie County PHA dataset, 2008; 2000 U.S. Census.
*p < .05, **p < .01, ***p < .001.

Those voucher holders who are hard to house because of a disability or because they are large households had an odds ratio of 2.279 (p<.001). They were more than twice as likely to live in Buffalo as households which were not hard to house. This finding supports research conducted in Erie County on the impediments to fair housing choice which found that larger families, especially those with teenagers and people with disabilities, had more difficulty finding and acquiring fair and affordable housing outside of Buffalo in Erie County (Patterson and Silverman 2011). Many of the complaints that residents with larger families had, centered around landlords not being willing to rent to them because they had older children who are feared to cause more damage and be involved in gang activity. Those with disabilities also encountered difficulties with landlords who were not willing to make apartments accessible because of perceived costs. Therefore, these groups were more likely to live in Buffalo where the barriers to fair and affordable housing were fewer. The unwillingness of landlords outside of the city to rent to these two groups partly explains this variable's significance as well as its direction.

Gender and income were the only voucher holder characteristics with negative coefficients. For gender, the odds ratio was .581 (p<.001). This meant that men were more likely to live in Buffalo than women when all other socio-demographic variables were held constant. Men's experiences with housing vouchers are rarely explored in scholarly literature, possibly because it is largely perceived that vouchers go to women and their families. While women do represent 83% of the voucher holders in Western New York, there are 1,480 men who hold vouchers and whose experiences on the program may be much different from women. This is of particular interest when considered in the context of housing options for black and Hispanic men. In cities like Buffalo, where a substantial segment of HCV recipients are minorities and men, there is a need to understand how well PHAs serve the needs of all groups receiving housing assistance. The concentration of males, the hard to house, and minority HCV recipients in the inner-city suggests that there is a need for expanded resources and services.

These findings were reinforced by other significant variables in the model. Recipients' incomes were highly significant in the third model. For every dollar increase in personal income, the likelihood that voucher holders would live in Erie County increased by .711 (p<.001). This is not surprising since rents and incomes are higher in Erie County than they are in Buffalo. The only housing and program variable that remained significant in the third model was years on the program. The number of years on the program significantly reduces the probability of living in Buffalo. This variable has an odds ratio of .986 (p<.05). This is potentially problematic since it suggests that more recent voucher holders are living in Buffalo's poor neighborhoods despite additional efforts by HUD to increase its incentive program for PHAs to place voucher holders in non-impacted neighborhoods (U.S. Department of Housing and Urban Development 2001). Lastly, the third model added neighborhood characteristics. Median contract rent was significant and in the expected direction. The odds ratio for this variable was .985 (p<.001). An increase in rental price reduced the probability of living in Buffalo. On the other hand, the median gross rent as a percentage of income variable had an odds ratio of 1.262 (p<001). This indicated that if tenants were paying a higher percentage of income on rent they were 1.3 times as likely to live in Buffalo. This is apparent since the average percent of personal income paid in rent was 37% in Buffalo and 31% in Erie County (ACS 2008).

## Conclusions

The results from the logistic regression analyses reveal that race is the strongest, most significant factor in determining where HCV holders will live in Erie County despite the fact that market forces are amenable to deconcentration. Unlike other metropolitan areas, where tight housing markets constrain voucher holders' options, rental costs in the suburbs of metropolitan Buffalo should not constitute a barrier to deconcentration. Regardless, some groups remain spatially concentrated. These groups include the hard to house, men, minorities, the poorest of the HCV population, and those newest to the program. This suggests that HUD and local PHAs need to augment resources and target services to these underserved HCV recipients.

At the federal level, the institution of SEMAP has improved the monitoring process and made local PHAs more accountable when it comes to deconcentration efforts. However, HUD may need to enhance those efforts by focusing more closely on the groups that are concentrating so that the awarding of points more closely corresponds to their increased needs. For example, in Buffalo, black men have a particularly hard time locating outside of areas of high poverty and racial concentration. Based on Buffalo's long history of racial divisions and discrimination (Taylor 1990, Krause 2000, Trudeau 2006) it is not difficult to imagine that black men confront real and/or perceived hostility from landlords in non-poor neighborhoods. The same holds true for Hispanic men. For this reason, HUD should consider awarding PHAs that successfully place these men outside of impacted areas, extra bonus points in their assessment. HUD should also better inform local PHAs of the special needs of these groups, and the possible barriers they face in their search for housing so that PHAs can more effectively assist them. Additionally, because of the barriers they encounter, black and Hispanic men may need more time finding housing. Certain groups such as people with disabilities, who obtain set aside vouchers through the Mainstreaming People with Disabilities Program, automatically receive 120 days to search for suitable housing (Devine 2000). HUD should consider extending the search time from 60 to 120 days for black and Hispanic men also.

Although HUD does make special efforts to assist people with disabilities with set aside vouchers, this may not be enough to improve their chances of living outside of impoverished neighborhoods. The hard to house population in Buffalo and Erie County are much more likely to live in Buffalo than in the non-poor neighborhoods in Erie County. Although this variable is problematic because it also includes households with three or more children, which may have confounded the results, a previous study found that low income persons with disabilities did encounter several barriers to fair housing in Erie County (Patterson and Silverman 2011). This group complained of lack of knowledge about available accessible units, the inferior quality of available units, the refusal of landlords to make units accessible, and discrimination by landlords (Patterson and Silverman forthcoming). Hence, this group needs more than just extra time for their housing search. They need additional information about available accessible housing outside of concentrated tracts and assisted living complexes and assistance in dealing with area landlords. Since PHAs often lack the capacity to provide additional services, it is incumbent on federal policymakers to expand programs like Mainstreaming People with Disabilities by increasing the funding and the scope of the program to include additional services.

Likewise, large families are another group who face discriminatory barriers when they search for housing outside of Buffalo. In Erie County, local public administrators conceded that landlords do discriminate against large families especially if they are poor and especially if there are teenagers (Patterson and Silverman 2011). This is supported in the current study in two ways. First, large families are significantly more likely to live in Buffalo in all three models. Second, the presence of children under six was not significant in any of the models. Families with a number of older children need additional assistance finding affordable housing outside of poor neighborhoods. Aiding this population should be a priority for HUD since it is these very families who are found to benefit most from living outside of minority and poverty concentration (Turner and Ellen 1997, Leventhal and Brooks-Gunn 2000, Goering et al. 2002, Goering 2003). Providing vouchers that come with additional support services could be a first step in dealing with these vulnerable families.

Although HUD should continue to improve its efforts when it comes to these particular at-risk groups, local PHAs must also improve their effectiveness when dealing with these groups. Communication is one area that even lower capacity PHAs could improve upon with few additional resources since one of the main criticisms leveled against local PHAs is that they fail to effectively communicate the availability of affordable housing outside of impoverished neighborhoods (Turner et al. 1999). It has been shown that poor people lack information mostly because they have problems accessing information (New York State Advisory Committee 1999, Servon and Nelson 2001). Therefore, PHAs should provide voucher recipients with clearer, more informative materials at start-up and offer enhanced orientations which focus mainly on the benefits of living outside of concentrated neighborhoods, giving actual examples of those neighborhoods and discussing availability in those neighborhoods.

Mobility counseling has been shown to improve locational outcomes for the general population of voucher holders (Goering et al. 1995, Turner and Williams 1998, Varady et al 2001, Cunningham and Sawyer 2005). As a result of the *Comer vs. Cisneros* lawsuit, HUD ordered the creation of a mobility center in Buffalo, NY. All recipients of vouchers, as a result of that case, were required to go to mobility counseling and prompted to move outside of poor neighborhoods. Analyzing a subset of that group, Trudeau (2006) found that a majority of those households relocated to poor inner city neighborhoods for three main reasons: concerns for accessibility to public transportation, the need to remain close to family, and the desire for neighborhood safety. The continued existence of the mobility center is something that PHAs in Buffalo should take better advantage of. Although current voucher recipients are not required to utilize its services, PHA administrators should consider making counseling mandatory for the most at-risk groups. This should be done with an understanding that for many of them there are legitimate concerns about moving outside of Buffalo. Administrators need to work proactively with counselors from the mobility center to identify those voucher recipients who could benefit the most from assistance and from moving outside of poverty and minority concentration.

The persistence of race and class segregation in Buffalo and Erie County is the result of the geographic concentration of African Americans in poor neighborhoods. It has been shown that these types of neighborhoods have a range of detrimental effects on well being and do not provide residents with the same opportunities for social and economic mobility as neighborhoods that are not segregated and poor. As HUD's primary mechanism for meeting the housing needs of the poor, the HCV program could have more impact addressing these troubling and persistent patterns. It starts at the federal level with federal policy makers continuing to push for greater accountability at the local level, expanding the scope of programs to reach more targeted, at-risk groups, and increasing funding levels. At the local level, PHAs need to be creative about enhancing their programmatic efforts with limited resources. These changes would go a long way in strengthening the HCV program and its administration as well as creating better outcomes for voucher recipients.

*References*

Cunningham, Mary K., Susan J. Popkin, Janet L. Smith, and Anne Knepler. 2002. *CHAC mobility counseling assessment. Final report.* Washington, DC: Urban Institute.

Cunningham, Mary K. and Noah Sawyer. 2005. "Moving to Better Neighborhoods with Mobility Counseling." Washington, DC: Urban Institute.

Devine, Deborah. 2000. "Persons with Disabilities Assisted Under the Section 8 Mainstream Set-Aside Program." *Cityscape* 5(1): 231–235.

Devine, Deborah J., Robert W. Gray, Lester Rubin, and Lydia B. Taghavi. 2003. *Housing Choice Voucher Location Patterns: Implications for Participants and Neighborhood Welfare.* Washington, DC: U.S. Department of Housing and Urban Development.

Eggers, Frederick J. and Fouad Moumen. 2008. "Trends in Housing Costs: 1985–2005 and the 30-Percent-of-Income Standard." Washington, DC: U.S. Department of Housing and Urban Development.

Ellen, Ingrid Gould and Margery Austin Turner. 1997. "Does Neighborhood Matter? Assessing Recent Evidence." *Housing Policy Debate* 8(4): 833–66.

Goering, John, Helene Stebbins and Michael Siewert. 1995. *Promoting Housing Choice in HUD's Rental Assistance Programs: Report to Congress.* Washington, DC: U.S. Department of Housing and Urban Development.

Goering, John, Joan Kraft, Judith D. Feins, Debra McInnis, Mary Joel Holin and Huda Elhassan. 1999. *Moving to Opportunity for Fair Housing Demonstration Program.* Washington, DC: U.S. Department of Housing and Urban Development.

Goering, John. 2000. "Opening Housing Opportunities: Changing Federal Housing Policy in the United States." Pp. 84–97 in F. Boal, editor, *Ethnicity and Housing: Accommodating Differences.* Brookfield, VT: Ashgate.

Goering, John, Judith D. Feins, and Todd Richardson. 2002. "A Cross-site Analysis of Initial MTO Demonstration Results." *Journal of Housing Research* 13(1): 1–30.

Goering, John. 2003. "The Impacts of New Neighborhoods on Poor Families: Evaluating the Policy Implications of the Moving to Opportunity Demonstration." *Economic Policy Review* 9(2): 113–140.

Goetz, Edward G. 2002. "Forced Relocation vs. Voluntary Mobility: The Effects of Dispersal Programs on Households." *Housing Studies* 17(1): 107–23.

Hartung, John and Jeffrey Henig. 1997. "Housing Vouchers and Certificates as a Vehicle for Deconcentrating the Poor: Evidence from the Washington, DC, Metropolitan Area." *Urban Affairs Review* 32(3): 403–419.

Jargowsky, Paul A. 1997. *Poverty and Place: Ghettos, Barrios, and the American City.* New York: Russell Sage Foundation.

Joint Center for Housing Studies. 2008. "America's Rental Housing: The Key to a Balanced National Policy." Cambridge, MA: Harvard University's Joint Center for Housing Studies.

Katz, Lawrence F., Jeffrey R. Kling, and Jeffrey B. Liebman. 2001. "Moving to Opportunity in Boston: Early results of a Randomized Mobility Experiment." *The Quarterly Journal of Economics* 116(2): 607–54.

Khadduri, Jill. 2001. "Deconcentration: What Do We Mean? What Do We Want?" *Cityscape* 5(2): 69–84.

Kraus, Neal. 2000. *Race, Neighborhoods, and Community Power: Buffalo Politics 1934–1997.* Albany, NY: State University of New York Press.

Kunkle, Fredrick. 2002. "Housing Vouchers No Magic Key." *Washington Post* (August 5): Section "A." Retrieved from <www.washingtonpost.com/ac2/wp-dyn/A43828-2002July30?language= printer.>

Leventhal, Tama and Jeanne Brooks-Gunn. 2000. "The Neighborhoods They Live in: The Effects of Neighborhood Residence on Child and Adolescent Outcomes." *Psychological Bulletin* 26(2): 309–337.

Lieberson, Stanley. 1981. "An Asymmetrical Approach to Segregation." Pp. 61–82 in C. Peach, V. Robinson, and S. Smith, editors, *Ethnic Segregation in Cities.* London, UK: Croom Helm.

Massey, Douglas and Nancy Denton. 1988. "The Dimensions of Residential Segregation." *SocialForces* 67: 281–315.

Massey, Douglas, Andrew B. Gross and Mitchell L. Eggers. 1991. "Segregation, the Concentration of Poverty, and the Life Chances of Individuals." *Social Science Research* 20(4): 397–420.

Massey, Douglas and Nancy Denton. 1993. *American Apartheid: Segregation and the Making of the Underclass.* Cambridge, MA: Harvard University Press.

Mitchell, J. Paul, ed.1985. *Federal Housing Policy and Programs.* New Brunswick, NJ: Center for Urban Policy Research Press.

National Low Income Housing Coalition. 2008. "Out of Reach." Washington, D.C.: National Low Income Housing Coalition.

New York State Advisory Committee to the U.S. Commission on Civil Rights. 1999. *Equal Housing Opportunities in New York: An Evaluation of Section 8 Housing Programs in Buffalo, Rochester, and Syracuse.* Washington, DC: U.S. Commission on Civil Rights.

Patterson, Kelly L. and Robert Mark Silverman. 2011. "Public Administrators, Nonprofit Providers and Elected Officials Perceptions of Impediments to Fair Housing in the Suburbs: An Analysis of Erie County, New York." *Housing Policy Debate* 21(1): 165–188.

Pendall, Rolf. 2000. "Why Voucher Holder and Certificate Users Live in Distressed Neighborhoods." *Housing Policy Debate* 11(4): 881–910.

Popkin, Susan J., Larry F. Buron, Diane K. Levy, and Mary K. Cunningham. 2000. "The Gautreaux Legacy: What Might Mixed Income and Dispersal Strategies Mean for the Poorest Public Housing Tenants?" *Housing Policy Debate* 11(4): 911–942.

Popkin, Susan J., and Mary K. Cunningham. 2000. *Searching for Rental Housing with Section 8 in the Chicago Region.* Washington, DC: Urban Institute. Retrieved from <http://www.urban.org/UploadedPDF/ 410314.pdf.>

Popkin, Susan J., Mary K. Cunningham, Erin Godfrey, Beata Bednarz, Alicia Lewis, Janet L. Smith, Anne Knepler, and Doug Schenkleberg. 2002. *CHA Relocation Counseling Assessment.* Washington, DC: Urban Institute.

Popkin, Susan J., George Galster, Kenneth Temkin, Carla Herbig, Diane K. Levy, and Elise Richer. 2000. "Baseline Assessment of Public Housing Desegregation Cases." Washington, DC: The Urban Institute.

Rosenbaum, Emily, and Laura E. Harris. 2001. "Residential Mobility and Opportunities: Early Impacts of the Moving to Opportunity Demonstration Program in Chicago." *Housing Policy Debate* 12(2): 321–46.

Rubinowitz, Leonard S., and James E. Rosenbaum. 2000. *Crossing the Class and Color Line: From Public Housing to White Suburbia.* Chicago: University of Chicago Press.

Servon, Lisa and Marla Nelson. 2001. "Community Technology Centers and the Urban Technology Gap." *International Journal of Urban and Regional Research* 25(2): 419–426.

Taylor, Henry. 1990. *African Americans and the Rise of Buffalo's Post Industrial City, 1940 to Present.* Buffalo, NY: Buffalo Urban League.

Trudeau, Daniel. 2006. "The Persistence of Segregation in Buffalo, New York: Comer vs. Cisneros and Geographies of Relocation Decisions among Low-income Black Households." *Urban Geography* 27(1): 20–44.

Turner, Margery Austin. 1998. "Moving Out of Poverty: Expanding Mobility and Choice through Tenant-Based Housing Assistance." *Housing Policy Debate* 9 (2): 373–94.

Turner, Margery Austin and Ingrid Gould Ellen. 1997. "The Effects of Neighborhoods on Families and Children: What We Can Learn from MTO." Paper presented at the U.S. Department of Housing and Urban Development's Moving to Opportunity Research Conference, November 20, Washington, DC.

Turner, Margery Austin and Kale Williams. 1998. *Housing Mobility: Realizing the Promise.* Washington, D.C.: The Urban Institute.

U.S. Census Bureau. 2003. *Census 2000, Summary File 3, Census of Population and Housing.* Washington, DC: U.S. Department of Commerce.

U.S. Census Bureau. 2008. American Community Survey. Retrieved from <http://factfinder.census.gov/servlet/DTGeoSearchByListServlet?ds_name=ACS_2008_1YR_G00_&_lang=en&_ts=298747164081.> (Accessed July 20).

U.S. Department of Housing and Urban Development, Office of Policy Development and Research. 2001. "Voucher Program Guidebook: Housing Choice." Washington, DC: U.S. Department of Housing and Urban Development.

Varady, David P., Carole A. Walker, and Xinhao Wang. 2001. "Voucher Recipient Achievement of Improved Housing Conditions in the U.S.: Do Moving Distance and Relocation Services Matter?" *Urban Studies* 38(8): 1273–1304.

Varady, David and Carole C. Walker. 2003. "Housing Vouchers and Residential Mobility." *Journal of Planning Literature* 18(1): 17–30.

Wilson, William J. 1987. *The Truly Disadvantaged: The Inner City, the Underclass, and Public Policy*. Chicago, IL: University of Chicago Press.

Xinhao, Wang and David P. Varady. 2005. "Using Hot-Spot Analysis to Study the Clustering of Section 8 Housing Voucher Families." *Housing Studies* 20(1): 29–48.

Yin, Li. 2009. "The Dynamics of Residential Segregation in Buffalo: An Agent-based Simulation." *Urban Studies* 46(13): 2749–2770.

## Case Cited

*Comer vs. Cisneros*. 1994. 37F.3d 775.

# SHOULD LOW-INCOME HOUSING TAX CREDITS AND HOUSING CHOICE VOUCHERS BE FUNGIBLE?

## Kirk McClure

### *Introduction*

Communities throughout the U.S. labor to resolve housing affordability issues for low-income renters. There are a great many tools that they employ in this work, but the federal government continues to be the dominant provider of funds for these efforts. The federal government's two most active programs for these initiatives are the Housing Choice Voucher (HCV) and the Low-Income Housing Tax Credit (LIHTC) programs. Other programs exist, such as public housing, but these programs are in the process of slow contraction as their portfolios age and eventually fall out of service. The HCV and LIHTC programs operate, more or less, independently of each other. In this chapter I ask whether this should be the case.

These two major housing assistance programs are not fungible, and perhaps they should be. Possibly states or communities should be able to trade in dollars from one program for dollars from the other. Should communities be able to trade in LIHTC dollars for more voucher dollars or vice versa if their market conditions and affordable housing needs suggest this approach?

If the market is in short supply with too few units relative to the scale of the demand, then there is a strong argument for additional production. This suggests that it would be a beneficial strategy for the community to direct scarce resources toward producing more affordable units even if that meant foregoing some funds for vouchers. If the market has a surplus of affordable units and affordability problems are more a function of inadequate income on the part of the population, then there is a strong argument for additional vouchers. It could be a beneficial strategy for the community to direct housing resources toward providing more income assistance earmarked for housing consumption even if that meant foregoing some funds for low-income housing tax credits.

Closely related to exchanging funds between programs is the need to facilitate successful mergers of these programs. There is no mechanism for a community to creatively partner the two programs together, and perhaps there should be. Should communities be able to join the two programs together as a way to resolve affordable housing problems where neither program can succeed individually?

If the market has a need for additional production and the market is unable to provide affordable housing opportunities for the poorest renter households, then joining the HCV and the LIHTC program makes sense. The LIHTC program produces units where the market would not, but it serves the least worst off of the poor. The HCV program servers the poorest of the poor, but only where a landlord is willing and able to accept a voucher. Joining these programs can provide additional units for the poorest of the poor where these units are needed.

These problems are not the only forms of the housing affordability problem. A community may experience a combination of the two. The nation's housing markets are not neat and tidy places; there is a wide array of problem types as market conditions differ widely. Markets can simultaneously suffer from both a supply shortage as well as inadequate income on the part of the households in need of affordable housing. To resolve these problems, it would be helpful if communities could better tailor these programs to fit the housing market conditions that exist locally.

### Review of the Programs: Two Major Programs are Now Active and Serving Low-Income Renters

*Housing Choice Vouchers: Quick History of the Program*

The Housing Choice Voucher program is the nation's largest program for low-income renters. It was previously known as the Section 8 Existing Housing program. It was created as part of the landmark Housing and Community Development Act of 1974 which ended urban renewal and began a new era of housing for the poor. With only a few relatively minor exceptions, federal ventures into assisted rental housing prior to this act were all project-based programs, where the subsidy was attached to the unit. This was true whether the housing was owned by a branch of local government, such as a public housing authority, or was owned by private investors such as with the Section

236 interest reduction subsidy program. The Act adopted the notion of tenant-based housing assistance where the subsidy is attached to the household in the form of an income supplement helping them to consume existing housing in the marketplace. The Existing Housing program offered certificates that could be accepted by landlords in partial payment of rent. The certificates were later renamed vouchers after minor adjustments in the programs rules.

The Act of 1974 did not abandon the concept of project-based housing; it simply modified the approach. In addition to the Section 8 Existing Housing program, the Act included a second version of the Section 8 program, the New Construction/Substantial Rehabilitation program. As its name implies, this project-based program attached Section 8 certificates to units either newly built or rehabilitated for low-income occupancy. The certificate was attached to the unit for at least 15 years which permitted the owner to leverage a loan to finance the development. This program was actively implemented by the Carter administration only to be canceled by the Reagan administration.

The existing housing program has continued since its inception and has grown in funding during most years, but it has also suffered from some periods of unstable funding. As might be expected with any program as it matures over multiple decades, alternative approaches are implemented. There are ten different versions of the Housing Choice voucher. The program permits vouchers to be used to help very low-income households purchase a home rather than the more conventional use to help rent a unit. The homeownership vouchers have rarely been used. The program has specialized vouchers for various sub-populations such as the disabled, those threatened with homelessness, and those who are participating in the Welfare-to-Work program. Despite these variants, over 96 percent of all vouchers are in the conventional tenant-based program in which the household is free to rent any unit that passes program rules.

*Housing Choice Vouchers: Workings of the Program*

The Housing Choice Voucher program helps about 2.25 million households nationwide. Despite its $17 billion annual price tag (U.S. Department of Housing and Urban Development 2009), this is far less than what is needed. Thus, among the most important features of the HCV program is that it is subject to budget discretion. It is not an entitlement, and must be rationed. The program is administered by over 2,700 public housing authorities (PHAs) (Sard 2001). Each PHA maintains a waiting list for vouchers as they become available. Rather than first-come-first-served, the waiting lists are managed with a set of priorities that permit certain especially deserving households to rise more quickly to the top of the list. The priorities are both mandated by the federal government and by local decision making.

As Congress provides funding for additional new vouchers, they are allocated on a competitive basis and the full allocation to each jurisdiction is relatively stable over time. Local PHAs may apply for funding to operate Section 8 programs by responding to Notices of Funding Availability (NOFA) published in the *Federal Register*. Each NOFA identifies allocation areas, amounts of funds available per area, and the selection criteria for rating and ranking applications (U.S. Department of Housing and Urban Development 2010b).

The program permits households to participate in the program if their household income falls below 80 percent of the metropolitan Area Median Family Income (AMFI) or, if located in a non-metropolitan area, below 80 percent of the median county AMFI. However, eligibility for the program is effectively much more limited. The law requires that 75 percent of the households assisted by a PHA must have an income that does not exceed 30 percent of the AMFI. Given this constraint, the program is intended to help the poorest of the poor. The average household in the HCV program is in the 22nd percentile of AMFI.

A household that is issued a voucher must find a unit that is acceptable to the program. This may be the unit already occupied by the household, or the household is free to move elsewhere, including outside the jurisdiction of the PHA. The unit must pass a physical inspection to ensure that it meets minimum standards of health and safety. The rent charged for the unit along with the cost of any tenant-paid utilities must pass a test for reasonableness. The household normally pays 30 percent of its income toward housing costs and the program pays the remainder, but there are limits to this subsidy contribution.

The PHA sets what is called a payment standard. This is the amount generally needed to rent a moderately-priced rental unit in the local housing market. The payment standard is used to calculate the amount of housing assistance a household will receive, but it does not limit the amount of rent a landlord may charge or the amount a family may pay. A household can select a unit with a rent that is above or below the payment standard. In either case, the housing voucher household must pay at least 30 percent of its income for rent and utilities, but if the rent is greater than the payment standard the household must pay the additional amount but may not pay more than 40 percent of its income for rent (U.S. Department of Housing and Urban Development 2010a).

The payment standard is initially set according to what are called Fair Market Rent (FMR) levels. The FMRs are established either across an entire metropolitan area or a non-metropolitan county. The FMR is set at the 40th percentile of the rents in the market. Set at this level, the program is not designed to allow households to enter into any apartment but only those apartments offered at moderate rent levels (U.S. Department of Housing and Urban Development 2007). Some markets are given FMRs set at a higher 50th percentile reflecting the tighter market conditions. PHAs are also allowed to set payment standards that are 10 percent higher or 10 percent lower than the FMR at their discretion. With approval from the U.S. Department of Housing and Urban Development (HUD), a PHA may move beyond the 110 percent limit.

## Housing Choice Vouchers: Evaluation of the Program's Strengths

Like any federal program, the HCV program has its critics, but despite all of this, the program works. It has existed for over 35 years, operates nationwide, and helps millions of people. The subsidy is the difference between the payment standard (based upon rents found in the metropolitan area or non-metropolitan counties) or the gross rent, whichever is lower. This effectively excludes many rental units because about one-half charge rents above the Fair Market Rents. Thus, a finite amount of money (the $17 billion in the federal budget) gets divided across only as many households as can be subsidized given their low income (typically about $13,000 but $12,000 when adjusted by HUD) and the cost of renting (typical gross rent is $890 dollars per month). This yields a typical subsidy cost per household of $550 per month.

The process of setting fair market rents for every county in the United States along with setting payment standards and exceptions to them is hardly simple. However, it is a process that has proven to be manageable. The program is working in all parts of the nation and in most neighborhoods. There are about 210,000 census block groups in the nation with 98 percent containing rental units and 88 percent containing rental units offered at rents below the applicable FMRs.

The HCV program makes entry into 70 percent of the total block groups, a high level of market entry (McClure 2010).

The HCV program offers mobility, and this mobility is popular. "Its most important advantage is that vouchers give recipients the freedom to choose the kinds of housing and the locations that best meet their needs" (Turner 2003). This mobility means that the HCV program enjoys high levels of satisfaction among its participating households, especially for those who use the voucher as a means to move to a neighborhood with reduced crime and improved access to services (Comey et al. 2008; Briggs and Turner 2006; Varady and Walker 2003). Very low-income households with vouchers are far less likely to be paying unaffordable housing cost burdens, and more likely to be living in decent quality housing than their poor counterparts (U.S. Department of Housing and Urban Development 2000). The vast majority pay 30 percent of income for housing. About 17 percent pay more than 40 percent of income for housing and this appears to be due to short-term fluctuations in income rather than an inability of the program to accommodate variations in the marketplace (McClure 2005).

The bottom line is that the program is relatively efficient; nearly all of the federal tax expenditure goes into the consumption of housing. Unlike a direct income supplement, the HCV program compels consumption of housing that meets or exceeds standards for minimum physical condition. The program serves the poorest of the poor, helping those in need while permitting some local identification of priorities. Generally, the program makes the consumption of this housing affordable for these participating households and provides the means to move to good neighborhoods.

*Housing Choice Vouchers: Evaluation of the Program's Weaknesses*

The program is not without its failings. Many households who rise to the top of the waiting list are given vouchers only to fail to find a unit that meets program guidelines. Generally, only about 69 percent of households given vouchers are successful in finding a unit that will pass inspection and rent reasonableness tests and signing a lease with a landlord. This success rate is down from 81 percent in the late 1980s (Finkel and Buron 2001). Market conditions may contribute to this reduced success rate as many housing markets were suffering from low vacancy rates during the late 1990s and the first decade of the 2000s.

The tight market conditions could make it harder for households to find rental units acceptable to the HCV program.

While the freedom to choose where to live may be the greatest strength of the program, this strength has not translated into a level of mobility that might have been expected. Racial and economic segregation remain strong in the nation's housing markets. The poor tend to be spatially concentrated, and this is compounded by the segregation of racial and ethnic minorities who tend to be disproportionately poor and subject to further discrimination in housing markets.

Table 1 reports on the over 200,000 census block groups nationwide, which are proxies for neighborhoods. The 2000 Census found that about 14 percent of the population lived below poverty. Yet, over one-half of the neighborhoods in the United States enjoy low levels of poverty, less than 10 percent. These low-poverty neighborhoods do not contain rental housing in comparable shares. Low-poverty neighborhoods are 52 percent of all neighborhoods, but they contain only 38 percent of all rental housing. This indicates that voucher households will not be able to exercise the freedom to move to less disadvantaged neighborhoods without confronting difficulties; disproportionately fewer units are available. The HCV program introduces one additional problem in that the limitation on rents from the FMRs further reduces the available units, and again, the reduction is disproportionately large in the desirable low-poverty neighborhoods. The low-poverty neighborhoods contain 38 percent of all rental housing, but they contain only 28 percent of the units offered below the FMR. Thus, this 28 percent figure becomes a benchmark against which to assess the workings of the HCV program. Are the poor households in the HCV program gaining entry into low-poverty neighborhoods in proportion to the availability of affordable rental housing?

It appears that HCV households are entering the more desirable low-poverty neighborhoods roughly on a par with the availability of units rented at or below the FMR. About 28 percent of these units are found there, and a comparable 27 percent of HCV households enter into these neighborhoods. Sadly, race appears to be a factor. White households with vouchers manage to enter the low-poverty areas in greater proportion than would be expected, sending 35 percent into these areas. This is just three percentage points below the share of all rental units, independent of price, that are found in the low poverty neighborhoods and eight percentage points above the share of rental units offered below the FMR. This indicates that non-Hispanic white

HCV households, who presumably confront no racial or ethnic discrimination, are able to gain entry into these desirable neighborhoods
and to overcome the disproportionately low share of units that are
available at rents below the FMR. Non-Hispanic whites are able to
enter low-poverty neighborhoods with a share that is 12 percentage
points greater than the share of black HCV households. Blacks, at 23
percent, and Hispanics, at 20 percent, both enter these more desirable
neighborhoods at levels that are less than the availability of units.

This suggests that the HCV program is not doing all that it could
and should do to facilitate the movement of poor households out of
areas with high poverty and into areas with lower poverty. It is performing relatively well for poor white households, but decidedly less
well for racial and ethnic minorities.

*Low-Income Housing Tax Credit: Quick History of the Program*

The LIHTC program was created as part of the Tax Reform Act of
1986. Two forces were at work to support the creation of this program.
First, the Reagan administration had previously stopped funding the
Section 8 New Construction/Substantial Rehabilitation program, the
project-based component of the Section 8 programs. This meant that
there was no major program for the production of affordable rental
housing, and proponents for this type of housing were calling for either
the restoration of funding for the project-based program or the development of a replacement program. Second, the pressure for tax reform
was mounting, calling for the closing of what were deemed to be excessive loop-holes in the tax code. Beneficial treatment of income from
real estate was among these loop-holes. Many called for flat taxes,
President Reagan among them. The Act that passed in 1986 did not
result in flat taxes, but it did significantly flatten them, a move that
would have cost the federal government a huge amount of revenue had
it not been for the removal of many tax benefits, especially those for
investment in real estate. Unfortunately, the removal of tax benefits for
real estate in general also removed many of the tax benefits that helped
build affordable housing. These benefits included accelerated depreciation and the capacity to shelter active income from non-real estate
sources with paper losses from the accelerated depreciation of real
estate. The proponents of affordable housing called for and received a
provision in the tax code that would grant tax credits to some rental
units that were developed for occupancy by low- or moderate-income

Table 1. Housing Choice Vouchers in Block Groups during 2008 by Level of Poverty in the Block Group

| | Level of poverty in block group | | | | |
| --- | --- | --- | --- | --- | --- |
| | Low Less than 10% | Average 10 to 14% | Moderate 15 to 39% | High 40+% | All block groups |
| All block groups | 108,253 52% | 32,767 16% | 57,537 27% | 11,317 5% | 209,874 100% |
| All rental units | 14,655,207 38% | 6,777,727 18% | 14,163,762 37% | 3,111,081 8% | 38,707,777 100% |
| Rental units with rents | 5,214,971 | 3,130,707 | 8,230,228 | 1,999,783 | 18,575,689 |
| Below fair market rent | 28% | 17% | 44% | 11% | 100% |
| HCV households in 2008 | 589,023 | 364,712 | 1,010,089 | 202,174 | 2,165,998 |
| Percent of all HCV households | 27% | 17% | 47% | 9% | 100% |
| HCV households by race/ethnicity | | | | | |
| Non-Hispanic Whites | 35% | 21% | 40% | 4% | 100% |
| Non-Hispanic Blacks | 23% | 15% | 50% | 12% | 100% |
| Non-Hispanic Asian race | 32% | 18% | 43% | 7% | 100% |
| Non-Hispanic other race | 29% | 17% | 48% | 6% | 100% |
| Hispanics any race | 20% | 14% | 52% | 14% | 100% |

*Source:* U.S. Bureau of the Census, Census 2000, SF3; U. S. Department of Housing and Urban Development, 2008.

households. This provision, incorporated in Section 42 of the tax code, is what we know today as the LIHTC program.

Since its inceptions in 1986, the program has placed in service over 1.6 million units in about 2,900 developments through 2006. Typically, the program produces between 90,000 and 100,000 units per year in all 50 states, plus the District of Columbia, Puerto Rico and the Virgin Islands. These developments range from as small as a single unit to quite large developments. The median development is 32 units with one-half of all developments containing between 12 and 64 units.

The annual cost of the LIHTC program is unclear as tax credits do not appear as a budget line item. However, costs are estimated to be in excess of $6 billion per year. This figure is a little hard to calibrate as each annual allocation represents credits that will be claimed by investors over a 10-year period.

*Low-Income Housing Tax Credit: Workings of the Program*

The amount of subsidy provided annually by the LIHTC program is statutory. This is a strength of the program in that the amount of the tax credits given to each state is specified in the law making it relatively immune from annual budget battles. This is a weakness in that housing projects that might meet the requirements of the program are not automatically entitled to the credits. The amount of credits awarded to each state is much less than the amount that is sought, making these tax credits a scarce resource. Project proposals must compete for the limited available funding. This competition is conducted, usually annually or semi-annually, by each state's housing finance agency.

The winning projects must complete the development, whether new construction or rehabilitation of existing properties. When the project is occupied, the property owners receive tax credits over a 10-year period, provided that the units maintain restricted-income occupancy for at least 15 years. Projects built since 1990 must pledge to maintain low-income occupancy for a period of 30 years, but after 15 years, the owners may notify the state housing finance agency of their intention to sell the property. The state agency then has one year to find a buyer who will pay a price specified in the statute and who is willing to maintain the property in income-restricted occupancy. This price requires repayment of the original owners' equity investment (even though this has already been repaid by receipt of the tax credit) as well as remaining debt. Given this double payment of equity, the price is generally too high for any buyer. When no buyer is found, the owners may sell or, as is more common, seek to win another set of tax credits on the property with a modified set of owners. This starts the 15 year compliance period over again.

The owners of the property receiving LIHTCs may claim credits only against units occupied by income-eligible households. No credits may be claimed unless:

1. At least 20 percent of the units are occupied by households whose income is less than 50 percent of the metropolitan area's median family income,

   or

2. At least 40 percent of the units are occupied by households whose income is less than 60 percent of the metropolitan area's median family income.

The developer must choose to meet one of these two standards before the housing begins operations. As the program does not grant any greater benefits for serving households whose income is below the 50th percentile, the less restrictive 60th percentile is more popular except where states mandate the lower figure.

The amount of the credits that can be claimed by an individual project are a function of the costs of the building construction, site improvements, and equipment, which comprise the credit basis. These include most development costs other than land plus a few other development expenses. Credits are allowed either in the amount of about nine percent of the credit basis or four percent. The higher figure is allowed if the development is not financed through the use of bonds with interest that is exempt from federal taxation. If tax exempt bond financing is used, then the lower 4 percent credit amount is applied to the credit basis. One other important distinction is that only the nine percent tax credits are subject to the limited amount of tax credits allocated to each state. The four percent credits are limited by the ceiling on the amount of private activity bonds that each state may issue annually.

Rents on the units against which credits are claimed are determined according to affordability standards set for the metropolitan area or non-metropolitan county. These rents are based on what an income eligible family could afford if it paid 30 percent of its income for housing, including contract rent plus tenant-paid utility expenses. These rents vary with the number of bedrooms in the unit. The allowed rents are based on metropolitan household income and expense criteria, not the income or utility expenses of the actual tenant residing in the unit. As a result, the program does not guarantee that an individual tenant household will not have to pay more than 30 percent of its income for rent, only that the rent will be held down to a level considered affordable for a household at the top of the eligible income category. The state housing finance agency enforces the income and rent limits and is responsible for periodic inspection of the physical condition of the units. If the development is failing to comply with any of the program's provisions, then a notice of noncompliance may be issued. If noncompliance becomes sufficiently severe, tax credits may be recaptured and penalties imposed on the property owners.

### Low-Income Housing Tax Credit: Evaluation of the Program's Strengths

#### Strong Portfolio

The LIHTC program is now the nation's primary mechanism for the production of newly constructed or rehabilitated rental housing for low-income households (U.S. Department of Housing and Urban Development 2005). The program was, until very recently, healthy and producing in excess of 90,000 units per year in about 1,300 projects. Occupancy levels are good at 95 percent, compared to 90 percent for rental housing nationwide (Joint Center for Housing Studies 2005, Multi-Housing News 2004). LIHTC projects were generating high levels of net operating income relative to their loan obligations. The vast majority of these developments are producing positive case flows annually, and the foreclosure rate is extremely low at 0.01 percent (Multi-Housing News 2004).

#### Quality of the Neighborhoods Entered

The history of project-based housing assistance is a story of projects placed in less than desirable neighborhoods. Project-based assisted housing for the poor is all too often located in neighborhoods with high concentrations of the poor and minorities (Rohe and Freeman 2001). The location of assisted housing developments remains a problem, but the LIHTC program has proven to be an improvement in this regard. Newman and Schnare (1997) compared the characteristics of neighborhoods where project-based developments are located with those of other renter households. They found that project-based programs do little to improve the quality of the assisted household's neighborhood conditions and that public housing actually makes things worse. Compared with all rental units, units in project-based developments are significantly more concentrated in low-income neighborhoods. Thus, project-based housing programs have not contributed to reducing concentrations of poverty; in fact, they appear to have exacerbated the problem.

Freeman (2004) re-examined this issue comparing LIHTC units with other project-based developments. He compared the neighborhoods where LIHTC developments are located with the neighborhoods of other project-based programs. He found that LIHTC units are disproportionately located in the suburbs and suggested that the capacity to penetrate into the suburbs is due, at least in part, to fewer political constraints on these developments. The LIHTC program seems to be more acceptable to suburban communities than its predecessor project-based programs. Freeman (2004) also found that LIHTC units are located in neighborhoods where the incidence of poverty is higher than it is for the population as a whole. However, those LIHTC units that did locate in the suburbs were located in neighborhoods with higher median incomes and lower levels of poverty than the central-city neighborhoods where other LIHTC units were located. Freeman states, "Taken together, then, the results…tell a consistent story. LIHTC neighborhoods are not as economically disadvantaged as those with traditional federally assisted housing developments" (2004;9).

Table 2 looks at where LIHTC units are located in terms of the concentration of poverty. One might expect the program to follow the pattern of other project-based programs and further the concentration of the poor into areas with high levels of poverty. Instead, the LIHTC program appears to have performed on a par with the tenant-based HCV program. The LIHTC program located 26 percent of its units in the low-poverty neighborhoods of the nation, only a single percentage point behind the HCV program. Both programs send about 60 percent or more of their households into the neighborhoods with average and moderate levels of poverty. The LIHTC does make greater entry into high-poverty neighborhoods than does the HVC program. About 14 percent of the LIHTC units are located there, compared to only five percent for voucher households. The low presence of vouchers in these highly impoverished neighborhoods may reflect the mobility granted to households in the HCV program. The higher presence of LIHTC units may reflect the desire of developers, communities, and nonprofit organizations to serve the population in these distressed neighborhoods.

Table 2. Low-Income Housing Tax Credit Units Put in Place through 2006 by Level of Poverty in the Block Group

| | Level of poverty in block group | | | | |
|---|---|---|---|---|---|
| | Low less than 10% | Average 10 to 14% | Moderate 15 to 39% | High 40+% | All block groups |
| All block | 108,253 | 32,767 | 57,537 | 11,317 | 209,874 |
| groups | 52% | 16% | 27% | 5% | 100% |
| All rental | 14,655,207 | 6,777,727 | 14,163,762 | 3,111,081 | 38,707,777 |
| units | 38% | 18% | 37% | 8% | 100% |
| LIHTC | 368,584 | 210,450 | 625,466 | 198,499 | 1,402,999 |
| units | 26% | 15% | 45% | 14% | 100% |

*Source:* U.S. Bureau of the Census, Census 2000, SF3; U. S. Department of Housing and Urban Development, 2008.

*Investment Returns*

A quick history of the LIHTC program as a form of investment can be found in the prices earned in the marketplace for each dollar of tax credit. When the program began in the late 1980s, the tax credits were deemed to be high risk investments. Investors paid only 45 cents per dollar of tax credit. This translates into the investors demanding yields of 17 to 19 percent. This fell through the 1990s and into the first decade of the new millennium. Tax credits earned prices upwards to 90 cents on the dollar which translates into yields as low as three percent, effectively equivalent to the yield on 10-year government bonds. The perception of risk clearly had fallen, perhaps too far.

*Low-Income Housing Tax Credit: Evaluation of the Program's Weaknesses*

*The Financial Crisis*

This successful trend in rising prices (falling yields) on tax credits came to a halt in 2008 and 2009 when the financial crisis hit. As Fannie Mae and Freddie Mac, two of the largest purchasers of tax credits, went into receivership, and as many of the largest banks, who also purchased large quantities of tax credits, ceased to be profitable, few buyers existed for tax credits. The problem was not only that the price of credits fell, but also that credits simply went without buyers. Developments could not close loans and go into construction because they could not secure the crucial syndication proceeds from the sale of tax credits.

In response to this problem, the American Recovery and Reinvestment Act of 2009 provides states with a pair of temporary programs to offset declining investor interest for housing tax credits. These include:

- The Tax Credit Assistance Program (TCAP) which provides grants or loans over and above the tax credits to help projects move forward that were stalled by the financial crisis, and
- The Tax Credit Exchange Program (TCEP) which allows states to exchange a portion of 2008 and 2009 credit allocations for cash with the cash available to make grants or loans to projects to make them feasible.

It is too early to know how well these two programs worked, but their mere presence signals the vulnerability of the LIHTC program to many problems found in credit markets.

*Failure to Create Mixed-Income Housing*
Critics of the LIHTC program call for it to play a larger role in providing mixed-income housing (American Bankers Association et al. 2004, Freeman 2004). The program was initially viewed as an incentive that would cause developers to set aside a fraction of their newly built or rehabilitated units for households with low income. The tax credit rules call for a minimum of 20 percent of units to be set aside for those whose income is less than 50 percent of the AMFI or a minimum of 40 percent of the units to be set aside for those whose income is less than 60 percent of the AMFI. If the goal was to develop mixed-income housing, then setting minimums may have been the wrong approach. About 84 percent of LIHTC developments placed in service through 2002 have tax credits applied to all units (U.S. Department of Housing and Urban Development 2005). With nearly all LIHTC units located in developments occupied entirely by low-income households, there is very little income mixing within the developments; the residents are all very low-income households.

*Failure to Serve the Truly Needy*
The LIHTC program is not designed to directly serve the poorest of the poor. It serves households with incomes below 60 percent of the AMFI, although the owner may choose to serve only those with incomes under 50 percent. LIHTC developments generally charge rents that are at or close to the maximum permitted by the program. The rents are not directly tied to the household's income as is true with

the HCV program. Rather, units are leased only to any income eligible household with enough income to afford the rent. A study of LIHTC developments found that resident households that did not receive vouchers or other rental assistance subsidy had incomes placing them at 45 percent of the AMFI (Ernst & Young LLP, Kenneth Leventhal Real Estate Group 1997). By comparison, among HCVP households, the average income is 22 percent of the AMFI (McClure 2005).

Because rents in the program are set for households with incomes at 60 percent of the AMFI, LIHTC units are generally too expensive for the renter households with incomes below the 30 percent level unless they receive additional subsidy, such as through vouchers. Nationally, a renter household in 2000 with income placing it at the 30th percentile of median family income could afford a gross rent of no more than about $390. While the rents of LIHTC units are not known with precision, the typical LIHTC development in 2000 had rent limits ranging from $700 to $900, depending upon unit size and which income limitation was selected. Knowing that the LIHTC program creates incentives for property owners to charge rents close to this maximum, the rents in LIHTC developments are considerably above what a household could afford with income below the 30 percent level.

*Building in Markets with a Surplus of Similarly Priced Units*
Ideally, the LIHTC program is placing units into neighborhoods where there is unmet demand for such housing. This is the idea behind the market analysis requirement imposed on all developers' applications for tax credits (Guggenheim 2003). Unmet demand means that there are households in the immediate market who are not served by the existing supply of rental housing.

The unmet demand for affordable rental housing is estimated for all census tracts across the country for the year 2000, using decennial census data. The unmet demand is calculated as the number of renter households whose income falls between 30 percent and 60 percent of the AMFI for the metropolitan area or non-metropolitan county minus the number of rental units affordable to these households. Table 3 lists the extent to which the LIHTC program located units in the years immediately after the 2000 census to resolve the problems arising from this demand in excess of supply.

The table shows that the LIHTC program is not directing units to markets with a shortage of units in the price range served by the program. Rather, the program is adding units in those markets that have a surplus of units in this price range. Only 6.5 percent of LIHTC units are being built where there is a shortage of housing in the price range served by the program. Nearly half are being built in census tracts where there is already a surplus of over 200 units.

These results suggest that the implementation of the LIHTC program is not working well. The tax credits are allocated to developers through competitions held by state housing finance agencies. The agencies allocate these units based upon a Qualified Allocation Plan (QAP), which is supposed to direct these housing tax credits to the greatest areas of need. While this plan is federally mandated, states are granted wide latitude to use the federal tax credits in the manner best suited to the needs identified by each state. The analysis shown here suggests that the QAPs do not seem to be doing their job.

*Market Need*
The American Housing Survey for 2007 finds that there is a shortage of units only for households with the lowest income (U.S. Census Bureau 20010a). See Table 4. The survey reports that there were about 11.8 million renter households with income below 30 percent of AMFI.

Table 3. Count of LIHTC Units Developed 2000–2004 in Tracts by Category of Shortage or Surplus of Rental Units for Renter Housings with Income between 30 and 60 Percent of AMFI

| Category of surplus (shortage) of affordable units | LIHTC units developed | Percent of units developed | Tracts entered | Percent of tracts entered |
|---|---|---|---|---|
| Shortage greater than 100 units | 3,823 | 0.8% | 36 | 0.3% |
| Shortage less than 100 units | 26,269 | 5.7% | 411 | 3.1% |
| Surplus less than 100 units | 111,768 | 24.4% | 3,614 | 27.1% |
| Surplus 100 to 199 units | 104,255 | 22.7% | 3,682 | 27.6% |
| Surplus 200+ units | 212,401 | 46.3% | 514 | 3.9% |
| Total | 458,516 | 100.0% | 13,349 | 100.0% |

*Source:* U.S. Bureau of the Census, Census 2000, SF3; U. S. Department of Housing and Urban Development, 2008.

This group is known as the extremely low-income population. A household at the 30th percentile in 2007 had an income of about $17,700. These households could afford gross rents (contract rent plus tenant-paid utilities) of no more than $443 per month. There are only 5.2 million rental units in the nation renting below that level, far less than the number of extremely low-income households. This results in a shortfall in 2007 of about 6.6 million rental units. This number can be reduced by the 2.2 million households in the HCV program as the Census Bureau reports rents before subsidy, but this still leaves over 4 million extremely low-income households without affordable housing. Interestingly, there is a surplus of units in the category serving renter households with income between 30 and 60 percent of AMFI. The LIHTC program is adding to this sector of the rental housing stock, a stock that is in surplus.

## Statement of the Problem

### The Need for Additional Housing for the Poorest of the Poor

There is a shortage of housing for the poorest of the poor (those with incomes below 30 percent of AMFI) but a surplus for the low-income (those with incomes between 30 and 60 percent of AMFI). There are

Table 4. Renter Households by Income Level and Rental Units Affordable to These Households

|  | Year | |
| --- | --- | --- |
|  | 2000 | 2007 |
| Renter households (000s) | | |
| Income below 30% of AMFI | 9,913 | 11,869 |
| Income between 30 and 60% of AMFI | 9,659 | 10,839 |
| Rental units with rents affordable to households (000s) | | |
| Income below 30% of AMFI | 6,769 | 5,222 |
| Income between 30 and 60% of AMFI | 20,659 | 15,306 |
| Surplus or deficit (000s) | | |
| Income below 30% of AMFI | -3,144 | -6,647 |
| Income between 30 and 60% of AMFI | 11,000 | 4,467 |

Source: U.S. Bureau of the Census, Census 2000; U.S. Bureau of the Census, American Housing Survey 2007.

11.9 million extremely low-income renter households, and the vast majority of these pay more than 30 percent of income on housing and do not receive assistance to reduce this housing cost burden. Despite the level of federal spending on housing assistance the government serves only about 1 in 5 households in need. Turner (2003) suggests that we are doing better serving 1 in every 3 households in need when examining other forms of assisted housing.

*Problems with the HCV Program*
The HCV is performing well. It effectively reduces the housing cost burden for millions of households who are of extremely low income. It provides mobility to households, helping them move to neighborhoods with low levels of poverty. Unfortunately, only white households are able to move into these low-poverty neighborhoods at a rate exceeding the availability of affordable units; the HCV program has not broken down all of the racial and ethnic barriers that inhibit living in these markets.

The nation funds about 2.2 million vouchers, yet it is unlikely that this number will change in any significant way. Incremental growth and stagnation is the history of funding for tenant-based assistance. The portfolio of HCV households has shown uneven growth over time. The program began with 600,000 households and, with a few plateaus, inched up, adding 50,000 to 60,000 additional households each year. There is no indication that it will grow by the whole multiples needed to serve all or even most of the needy households.

Where the HCV program fails is in the rate at which its participating households are able to find units at all. Too many fail to find a unit when given a voucher, and when they find that unit, too often the unit is located in a distressed neighborhood with concentrated poverty and few opportunities for good employment or high quality education.

*Problems with the LIHTC Program*
The LIHTC program, although complex with its system of selling tax credits to investors, can produce housing developments that will leverage investments and these investments will perform well. In addition, these developments are making entry into low-poverty neighborhoods on a par with the HCV program and much better than project-based housing programs of the past.

However, these LIHTC developments are not serving the goal of providing mixed-income housing. Rather, the LIHTC program is repeating mistakes of the past by concentrating low-income people into a project housing only other low-income people, denying the income mixing that is needed and furthering the stigma attached to low-income housing projects. In addition, the LIHTC program is building units in markets where there is little or no need for additional units in this program range. Finally, the program is building units for a segment of the low-income population for which there are sufficient units. The program is not serving the poorest of the poor.

## Solutions

Solutions to some of these problems require a huge budget commitment. Significantly expanding the level of funding to the HCV program is unlikely. However, some of the solutions are revenue neutral or at least close to it and these are well worth exploring.

### Modifications to the HCV Program

#### Improved Counseling of Participating Households

The PHAs that administer the HCV program perform well. They work with a large volume of clients, work with a nearly as large volume of landlords, inspect millions of apartments, and process a huge number of payments. Unfortunately, the current administrative procedures used in the HCV program provide little guidance to the households admitted to the program. The level of individual counseling given to each entering household is little more than an explanation of the rules of the program. More intensive counseling has shown itself to be beneficial to the households, especially when this counseling moves to the level of case management and guidance in more than just finding and leasing a home (Johnson 2005; Cunningham et al. 2002; Shroder 2002). In fact, counseling is crucial if adopting requirements that the households move to high opportunity neighborhoods. The Gautreaux and the Moving to Opportunity programs demonstrate that successful movement is dependent upon adequate counseling (Rubinowitz and Rosenbaum 2000; Rosenbaum and Harris 2001). If the HCV program is truly to achieve the mobility that its designers hoped for, it is clear that improved household counseling and case management are needed.

### Metropolitan Scale Administration

Katz and Turner (2001) recommend that the HCV program be administered by agencies serving entire metropolitan areas, rather than PHAs who serve an individual municipality. They argue that the program can only achieve its full potential if it is administered in a manner that helps households to overcome the barriers to entry into desirable housing markets. The current system of administration by local PHAs reinforces these market barriers. The fragmented structure of administration, with many PHAs operating within a single metropolitan area, undermines the mobility of households beyond the boundaries of individual cities. It also inhibits outreach to landlords throughout the metropolitan area, especially in desirable low-poverty neighborhoods that may lie beyond the city limits of the individual PHAs' cities. If the HCV program could be administered at the metropolitan scale, it could facilitate and enhance the poverty deconcentration that is slowly taking place through the program.

*Raise the FMRs*
One-half of the neighborhoods in the nation are low-poverty markets, but only about one-fourth of the rental units offered below the FMRs are found in these neighborhoods. Too many households, 30 percent and more, are unsuccessful in finding a suitable rental unit when given a voucher. HUD already has a mechanism in place permitting PHAs to raise payment standards by 10 percent at their own discretion. HUD can also grant exceptions to raise payment standards further. At this point, the analysis for raising payment standards examines the entire market. HUD should begin to examine smaller submarkets in its consideration of raising market standards. These submarkets should be high opportunity neighborhoods with low poverty and good schools and jobs. Where these high opportunity neighborhoods offer few rental units with rents below the FMRs, the exceptions should be considered.

*Redesign Incentives in the LIHTC Program*

*Direct LIHTC Units to Markets with a Need*
Perhaps the government should re-examine the implementation of the LIHTC program. It may be time to recognize that not all markets need additional units. Katz and Turner (2007) called for revising the system through which the tax credits are allocated. They suggested that credits should be directed to markets where there is a demonstrable need for production of units. Many markets need resources to renovate existing units, which is possible within the LIHTC program. However, this means that the QAPs need to direct the developers into this approach

of renovating existing rather than adding units to submarkets that already have a glut of units. The LIHTC program is a highly decentralized program depending upon state housing finance agencies to monitor the developers. But who is monitoring the state housing finance agencies? These agencies are showing a collective disregard for the market analysis requirements of the program. Congress should consider stiffening the mandates associated with the QAPs. They need some teeth; if a need for additional units is not found in a market, the agency should not award tax credits. Unfortunately, states are in a "use-it-or-lose-it" frame of mind in the use of tax credits. They would rather use the tax credits poorly than turn away federal housing subsidies for their state. The federal government needs to offer alternatives to states so that these scarce housing resources are better utilized in ways that fit local market conditions.

*Help the LIHTC Program Serve Extremely Low-Income Households*
The LIHTC program could be made to serve extremely low-income households by pairing it with Housing Choice Vouchers. While this can be done now, the two programs are not designed to facilitate this process. A developer cannot easily attach vouchers to tax credit units to serve the neediest households. Right now HUD is experimenting with ways to attach vouchers to units that may provide solutions to this problem.

PHAs are permitted to allocate up to 20 percent of their vouchers for use as Project-Based Vouchers (PBVs), but this approach is not widely used. The value of attaching vouchers to buildings is that it provides the income stream that building owners need in order to leverage private financing. This was done successfully in the late 1970s and early 1980s with the Section 8 New Construction/Substantial Rehabilitation programs. While these projects were able to raise private capital, too often they concentrated poverty. The PBV program overcomes this problem by permitting vouchers to be attached to not more than 25 percent of the units in a development unless it serves a special needs population, such as the elderly or the disabled. Also new with the PBV is the ability of the participating household to move from the development but continue to receive rental assistance. After one year in the PBV unit, the household may move with a voucher from the PHA, and the PHA fills the vacant unit with a family from its waiting list. HUD is expanding this PBV idea by allowing PHAs to convert public housing into PBV units so as to tap into the private credit markets. This would reduce the demand upon the public housing funds, and increase use of rental assistance for these units in order to leverage private loans for improving units (Sard 2001).

These initiatives could be applied to LIHTC development as well. Project-based vouchers could be offered as a means to help LIHTC projects serve a poorer population and to help leverage private financing. The vouchers serve a population with lower income than can be served by the LIHTC program alone. The vouchers would also provide a stable source of income that will appeal to lenders who seek confidence that the project's debt will be repaid on schedule.

There is little question that there are too few rental units priced at levels low enough to be affordable to the poor. What is not clear is whether or not the answer to this problem is to build more units serving this price range, which would require deep subsidy, or to simply give vouchers to the poor so that they could afford rental units existing in the marketplace that are priced out of the reach of the poor. Attaching vouchers to tax credit units would deepen the reach of the LIHTC program so that it can serve truly poor households. Currently it is estimated that one-third of LIHTC units are occupied by households with vouchers (Ernst & Young 1997). However, these vouchers are nearly all tenant-based vouchers that move with the household. It could help the reach of LIHTC projects if vouchers could be set aside for use with LIHTC developments. LIHTC projects would then be little different from the earlier Section 8 New Construction/Substantial Rehabilitation program which did serve a more needy population. These LIHTC projects assisted by some vouchers could also serve very special needs such as locating affordable units in low-poverty neighborhoods that offer safety, good schools and high employment opportunities. Very often, these are neighborhoods that will not provide affordable options without direct program intervention.

*Incentivize Mixed-Income Housing*

Mixed-income housing can be beneficial to all involved. Although more is unknown than known about the costs and benefits of mixed-income housing, there is evidence that it can reduce, even eliminate, the stigma attached to low-income developments. The success of mixed-income housing depends heavily upon the market conditions in the receiving neighborhood (Schwartz and Tajbakhsh 1997). Where poverty is low and where market rents are above the levels charged for units in the LIHTC program, the opportunities are right for the creation of mixed-income housing. Unfortunately, the LIHTC program too often misses these opportunities and attempts to develop projects that are to be completely occupied by low-income households. This could be avoided with some changes to the program, changes that offer bonuses to developments that provide a mix of units for low-income tenants as well as tenants who can afford market-rate units. This could even be refined further by using vouchers to encourage the use of a small portion of the units by extremely low-income households. The vouchers offer the certainty that the units will be occupied nearly all of the time, making them appealing. Such vouchers could be offered but with a provision that they could be attached to no more than 10 percent of the tax credit units. These units would serve households with incomes below 30 percent of AMFI. Another 10 percent of the units could also be covered by tax credits but without vouchers. These would serve renter households in the 30 percent to 60 percent of AMFI. If the development utilized tax credits on a proportion of all units that was no more than some ceiling, such has 20 percent, then a bonus could be offered. Bonuses are offered now in the LIHTC program for certain high cost areas and especially poor neighborhoods. This would extend the bonus rewards to those developments that foster mixed-income housing in high opportunity neighborhoods.

*Permit Fungibility between the LIHTV and HCV Programs*
Perhaps it is time to admit that the production-based LIHTC program is not doing the right job. It is building units for a segment of the market that already has enough units, builds most of these units where surpluses already exist, and is not offering units at rents affordable by the households truly in need. This suggests that states may want to consider exchanging tax credits for vouchers.

The typical LIHTC unit receives nine percent credits against newly developed rental units that cost about $120,000. After deducting the value of the land and other ineligible expenses, the typical newly developed rental unit has a credit basis of about $100,000. With a nine percent credit applied to this basis, this unit will cost the federal government about $9,000 per year in tax credits each year, for 10 years, for a total of $90,000. This will bring about the provision of 15 years of housing for a household with income between 30 to 60 percent of AMFI. Thus the cost is around $6,000 per year.

The typical HCV household has a gross rent of $890 per month of which the federal government pays $550 per month. This means that the program costs about $6,600 per year now with inflation of this figure over time. This crude arithmetic suggests that it might be plausible to permit trading dollars of tax credits for dollar of vouchers. If more precise calculations are made, then an exchange rate can be established adjusting the rate at which tax credits are traded in for vouchers.

*Is Fungibility Too Much Like Block Grants for Housing?*
Fungibility between the HCV and LIHTC programs begins to sound akin to the Bush era proposal to give states block grants and let them decide how to use the funds to resolve housing affordability problems. This proposal was opposed by many on the grounds that a block grant "does nothing to address these challenges and indeed could make them harder to overcome" (Turner 2003).

It was argued that states might reduce subsidy payments to households in order to serve more families. This could limit the range of location options for participating households, undermining the program's effectiveness in making decent housing affordable for the poorest households. States could impose time limits in hopes of encouraging self-sufficiency, leaving working poor families to face unaffordable market rent levels. States might divert voucher funds to build new housing projects ear-marked for the poor, potentially exacerbating the concentration of assisted housing in poor and minority neighborhoods. These alternative uses of the housing funds may lack the rigorous evaluation necessary to assess the effectiveness of alternative program models (Khadduri 2003; Turner and Popkin 2000).

It is possible that states and municipalities should not be trusted with unchecked discretion on the use of housing resources between types of applications (i.e., allocating some funding to tenant-based vouchers and some funding to project-based tax credits). Decisions should be made on the basis of market need and market condition, and not political pressure from interest groups. For example, homebuilders tend to favor project-based subsidy even in a glutted market while advocates for the poor favor additional vouchers even in a very tight market where they cannot be well implemented. Prior efforts to trust localities with the allocation of resources to meet market conditions have shown a bias that cannot be reconciled with market conditions. HOME funds show a heavy bias toward production programs when market conditions suggest that tenant-based programs should be favored (The Urban Institute 1995). This suggests that HUD should have oversight of any exchanges between the two programs and should ensure that the exchange is appropriate and beneficial to the markets served.

*How Would Fungibility Work with Proposals to Make Vouchers an Entitlement?*

Calls to alter the HCV program have been heard from across the political spectrum (Olsen 2001; Quigley 2008). Olsen suggests that the nation could make vouchers an entitlement program by taking all production subsidy funds (public housing and LIHTC) and placing them into the voucher program. If the program received all this funding, it could serve all very low income households suffering from a severe housing hardship, although providing fewer subsidy dollars per household per year. This would lower the amount of dollars of rent subsidy per household per month compared to what is now being paid by the program, but it would provide this smaller level of subsidy to all eligible households.

Quigley (2008) makes a similar proposal. He suggests that, if the nation was starting from scratch to build the right housing program to serve current rental housing needs, we would: make the program an entitlement rather than the lottery we have now; tighten eligibility rules to serve only the most needy; and administer the program though the IRS income tax returns by granting refundable tax credits to all eligible households. This would generate a total cost to government of $22 billion (in 2006 dollars) which could be achieved at current funding levels assuming the removal of subsidies from households with incomes above the threshold of need.

These proposals seek rather radical changes. Both would reduce or even eliminate the HCV program and, perhaps, the LIHTC production program as well. This approach is an abandonment of the housing and neighborhood goals of our two primary housing programs. These programs can add to the stock of housing in markets where there is need. These programs can help extremely low- and low-income households consume good quality rental housing at affordable rents if the program is properly administered. These programs can help to further the goals of poverty deconcentration and racial integration, if well administered. It is doubtful that any of this would be accomplished if these programs are reduced to refundable tax credits realized by the poor every April 15th.

## Concluding Discussion

Experience instructs us not to trust state and local governments to make the allocations on their own. HUD should negotiate with states individually to design the funding allocation between vouchers and tax credits. HUD can make some of the funds competitive, calling for innovative approaches to new developments that are both mixed-income and supportive of poverty deconcentration.

State housing finance agencies are production oriented, but they can be made to shift toward mixed-income housing and toward better market analysis. HUD should demand more of them so that tax credit developments enter markets with a real need and should offer vouchers that can improve the quality of this reach. States can also lead the way in assembling metropolitan scale administration of vouchers to assist in breaking down the racial and income barriers that prevent the poor from gaining access to better neighborhoods.

## References

American Bankers Association, America's Community Bankers, Mortgage Bankers Association, National Association of Homebuilders, and National Association of Realtors. 2004. *Housing Policy for the 21st Century*. Washington, DC.

Briggs, Xavier deSousa, and Margery Austin Turner. 2006. "Assisted Housing Mobility and the Success of Low-Income Minority Families: Lessons for Policy, Practice, and Future Research." *Northwestern Journal of Law & Social Policy* 1(1): 25–61.

Comey, Jennifer, Xavier de Souza Briggs, and Gretchen Weismann. 2008. *Struggling to Stay Out of High-Poverty Neighborhoods: Lessons from the Moving to Opportunity Experiment*. The Urban Institute, Metropolitan Housing and Communities Center Brief No. 6. Accessed at http://www.urbaninstitute.org/UploadedPDF/411635_high-poverty_neighborhoods.pdf.

Cunningham, Mary K., Susan J. Popkin, Erin B. Godfrey, and Beata A Bednarz. 2002. *CHAC Mobility Counseling Assessment: Final Report*. The Urban Institute. Accessed at http://www.urban.org/publications/410588.html.

Ernst & Young LLP, Kenneth Leventhal Real Estate Group. 1997. *The Low-Income Housing Tax Credit: The First Decade*. Boston.

Finkel, M., and L. Buron. 2001. *Study on Section 8 voucher success rates*. Vol. I, *Quantitative Study of Success Rates in Metropolitan Areas*. Washington, DC: U.S. Department of Housing and Urban Development.

Freeman, Lance. 2004. *Siting Affordable Housing: Location and Neighborhood Trends of Low-Income Housing Tax Credit Developments in the 1990s*. Washington, D.C.: Brookings Center on Urban and Metropolitan Policy, Census 2000 Survey Series. Retrieved from www.brookings.edu/urban/pubs/20040405_Freeman.pdf.

Guggenheim, Joseph. 2003. *Tax Credits for Low Income Housing: Opportunities for Developers, Non-Profits, Agencies and Communities Under Expanded Tax Code Provisions*, 12th Edition. Glen Echo, Maryland: Simon Publications.

Johnson, Michael P. 2005. "Spatial Decision Support for Assisted Housing Mobility Counseling." *Decision Support Systems* 41(1): 296–312.

Joint Center for Housing Studies. 2005. *The State of the Nation's Housing 2005*. Cambridge, Massachusetts: Graduate School of Design and John F. Kennedy School of Government, Harvard University.

Katz, Bruce and Margery Austin Turner. 2001. "Who Should Run the Housing Voucher Program? A Reform Proposal." *Housing Policy Debate* 12(2): 239–262.

Katz, Bruce, and Margery Austin Turner. 2007. *Rethinking U.S. Rental Housing Policy. Joint Center for Housing Studies, Harvard University.* Accessed at http://community-wealth.com/_pdfs/articles-publications/cdcs/paper-katz-turner.pdf.

Khadduri, Jill. 2003. "Should the Housing Voucher Program Become a State-Administered Block Grant?" *Housing Policy Debate* 11(3): 235–269.

McClure, Kirk. 2010. *Housing Choice Voucher Marketing Opportunity Index: Analysis of Data at the Tract and Block Group Level.* A research report prepared for the U.S. Department of Housing and Urban Development, Office of Policy Development and Research.

McClure, Kirk. 2005. "Rent Burden in the Housing Choice Voucher Program." *Cityscape: A Journal of Policy Development and Research* 8(2): 5–20.

Multi-Housing News. 2004. "E&Y Confirms Positive Returns, Performance of LIHTC Housing." *Multi-Housing News.* August 2004, p. 6.

Newman, Sandra J. and Ann B. Schnare. 1997. "'… And a Suitable Living Environment': The Failure of Housing Programs to Deliver on Neighborhood Quality." *Housing Policy Debate* 8(4): 703–741.

Olsen, Edgar O. 2001. *Hearing on Housing and Community Development Needs: The FY 2003 HUD Budget.* Testimony before the U.S. Senate Committee on Banking, Housing, and Urban Affairs.

Quigley, John. 2008. "Just Suppose: Housing Subsidies for Low-Income Renters." In *Revisiting Rental Housing: Policies, Programs, and Priorities*, Nicolas P. Retsinas and Eric S. Belsky, Editors. Cambridge, MA and Washington, DC: Joint Center for Housing Studies, Harvard University and Brookings Institution Press. Pp. 300–318.

Rohe, William M. and Lance Freeman. 2001. "Assisted Housing and Residential Segregation The Role of Race and Ethnicity in the Siting of Assisted Housing Developments." *Journal of the American Planning Association* 67(3): 279–292.

Rosenbaum, Emily, and Laura E. Harris. 2001. "Residential Mobility and Opportunities: Early Impacts of the Moving to Opportunity Demonstration Program in Chicago." *Housing Policy Debate* 12(2): 321–346.

Rubinowitz, Leonard S., and James E. Rosenbaum. 2000. *Crossing the Class and Color Lines: From Public Housing to White Suburbia.* Chicago: University of Chicago Press.

Sard, Barbara. 2001. "Housing Vouchers Should Be a Major Component of Future Housing Policy for the Lowest Income Families." *Cityscape: A Journal of Policy Development and Research* 5(2): 89–110.

Schwartz, Alex, and Kian Tajbakhsh. 1997. "Mixed-Income Housing: Unanswered Questions." *Cityscape: A Journal of Policy Development and Research* 3(2): 71–92.

Shroder, Mark. 2002. "Locational Constraint, Housing Counseling, and Successful Lease-up in a Randomized Housing Voucher Experiment." *Journal of Urban Economics* 5(2): 315–338.

Turner, Margery Austin. 2003. *Strengths and Weaknesses of the Housing Voucher Program.* Congressional Testimony of Margery Austin Turner, Director, Metropolitan Housing and Communities Policy Center, The Urban Institute, prepared for the Committee on Financial Services, Subcommittee on Housing and Community Opportunity, United States House of Representatives, June 17, 2003.

Turner, Margery Austin. 2003. *The Federal Housing Choice Voucher Program: Strengths and Challenges.* Testimony before the Committee on Financial Services, Subcommittee on Housing and Community Opportunity of the U.S. House of Representatives, June 17, 2003. Retrieved from http://financialservices.house.gov/media/pdf/061703mat.pdf.

Turner, Margery Austin, and Susan Popkin. 2000. "Comment on Jill Khadduri's Should the Housing Voucher Program Become a State-Administered Block Grant?" *Housing Policy Debate* 11(3): 271–281.

U.S. Bureau of the Census. 2010a. *American Housing Survey 2007*. Retrieved March 16, 2010 from http://www.census.gov/hhes/www/housing/ahs/ahs07/ahs07.html.

U.S. Bureau of the Census. 2010b. *Census 2000, Summary File 3*. Retrieved March 16, 2010 from http://www.census.gov/Press-Release/www/2002/sumfile3.html.

U.S. Department of Housing and Urban Development. 2010a. Retrieved March 16, 2010 from *Housing Choice Vouchers Factsheet* http://www.hud.gov/offices/pih/programs/hcv/about/fact_sheet.cfm.

U.S. Department of Housing and Urban Development. 2010b. *Housing Choice Voucher Program (Section 8)*. Retrieved March 16, 2010 from http://portal.hud.gov/portal/page/portal/HUD/topics/housing_choice_voucher_program_section_8.

U.S. Department of Housing and Urban Development. 2009. *FY2010 Budget: Road Map for Transformation*. Retrieved from http://www.hud.gov/budgetsummary2010/fy10budget.pdf.

U.S. Department of Housing and Urban Development. 2008. Unpublished data on Housing Choice Voucher households nationwide.

U.S. Department of Housing and Urban Development. 2007. *Fair Market Rents for The Section 8 Housing Assistance Payments Program*. Retrieved March 16, 2010 from http://www.huduser.org/portal/datasets/fmr/fmrs/docsys.html&data=fmr07.

U.S. Department of Housing and Urban Development. 2005. "New Low-Income Housing Tax Credit Project Data Available." *U.S. Housing Market Conditions 1st Quarter 2005*. Washington, D.C.: U.S. Department of Housing and Urban Development, Office of Policy Development and Research.

U.S. Department of Housing and Urban Development. 2000. *Section 8 Tenant-Based Housing Assistance: A Look Back After 30 Years*. Washington, D.C.: U.S. Department of Housing and Urban Development.

The Urban Institute. 1995. *Implementing Block Grants for Housing: An Evaluation of the First Year of HOME*. Washington, D.C.: U.S. Department of Housing and Urban Development.

Varady, David, and Carole Walker. 2003. "Using Housing Vouchers to Move to the Suburbs." *Urban Affairs Review* 39(2); 143–180.

PART FOUR

THE RISE AND STALL OF HOMEOWNERSHP

# THE HISTORICAL ROOTS OF THE CRISIS IN HOUSING AFFORDABILITY: THE CASE OF BUFFALO, NEW YORK 1920-1950

## Henry Louis Taylor, Jr.

A crisis of housing affordability emerged in the 1970s that caused the housing challenge to become one of the nation's top domestic issues (Kain 1983, Downs 1988/89). This affordability problem meant that, increasingly, households had to pay more than a third of their income on lodging, thereby making the quest to meet other family needs— food, healthcare, clothing, childcare and transportation—exceedingly difficult (Feldman 2002). Thus, because of the high cost of housing, finding a place to live and making ends meet became a daily struggle to survive in the city, especially for blacks, Latinos, and low-income whites. To understand why this crisis in housing affordability emerged in the 1970s, we have to recast the 1920s, 1930s and 1940s as a critical period in (1) the formation of a new vision of the American city, (2) the building of a local and national political coalition empowered to realize the vision, and (3) the construction of a public policy and institutional framework to make it happen (Heathcott 2008). In the first half of the 20th century, local and national leaders thought and acted in metropolitan terms, and their new urban vision was based on the idea of turning the central city, suburbs and outlying areas into one big city—an American metropolis (Taylor 2000).

During the thirty-year period between 1920 and 1950, urban leaders laid the theoretical, organizational, institutional and policy groundwork needed for the construction of this new American metropolis, which they built during the 1950s and 1960s. The creation of this metropolis gave birth to the contemporary crisis in housing affordability. Within this context, housing affordability and fair housing became intertwined issues because the growing economic rationalization of urban space created the desire to keep out people of neighborhoods who might devalue property. This thesis is explored by examining the experiences of Buffalo, New York, between 1920 and 1950.

Buffalo is an ideal city to investigate the historical roots of the housing affordability crisis. A medium size, bi-national city located on the

Upper Great Lakes, where the Niagara River joins Lake Erie, Buffalo became one of the nation's leading manufacturing centers in the late 19th and early 20th centuries (Goldman 1983). Its history, then, mirrors that of other Great Lakes, mid-western and eastern seaboard cities. Today, in Buffalo, housing affordability is a big issue, with a significant number of households paying more than 30% of their income on lodging. For example, in five of the city's nine council districts, more than 50% of the households pay more than 30 percent of their income on lodging (City of Buffalo 2003). At the same time, reports from Buffalo's Housing Opportunities Made Equal (HOME) indicate that fair housing, especially in the suburban region, is still problematic (Patterson and Silverman 2005).

*The Need for a New Urban Vision: Life in the Unregulated City*

Industry triumphed in the late 19th century, and manufacturing became the engine that drove the development of American society. This economic victory triggered a period of spectacular urban growth during the late 19th and early twentieth century. For example, New York City grew from less than one million inhabitants in 1860 to more than 5.5 million in 1920. Chicago, which was a place with less than 100,000 residents in 1860, soared toward the three million mark in 1920. Everywhere, urban centers grew. From Atlanta, Birmingham, and Louisville, to St. Louis, Milwaukee, Cincinnati, Cleveland, Buffalo, Kansas City, and Omaha, to Philadelphia, Baltimore, and Washington, D.C., to Denver, Los Angeles, San Francisco and Seattle, people flocked to the city. By 1920, for the first time, the U.S. census revealed that more than 50 percent of all Americans lived in urban areas (Taylor 2000).

The astounding growth of American cities was informed by a vision of the city and a city building process that had remained virtually unchanged throughout the 19th and early 20th centuries. Thus, although cities became much larger, the process used to build them remained essentially the same. Of course, over this period, residential areas became increasingly segregated by class, the suburban regions became more built up, industry became more concentrated, building codes became more restrictive, and cities began to introduce zoning and subdivision regulations (Teaford 1986). These, however, were quantitative, not qualitative changes in the city building process. Throughout the 19th and early 20th centuries, cities continued to be developed in an unregulated urban environment, and the vision of the city was framed within a central city rather than metropolitan context (Fairbanks 1988). This started to change in the opening decades of the 20th century when population growth and technological innovation brought the city building question to the forefront of American urban development.

In the unregulated environment, the rapid growth and development of urban centers challenged the sensibilities of existing strategies of city building and forced leaders to rethink their vision of the city. For example, the lack of a strong system of land use regulation meant that factories and "substandard" dwelling units could be built anywhere, including in exclusive residential districts (Taylor 1993). In this setting, where work was still the main determinant of where people lived, the working class home sphere was typically a place where factories, businesses, railroad facilities and dwelling units were intermingled in a landscape of shared space (Emergency Work Relief Bureau 1934). In the working class home sphere homeownership was viewed as a cultural artifact that offered greater security than renting. The geographer, Jon Goss, says that a building, including housing, is more than it seems: "It is an artifact—an object of material culture produced by society to fulfill particular functions determined by, and thus embodying or reflecting, the social relations and level of development of the productive forces of that society" (Goss 1988:392). In this sense, housing not only reflects the culture of an era, but also reflects the reproduction of social relations. Within this context, during the unregulated era, among workers, housing represented an opportunity to acquire a 'secure' living place in a complex and uncertain world (Harris 1996).

Restrictive covenants were used to protect the integrity of elite residential districts, but their application across the metropolitan region was limited (Self 2001; Gotham 2000). Without being able to protect residential districts and segregate housing based on type and cost, a growing number of urban leaders believed that owning a home would never become a good economic investment (Taylor 1993). During this same period, the automobile combined with the decentralization of manufacturing to spawn a suburbanization movement that made city building even more complex. As early as 1915, Graham Romeyn Taylor, in his classic study of *Satellite Cities*, described this suburbanization trend. "Huge industrial plants," he said, "are uprooting themselves bodily from the cities. With households, small stores, salons, lodges, churches, schools clinging to them like living tendrils, they set themselves down ten miles away in the open" (Taylor 1915:1).

This intra-urban migratory movement was an extraordinarily democratic one, which was led by factory workers and the white-collar workers that followed them (Harris 1996). African Americans also joined the trek, as they moved into the suburban hinterland in search of improved housing and a place of their own (Wiese 2004). By 1920, the rate of suburban population growth not only exceeded that of the central city, but brought the hinterland into the vortex of urban development, thereby, creating a new urban metropolis that consisted of an increasingly integrated central city, suburban hinterland, and rural areas (Teaford 1986; Harris and Lewis 2001).

*City Building in Buffalo*

City building in Buffalo, New York, took place in an unregulated environment during the opening decades of the twentieth century. By 1930, the Queen City, one of the nation's leading industrial centers, was divided into three sectors: West Side, East Side, and South Buffalo. Main Street split the city into West and East Sides, while the Buffalo River formed the northern boundary of South Buffalo. There were 998 manufacturing firms in the city proper. These firms were free to locate anywhere. Consequently, they could be found in every section of the city. Yet, the historical landscape of the West Side differed from that of the East Side and South Buffalo.

The reason for this difference in historical landscape is that on the West Side, an industrial belt formed along Niagara Street, near the Black Rock Canal and Upper Black Rock Canal, and then culminated in an industrial district in the Black Rock community, in the Military Road area. This location placed the West Side manufacturing firms close to the Niagara River and Lake Erie, which they accessed via the Black Rock Canal. There were virtually no West Side industries located outside this area. The reason is the presence of the Olmsted Park and Parkway System combined with the existence of the Buffalo Teachers College, the New York State Hospital Campus, and neighborhoods of the elites to discourage the location of West Side factories outside of this industrial belt.

The story of industrial development on the East Side was very different. In this part of town, factories could and did locate anywhere. Large clusters of manufacturing firms were scattered across the face of the East Side, with the heaviest concentration of factories found below East Delavan Avenue, especially adjacent to downtown Buffalo and along the waterfront. The South Buffalo factory district was actually located in Lackawanna, NY, a small industrial suburb that formed on South Buffalo's southern border.

### The Home Sphere and the Housing Delivery System

Working class neighborhoods developed in the shadow of these manufacturing plants and railroad facilities. This happened on both the East and West Sides, as well as in South Buffalo. Thus, in the unregulated city, the working class home sphere often consisted of a mixed land use environment, where the homes of unskilled, semi-skilled and skilled workers co-existed with the manufacturing plants, commercial corridors and tangled webs of railroad tracks. The landscape of work also shaped the city's population distribution. For example, the Italians were overrepresented in the lower East Side, where they worked on the docks, while the Polish, Germans, blacks, Russians, Irish and Czechoslovakians were overrepresented on the East Side. American-born whites, the British and the Canadians were overrepresented on the East Side.

I use the term *home sphere* to capture the complex nature of the industrial city residential environment, where social interactions took place at multiple levels (Lewis 1991). In this framework, home refers to the household and the community. In this environment, the neighborhood was composed of several sub-communities—black, Italian, Russian Jews, Polish, Irish and other ethnic groups. Physical proximity in the home sphere meant that racial and ethnic groups interacted within and across 'communities.' The term *home*, then, is meant to capture the complexity of an interlocking web of multiple households and communities socially interacting within the same spatial margin. The word *sphere* seeks to capture the neighborhood environment in all its complexity. This concept not only includes the household and community, but also the place of work and commercial corridors, along with the tangled web of interactions that occur in a multi-racial, ethnic and cultural setting where social interaction is omnipresent. Thus, Buffalo's home sphere represented an environment that existed at several different, but highly interactive levels—household, workplace, neighborhood, shopping, recreation, and community (Williams 2001).

This brings us to a discussion of the housing delivery system, which was driven by micro-home construction firms. These small firms operated in an economically non-rational housing market. By this, I mean the market was not structured to maximize profits and most companies operating in it barely made ends meet. According to a survey by the Commerce Department in 1929, approximately 80 percent of the builders did an annual business of less than $9,000 (Radford 1996). In Buffalo, the cost of constructing a 'standardized' home was about $5,000 (Milliken 1937). Thus, the typical builder constructed only about one or two houses a year, which kept home building from being a profitable business for most firms. Still, there was no shortage of builders. This was an easy field to enter, since many people knew the fundamentals of simple wood framing and expensive machinery was not required (Radford 1996). This explains why there were so many small enterprises and why cities, such as Buffalo, had no problems producing a sufficient supply of housing to meet the demand of a growing population.

Although the evidence on home construction is fragmentary, it seems that most financing and building took place on a piecemeal basis. Individuals would acquire a parcel of land and hire a builder to put up a specific structure on it. In some instances, depending on the owner's resources, the house was constructed in a bit by bit fashion. The owner would build one room, move in, and as resources increased, they would add more units to the house. People normally financed the operation using some combination of saving and personal loans (Radford 2006; Taylor 1993; Taylor 1979).

In Buffalo, unlike New York City, Cincinnati and Philadelphia, builders mostly constructed small wooden single- and two-family housing units. Families were almost equally distributed between these two types of dwelling units. Among cities with 500,000 or more residents, for example, Buffalo had the largest proportion (43%) of its families living in two-family dwelling units (Behrens 1939). Typically, in the working class home sphere, the dwelling units were built on small lots, very close to each other. These bungalows were usually very long structures, consisting of three to five rooms, with no hallway (Radford 1996). In this unregulated residential setting, sometimes, to reduce the cost of construction by eliminating the purchase of a new building lot, owners would construct two houses on a single lot. The second house was typically built to provide lodging for a relative or immediate family member (Housing Committee, Civic League of

St. Louis 1908). Working class neighborhoods were anchored by a commercial district that provided goods and services to community residents. Apartments were located above many of the business establishments in the locale, thereby turning the commercial district into a live/work neighborhood. In Buffalo, these live/work neighborhoods anchored most communities (Behrens 1939; Buffalo Planning Board 1940).

The work of owner-builders augmented the building activity of these small producers. According to the Geographer, Richard Harris (1997:252), by 1949 one-quarter of all new single-family homes in the United States were owner built. Owner builders not only constructed houses in the city, but also in the suburban hinterland. During this period, the urbanization process increasingly converted large tracts of land from rural to urban uses. These workers, in turn, either built their own homes, or hired a carpenter to build a house for them. In addition to constructing their own homes, owners often added new rooms by subdividing their existing home or building new rooms onto the house. Home building and conversions, as the practice of subdividing or adding rooms to a structure was called, then, formed a significant part of the landscape of working class residential districts in both the central city and suburbs (Taylor 1979; Harris 1996; Wiese 2004).

### Race and the Working Class Home Sphere

In the 1930s, the Buffalo Municipal Housing Authority, as part of their studies of 'slum' conditions in the Queen City, produced a series of dot maps, overlying census tracts, which showed the residential location of racial and ethnic groups in Buffalo. Based on these maps, it is not only possible to determine where in the city African Americans lived, but also to be able to determine who were their neighbors.

The data showed that while blacks and white ethnic groups were underrepresented in some neighborhoods and overrepresented in other neighborhoods, work, rather than race or ethnicity, seemed to determine where within the city a person lived. Within this setting, the lower East Side industrial neighborhood was the most diverse in the city. The neighborhood was situated adjacent to downtown Buffalo and fell within census tracts 12, 13, 14, 15, 25 and 26. This neighborhood had the largest concentration of industry in the city. For example, there were about 15 large manufacturing plants, which employed more than 100 workers and more than 221 smaller manufacturing firms that employed less than 100 workers.

The neighborhood had a remarkable racial and white ethnic population composition. Here, about 16,000 African Americans shared the neighborhood with about 71,000 Polish, Italians, Germans and Russian workers, along with a handful of Canadians, British, Irish, Austrians, and Hungarians. Blacks and white ethnics not only lived side by side, but sometimes they even lived in the same dwelling unit. As late as 1953, some blacks and whites were still living together in the same dwelling unit.[1] For example, at 531 Clinton Street, four blacks and one white lived together. Nearby, at 490 Eagle Street, five whites and three blacks lived in the same building. At 506 Eagle Street, half of the sixteen residents in the building were white. Thus, on the eve of the 1954 Supreme Court decision that outlawed school segregation, in Buffalo's working class neighborhoods, blacks and whites could still be found living in the same residential building (Buffalo Municipal Housing Authority 1953).

Racial residential segregation did not occur in working class neighborhoods because no economic incentive existed to exclude blacks from these communities. In the unregulated city, with its slack building codes and weak zoning laws, the housing market was an economically non-rational one. This gave rise to a working class home sphere with three distinct characteristics. First, housing was a cultural artifact, rather than a commodity to be bought and sold. Second, the housing inventory was built to meet the demand of all workers—unskilled, semi-skilled and skilled. In this mixed land-use environment, any type of residential structure was allowed. As a result, owner- and renter-occupied units stood side by side, along with cheap and expensive housing units (Radford 1996, City of Buffalo 1940).

Third, housing was not separated on the basis of type and cost, which meant boarding housing were next to single family units, very cheap housing and more moderately price structures were intermingled. Thus, although African Americans lived in the cheapest and poorest quality housing, they were not separated from white workers, and there was no demand to exclude them from the neighborhood

---

[1] In the 1950s, the city's extensive urban renewal campaign required the purchase of numerous residential buildings. To complete this task, the City gathered extensive information about the residents of the buildings they planned to purchase.

(City of Buffalo 1940). The reason for this is that the value of housing was not attached to residential homogeneity and exclusivity. In this moment, in working class neighborhoods, no correlation existed between property values and population composition (Hayden 1980, Cohen 1989, Wheelock 2008). Consequently, white property owners had no economic incentive to keep out blacks, so they did not protest their presence in the neighborhood (Radford 1996). Buffalo was not an anomaly, neighborhoods similar to the lower East Side could be found in most American cities.

The situation was different in affluent white neighborhoods. In this setting, owners used restrictive housing covenants not only to keep out blacks, but also to exclude working class whites and non-residential forms of land-use (Gotham 2000). Even in a non-rationale economic market, they sought to protect the affluence and exclusivity of their communities. This suggests that during the late 19th and early 20th centuries, residential development was different in elite and working class neighborhoods and that the ideals of racial residential segregation had its origin in elite neighborhoods, rather than in the working class home sphere (Weaver 1944).

*Housing Affordability: Finding a Place to Call Home*

Although the data on housing affordability is sketchy, it is still possible to gain some insight into the issue. The 1939 housing market analysis estimated that the average Buffalo worker made about $1,000 annually in 1935 and that only one family in four paid as much as $30 a month for rent (City of Buffalo 1940; Bureau of Intelligence 1942; Behrens 1939). This suggests that many workers might have paid less than 30% of their income on housing. The problem is that without having accurate information of the ratio of income to housing for workers at the various skill levels, we cannot really determine the degree to which affordability was a problem. However, the available data do suggest that in the unregulated city, workers had many options for dealing with the affordability issue. Thus, housing quality notwithstanding, these options helped workers make ends meet and survive the city.

To start, the weak system of land-use regulation meant that builders, including owner-builders, could construct any type of dwelling units they desired, depending on the resources available to them. This option made it possible for any worker to build a house within their price range. For example, between 1895 and 1914, the cost of residential building increased by 50% as the acceptable minimum standard for new housing increased with the change in housing preferences. In this new setting, the enforcement of building codes became more stringent and indoor plumbing and bathrooms became the new 'standard' in housing construction (Radford 1996).

Even so, in the unregulated environment, workers could still get away with constructing new housing units that did meet the new standards. They could choose to operate within the formal or informal housing market or operate betwixt and between the two. On this point, in Buffalo, builders used non-union workers to construct small houses, and the wages of these laborers were about 20% lower than unionized labor, thereby leading to a substantial reduction in the cost of the housing unit (Behrens 1939). Moreover, when they employed a carpenter, families and their friends often built a significant portion of their own home, which greatly reduced the cost of housing construction. Families also had the choice of building more than one house on a residential lot, thereby reducing the cost of the second home. In some instances, in places like Milwaukee, builders would construct as many as three houses on a single lot, which was designed to reduce the price. Indeed, lot crowding was a characteristic feature of the unregulated city (Hageman 1916).

In Buffalo's economically non-rational housing market, builders constructed housing units targeted for the low end of the market. In 1934, for instance, about 95% of the inventory for family houses was aimed at the lower end of the market, where units were rented monthly for $49 and less. Within this framework, about 22% of Buffalo's housing inventory was aimed at the very lowest end of the market, those units for rent under $15 a month (Behrens 1939). This was a city in which most workers labored in the low-wage sector of the labor market and the economic non-rationale housing market was designed to construct products for them.

Suburbanization also increased the housing options available to workers. In Cincinnati, Buffalo and other places, workers, including African Americans, purchased suburban lots and built housing on them. This process was facilitated by roving land speculators, who went from city to city, purchasing rural lands and subdividing them into unimproved residential lots and then selling them to workers, mostly with low-incomes. The workers, in turn, would build a house on the lot. If they did not have the resources to complete the house, they would often build one room, move in, and add onto the unit as their resources increased (Taylor 2000). As the historian Richard Harris (1997) has noted, owner-built dwellings, in both the central city and suburban region, shaped the landscape of the pre-1950 American industrial city.

Once workers obtained lodging, they could find even more ways to reduce housing costs. For example, a number of workers routinely took in boarders to increase their incomes. In Buffalo, about four percent of all dwellers' units contained boarders (5,825), where 66% of those units containing boarders were tenant-occupied. The proportion of dwelling units with renters was probably higher. For example, about 49% of the city's 30,865 two-family, double-deckers were owner-occupied. These units normally had separate entrances, and the owner probably rented out the second unit. Secondly, property-owners sometimes subdivided their dwelling units into multiple units or simply built additional units onto the structure. Of the 7,716 partially or fully converted single family units in Buffalo, about 58% were owner-occupied. The fact that most of these conversions took place between 1930 and 1939 suggests that people were converting their homes for economic reasons (City of Buffalo 1940). Lastly, on the commercial corridors, many small business owners had the option of living above their businesses or renting out the apartment to reduce housing costs.

The renting of rooms in their homes to tenants had an impact on housing affordability in two interactive ways. First, it reduced the cost of housing for the homeowners and tenants who took in boarders. Second, it provided an inexpensive place to live for the boarder (Buffalo Municipal Housing Authority 1953, City of Buffalo 1940). Thus, in the unregulated city, residents had many options with which to deal with the affordability issue. This explains why housing experts of that time never mentioned 'homelessness' as an issue in their discussion of the housing problem. In the unregulated city, everyone could find a place to call home, even if the quality of that place was poor.

### Building the Regulated City

In the late 19th century, Buffalo's leaders defined the city's main urban problem in terms of the housing conditions of the poor and city beautification (Charity Organization Society of Buffalo 1927, Charles Mulford Robinson 1902). In this epoch, they believed that solving the

housing problem and improving the visual image of the city were central to building a great city. This viewpoint changed during the opening decades of the 20th century. The forces of industrialization,
urbanization and population growth combined to force leaders to
redefine the urban problem as they confronted a series of unprece-
dented challenges associated with the city's dramatic growth.

In this new setting, locally and nationally, urban leaders now defined
unregulated growth and development as the most daunting problem
facing cities. To them, the haphazard, chaotic and unpredictable
approach to city building threatened the city's future and posed huge
obstacles to its ability to meet the challenges of 20th century urban life.
Within this context, developing a new vision and approach to city
building became Buffalo's two most urgent tasks. City leaders started
working on these two tasks as early as 1911. That summer, members of
the Common Council began debating the importance of city planning.
The following year, The Civic Improvement Committee drafted a bill
for the establishment of a City Planning Committee in Buffalo. In the
introduction, Dr. Matthew D. Mann, a local civic leader, outlined the
importance of city planning:

> An ounce of city planning is worth a pound of city re-planning. A city
> without a city plan is like a ship without a rudder. Instead of leaving the
> future improvements to the whims of future city officials, influenced per-
> haps by personal motives, utterly lacking in broad vision and without
> special training, it will substitute a carefully considered program, which
> can be changed only by the vote of some of the most competent and best-
> trained of our officials and citizens, after careful study and deliberation.
> (Mann 1912:27)

Mann was talking about using 'official' city plans to overcome the
problem of building cities in an unregulated urban environment where
business, industry, building, retail establishments, and poorly constructed dwelling units could locate anywhere. Without city plans to
guide and direct growth and development, urban leaders felt that
Buffalo would become a "city of dis-ordered physical growth," incapa-
ble of meeting the 20th century urban challenge. By 1920, the development and implementation of a city building strategy based on "official"
city planning and land-use regulation was a top priority (Buffalo
Department of Public Works 1910–1911).

During this period, leaders viewed Buffalo, Erie and Niagara counties as one big city, which should be developed as a single geographic
unit called the *Greater City of the Niagara Frontier*. This vision was
spelled out in the City Planning Committee's first Annual Report in

December 1919: "The time is not far distant when Buffalo, Lockport, the Tonawandas and Niagara Falls will be one, large industrial community. There will be 400 square miles of manufacturing plants in this community, operated solely by electric power. The population will total 6,000,000 and there will be one horsepower developed for every three persons..." (City Planning Committee 1919:19).

This broader vision caused urban leaders to shift emphasis from 'city planning' to 'regional planning' as they sought to realize in practice their dream of The Greater City of the Niagara Frontier. At a meeting to organize the Niagara Frontier Planning Board, which was held in Tonawanda, New York, on September 29, 1924, Governor Alfred E. Smith outlined the importance of regional planning: "This Region is sure to grow, certain to change. Nothing that we can do is going to prevent that growth and change, but what we can do is to prevent that growth from becoming a haphazard one. What we can do is to guide that growth and to plan it" (Niagara Frontier Planning Board 1925). Later that year, in its First Annual Report, the Niagara Frontier Regional Planning Board outlined its strategy for creating the infrastructure necessary to build the Greater City of the Niagara Frontier: "The Niagara Frontier Regional Plan proposes to develop new communicating highways, parks, and rapid transit facilities, and regional zoning to provide for the proper location of industrial and residential areas, the location of bridges within the Region and across the Niagara River, the furtherance of parkways, boulevard extensions, water supply, sewage disposal and harbor and canal improvements" (Niagara Frontier Planning Board 1925:8).

The goal of building a metropolitan city was based on two beliefs or assumptions. Urban leaders were aware of the gradual shift in the center of population growth from the central city to the suburban region. For example, between 1900 and 1920, the population of the City of Buffalo increased by 44%, while the suburban population of Erie County increased by 58%. While the number of people moving to the city (N=154,388) was much greater than the number of people moving to the suburbs (N=46,714), the rate of population growth in the suburbs was greater (U.S. Census Bureau 1900–1920). Urban leaders not only believed that this trend would continue, but that it would intensify over time (Niagara Frontier Planning Board 1925, Smith 1926).

Within this context, the *one big city* ideal would enable them to 'capture' this growth and guide its development and use homeownership as the anchor to the new urban metropolis. In this model, urban leaders envisioned a monocentric region in which Buffalo's Central Business District (CBD) would remain a major employment center and the hub of the metropolitan region. The central goal was to build a monocentric regional city (1) that was anchored by homeownership and the single-family dwelling unit; (2) that had a modern transportation system which facilitated population movement to and from the central city; (3) that segregated land-use and (4) that concentrated blacks and low-to-moderate income white workers in the central cities, while higher income white workers and the middle-classes lived in the suburbs. In this new residential environment, urban leaders intended to segregate housing units based on type and cost (Niagara Frontier Planning Board 1925; City Planning Commission 1919).

*Making it Happen: The Depression and the Federal/Local Partnership*

The dreams and aspirations of local leaders notwithstanding, building a metropolitan city anchored by a modern residential environment and homeownership could not happen without a partnership among the federal, state and local governments. The reason is that a modern residential environment undergirded by homeownership required not only the establishment of a regulated city (zoning laws, building codes and subdivision regulations), but also the creation of a banking system based on the amortized mortgage, easy access to capital, and a theory of neighborhood development to guide the investment decision of underwriters and mortgage brokers, along with a method of evaluating neighborhood conditions (Taylor 1993). Building the regional city also required the allocation of millions in federal and state aid to construct an inter-metropolitan arterial system to tie the metropolis together and to facilitate transportation from the central core to the outer-lying region. This process not only included the widening of roads and the building of new bridges, tunnels, streets, parkways, thoroughfares and thruways, but also the acquisition and demolition of thousands of structures and the relocation of people and businesses (Rae 2003).

The Great Depression and World War II created the condition that made possible the development of a partnership between the federal, state and local governments. This partnership enabled local leaders in Buffalo and elsewhere to build a regulated urban metropolis anchored by homeownership. This metropolitan city building process involved three episodes of federal-local activity. In the first episode, the federal government set up the policies, established the institutions, and made the necessary changes in the money mortgage system, while local government developed regional plans to guide the metropolitan building process. In the second episode there was the onset of the massively subsidized construction of low-income public housing projects which accelerated the process of racial residential segregation, and in the final episode there was the urban renewal and highway construction process of the 1950s and 1960s. Also, during this period, in many localities, the process of building public housing units was completed. These three episodes not only led to the construction of the contemporary urban metropolis, but they also triggered the development of fair housing and housing affordability as major issues in American society.

## The First Episode

The Great Depression spawned an epidemic of foreclosures, and this created the opportunity for federal and local leaders to realize in practice their dream of building a modern residential environment anchored by homeownership and the single family dwelling unit. To achieve this goal, the federal government established the Federal Home Loan Bank System (1932), the Federal Home Owners Loan Corporation (HOLC 1933) and the Federal Housing Administration (FHA) in 1934 to stabilize the housing market and build the institutional base needed to stimulate mass homeownership (Henderson 2000). These three institutions provided the foundation for the homeownership movement by providing citizens with easy access to capital and by developing the self-amortized mortgage, which revolutionized the money mortgage system.

The HOLC, which operated under the supervision of the Federal Home Loan Bank Board, developed the long-term, self-amortizing mortgage in 1933. HOLC refinanced mortgages at 5% interest over 15 years, thereby making homeownership feasible for those who had been previously unable to afford short-term mortgages at high interest rates. Before 1930, home buying was a risky financial journey. Institutions required large down payments, charged high interests rates, and demanded the repayment of loans within a very short period, typically from two to five years. So, when a family used its savings to purchase a house, a big economic investment in the dwelling was being made.

This investment was risky because rising or falling property values determined the home buyer's fate (Henderson 2003, Taylor 1993).

Only a few people could pay off their mortgage within two to five years, so most owners counted on having it renewed again and again as needed. But mortgage renewal was not automatic. If a lending company believed that neighborhood conditions were declining and that housing values were depreciating, it might not renew the mortgage. If that happened, the home buyer might lose both the house and the money invested in it. This possibility undergirded the view that zoning and building code regulations were essential to the development of an economically rational housing market. In Cincinnati, Ohio, for example, the city's Better Housing League said that in addition to strict building codes, comprehensive zoning codes were required to protect residential neighborhoods from invasion by undesirable structures. In its 1921 report, the League stated, "It would be a short-sighted policy to encourage the construction of small homes and to foster home ownership and at the same time fail to take every precaution to see to it that the residential districts are not properly protected" (Taylor 1993:170).

By building houses that maintained the class character of neighborhoods and by keeping out bad houses, factories, and businesses, home buyers could maintain property values and protect the home investment. Thus, zoning laws and building codes were essential tools in the construction of a modern residential environment anchored by homeownership. Alone, however, building codes, zoning laws, amortized mortgages and access to capital were not sufficient to build a sustainable economically rational housing market within which homeownership was embedded (Radford 1996). The missing part of the equation was a theory of neighborhood development, along with a method of appraising the real estate risks in urban settings, which underwriters and insurance companies could use in making investment decisions. For the economically rational housing market to operate efficiently and effectively, insurance companies and mortgage brokers needed a 'rational' basis on which to make their investment decisions (Metzger 2000).

This is where the work of the economist Frederick M. Babcock comes in. Before joining the HOLC as its chief underwriter in 1936, Babcock, in his influential text book, the *Valuation of Real Estate*, urged realtors to analyze the future histories of neighborhoods when appraising them:

A residential district seems to go through a very definite and inevitable course of development when not affected by forces which can entirely change its use. This cycle is characterized by the gradual decline in *quality of people* [emphasis added] through the years accompanied by population increases and the more intensive residential use of ground. (Babcock 1932:75)

Babcock's neighborhoods life-cycle theory suggests that a linear relationship exists between race, class and neighborhood decline. For instance, when talking about a "gradual decline in quality of people," he was referring to the influx of blacks, foreign-born, and/or low-income white workers into neighborhoods, which changed their class composition, thereby resulting in an "inevitable ultimate condition" of becoming either "a poor, blighted, or decadent district," or even worse, a district of "a slum character" (1932:76). Babcock's language about the inevitability of neighborhood decline became a vital principle in the FHA *Underwriting Manual*. In 1935, based on Babcock's neighborhood life-cycle theory, the HOLC conducted a study of neighborhood conditions in 239 cities to unearth principles to guide the underwriting decisions of insurance companies and mortgage lenders. The goal was to establish a method for appraising real estate risks in urban neighborhoods. Toward this end, HOLC fieldworkers sought to determine where in the lifecycle a neighborhood was situated (Rae 2003).

The fieldworkers were given extensive instructions on how to carry out their confidential survey of neighborhoods. They gathered comprehensive information on the kind of structures located in the community, including data on the type, age, condition, and value, and they were instructed to evaluate the entire neighborhood, not just the dwelling units. So, they were asked to identify a neighborhood's positive and negative features. For example, did the community have parks, recreation centers, schools, churches and good transportation linkages? Were the streets and sidewalks in good shape and were manufacturing plants, especially those with noxious odors, located in or near the community (HOLC Security Maps of Buffalo 1937)?

HOLC fieldworkers were particularly concerned with the socioeconomic composition of neighborhoods. They wanted to know the race, ethnicity, occupation, and family income of people living in each community, or that might potentially move into the neighborhood, especially the number of blacks, foreign-born whites, or "low-grade populations" (Home Owners Loan Corporation, 1937: N.P.). If blacks, or other low-grade populations, had started to move into a

neighborhood, the fieldworkers estimated the rapidity of the in-migra-
tion. They concluded their assessment by projecting the trend of desirability for the neighborhood over a ten to fifteen year period. Based on
this thorough examination, a color-coded grade was assigned to each
residential area which ranged from first to fourth. First grade areas
were coded green, second grade areas blue, third grade areas yellow,
and fourth grade areas red. Neighborhoods coded green and blue were
considered highly desirable communities, while neighborhoods coded
yellow and red were considered undesirable communities on a downward trajectory. Neighborhoods coded in red were considered slum
areas, which had already reached the point of no return (Rae 2003).

In Buffalo, the HOLC survey revealed two things about residential
development. First, most of the neighborhoods in the city were declining. Over half the 58 residential areas designated by the HOLC in 1937
were coded yellow (36%) and red (16%),[2] with the majority (83%) of
these *yellow-red* neighborhoods found on the West and East sides,
below West and East Delavan Avenue where the many of the city's
industries were located (Hillier 2003). Indeed, the HOLC coded all the
neighborhoods situated along Buffalo's industrial zones on both the
East and Lower West sides as either yellow or red. Here, it should be
recalled that the HOLC fieldworkers were asked to look unfavorably
on the neighborhoods where industries were located. These yellow and
red coded neighborhoods covered most of the city's land area. There
were only four (7%) neighborhoods in the city coded green or first
grade, and these residential districts were situated on the northern
fringe, near Amherst, a bucolic suburban area.[3] On the flip side, the
East Side industrial neighborhood, where blacks shared residential
space with white ethnic workers, was coded mostly red, indicating that
multiracial neighborhoods near manufacturing plants were the most
undesirable in the city.

Second, the HOLC survey confirmed that most of the building lots
in Buffalo had been exhausted and there existed little or no room for
the development of new subdivisions. A study, conducted at the same
time the HOLC survey was taken, indicated that about 89% of the city's
land parcels (107,000 out of 120,000) had structures on them (Deane

---

[2] It is not clear what guidelines the fieldworkers used to establish the residential
areas, and each area can vary greatly in terms of size.
[3] Division of Research and Statistics, Appraisal Department, Home Owners Loan
Corporation, HOLC Residential Security Map, Buffalo, New York, April 1937.

and Milliken 1936). Thus, by 1930, in Buffalo, most of the undeveloped land suitable for residential development had disappeared. Therefore, without extensive demolition, there were no sites on which to develop new subdivisions. The built-up character of Buffalo meant the construction of new owner-occupied, single-family dwelling units would have to take place mostly in the suburban hinterland. Buffalo was no anomaly. In most places, in the 1930 to 1970 period, population growth and new residential development took place in the suburbs (Teaford 1979, Burgess 1994).

The central role of suburban development was reflected in the design of Greater Buffalo's metropolitan arterial system. Regional studies of automobile registration and suburban population growth reinforced the notion that the center of population growth and residential development had shifted to the suburban region. In its first annual report, the Niagara Frontier Planning Board speculated that by 1960 almost 1.6 million people would be living in the Erie and Niagara counties and that Buffalo would be the hub of this great metropolitan city (Niagara Frontier Planning Board 1925). While this vision proved overly optimistic, the suburban region did become the center of population growth in metropolitan Buffalo. For example, between 1920 and 1960, Erie County's suburban population grew from 127,913 to 531,929, an increase of 404,016 residents (a 316% increase). During this same period, the population of Buffalo grew from 506,775 to 532,759, an increase of only 25,000 or five percent (Table 1).

During the 1970s, for the first time, Buffalo experienced negative growth, while the suburban population grew by 119,000, an increase of 22% (Table 1). In the first half of the 20th century, operating in the context of the One-Big City view of urban development, leaders believed the future of metropolitan Buffalo centered on suburban population growth, and they sought to create an arterial system to facilitate traffic flow from the central city to the suburbs. Thus, in Buffalo and elsewhere, transportation planning, regional planning, and suburban population growth marched in unison.

This process of regional city building intensified racial segregation and spawned the rise of a bifurcated *de-facto* metropolitan city in which whites (the elites, middle-class and higher-paid workers) would be overrepresented in the suburbs, and blacks, foreign-born whites and low-income workers would be overrepresented in the central city. In 1900, whites comprised 99% of the city's population. By 1970, the proportion of whites living in Buffalo dropped to 79%, while the

Table 1. Population Growth in Buffalo and Erie County, 1900–2000

| Year | Buffalo | Suburb | Percent city |
|------|---------|--------|--------------|
| 1900 | 352,387 | 81,199 | 81.27 |
| 1910 | 423,715 | 105,270 | 80.09 |
| 1920 | 506,775 | 127,913 | 79.84 |
| 1930 | 573,076 | 189,332 | 75.16 |
| 1940 | 575,901 | 222,476 | 72.13 |
| 1950 | 580,132 | 319,106 | 64.51 |
| 1960 | 532,759 | 531,929 | 50.03 |
| 1970 | 462,768 | 650,732 | 41.56 |
| 1980 | 357,870 | 650,723 | 35.24 |
| 1990 | 328,123 | 640,049 | 33.89 |
| 2000 | 292,648 | 657,617 | 30.80 |

Source: U.S. Census Bureau, Population of Census.

percentage of blacks living in the city increased to 20%. The die was cast. The suburbanization process was sorting and sifting the population by race.

In retrospect, the rise of homeownership combined with land-use regulation, the amortized mortgage, and easy access to capital, birthed the fair housing issue and planted the seeds that grew into the post 1970 housing affordability problem. The reason is that the HOLC system sent a powerful message to bankers that black and low-to-moderate income white neighborhoods were high risk places, for which prudent investors should withhold credit for the purchase, repair or renovation of housing. According to the neighborhood life-cycle theory, African Americans were prime triggers of neighborhood decline, thereby making them the most undesirable residents in the metropolis. Therefore, black neighborhoods, in particular, should be avoided by financial institutions and African Americans should be kept out of the most desirable communities (Metzger 2003). Consequently, the HOLC rating system, combined with the rise of homeownership, operated in the context of an economically rational housing market to transform neighborhoods into defended territories where residents sought to keep out undesirables, especially African Americans. Thus, maintaining property values and protecting the home investment became part of the cult of homeownership and neighborhood culture, and this changed fundamentally the nature of race and class relations in the urban metropolis (Massey and Denton 1993).

## The Second Episode

In the second episode, the multiracial East Side industrial neighborhood was broken-up, thereby opening up the age of racial residential segregation in Buffalo. During the opening decades of the 20th century, most blacks lived in the East Side industrial neighborhood, along with a plethora of white ethnics. Outside this neighborhood, the only other concentration of blacks was found in Cold Springs, which was situated between Best Street and East Delavan, and Main Street and Jefferson Avenue on the east and west. The remainder of the African American population was scattered across the city, where they resided largely in neighborhoods dominated by white ethnic groups. During these years, racial residential segregation did not exist in Buffalo. Even in those communities where blacks were concentrated, they did not dominate residential space (BMHA 1934).

In those days, blacks were at the bottom of the city's socioeconomic order. They were mostly a low-income group comprised primarily of domestic servants and unskilled and semi-skilled laborers. Twelve percent held skilled laborer jobs, while only seven percent were employed as professionals—musicians, ministers, social workers, doctors, dentists and lawyers. There were no black bankers, financiers or brokers. Although blacks shared residential space with whites, they lived under deplorable housing conditions. For example, about 75% of the black population lived in housing that was designated as substandard in the city's 1937 Real Property Survey, which explains, in part, why most of the neighborhoods in which blacks lived were colored red by the HOLC (City of Buffalo 1940). Between 1940 and 1970, Buffalo's black population exploded as it jumped from 17,694 to 94,540, an increase of more than 77,000, representing a jump from 3% to 20% of the population.[4] As African Americans moved into the City, an even larger number of whites moved to the suburbs. During this same period, the suburban population grew by more than 428,000 as it zoomed from

---

[4] This movement of blacks to Buffalo was part of the Second Great Migration of blacks out of the South. More than 2 million African Americans moved to urban centers in the North and also millions left the farms for southern cities as well.

222,500 to 650,700, while the city's population declined by a little over 113,000 residents (Taylor 1990).

The city used a twofold strategy to house this rapidly growing black population, and their approach spawned the growth of racial residential segregation in Buffalo. The first strategy focused on the use of filtered-down East Side housing to provide lodging for African Americans. Most of the 77,000 blacks moving into Buffalo between 1940 and 1970 settled in the spatial margin between East Delavan and Eagle Street and between Main Street and Jefferson Avenue, where they moved into housing that had been previously occupied by whites. According to the HOLC survey, the neighborhoods into which African Americans were moving were declining communities that had been coded yellow. Thus, in Buffalo's transitional city, a housing filtration strategy was used to meet the demands of African Americans, while white newcomers and old timers were being steered into new suburban neighborhoods with good housing and amenities. Policy makers believed that blacks could not afford the new housing being constructed in the suburban region and would devalue the war housing units being constructed in white neighborhoods, so they tried to keep them out. The de facto process of separating blacks and whites in residential space was starting.

The second strategy to cope with the increase in black population, involved using public housing to provide lodging for African Americans. This approach did provide African Americans with higher quality housing, but it also forced them to live in a segregated residential environment. In the middle 1930s, urban leaders and real estate industry spokespersons, especially those affiliated with the National Association of Real Estate Boards (NAREB), began calling for the federal government to curb the ruinous effects of urban decay, to revitalize the central city, and to protect downtown real estate investments. Much of the real estate industry's lobbying efforts from the 1930s through the 1950s included the development of a series of policy proposals to facilitate the public acquisitions of slum land in blighted areas for clearance and resale to private builders. These proposals included state acts empowering municipalities to redevelop blighted areas, public-private coordination of urban land-use and controls, long-term federal loans to cities at low interest rates, and generous tax subsidies and write-offs for local redevelopment proposals. The 1949 and 1954 Housing Acts provided federal funds for local redevelopment authorities to designate 'blighted' areas, acquire and clear land, and then sell the land to private developers or local housing authorities for public housing (Gotham 2001).

Public housing was not meant to provide housing solely for African Americans. Rather, it was considered transitional housing for working class families, white and black, who were experiencing temporary financial difficulties. They were built to high construction standards and meant to provide residents with good living conditions, as well as a social atmosphere conducive to the development of good citizenship. However, within this context, the federal and state governments allowed local government to organize public housing units along racial lines. As a result, local housing authorities in Buffalo, Chicago and other cities frequently segregated residents according to race, and so they built housing developments in areas where blacks were heavily concentrated (Kraus 2004).

Starting in 1934, Buffalo's public housing developments were built in several locations around the city and in the suburbs, but African Americans were allowed to live only in those developments built on the lower east side, the Willert Park apartments (Kraus 2004). The issue of whether to allow blacks to live in public housing in predominantly white residential areas came to a head in 1941. That year, several white neighborhoods successfully mobilized opposition to housing for African Americans, who were employed in war-related industries that were located in their neighborhoods. Thus, growing white opposition to blacks in their neighborhoods caused new war housing to be built in the shadow of the Willert Park apartments, thereby reinforcing the growing pattern of racial residential segregation. Moreover, this action demonstrated that strong opposition existed to black presence in white neighborhoods, and policy makers would use this knowledge to influence future decisions on where to construct public housing units (Kraus 2004).

The city and regional building process initiated in the 1930s in Buffalo, and elsewhere, altered the social geography of the metropolitan region by creating an urban duality between the central city and the suburban hinterland. The suburbs became the residential center of higher income groups, living in new single family dwelling units, while the central city became the place where blacks and low-income workers were overrepresented. In this new setting, racial residential segregation became the norm. In 1968, the Kerner Commission, in its report on urban riots, said the United States is moving toward the development of two societies, "one largely Negro and poor, located in central

cities; the other predominantly white and affluent, located in the suburbs" (in Massey and Denton 1993:3–4).

The quest to build a regional city based on a system of homeownership, operating in the context of an economically rational housing
market, was the culprit. This approach to city and regional building
dramatically changed the urban metropolis and the way in which
neighborhoods were organized. For example, between 1940 and 1970,
the national rate of homeownership jumped from 43% to 63%, an
increase of 47%. In New York State, during the same time, the homeownership rate jumped from 30% to 47%, an increase of 57%. Not only
did the rate of homeownership change, but even more importantly, the
emergence of the economically-rational housing market transformed
the owner-occupied dwelling unit into a commodity to be bought and
sold for a profit (U.S. Census of Housing 1940–2000).

This shift of owner-occupied housing from a cultural artifact to a
commodity is reflected in the dramatic increase in the value of housing, both nationally and in New York State. Nationally, between 1940
and 1970, in constant dollars, the value of housing jumped by 110%, as
it increased from $31,000 to $65,000. In New York State, the value of
housing increased by 87%. In other places, the increase was even more
dramatic. For example, in Tennessee, the value in housing increased by
153% during the same time frame, and in Illinois, the value of housing
jumped by 124%, as it increased from $34,000 to $76,000 (U.S. Census
of Housing, 1940–2000). Overall, nationally, between 1940 and 2000,
the value of housing increased by 287%, as it jumped from $31,000 to
$120,000 (Figure 1).

The great irony is that increments in the cost of housing ultimately
placed homeownership beyond the reach of many Americans, thereby,
thwarting the original goal of mass homeownership. For example,
between 1940 and 1960, the rate of homeownership increased by 32%,
while in the forty year period between 1960 and 2000, the homeownership rate increased by only 6.4%. On the other hand, the cost of housing increased by 103% over the same period. The ratio between cost
and homeownership helps to explain why race was a factor in this
quest. Between 1940 and the present, as owner-occupied housing
morphed into a commodity, it became a major source of wealth accumulation in the United States. However, the income disparity between
blacks and whites produced a disparity in homeownership between the
two groups. The gap between homeownership rates among white
households and black households has exceeded 20 percentage points

**Median Home Values: 1940 to 2000**

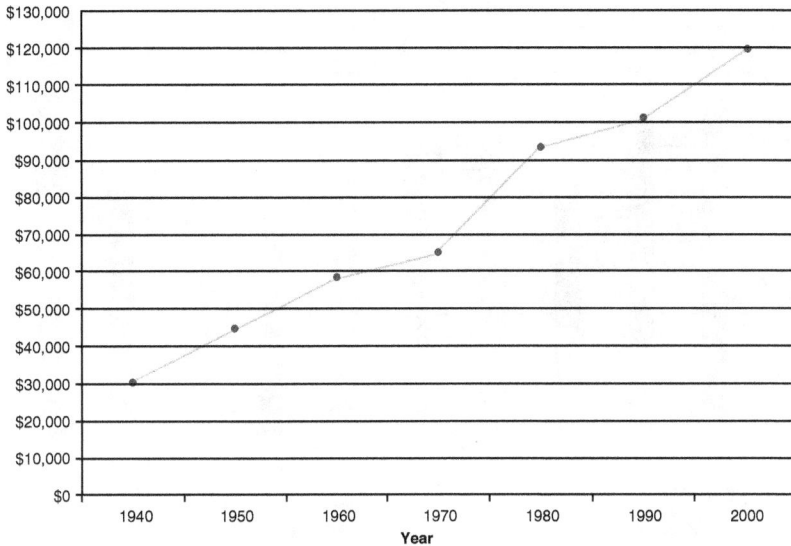

Figure 1. Median Home Values 1940-2000 (in 2000 dollars)
*Source:* U.S. Census of Housing, Historical Census of Housing Graphs,
http://www.census.gov/hhes/www/housing/census/historic/hvgraph.html.

every year since 1940, and in 2000 that gap was 26% (Leigh and Huff 2007). In that census year, about 71% of whites owned the home within which they lived, while about 46% of African Americans and 45% of Latinos owned their homes (Figure 2). So, for whites, mass homeownership became a reality, while for blacks and Latinos it remains a dream deferred. In terms of value, the median value of homes for whites is $123,000, for blacks it is $81,000 and for Latinos it is $105,000.

## The Third Episode

During the first half of the 20th century, urban leaders in Buffalo and elsewhere forged their dream of building a metropolitan city and then formulated plans to guide its development. Between 1950 and 1970, cities, including Buffalo, began the process of implementing these plans. The legislative engine that drove this effort was the Housing Act of 1949 and the 1956 Federal-Aid Highway Act (Lang and Sohmer 2000). The 1949 Housing Act provided local government with funding for slum clearance programs associated with urban renewal projects

270                          HENRY LOUIS TAYLOR, JR.

Homeownership Rates by Race and Hispanics Origin of Householder: 2000

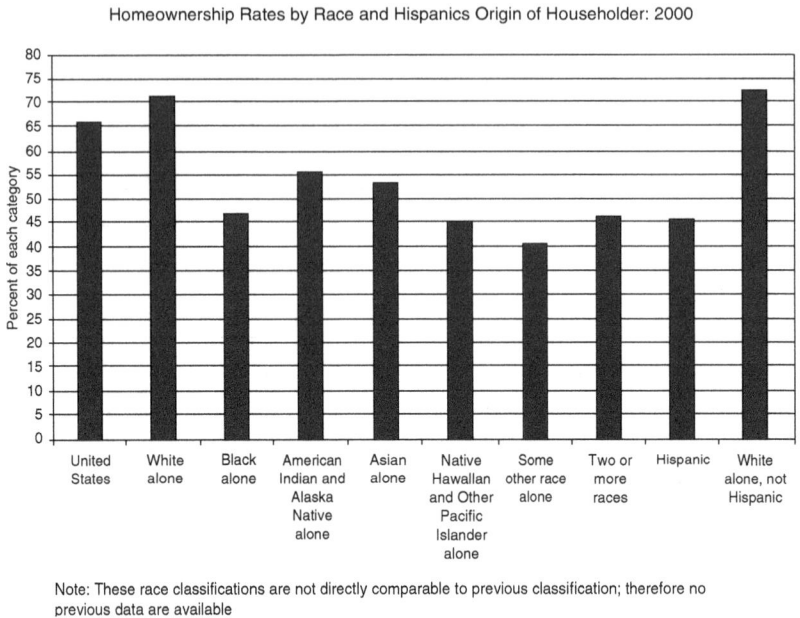

Note: These race classifications are not directly comparable to previous classification; therefore no
previous data are available

Figure 2. Homeownership Rates by Race and Hispanic Origin of
Householder, 2000
*Source:* U.S. Census of Housing, Historical Census of Housing Graphs,
http://www.census.gov/hhes/www/housing/census/historic/racegraph.html.


in American cities, increased authorization for the Federal Housing
Administration (FHA) mortgage insurance, and extended federal
money to build more public housing units. The Federal-Aid Highway
Act gave state and federal government complete control over new
highways, which were often directed through vibrant urban neighborhoods, especially those where African Americans lived. The fundamental goal of the Highway Act was to create an arterial system that
moved traffic in and out of central cities as efficiently and effectively as
possible (Levine 1959).

This metropolitan city-building process had a dual impact on the
urban metropolis. On one hand, the slum clearance and highway
construction strategy led to the destruction of many of the central
city's vibrant working class and African American communities and
intensified the outmigration of whites. For example, in Buffalo, between
1950 and 1970, the central city population dropped by 20%, as the
number of people living in Buffalo fell from 580,132 to 462,768. Most
of the residents leaving the city were white. For instance, during this
twenty year period, 178,065 whites left the City, as their number fell

from 542,432 to 364,367, a decline of 33%. Concurrently, the city's African American population increased by 57,584 (or 157%) as their numbers grew from 36,745 to 94,329 (Taylor 1990).

In Buffalo, the highway construction process wreaked havoc in the black community. Policymakers routed most of the new highway construction through the East Side, where the growing black population was settling. For example, the construction of the Niagara Thruway to connect the Buffalo Niagara Frontier to the Erie Thruway was built through portions of the East Side Industrial neighborhood, and the building of the Kensington Expressway to link downtown Buffalo to the regional airport and to provide rapid transit from the northeastern suburbs to the CBD, led to the destruction of the beautiful Humboldt Park and cut through Hamlin Park, an emerging black middle class community. As the Kensington Expressway moved through the black community, it divided neighborhoods, demolished hundreds of dwelling units, devalued property and accelerated the process of neighborhood decline (Taylor 1990).

On the flip side, omnipresent demolition combined with new highway construction and road widening to facilitate suburban growth and development. Thus, while blacks were moving into public housing and declining neighborhoods, whites were moving into the rapidly developing suburban region. For example, between 1950 and 1970, the Erie County suburban population increased by 331,617, an increment of 104%. By 1970, in Buffalo and across the United States, for the first time, the suburban population outnumbered the central city population (Taylor 1990).

The residential dominance of the suburbs over the central city marked the dawning of a new age in urban development. This new urban metropolis was characterized by a duality in which blacks, people of color and low-income groups were overrepresented in the core, while whites were overrepresented in the suburban region. Not only this, but the suburbs became associated with homeownership, upward social mobility and the good life, while the central city became increasingly associated with blacks, crime, and the urban crisis (Massey and Denton 2003).

## Reflection

The Buffalo vision of transforming the central city and suburb into One Big City never happened. Instead, the metropolitan city-building process created an urban duality and spawned the problems of fair housing and housing affordability. Before the economic rationalization of the housing market, while blacks and other groups experienced housing discrimination, racial factors did not shape the social geography of the urban environment. Back then, when housing was a cultural artifact, the value of housing in working class neighborhoods was not tied to racial exclusion. In this setting, although blacks might be over-represented in one part of the neighborhood and whites in another, the two groups nonetheless shared residential space.

The commoditization of housing and the rise of homeownership changed this. When the economically rational housing market supplanted the non-economically rational market, housing was transformed from a cultural artifact to a commodity. When this happened, increasingly, the goal of homeownership was to make a profit on the building and selling of dwelling units, and homeownership became the major source of wealth acquisition in the United States. To make possible the building of homogenous neighborhoods and to protect owner-occupied housing, cities used zoning laws, building codes and subdivision regulations to build the regulated city and to develop neighborhoods stratified based on housing cost and type. These regulations transformed neighborhoods into defended territories, where residents sought to keep out people and land-uses that might devalue property. The work of the Homeowners Loan Corporation reinforced this growing trend with its neighborhood life-cycle theory. By declaring that blacks were a major cause of neighborhood decline, HOLC actually encouraged racial discrimination in the sale, rental and financing of housing, thereby, wittingly or unwittingly, making fair housing an urban problem.

Concurrently, although housing affordability did not emerge as a problem until after 1970, the seeds were planted during the regional city-building era. The commoditization of housing meant that one critical purpose of home owning was to accumulate wealth from the buying and selling of property. Thus, in the decades after 1950, the value of housing grew exponentially, especially from 1970 onward. For example, nationally, between 1950 and 1970, the median value of housing increased from $45.000 to $65,000, an increase of about 44%. However, between 1970 and 2000, the median value of housing increased from $65,000 to $120,000, an increase of 85%. Overall, between 1940 and 2000, the value of housing increased by 167%, while ownership increased by 50%, with most of that increment coming between 1940 and 1960. In the forty years between 1960 and 2000, homeownership rates increased by only four percent. Thus, the commoditization of housing placed profit-making at the center of the production and sale of housing in the United States. The increasing cost of housing meant that fewer and fewer people could purchase their homes and renters had to pay an increasing portion of their income on housing.

*References*

Babcock, F. M. 1932. *The Valuation of Real Estate.* New York: McGraw-Hill.

Behrens, C. F., Curtis P. Summers, Richard M. Creath. April, 1939. *Analysis of the Housing Market, Buffalo, NY.* Washington: Division of Economics and Statistics, Federal Housing Administration.

Bettman, A. 1924. "Constitutionality of Zoning." *Harvard Law Review* 37(7): 834–859.

Bullard, R. D. 1984. "The Black Family: Housing Alternatives in the 80s." *Journal of Black Studies* 14(3): 341–351.

Buffalo Municipal Housing Authority. 1953. *Buffalo–New York State-61: Site B Parcels.* UB Center for Urban Studies, School of Architecture and Planning, University at Buffalo.

Burgess, P. 1994. *Planning for the Private Interests: Land Use Controls and Residential Patterns in Columbus, Ohio, 1900–1970.* Columbus: Ohio State University Press.

Bureau of Intelligence. 1942. *Progress Memorandum on Treasury Study in Buffalo.* Record Group 44: Records of the Office of Government Reports, Records of the Bureau of Special Service, Report of the Survey Division, 1942–1944, Office of War Information.

Charity Organization Society of Buffalo. 1927. "Fifty Years of Family Social Work, 1877–1927." Pp. 37–66 in F. S. Palen (Ed.), *Buffalo City Planning: Selected Materials, 1880–1960.* Buffalo: School of Architecture and Planning, University at Buffalo.

Cohen, L. 1989. "Encountering Mass Culture at the Grassroots: The Experience of Chicago Workers in the 1920s." *American Quarterly* 41(1): 6–33.

City of Buffalo. 1940. *Real Property Survey and Supplementary Low-Income Housing Area Survey.* Buffalo.

City Planning Committee of the Council. 1925. "Extract of Proposed Zoning Ordinance for Buildings and Uses Buffalo." Pp. 1–10 in F. S. Palen (Ed.), *Buffalo City Planning: Selected Materials, 1880–1960.* Buffalo: School of Architecture and Planning Library, University at Buffalo.

City Planning Committee of the Council. December 31, 1920. "Second Annual Report." Pp. 7–19 in F. S. Palen (Ed.), *Buffalo City Planning: Selected Materials, 1880–1960.* Buffalo: School of Architecture and Planning Library, University at Buffalo.

City Planning Committee of the Council. 1919. "First Annual Report." Pp. 9–30 in F. S. Palen (Ed.), *Buffalo City Planning: Selected Materials, 1880–1960.* Buffalo: School of Architecture and Planning, University at Buffalo.

City Planning Department. 2003. *Census 2000 SF3 Summary Statistics, Erie County, City of Buffalo and Buffalo Council Districts.* Buffalo, New York: City of Buffalo.

Civic League of St. Louis. 1908. *Housing Conditions in St. Louis: Report of the Housing Committee of St. Louis.* St. Louis.

Deane, A .G., F. Milliken., Jr. 1936. Confidential Report of a Survey in Buffalo, New York. Buffalo, New York: Mortgage Rehabilitation Division, Home Owners Loan Corporation, Washington, D.C., January 25. UB Center for Urban Studies, School of Architecture and Planning, University at Buffalo.

Department of Public Works. 1913-1914. "22nd Annual Report, 1913-1914." Pp. 63-68 in F. S. Palen (Ed.), Buffalo City Planning: Selected Materials, 1880-1960. School of Law, University at Buffalo.

Downs, A. 1988/1989. "The Housing Challenge." *The Brookings Review* 7(1): 34-35.

Emergency Relief Bureau, Work Division. 1934. *Maps and Charts: Slum Area Determination Study*. Buffalo: Buffalo Municipal Housing Authority. UB Center for Urban Studies, School of Architecture and Planning, University at Buffalo.

Fairbanks, R. B. 1988. *Making Better Citizens: Housing Reform and the Community Development Strategy in Cincinnati, 1890-1960*. Urbana and Chicago: University of Illinois Press.

Feldman, R. 2002. "The Affordable Housing Shortage: Considering the Problem, Causes and Solutions." Bank and Policy Working Paper 02-2: Federal Reserve Bank of Minneapolis, 1-43.

Goldman, M. 1983. *High Hopes: The Rise and Decline of Buffalo, New York*. Albany: State University of New York Press.

Gordon, A. 2005. "The Creation of Homeownership: How New Deal Changes in Banking Regulation Simultaneously Made Homeownership Accessible to Whites and out of Reach for Blacks." *The Yale Law Journal* 115(1): 186-226.

Gotham, K. F. 2000. "Urban Space, Restrictive Covenants and the Origins of Racial Residential Segregation in a US City, 1900-1950." *Internal Journal of Urban and Regional Research* 24(3): 616-633.

Gotham, K. F. 2001. "A City Without Slums: Urban Renewal, Public Housing and Downtown Revitalization in Kansas City, Missouri." *American Journal of Economics and Sociology* 60(1): 285-316.

Goss, J. 1988. "The Built Environment and Social Theory: Toward an Architectural Geography." *Professional Geographer* 49(4): 392-403.

Hageman, W. 1916. *City Planning for Milwaukee: What it Means and Why it Must be Secured*. Milwaukee: The Wisconsin Chapter of the American Association of Architects.

Hallauer, F. J. 1934. "Population and Building Construction." *The Journal of Land & Public Utility Economics* 10(1): 35-41.

Hallauer, F. J. 1937. "Prospective Residential Construction." *The Journal of Land & Public Utility Economics* 13(1): 14-19.

Harris, R. 1996. *Unplanned Suburbs: Toronto's American Tragedy, 1990 to 1950*. Baltimore and London: The Johns Hopkins University Press.

Harris, R. 1997. "Reading Sanborns for the Spoor of the Owner-Builder, 1890s-1950s." *Perspectives in Vernacular Architecture* 7: 251-267.

Harris, R., Robert Lewis. 2001. "The Geography of North American Cities and Suburbs, 1900-1950: A New Synthesis." *Journal of Urban History* 27(3): 262-292.

Hayden, D. 1980. "What Would a Non-Sexist City Be Like? Speculations on Housing, Urban Design, and Human Work." *Signs* 5(3): S170-S187.

Heathcott, J. 2008. "The City Quietly Remade: National Programs and Local Agendas in the Movement to Clear the Slums, 1942-1952." *Journal of Urban History* 34(2): 221-242.

Henderson, A. S. 2000. *Housing and the Democratic Ideal: The Life and Thought of Charles Abrams*. New York: Columbia University Press.

Home owners Loan Corporation. 1937. "Area Descriptions-Security Maps of the Buffalo Area-New York: Buffalo, New York." UB Center for Urban Studies, School of Architecture and Planning, University at Buffalo.

Hillier, A. E. 2003. "Redlining and the Home Owners' Loan Corporation." *Journal of Urban History* 29(4): 394-420.

Housing Committee 1908. *Housing Conditions in St. Louis*. St. Louis: Civic League of St. Louis.

Kain, J. F. 1983. America's Persistent Housing Crises: Errors in Analysis and Policy. *Annals of the American Academy of Political and Social Science* 465: 136-148.

Kraus, N. 2004. "Local Policymaking and Concentrated Poverty: The Case of Buffalo, New York." *Cities* 21(1): 481–490.

Lang, E. R, Rebecca R. Sohmer. 2000. "Legacy of the Housing Act of 1949: The Past, Present, and Future of Federal Housing and Urban Policy." *Housing Policy Debate* 11(2): 291–298.

Leigh, W. A., Danielle Huff. 2007. "African Americans and Homeownership: Separate and Unequal, 1940–2006." *Joint Center for Political and Economic Studies*. November. http://www.jointcenter.org/index.php/publications_recent_publications/economics_business/african_americans_and_homeownership_the_subprime_lending_experience_1995_to_2007_november_2007_brief_2.

Levine, D. R. 1959. "Federal Aspects of the Interstate Highway Program." *Nebraska Law Review* 38: 377–406.

Lewis, E. 1991. *In Their Own Interests: Race, Class, and Power in Twentieth-Century Norfolk, Virginia*. Berkeley, Los Angeles and Oxford: University of California Press.

Mann, M. D. 1912. "The New City Planning Bill: Introduction." Pp. 27–29 in F. S. Palen (Ed.), *Buffalo City Planning: Selected Materials, 1880–1960 (Vol. 1)*. Buffalo: University at Buffalo, School of Law.

Massey, D.S., Nancy A. Denton. 1993. *American Apartheid: Segregation and the Making of the Underclass*. Cambridge and London: Harvard University Press.

Metzger, J. T. 2000. "Planned Abandonment: The Neighborhood Life-Cycle Theory and National Urban Policy." *Housing Policy Debate* 11(1): 7–40.

Milliken, F. Jr. 1937. Bulletin on Buffalo Area–New York: Record Group 44: Records of the Office of Government Reports, Record of the Bureau of Special Service, Report of the Survey Division, 1942–1944. UB Center for Urban Studies, School of Architecture and Planning, University at Buffalo.

Monchow, H. C. 1939. "A Yardstick of Residential Lot Needs." *The Journal of Land & Public Utility Economics* 15(4): 474–477.

Niagara Frontier Planning Board. 1925. First Annual Report of the Niagara Frontier Planning Board. Buffalo, New York: New York State Bureau of Housing and Regional Planning. Frank S. Palen, Niagara Frontier Planning Board, Annual Reports, UB School of Architecture and Planning Materials, 1880–1960.

Patterson, K. L., Robert M. Silverman. 2008. *Analysis of Impediments to Fair Housing Choice in Erie County, NY*. The Erie County Development Block Grant (CDBG) Consortium, and in towns of Amherst, Cheektowaga, and Tonawanda.

Quigley, J. M., S. Raphael. 2004. "Is Housing Unaffordable? Why Isn't It More Affordable?" *The Journal of Economic Perspectives* 18(1): 191–214.

Radford, G. 1996. *Modern Housing for America: Policy Struggles in the New Deal Era*. Chicago: University of Chicago Press.

Rae, D. W. 2003. *City: Urbanism and Its End*. New Haven: Yale University Press.

Richardson, J. (Cartographer). 1900. Buffalo Historical GIS. http://history.buffalostate.edu/BuffaloGIS/StartGIS.htm.

Self, R. 2001. "Writing Landscapes of Class, Power, and Racial Division: The Problem of (Sub)Urban Space and Place in Postwar America: A Review Essay." *Journal of Urban History* 27(2): 237–250.

Smith, G. 1926. "Buffalo vs. Buffalo." *Survey* 57(2): 92–94, in Frank S. Palen, *Buffalo City Planning*, Vol. 91. Law School, University at Buffalo.

Stutz, F. P., Arthur E. Kartman. 1982. "Housing Affordability and Spatial Price Variations in the United States." *Economic Geography* 58(3): 221–235.

Taylor, G. R. 1915. *Satellite Cities: A Study of Industrial Suburbs*. New York and London: D. Appleton and Company.

Taylor, H. L., Jr. 1979. *The Building of a Black Industrial Suburb: The Lincoln Heights, Ohio Story*. Unpublished Dissertation. University at Buffalo, Buffalo.

Taylor, H. L., Jr. 1990. *African Americans and the Rise of Buffalo's Post-Industrial City, 1940 to Present*. Vol. 2. Buffalo: Buffalo Urban League.

Taylor, H. L., Jr. 1993. "City building, Public Policy, the Rise of the Industrial City, and Black Ghetto-Slum Formation in Cincinnati, 1850–1940." Pp. 156–192 and 167 in J. Henry Louis Taylor (Ed.), *Race and the City: Work, Community, and Protest in Cincinnati, 1820–1970*. Urbana and Chicago: University of Illinois Press.

Taylor, H. L., Jr. 2000. "Creating the Metropolis in Black and White." Pp. 51–71 in Henry Louis Taylor, Walter Hill (Ed.), *Historical Roots of the Urban Crisis: African Americans in the Industrial City, 1900–1950*. New York and London: Garland Publishing, Inc.

Taylor, H. L., Jr. 2000. "Creating the Metropolis in Black and White: Black Suburbanization and the Planning Movement in Cincinnati, 1900–1950." Pp. 51–71 and 52 in H. L. Taylor, Jr. and Walter Hill (Ed.), *Historical Roots of the Urban Crisis: African Americans in the Industrial City, 1900–1950*. New York and London: Garland Publishing, Inc.

Taylor, H. L., Jr., Walter Hill. 2000. "Prologue." Pp. xiii-xxii in Henry Louis Taylor and Walter Hill (Ed.), *Historical Roots of the Urban Crisis: African Americans in the Industrial City, 1900–1950*. New York and London: Garland Publishing.

Teaford, J. C. 1979. *City and Suburb: The Political Fragmentation of Metropolitan America, 1850–1970*. Baltimore and London: The Johns Hopkins University Press.

Teaford, J. C. 1986. *The Twentieth Century American City: Problem, Promise and Reality*. Baltimore: The Johns Hopkins Press.

The Buffalo City Planning Association. November 1924. "What Zoning Means." Pp. 1 in F. S. Palen (Ed.), *Buffalo City Planning: Selected Materials, 1880–1960*. Buffalo: School of Architecture and Planning Library, University at Buffalo.

U.S. National Advisory Commission on Civil Disorders. 1968. "The Kerner Report." P. 4 in Massey, D. S., Nancy A. Denton. *American Apartheid: Segregation and the Making of the Underclass*. Cambridge and London: Harvard University Press.

U.S. Census Bureau. 1940–2000. Historical Census of Housing Tables. from U.S. Census Bureau. http://www.census.gov/hhes/www/housing/census/histcensushsg.html.

Weaver, R. C. 1944. "Race Restrictive Housing Covenants." *The Journal of Land & Public Utility Economics* 20(3): 183–193.

Wheelock, D. C. 2008. "The Federal Response to Home Mortgage Distress: Lessons from the Great Depression." *Review* 90(3, Part 1): 133–148.

Wiese, A. 2004. *Places of Their Own: African American Suburbanization in the Twentieth Century*. Chicago and London: University of Chicago Press.

Williams, L. S. 1999. *Strangers in the Land of Paradise: The Creation of an African American Community, Buffalo, New York*. Bloomington and Indianapolis: Indiana University Press.

# SEGREGATION AS A DRIVER OF SUBPRIME LENDING AND THE ENSUING ECONOMIC FALLOUT[1]

## Gregory D. Squires

### Introduction

Dramatic changes have taken place in the U.S. mortgage lending markets in recent years. Passage of the Community Reinvestment Act (CRA) in 1977, enforcement of the federal Fair Housing Act (FHA), and compliance with a range of local, state, and national fair lending rules have increased access to credit for many households and communities long denied conventional financial services. Within the past decade, the rise in subprime and predatory lending has put many families and neighborhoods in financial jeopardy. This has been particularly problematic in minority and low-income areas where default and foreclosure rates are skyrocketing at the time of this writing. Fingers are pointed in several directions: greed on the part of families trying to buy homes they could not afford, lax underwriting by originators, inaccurate appraisals, fraudulent practices by investment bankers, inattention by regulators, and more. Community groups, elected officials, bank regulators and mortgage lenders themselves are debating how the nation should respond.

Lost amidst recent debates is the central role that surging economic inequality and persistent racial segregation have played. The concentration of income and wealth at the top coupled with the concentration of poverty and persisting levels of segregation and hyper-segregation have nurtured significant increases in subprime and predatory lending among vulnerable communities. Reforming the regulation of financial services is a necessary but insufficient step for ameliorating the crises created by recent lending practices. Broader macro-economic policies that directly address various trajectories of economic inequality and

---

[1] This Chapter is based on comments made by the author before the Joint Economic Committee of the U.S. Congress, June 25, 2009. The comments were made in the hearing titled, "Predatory Lending and Reverse Redlining: Are Low-income, Minority and Senior Borrowers Targets for Higher Cost Loans?"

dynamics of discrimination and segregation must complement progressive banking and bank regulatory reforms if emerging challenges are to be met (Squires 2008/9). In this chapter I examine the impact of inequality on subprime and predatory lending and offer a range of policy responses to the emerging problems confronting metropolitan areas across the U.S.

## Surging Inequality

By virtually any measure, economic inequality has increased in recent decades. Between 1967 and 2007, the share of income in the U.S. going to the top quintile of all households increased from 43.6% to 49.7%, while the share going to the bottom fifth dropped from 4.0% to 3.4% (Walt-Denavas 2008). Since the mid 1970s, compensation for the 100 highest paid chief executive officers increased from $1.3 million, or thirty-nine times the pay of the average worker, to $37.5 million, or more than 1,000 times the pay of a typical worker (Krugman 2002). In 2004, those in the top 1% enjoyed a 12.5% increase in their incomes compared to 1.5% for the remaining 99% (Krugman 2006).

Wealth, of course, has long been much more unequally distributed than income, and that inequality has increased over time. Between 1983 and 2001, the share of wealth going to the top 5% grew from 56.1% to 59.2%. While African Americans and Hispanics earn approximately two-thirds of what whites earn, wealth holdings for the typical non-white family are approximately one-tenth that of the typical white family (Shapiro 2006, National Community Reinvestment Coalition and the Woodstock Institute 2006).

City residents have been falling behind their suburban counterparts, and non-white neighborhoods have been falling behind white communities. In 1960, per capita income in cities was 105% that of suburbanites, but in 2000, urban residents were earning just 84% of those in the suburbs (Cisneros 1999, Logan 2002b). The median census tract income for the typical black household in 1990 was $27,808 compared to $45,486 for whites, a gap of $17,679. A similar pattern holds for Hispanics (Logan 2002a).

Between 1970 and 2000, the number of high poverty census tracts (those where 40% or more of the population is poor) grew from 1177 to 2510, and the number of people living in those tracts grew from 4.1 million to 7.9 million (Jargowsky 1998; Jargowsky 2003). The isolation of rich and poor families is also reflected by the declining number of middle income communities (Booza et al. 2006). Between 1970 and 2000, the number of middle income neighborhoods (census tracts where the median family income is between 80% and 120% of the median family income for the metropolitan area) dropped from 58% to 41% of all metropolitan area neighborhoods (Booza et al. 2006). And whereas more than half of lower-income families lived in middle income neighborhoods in 1970, only 37% of such families did so in 2000 (Booza et al. 2006). The share of low-income families in low-income areas grew from 36% to 48% (Booza et al. 2006). Even longer standing patterns of racial segregation persist.

Nationwide, the black/white index of dissimilarity declined from .73 to .64 between 1980 and 2000 (Iceland et al. 2002; Timberlake and Iceland 2007).[2] Scores above .60 are widely viewed as reflecting high levels of segregation. But in the large metropolitan areas where the black population is most concentrated, segregation levels persist at high levels reaching at or near .80 in New York, Chicago, Detroit, Milwaukee, and many other urban communities. Lower levels exist primarily in western and southwestern communities with small black populations. For Hispanics and Asians, segregation levels are much lower, approximately .4 and .5, but they have remained at that level or actually increased slightly between 1980 and 2000 (Iceland et al 2002; Farley and Squires 2005).

*Inequality and Subprime Lending*

A wealth of research has documented the concentration of subprime loans in low-income and minority communities (Squires et al. 2009). Home Mortgage Disclosure Act (HMDA) reports reveal, for example, that for 2006, when subprime lending was at its peak, for first lien conventional home purchase loans, 46% of borrowers in low-income areas received a high-priced loan, compared to 16% in upper income areas. Among borrowers in predominantly non-white communities 49% received such loans compared to 18% in predominantly white

---

[2] This index varies from 0 to 1, where a score of 0 would indicate that each neighborhood had the same racial composition of the metropolitan area as a whole and a score of 1 would represent total segregation meaning every neighborhood was either all African American or all white.

areas. In that year, 53% of African Americans, 46% of Hispanics, and 22% of whites received high-priced loans. Subsequent research revealed that even after controlling on credit rating, income, and other financial characteristics, racial disparities persist (Calem et al. 2004).

Such patterns are no accident. The City of Baltimore recently sued Wells Fargo Bank for racially discriminatory predatory lending patterns in that community leading to high foreclosure rates and the heavy costs associated with those foreclosures. Plaintiffs found, for example, that the foreclosure rate for Wells Fargo loans was twice the city-wide average in African American communities while the rate in white neighborhoods was half the city-wide average (Mayor and City Council of Baltimore v. Wells Fargo Bank, U.S. District Court for the District of Maryland, Baltimore Division Case Number 1:2008v00062, January 8, 2008). Subsequent investigation revealed that Wells Fargo loan officers were provided financial incentives to steer borrowers from lower-cost prime loans to higher-cost subprime loans, referring to them as "ghetto loans" and to the borrowers as "mud people" (Powell 2009).

And racial segregation has an effect above and beyond that of race alone. Table 1 shows that the share of loans that are high-priced is considerably higher in highly segregated than in less segregated communities. The average share of such loans in the nation's ten most segregated communities is 31% compared to 20% in the ten least segregated.

Far more significant, however, is that racial and ethnic segregation remain statistically significant predictors of the level of high-priced loans even after controlling for credit rating, poverty level, percent minority, and education (see Tables 2 and 3). These data show, for example, that a 10% increase in black/white segregation (measured by the index of dissimilarity) is associated with an increase of 1.4% in high-cost lending. Every 10% increase in Hispanic/white segregation is associated with an increase of 0.6% in high-cost lending.

*Policy Responses*

Many proposals have been offered to change the way banks do business and the way they are regulated. Clearly, such reforms are necessary. But if the problems generated by subprime and predatory lending along with the foreclosures and other economic costs that followed

Table 1.  Top Ten Most and Least Segregated Metro Areas and Percent of High-Cost Loans

| Ten most segregated metropolitan regions | Black segregation index | % High-cost loans |
|---|---|---|
| Detroit-Warren-Livonia, MI | 84 | 34 |
| Milwaukee-Waukesha-West Allis, WI | 81 | 29 |
| Chicago-Naperville-Joliet, IL-IN-WI | 78 | 31 |
| Cleveland-Elyria-Mentor, OH | 77 | 28 |
| Flint, MI | 76 | 37 |
| Muskegon-Norton Shores, MI | 76 | 38 |
| Buffalo-Niagara Falls, NY | 76 | 25 |
| Niles-Benton Harbor, MI | 73 | 30 |
| St. Louis, MO-IL | 73 | 31 |
| Cincinnati-Middletown, OH-KY-IN | 73 | 25 |
| Average | 77 | 31 |
| Ten least segregated metropolitan regions | | |
| Coeur d'Alene, ID | 16 | 24 |
| Hinesville-Fort Stewart, GA | 18 | 39 |
| Santa Fe, NM | 21 | 17 |
| Prescott, AZ | 21 | 21 |
| Bellingham, WA | 22 | 16 |
| Boulder, CO | 23 | 10 |
| Jacksonville, NC | 24 | 22 |
| Blacksburg-Christiansburg-Radford, VA | 24 | 20 |
| Santa Cruz-Watsonville, CA | 24 | 14 |
| Missoula, MT | 24 | 15 |
| Average | 22 | 20 |

Source: Gregory D. Squires, Derek S. Hyra, and Robert N. Renner, *Segregation and the Subprime Lending Crisis*, paper presented at the Federal Reserve Board's Community Affairs Research Conference, (April 16, 2009).

require new policies to change lending practices of financial institutions and regulatory actions of enforcement agencies, the broader context of inequality and segregation must also be addressed.

Several politically feasible tools are available to respond to the overall surge in inequality. For example, the federal minimum wage should

GREGORY D. SQUIRES

Table 2.  Black Segregation

| Variables | Coefficients | Standard errors |
|---|---|---|
| Percent in poverty | −0.00 | 0.67 |
| Percent minority | 0.13* | 0.02 |
| Median home value | −0.11* | 0.03 |
| Black segregation | 0.14* | 0.02 |
| Percent low credit score | 0.23* | 0.06 |
| Percent with BA or higher | −0.48* | 0.04 |

N=354, R-Squared=0.6943, *p<.01.

Table 3.  Hispanic Segregation

| Variables | Coefficients | Standard errors |
|---|---|---|
| Percent in poverty | −0.05 | 0.07 |
| Percent minority | 0.12* | 0.02 |
| Median home value | −0.14* | 0.03 |
| Hispanic segregation | 0.06* | 0.02 |
| Percent low credit score | 0.25* | 0.07 |
| Percent with BA or higher | −0.48* | 0.04 |

N=354, R-Squared=0.6312, *p<.01.

be indexed to take into consideration the cost of living so that the recent increase that was approved in May 2007 does not continue to lose buying power as it has since the moment it went into effect in July 2007 (Atlas and Dreier 2006, Peirce 2007). Living wage ordinances, which mandate even higher wages, generally $8 to $10 per hour, frequently with fringe benefits, have been enacted in more than 100 jurisdictions with these rules applying to government contractors and recipients of economic development subsidies (Dreier 2007). More jurisdictions should follow this lead. The Earned Income Tax Credit could be expanded to lift more working families out of poverty (Mishel 2005). Enacting the Employee Free Choice Act, which allows workers to form a union when more than 50% of workers sign a card indicating their desire to do so in lieu of secret elections, would strengthen the role of unions in the U.S. and their positive impact on wage inequality (Kochan and Shulman 2007). A more provocative proposal, the Income Equity Act, offered by former Minnesota Representative Martin Sabo, would deny corporations tax deductions on any executive compensation exceeding twenty-five times the pay of the firm's lowest paid workers (Pierce 2007).

Expansion of several housing and land use policies would also reduce inequality. Tax-based revenue sharing, whereby a portion of the increasing property tax revenues in prosperous neighborhoods is used to invest in housing and other community development initiatives in distressed areas, has been implemented in Minnesota (Orfield 2002). Mobility programs have enabled thousands of families to leave ghettos and barrios for more prosperous outlying urban and suburban communities where they found safer neighborhoods, better schools, and better job prospects (Rubinowietz and Rosenbaum 2000; Goering and Feins 2003; Polikoff 2006).

Housing policies of the past have been linked with the concentration of minorities, particularly African Americans, in extremely segregated and impoverished communities (Massey and Denton 1993; Massey and Kanaiaupuni 1993; Carr and Kutty 2008). Today, much of the distressed public housing that once segregated minorities in inner city neighborhoods is being razed (Goetz 2003; Hyra 2008). Residents of these demolished buildings are receiving housing vouchers, a rent subsidy, to obtain private market rental units. Evidence suggests that voucher holders are ending up in other highly segregated communities (Hartung and Henig 1997; Fischer 2003). To prevent the continuing concentration of poverty and racial disadvantage, the U.S. Department of Housing and Urban Development's Housing Choice Voucher program must be reformed to provide greater opportunities for recipients to find units in less segregated and impoverished neighborhoods.

The Low Income Housing Tax Credit (LIHTC) program and inclusionary zoning laws are two other mechanisms for increasing the number of affordable rental units in non-poverty neighborhoods for voucher recipients. Traditionally, housing developments in low-income communities are given preferences for LIHTCs. This circumstance may indirectly increase or sustain prior levels of segregation by placing low-income residents and units in an already low-income community. To open up housing opportunities for low-income families, affordable housing developments in middle- and upper-income communities should be given priority for LIHTCs. Inclusionary zoning laws can also increase the stock of affordable housing in low-poverty areas. These local laws, which have been enacted in dozens of cities, require new developments to set aside a certain percentage of units for affordable housing. The federal government could provide financial incentives for municipalities to adopt zoning laws that promote the construction and redevelopment of more affordable units.

Housing market discrimination clearly contributes to segregation. To more effectively enforce fair housing laws already in place, the proposed Housing Fairness Act of 2009 (H.R. 476) should be enacted. This bill would increase funding for the Fair Housing Initiatives Program to $52 million and would fund a $20 million nationwide paired testing program providing for 5,000 tests, approximately 50 in each of the nation's 100 largest metropolitan areas. In paired-testing investigations, equally qualified white and non-white auditors posing as homebuyers or renters approach housing providers, such as real estate and rental agents, mortgage lenders, and insurance agents, and inquire about the availability of the same or similar housing units or housing related services like home insurance or mortgage loans. Any differences in treatment they receive likely reflect discrimination since these auditors or testers are assigned identical qualifications and interests. Such investigations have routinely revealed discrimination in approximately one out of every five initial visits to real estate or rental agents. Discrimination in insurance and mortgage lending has also been documented using similar investigative techniques (Smith and Cloud 1997; Turner and Skidmore 1999; Turner et al. 2002). If the real estate, mortgage and insurance industries knew these investigations were occurring more frequently, incidents of discrimination and levels of segregation might be reduced.

In addition to these general economic reforms and housing proposals, there are specific changes in the regulation of financial services that should be included in any reorganization of that regulatory function. For example, prepayment penalties and introductory teaser rates should be limited in all mortgage lending including the prime and subprime markets. Prepayment penalties make it more difficult for those that get behind in their payments to refinance or sell their homes. Even though these penalties provide banks with risk protection against early payment, it increases the likelihood that borrowers will default. Teaser rates (for example, 2/28 and 3/27 adjustable rate mortgages) frequently lead to late payments, defaults, and foreclosure (Quercia et al. 2007). Only when carefully underwritten and when there is a clear economic benefit for the borrower should these types of loans be permitted. These simple product restrictions might reduce the extent of subprime loans, defaults, and foreclosures throughout the country. The National Mortgage Reform and Anti Predatory Lending Act (H.R. 1728) would reduce substantially the provision of inappropriate products in the mortgage market.

State and local governments that receive federal funding for housing and community development are required to "affirmatively further fair housing" in the utilization of those funds. Recipients of Troubled Asset Relief Program (TARP) funds , bailout money, or any other federal financial support should be required to pursue this objective as well.

To ensure that these regulations and restrictions are followed, federal oversight is needed over the independent mortgage companies, the unregulated entities who originated the bulk of subprime mortgages and the affiliated institutions that are involved in the trading of mortgage-backed securities (Avery et al. 2007). Currently, the CRA applies only to depository institutions but passage of the CRA Modernization Act of 2009 (H.R. 1749) would bring unregulated mortgage lenders under its purview. Having greater oversight over independent mortgage companies, might help decrease the number of high-cost loans.

It has been argued that the CRA and related fair lending laws contributed to the foreclosure and related problems. But as the Federal Reserve Board and others have documented, this is simply not the case. CRA lenders made approximately 6% of all high-cost loans to low-income markets. Altogether just 5 % of loans made by CRA lenders were high-cost compared to 34% for non-CRA lenders. In fact, the Federal Reserve Board and others have found that the CRA is responsible for significant increases in the level of good loans in traditionally underserved markets (Kroszner 2008a; Kroszner 2008b; Squires 2008).

A promising step in the reform of financial services is the creation of the Consumer Financial Protection Bureau established by the Dodd-Frank Wall Street Reform and Consumer Protection Act, the major bank reform law passed in 2010. If given the tools to write and enforce strong regulations, the Bureau will prove to be an effective tool for eliminating abusive financial service industry practices.

## Conclusion

The housing and related economic crises that disproportionately impact poor and minority communities, but which are clearly now threatening many middle income families as well, are inextricably linked to specific financial industry practice as well as broader forces of inequality and uneven development. The policies and practices that have generated these patterns are no great secret. Neither are at least some of the remedies.

## References

Atlas, John and Peter Dreier. 2006. "Waging Victory." *The American Prospect.* November 10: Web Only <http://www.prospect.org/cs/articles?article=waging_victory>.

Avery, Rovert B., Kenneth P. Brevoort and Glenn B. Canner. 2007. "The 2006 HMDA Data." *Federal Reserve Bulletin* 93:73–109.

Booza, Jason C, Jackie Cutsinger, and George Galster. 2006. *Where Did They Go? The Decline of Middle-Income Neighborhoods in Metropolitan America.* Washington, DC: The Brookings Institution.

Calem, Paul, Kevin Gillen, and Susan Wachter. 2004. "The Neighborhood Distribution of Subprime Mortgage Lending." *Journal of Real Estate Finance and Economics* 29: 393–410.

Cisneros, Henry G., ed. 1993. *Interwoven Destinies: Cities and the Nation.* New York, NY: W.W. Norton and Company.

Walt-Denavas, Carmen, Bernadette D. Proctor, and Jessica C. Smith. 2008. *Current Population Reports, Pp.60–235, Income, Poverty, and health Insurance Coverage in the United States: 2007, Table A-3. Selected Measures of Household Income Dispersion 1967–2007.* Washington, DC: U.S. Census Bureau.

Carr, James H. and Nandienee K. Kutty. 2008. *Segregation and the Rising Costs for America.* New York, NY: Rutledge.

Dreier, Peter. 2007. "Community Organizing for What? Progressive Politics and Movement Building in America." Pp. 218–251 in *Transforming the City: Community Organizing and the Challenge of Political Change,* edited by Marion Orr. Lawrence, KS: University of Kansas Press.

Farley, John E. and Gregory D. Squires. 2005. "Fences and Neighbors: Segregation in 21st Century America." *Contexts,* Winter: 34–39.

Fischer, Paul. 2003. *Where are Public Housing Families Going?: An Update.* Chicago, IL: Woods Fund of Chicago.

Goering, John and Judith D Feins. 2003. *Choosing a Better Life?: Evaluating the Moving to Opportunity Social Experiment.* Washington, DC: Urban Institute Press.

Goetz, Edward. 2003. *Clearing the Way: Deconcentrating the Poor in Urban America.* Washington, DC: Urban Institute Press.

Hartung, John M. and Jeffrey R. Henig. 1997. "Housing Vouchers and Certificates as a Vehicle for Deconcentrating the Poor." *Urban Affairs Review* 32(3):403–419.

Hyra, Derek S. 2008. *The New Urban Renewal: The Economic Transformation of Harlem and Bronzeville.* Chicago, IL: University of Chicago Press.

Iceland, John, Daniel H. Weinberg, and Erika Steinmetz. 2002. *Racial and Ethnic Residential Segregation in the United States: 1980–2000, Table 1.* Washington, DC: U.S. Census Bureau.

Jargowsky, Paul A. 1998. *Poverty and Place: Ghettos, Barrios, and the American City*. New York, NY: Russell Sage Foundation.

Jargowsky, Paul A. 2003. *Stunning Progress, Hidden Problems: The Dramatic Decline of Concentrated Poverty in the 1990s*. Washington, DC: Brookings Institution Press.

Kochan, Thomas and Beth Shulman. *A New Social Contract: Restoring Dignity and Balance to the Economy*. Washington, DC: Economic Policy Institute.

Kroszner, Randall S. 2008a. *The Community Reinvestment Act and the Recent Mortgage Crisis*. Speech Delivered to the Confronting Concentrated Poverty Forum. Washington, DC: Board of Governors of the Federal Reserve System.

Kroszner, Randall S. 2008b. "Editorial, Mortgages and Minorities." *New York Times* 9, December.

Krugman, Paul. 2002. "For Richer." *New York Times Magazine* 20 October: 62–64.

Krugman, Paul. 2006. "Editorial, Left Behind Economics." *New York Times* 14 July: A19.

Logan, John R. 2002a. *Separate and Unequal: The Neighborhood Gap for Blacks and Hispanics in Metropolitan America*. Albany, NY: Lewis Mumford Center for Comparative Urban Regional Research, University at Albany.

Logan, John R. 2002b. *New Census Data Show Unyielding City-Suburb Economic Gap, and Surprising Shifts in Some Places*. Albany, NY: Lewis Mumford Center. For Comparative Urban Regional Research, University at Albany.

Massey, Douglas S. and Nancy Denton. 1993. *American Apartheid: Segregation and the Making of the Underclass*. Cambridge, MA: Harvard University Press.

Massey, Douglas S. and Shawn M. Kanaiaupuni. 1993. "Public Housing and the Concentration of Poverty." *Social Science Quarterly* 74(1):109–122.

Mishel, Lawrence, Jared Bernstein and Sylvia Allegretto. 2004/2005. *The State of Working America*. Washington, DC: The Economic Policy Institute.

National Community Reinvestment Coalition and the Woodstock Institute. 2006. *A Lifetime of Assets*. Washington, DC: National Community Reinvestment Coalition.

Peirce, Neal. 2007. "Congress' Minimum Wage Vote: Prelude to a Better Politics?" *Stateline.org*, Jan. 25, 2007. <http://www.stateline.org/live/details/story?contentId=174954&utm_source=feedburner&utm_medium=feed&utm_campaign=Feed%3A+StatelineorgRss-Stories+(Stateline.org+RSS+-+Stories)>.

Orfield, Myron. 2002. *American Metropolitics: The New Suburban Reality*. Washington DC: Brookings Institution Press.

Polikoff, Alexander. 2002. *Waiting for Gautreaux: A Story of Segregation, Housing, and the Black Ghetto*. Evanston, IL: Northwestern University Press.

Powell, Michael. 2009. "Bank Accused of Pushing Mortgage Deals on Blacks." *New York Times* 7 June: A-15.

Quercia, Robert G., Michael A. Stegman and Walter R. Davis. 2007. "The Impact of Predatory Loan Terms on Subprime Foreclosures: The Special Case of Prepayment Penalties and Balloon Payments." *Housing Policy Debate* 18(2):311–346.

Rubinowitz, Leonard S. and James E. Rosenbaum. 2000. *Crossing the Class and Color Lines: From Public Housing to White Suburbia*. Chicago, IL: University of Chicago Press.

Shapiro, Thomas M. 2006. *The Hidden Cost of Being African American: How Wealth Perpetuates Inequality*. New York, NY: Oxford University Press.

Smith, Shanna and Cathy Cloud. 1997. "Documenting Discrimination by Homeowners Insurance Companies through Testing." Pp. 97–118. In *Insurance Redlining: Disinvestment, Reinvestment, and the Evolving Role of Financial Institutions*, edited by Gregory D. Squires. Washington, DC: The Urban Institute Press.

Squires, Gregory D. 2008. "Scapegoating Blacks for the Economic Crisis." *Poverty & Race* 17(6):3–4.

Squires, Gregory D. 2008/9. "Urban Development and Unequal Access to Housing Finance Services." *New York Law School Law Review* 53(2):255–268.

Squires, Gregory D., Derek S. Hyra, and Robert N. Renner. 2009. "Segregation and the Subprime Lending Crisis." Paper Presented at the Federal Reserve Board's Community Affairs Research Conference, 16 April.

Timberlake, Jeffrey M. and John Iceland. 2007. "Change in Racial and Ethnic Residential Inequality in American Cities, 1970–2000." *City & Community* 6:335–365.

Turner, Margery T. and Felicity Skidmore. 1999. *Mortgage Lending Discrimination: A Review of Existing Evidence*. Washington, DC: The Urban Institute.

Turner, Margery T., Fred Freiberg, Erin Godfrey, Carla Herbig, Diane Levy and Robin Smith. 2002. *Mortgage Lending Institutions*. Washington, DC: The Urban Institute.

US Department of the Treasury. 2009. Financial Regulatory Reform. Washington, DC: US Department of the Treasury.

# BE IT EVER SO HUMBLE, THERE'S NO PLACE LIKE HOME: THE EXPERIENCES OF LOW-INCOME, MINORITY HOMEBUYERS[1]

Anna Maria Santiago, George C. Galster, Cristina M. Tucker, Ana H. Santiago-San Roman, and Angela A. Kaiser

## Introduction

Since the 1940s, federal housing policies have encouraged owner-occupancy over rental tenure using Federal Housing Administration (FHA) and Veteran's Administration (VA) mortgage loans as major catalysts of the post-World War II housing boom in suburban America (Stegman et al. 1991; Galster and Daniell 1996; Shlay 2006; Galster 2008). Over the last 30 years, however, federal policies have explicitly extended this encouragement to households of increasingly-lower incomes (Shlay 2006; Rohe and Watson 2007). During the Reagan Administration in the 1980s, the U.S. Department of Housing and Urban Development (HUD) piloted a homeownership program that sold public housing units to their occupants. In an attempt to ease liquidity, stability and affordability constraints in low-income and minority-occupied urban neighborhoods, Congress imposed goals for Fannie Mae and Freddie Mac as part of the Federal Housing Enterprises Financial Safety and Soundness Act of 1992 that required them to buy a minimum share of mortgages originated in these neighborhoods and to offer mortgages to low-income borrowers regardless of location. Soon thereafter, many innovations in mortgage instruments appeared that expanded access to low-income borrowers (Listokin et al. 2002; Gramlich 2007; Bostic and Lee 2008; Immergluck 2008). During the 1990s, the Clinton Administration set a national homeownership goal and in the 2000s the Bush Administration followed suit by making

[1] The research reported in this chapter is supported by grants from the Ford Foundation and the MacArthur Foundation. The views expressed in this chapter are the authors' and do not necessarily reflect those of these foundations or the Board of Governors of Wayne State University. We also express our gratitude to the Denver Housing Authority for their support of this research, particularly Ismael Guerrero, Stella Madrid and Renee Nicolosi.

the expansion of low-income and minority homeownership a corner-stone of HUD's mission (U.S. Department of Housing and Urban Development 2002; Retsinas and Belsky 2002). Since the 1990s, Congress has enacted pilot programs for homeownership education and counseling, individual development accounts for asset building, and the use of Housing Choice Vouchers for home-buying (Rohe et al. 2002; Locke et al. 2006; Grinstein-Weiss et al. 2008). Most recently, the fiscal stimulus package adopted under the Obama Administration in 2009 provided refundable tax credits for home purchases by low- and moderate-income households.

This consistent political and institutional emphasis, coupled with a generally favorable macroeconomic climate, produced remarkable increases in homeownership rates among low-income households and minority households from the mid-1980s through the first five years of the 21st century (Retsinas and Belsky 2002; Boehm and Schlottman 2003; Pitcoff 2003; Wiranowski 2003; Nothaft and Chang 2005; Kochar et al. 2009). In the 1990s, about 800,000 low-income households bought their first home (Retsinas and Belsky 2002), raising the home-ownership rates of non-elderly, households in the lowest income quin-tile, from 22 percent in 1989 to 28 percent in 2001 (Nothaft and Chang 2005). Mortgage loans to low-income borrowers almost doubled between 1993 and 1999 (Pitcoff 2003), raising their share of all home-purchase loans from 14 to 19 percent during this period (Wiranowski 2003). The average real value of home equity held by households with incomes below 80 percent of their metropolitan area's median increased rapidly, from $67,683 in 1985 to $76,505 in 1995 to $96,011 by 2001 (Nothaft and Chang 2005).

The rationale for expanding homeownership has been multifaceted (Rohe, van Zandt and McCarthy 2002; Shlay 2006). Some have viewed the benefits as primarily accruing to low-income homeowners them-selves. These have included increased: wealth, status, security of ten-ure, control over dwelling, pride, life satisfaction, and well-being (Rohe and Stegman 1994; Rohe and Stewart 1996; Rossi and Weber 1996; Rohe and Basolo 1997; Rohe et al. 2000; McCarthy et al. 2001; Rohe et al. 2003; Rohe and Watson 2007; Christy-McMullin et al. 2009). Others have seen benefits to children who are able to live in homes owned by their parents (Haurin 1992; Green and White 1997; Mayer 1997; Boehm and Schlottmann 1999; Aaronson 2000; Harkness and Newman 2002; 2003; Haurin et al. 2002a; 2002b; Dietz and Haurin 2003; Galster et al. 2007). Still others have emphasized external benefits to the larger society, such as enhanced home maintenance, civic engagement, and attachment to community (Cox 1982; Galster 1983; 1987; DiPasquale and Glaeser 1999; Rohe, McCarthy and van Zandt 2000; McCarthy et al. 2001; Rohe et al. 2002; Hoff and Sen 2005; Englehardt et al. 2010).

A variant of the pro-homeownership rationale focuses on its anti-poverty effects. Beginning in the early 1990s, advocates and analysts began re-framing the anti-poverty debate as one of asset acquisition instead of merely income support (Sherraden 1991; Blank 2002; McKernan and Sherraden 2008; Christy-McMullin et al. 2009). Given that a downpayment is typically highly leveraged by mortgage money, even modest appreciation of the home can produce substantial rates of return on the initial investment by the buyer. Add to this the favorable federal tax treatment of housing capital gains and potential deductibility of mortgage interest and local property taxes, and the wealth-building potential of homeownership appears even more powerful (Retsinas and Belsky 2005). Home equity is the most important and often only component of most low-income households' wealth. The 2001 Survey of Consumer Finances shows, for example, that the median net worth of homeowners earning less than $20,000 was $72,750, whereas that of renters in this income range was only $900 (Belsky et al. 2005). During the 1990s, low-income, minority homeowners saw their average home equity rise by $1,712 annually, but non-housing wealth of low-income, minority owners and renters alike did not change, on average (Boehm and Schlottmann 2003; 2004).

Owning a home is not necessarily an unmitigated financial benefit for minority households, of course. Five major limitations have been identified. First, minority home buyers may invest more in housing than is optimal compared to other assets, given the risk and return characteristics of various assets and the fact that the household's effective marginal federal tax rate is likely zero (Ambrose and Goetzmann 1998; Goetzmann and Spiegel 2002). Second, low-income minority homeowners are much less likely to pre-pay their mortgages (typically with refinancing) when interest rate declines make such options profitable (Van Order and Zorn 2002; Nothaft and Chang 2005), thereby foregoing potential gains in wealth. Third, unexpected major home repairs or loss of income through illness, injury, or layoff raise the specter of unsustainable financial stresses that potentially could culminate in mortgage delinquency and default, with concomitant psychological damages, loss of home equity, and destruction of consumer credit ratings (Haurin and Rosenthal 2005). Fourth, the homes purchased by minority buyers may not appreciate and may even decline in value, especially if they are located in troubled, declining neighborhoods (Harkness and Newman 2002; Ding and Knapp 2003; Woldoff and Ovandia 2008). Though there is no consensus on whether there are differential home appreciation rates at different price points (cf. Kiel and Carson 1990; Pollakowski et al. 1991; Poterba 1991; Seward et al. 1991; Delaney and Smith 1992; Mayer 1993; Case and Schiller 1994; Smith and Ho 1996; Quercia et al. 2000; Case and Marychenko 2002), simulation models consistently show the financial returns from homeowning and the probability of the borrower exercising the default option are highly sensitive to interest rates and price movements between purchase and sale dates (Haurin 1988; Belsky and Duda 2002; Boehm and Schlottmann 2004; Belsky et al. 2005; Haurin and Rosenthal 2005; Turner and Smith 2009). Fifth, minority homeowners may be more subject to victimization by predatory lenders, leading to erosion of equity through excessive refinancing fees or, in the worst case, default and foreclosure (Renuart 2004; Bowdler et al. 2010).

The latter three issues have been of pre-eminent concern (Meyer et al. 1994; Pitcoff 2003), because they challenge the premise that homeownership actually does lead to increased stability of tenure and the wealth acquisition associated with it. Boehm and Schlottmann (2004) found that once homeownership was attained, low-income and minority households were much less likely than higher-income White ones to maintain their homeowning status (Turner and Smith 2009). Haurin and Rosenthal (2005) found that disproportionate shares of low-income homeowners switch back into renting years after their home purchase: seven percent after three years, five percent more after five years, and two percent more after ten years. Thus, increasingly the policy discussion has evolved from considering only how more low-income households can *attain* homeownership (e.g., Galster et al. 1999; Nesslein 2000; Listokin et al. 2002) to also considering how more low-income and minority households can *sustain* homeownership (Wiranowski 2003; Shlay 2006; Herbert and Belsky 2008).

It is to this rising concern over the sustainability of minority homeownership that our chapter aims to contribute. In addition to examining administrative data from 152 low-income, minority homebuyers, we use in-depth quantitative and qualitative data gathered from retrospective surveys with 126 of these homeowners who purchased their homes in the period between 1995 and 2008 after participating in an extensive asset-building and homeownership education-counseling program offered by the Housing Authority of the City and County of

Denver (DHA), called HOP. Our information comes from retrospective telephone surveys and focus group discussions with both program graduates and program dropouts, which elicit these new homeowners' experiences with the benefits and costs of homeownership and the challenges of sustaining this tenure.

In this chapter, we investigate the following questions. What are the perceived benefits of homeownership? Have the original worries about homeownership held by these recent, low-income Latino and black[2] homebuyers been justified after several years of experience owning a home? What do they perceive as the major challenges to their continued ownership? What are their expectations regarding neighborhood quality and the value of their homes? How much have they maintained and improved their homes? To what extent have they been able to build assets? Have they experienced severe financial stresses and increased indebtedness? What have been their experiences with delinquent mortgage payments, foreclosures, refinancing, predatory lenders, and other purveyors of debt? Are there significant Latino-black differences for any of the aforementioned questions?

We begin the chapter with a review of the scanty extant evidence regarding low-income, minority homeowners' experiences, concerns, perceptions, and expectations. We then describe the DHA's Home Ownership Program (HOP) in which our all of our subjects participated as a means of buying their first home, although not all completed the program. We briefly describe the DHA administrative data employed as well as the surveys and focus groups we conducted in Denver. The bulk of the chapter then reports on the comprehensive battery of information we have collected from our sample of low-income, minority homebuyers. We conclude with a discussion of the implications of our findings for U.S. housing policy and directions for continued research.

*Literature Review*

Virtually all extant research related to the issue of low-income homeownership has been conducted by secondary analyses of general purpose surveys, such as the Panel Study of Income Dynamics

---

[2] For the purpose of this study, we use the term Black to refer to program participants who are African American or who are foreign born of African ancestry and identify themselves as Black.

(e.g., Boehm and Schlottmann 2004), the National Longitudinal Survey of Youth (Haurin and Rosenthal 2005; Reid 2004), the Survey of Income and Program Participation (Galster et al. 1999), the American Housing Survey (Belsky and Duda 2002; Flippen 2004), or the Survey of Consumer Finances (Nothaft and Chang 2005). Two notable exceptions, however, provide the context for the research presented here because they involve surveys of low-income households who recently purchased housing.

Mitchell and Warren (1998) interviewed 95 homeowners who had purchased their homes by participating in one of 19 Habitat for Humanity development efforts across the nation during the 1990s. Among this study's major findings:

- Monthly costs (mortgage, insurance and taxes) were generally not burdensome (averaging only 12% of buyers' incomes at time of closing), even though 77% of the Habitat homebuyers earned less than 80% of area median income and 43% earned less than 50% of area median income; the same held when maintenance and utility costs were included (7% of average income).
- Two-thirds of homebuyers saw their incomes increase since purchasing, though all housing costs currently consumed more of their income (27%, on average) than at time of purchase.
- Despite the low average expense burdens, over one-third of respondents reported that they had found it difficult to meet financial obligations at some point and one-fifth believed that they needed ongoing financial support from Habitat in order to continue as homeowners.
- Reported incidences of difficulties paying mortgages on time were inversely related to income (38% with incomes below 80% of area median vs. 14% with incomes above).
- Few homebuyers invested heavily in maintenance and repairs (which the authors attributed to the fact that respondents occupied homes that recently were substantially rehabilitated or newly constructed by Habitat).
- Before moving into homeownership, respondents perceived responsibility for maintenance and repairs as the greatest burden; many perceived no disadvantages from homeownership.
- The most common benefit from homeownership perceived by respondents was pride and increased stability and feelings of security of their tenure, though most also experienced a substantial increase in dwelling size as a consequence of buying.

- All agreed that advantages to homeownership outweighed disadvantages and that they would buy again.
- One in five believed that they were inadequately prepared for homeownership, and these were preponderantly lower-income families.
- Most believed that homeownership was having a positive impact on their families, especially through increased stability and privacy for children.

The second study was conducted by Rohe and Quercia (2003), who surveyed 477 persons who completed homeownership training classes in eight Neighbor Works organizations conducting pilot programs in 1999–2000, and then surveyed them again in 2002. The authors compared responses of those completing the program and buying a home within the prior two years to those who did not. Among their salient findings:

- Very few homebuyers (less than one percent) within the first two years of home purchase experienced delinquent payments on their mortgages; 15% took out a home-equity loan and 15% refinanced; however, eight percent of those who refinanced did so to catch up on mortgage payments.
- 48% of respondents had experienced major unexpected costs associated with the home.
- 63% of homebuyers reported that the greatest advantage of home-owning was building equity through house appreciation; the next most-frequent response was "sense of independence" (19%).
- The greatest challenges reported (by roughly a quarter of homebuyers) were increases in monthly housing-related expenses and finding time for maintenance; 16% perceived no challenges.
- Homebuyers were more satisfied with their lives and had larger social-support networks than continuing renters, controlling for other background characteristics, though there were no differences in levels of participation in voluntary associations, neighborhood satisfaction, self-esteem, or perceptions of opportunity.
- Homebuyers were more likely to see gains in the size of their residences, be more likely employed and more likely to have health insurance than otherwise-comparable continuing renters, though there were no differences in housing quality, housing payments, assets, income, and debts.

In sum, these two studies suggest that, for most low-income, minority families surveyed, owning a home proves to be a positive experience psychologically, socially, and economically. Potential challenges lurk, however, as nontrivial percentages of homeowners find themselves strapped by unstable incomes, rising housing expenses, and unexpected major repair needs.

Our research aims to expand our knowledge base by investigating similar sorts of issues with recent, low-income minority homebuyers in Denver. Unlike the Mitchell and Warren (1998) and Rohe and Quercia (2003) studies, however, our sample consists of: (1) former long-term recipients of public housing or rental subsidies, who (2) participated in a comprehensive, multi-year homeownership counseling and asset-building program run by a local housing authority, and (3) are comprised disproportionately of Latino and black families. We next turn to a description of this program.

*The Denver Housing Authority's Homeownership Program*

The DHA has operated its Homeownership Program since 1995, in conjunction with its federally funded Family Self-Sufficiency (FSS) program and since 2001, their Resident Opportunities for Self-Sufficiency (ROSS) program. The goal of HOP is to assist DHA tenants in enhancing their human, financial, and social capital, with the ultimate goal of buying their own home. All current DHA residents and Housing Choice Voucher (HCV) recipients are eligible to participate in HOP, regardless of whether they are living in DHA's conventional public housing, scattered-site units, or HCV subsidized units. Program participants are eligible for: homeownership assessments, free credit reports, credit repair and money management counseling, classes on a wide variety of topics (e.g., housing finance, home repairs, shopping for real estate and mortgages), individual development accounts with 1:1 matches up to $1,500, and for FSS Program participants, rent escrow accounts where increments in DHA rents associated with increasing tenant income are placed into escrow for use for a down-payment. Participants, working with program case management staff, develop individual training and services plans outlining their goals. Participants file monthly updates with their HOP technician and their overall plans are reassessed quarterly to ascertain client progress toward goals and compliance with program requirements.

During the final stage of the HOP program, eligible participants (i.e., those who are within a year of being able to purchase a home, have at least $500 in savings, and have employment stability) are invited to join the Home Buyer's Club. The primary purpose of the Club is to prepare participants for the purchase of a home. Participants are required to attend monthly Club classes, which provide intensive real estate and finance training, presentations by housing industry representatives, and peer support. Individuals with three absences or more in the 12-month period or who lose their jobs are terminated from the Club. Membership in the Club can provide special benefits such as low interest rates, discount fees, downpayment and closing cost assistance, and second mortgage assistance.

In any given year, between five and ten percent of HOP participants are in the Home Buyers Club. By 2008, a total of 270 participants reached this stage of the HOP. As of 2008, slightly more than half (N=136) of the participants had graduated from the program and purchased homes; approximately 13 percent had dropped out and purchased homes outside of the program; 27 percent had dropped out and did not purchase homes and 10 percent were still participating in the program.

Historically, the majority of HOP participants also participated (generally concurrently) in the FSS program. In 2001, the program was expanded to include non-FSS participants under the new, at the time, Resident Opportunities and Self-Sufficiency (ROSS) program. The two versions of HOP are similar in most respects, with the notable exception that the ROSS program does not involve rent escrow accounts. However, the ROSS program provides $1,000 in scholarship monies to program participants that can be applied to educational expenses and any related costs (e.g., child care, transportation expenses associated with attending school). At this writing, there were 329 DHA residents participating in the program, 88% of whom were receiving benefits from both the FSS and ROSS programs. Approximately 10% of the program participants were only in the ROSS program, and less than 2% were only in the FSS program.

Given that it is voluntary, it is not surprising that DHA's HOP program has attracted participants who differ systematically from other DHA tenants. In particular, significantly higher percentages of participants are under age 40 heads of mother-only, never-married families with children. Current and former HOP participants are less likely to

be of Latino (38%) and more likely to be black (34%) than the overall
DHA population. They also are less likely to be non-citizens, disabled,
or unable to speak English well.

## Data Collection Procedures

Three different sources of data were utilized to examine the experiences of low-income homebuyers in Denver. These include: administrative data from the Denver Housing Authority and Real Property
Offices; a Retrospective Homeowner Survey that was administered as
part of the *Denver Housing Study*, a longitudinal study of approximately 450 households who have participated in the HOP Program;
and five years of data derived from focus group discussions with homebuyers. Each of these data sources are described in more detail below.

### Administrative Data

The Denver Housing Authority provided information for all 109 Latino
and black individuals who participated in the HOP program during
the period between 1995 and 2007. Comparable data for 43 HOP program dropouts[3] were obtained from other DHA and HOP administrative sources. These administrative data include detailed information
about the home purchase as well as household demographic and
income characteristics of homebuyers at time of home purchase. We
use these data as baseline information for homeowners who are part of
our longitudinal study as well as to estimate the extent to which our
survey respondents are representative of the larger group of HOP
homebuyers. Additional information about the home purchase transaction as well as current ownership and home values was obtained
from on-line records for the Real Property and Tax Assessors Offices
in the counties where HOP homebuyers bought their homes.

---

[3] For the most part, HOP program dropouts were individuals who had completed
many of the requirements of the Home Buyers Club but did not purchase homes
through HOP. For some of these individuals, dropping out prior to completion
reflected loss of job stability or income, decisions to defer home purchase until after
schooling was completed or due to family problems such as illness or marital disruption. For others, the decision to drop out of HOP was associated with their impatience
with program duration: they simply did not want to wait to purchase a home. Finally,
some were terminated from the program because of noncompliance issues. Most of
the HOP dropouts in our study came from the first two categories of dropouts.
For further information on HOP program dropouts see Santiago et. al. 2009.

Finally, data on pre- and post-purchase neighborhood characteristics were obtained from the Geolytics *Neighborhood Change Database* for census tracts.

## Retrospective Homeowner Survey

All individuals who entered the Home Buyers Club during the period between January 1995 and December 2007 (N=270) were contacted and invited to participate in the longitudinal study by completing a 90-minute telephone interview. For this study, we restricted our analysis to the 109 Latino and black homebuyers who purchased their homes through the HOP Program and the 43 Latino and black HOP dropout homebuyers. From this group of minority homebuyers a total of 114 (75%) completed surveys which were administered between 2006 and 2009. Both groups of homeowners were asked about any financial assistance obtained for downpayments and closing costs; their concerns and experiences as recent homebuyers; their life satisfaction, goals and expectations, education and employment since becoming homeowners, household income and assets, child outcomes and social networks in their new neighborhoods.

## Focus Group Discussions

Between 2002 and 2006, we conducted annual focus group interviews with HOP program homeowners. In 2006, we held several groups with HOP program dropouts who nevertheless became homebuyers as well. A total of eight groups involving 37 Latino and black homeowners were conducted. These minority homebuyers were asked to reflect upon the things that enabled them to buy their homes, their initial experiences – positive and negative – with homeownership, their major worries as homeowners, mortgage payment histories, and their perceptions regarding how homeownership has affected them and their families. In addition, these new homeowners were asked to describe their current neighborhood conditions and relationships with neighbors relative to those experienced in their old neighborhoods. Further, they were asked to reflect on anticipated short-term changes within their new neighborhoods. Subsequent focus group discussions included questions on major issues homeowners have faced, asset building strategies and the threats to maintaining their financial assets, and their perceptions regarding how living in their neighborhood positively or negatively affects them and their children, and strategies employed to either reinforce positive effects or counteract negative effects.

Table 1 summarizes the home purchase and household characteristics of the full study sample of 152 HOP graduate and drop-out homebuyers at the time of home purchase, distinguished by ethnicity. Approximately seven out of ten minority homebuyers in the study graduated and purchased their homes as part of the HOP Program. More than six out of ten of study participants (63%) were Latino; 37% were black. The average age of our homebuyers at time of home purchase was 38.1 years. Approximately 88% of the Latino and 85% of black homebuyers were female (not shown). One out of five Latino and one out of four black homebuyers were immigrants. Approximately 71% of black and 55% of Latino homebuying households were headed by single parents. The average number of children or grandchildren under 18 residing in the household was 2.5 for Latinos and 2.1 for blacks. At time of home purchase, Latino homebuyers had slightly higher median household incomes than black homebuyers ($35,748 vs. $35,003). Latino homebuyers held higher median assets ($13,000) at time of purchase than blacks ($6,500). However, neither of these ethnic differences in economic characteristics was statistically significant. HOP Program participants were more likely to have participated in the Housing Choice Voucher Program or dispersed (scattered-site) public housing programs instead of the conventional DHA public housing (not shown). Finally, HOP Program participants had resided in DHA housing for an extended period of time: nearly 81 months for Latino homebuyers and 84 months for black homebuyers.

The median purchase price that respondents paid for their homes was $149,950 for Latinos and $148,750 for blacks. When compared to black homebuyers, Latinos were more likely to live in older, single-family detached homes. Approximately half of black and one-third of Latino homebuyers purchased homes located outside of Denver. Both Latino and black homebuyers moved considerable distance away from their DHA neighborhoods averaging 7.2 and 8.2 miles, respectively. Nonetheless, about twice as many Latino (8%) than black (4%) homebuyers bought homes within a mile of their previous neighborhoods.

We recognize that our sample for this study is limited in its generality. Since our sample represents low-income, minority parents who have: (1) received subsidized housing through a housing authority for an extended period; (2) chosen to participate in voluntary self-sufficiency and homeownership programs; and (3) purchased a

Table 1. Selected Home Purchase and Homeowner Characteristics at Time of Purchase, by Ethnicity (All HOP Home Buyer's Club Participants during Study Period)

| | All homebuyers (N=152) | Latino homebuyers (N=96) | Black homebuyers (N=56) |
|---|---|---|---|
| *Household characteristics of Time of Purchase* | | | |
| Average age of head of household (in years) | 38.1 | 36.8 | 38.8 |
| Percent single parent households[a] | 61.0 | 54.6 | 70.7 |
| Average number of children in household[b] | 2.3 | 2.5 | 2.1 |
| Percent immigrant | 21.9 | 21.4 | 24.1 |
| Median household income | $35,322 | $35,748 | $35,003 |
| Median assets | $11,114 | $13,000 | $6,500 |
| HOP program status (percent HOP graduates) | 70.5 | 71.1 | 69.6 |
| Median months residing in DHA | 80.9 | 80.8 | 84.0 |
| *Characteristics of home purchase* | | | |
| Median purchase price | $149,900 | $149,950 | $148,750 |
| Average distance in miles | 7.6 | 7.2 | 8.2 |
| Percent of homes purchased within 1 mile of last DHA address | 6.2 | 8.3 | 3.6 |
| Percent of homes purchased outside of the City and County of Denver[c] | 42.5 | 36.5 | 48.2 |
| Percent single-family, detached homes[d] | 84.2 | 91.3 | 75.9 |

*(Continued)*

Table 1.  *(Cont.)*

|  | All homebuyers (N=152) | Latino homebuyers (N=96) | Black homebuyers (N=56) |
| --- | --- | --- | --- |
| Median square footage | 1121 | 1121 | 1117 |
| Median year built[e] | 1967 | 1958 | 1974 |

*Sources:* Real Property records from the respective county real estate offices were used to assess property values at time of purchase as well as in 2008 or time of sale or fore-closure. Detailed homeowner demographic and financial characteristics were derived from DHA administrative records.

*Notes:* All of the following differences across groups are statistically significant at the p < .05 level. Please note that while median values are reported here for selected vari-ables, difference in means tests also were estimated for these indicators.
(a) The percentage of single parent households was significantly higher for black homebuyers relative to Latino homebuyers.
(b) The average number of children at time of home purchase was significantly higher for Latino homebuyers relative to black homebuyers.
(c) The percentage of homes located in the suburbs is significantly higher for Latino homebuyers relative to black homebuyers.
(d) The percentage of single-family detached homes owned by Latino homebuyers is significantly higher than that for black homebuyers.
(e) The age of the dwelling is significantly older for Latino homes.

home, there undoubtedly is a good deal of self-selection present here. Nevertheless, we believe that our sample can provide valid insights that can be generalized to the sort of households that represent the 'cutting edge' of public and nonprofit efforts to expand homeowner-ship opportunities via enhanced homeownership counseling and mortgage innovations (Listokin et al. 2002).

*Experiences, Perceptions and Expectations of Low-Income, Minority Homebuyers*

As shown in Table 2, low-income Latino buyers experienced signifi-cant gains in neighborhood quality with the purchase of their homes, when compared to the neighborhoods they experienced as a resident of DHA public housing or a holder of a Housing Choice Voucher. In addition to moving to more ethnically diverse neighborhoods with higher fractions of Anglo neighbors, Latino homeowners also moved to neighborhoods with fewer children per household and smaller shares of households headed by females. Further, Latino buyers moved into higher income neighborhoods comprised of higher percentages of homeowners, college graduates, and newer housing construction, and lower rates of poverty, unemployment, and housing vacancies. While black homebuyers also generally experienced gains in neighborhood quality, these gains were more modest. Black buyers also moved into neighborhoods characterized by proportionately more homeowners, newer homes, lower poverty rates, and fewer female-headed households. However, homeownership for black buyers did not result in appreciable improvements in neighborhood ethnic diversity or economic conditions. If we look at ethnic differences in the gains made in post-purchase neighborhood quality, we see that blacks resided in post-purchase neighborhoods that contained higher fractions of black residents and lower fractions of Latino and White residents. Relative to Latino buyers, black homebuyers also purchased in neighborhoods with higher fractions of female-headed households.

Neighborhood quality also varied by HOP Program status (data not shown). When compared to Latino dropouts, vacancy rates were higher in neighborhoods where Latino HOP graduates purchased homes. Average household income in post-purchase neighborhoods was significantly lower for Latino HOP graduates. Latino HOP dropouts purchased homes in neighborhoods with significantly lower poverty rates. Black HOP graduates were residing in neighborhoods with higher fractions of single parent households than were Latino HOP graduates.

Table 2. Selected Pre- and Post-Purchase Neighborhood Characteristics by Ethnicity (All HOP Home Buyer's Club Participants during Study Period)

| Neighborhood characteristic | All homebuyers (N=152) | | Latino homebuyers (N=96) | | Black homebuyers (N=56) | |
|---|---|---|---|---|---|---|
| | Pre | Post | Pre | Post | Pre | Post |
| Vacancy rate | 3.0 | 2.6* | 3.4 | 2.7* | 2.4 | 2.3 |
| Percent of owner-occupied housing units | 53.6 | 67.2* | 53.8 | 66.1* | 53.6 | 68.2* |
| Percent of housing units built before 1940 | 25.5 | 13.5* | 27.0 | 15.3* | 23.2 | 10.8* |

*(Continued)*

Table 2. *(Cont.)*

| Neighborhood characteristic | All homebuyers (N=152) | | Latino homebuyers (N=96) | | Black homebuyers (N=56) | |
|---|---|---|---|---|---|---|
| | Pre | Post | Pre | Post | Pre | Post |
| Average household income | $43,241 | $49,138* | $42,242 | $48,881 | $51,327 | $51,332 |
| Total poverty rate | 21.6 | 12.7* | 22.9 | 13.3* | 19.6 | 12.4* |
| Percent of college graduates | 18.4 | 18.9 | 13.7 | 22.4* | 26.0 | 20.2 |
| Unemployment rate | 8.7 | 7.0* | 9.6 | 7.1* | 7.4 | 6.9 |
| Percent Black[a] | 16.2 | 17.2 | 7.7 | 9.4 | 29.7 | 29.6 |
| Percent Latino[b] | 48.0 | 38.1* | 56.6 | 42.2* | 34.2 | 31.6 |
| Percent White[c] | 53.6 | 59.2* | 56.3 | 64.3* | 49.2 | 50.8 |
| Percent foreign born | 22.8 | 22.2 | 24.4 | 22.3 | 20.4 | 21.9 |
| Percent female-headed households[d] | 36.9 | 28.6* | 35.6 | 24.4 | 39.0 | 31.7* |
| Percent children 0–18 | 29.2 | 28.5 | 30.3 | 28.0* | 27.4 | 29.4 |
| Percent moved in last year | 25.5 | 24.8 | 25.2 | 23.7 | 26.0 | 26.5 |

*Sources:* Census tract level neighborhood data were derived from the Geolytics *Neighborhood Change Database* for 1990 and 2000.

Intercensal year data were interpolated between 1990 and 2000; extrapolated through 2007.

*Notes:* *Pre- and post-purchase paired sample t-tests for each specific ethnic group are significant at the $p < .05$ level where noted. Ethnic group comparisons also were estimated using independent samples t-tests for post-purchase indicators to assess the extent to which post-purchase neighborhood quality differed for Latino and black homebuyers. These differences are summarized as follows:
 (a) The difference in mean percentage black in post-purchase neighborhoods was significantly higher for black homebuyers relative to Latino homebuyers.
 (b) The difference in mean percentage Latino in post-purchase neighborhoods was significantly higher for Latino homebuyers relative to black homebuyers.
 (c) The difference in mean percentage White in post-purchase neighborhoods was significantly higher for Latino homebuyers relative to black homebuyers.
 (d) The percentage of female-headed households residing in post-purchase neighborhoods was significantly higher for black homebuyers relative to Latino homebuyers.

The improved quality of life in post-purchase neighborhoods was noted by our minority homebuyers. Nearly 75% of Latino and 60% of black buyers reported that their post-purchase neighborhoods were somewhat or much better than the neighborhoods they lived in while in the DHA. When asked to identify what was better about their new neighborhoods, respondents stated that they were safer (27%) and quieter (22%). Slightly less than one-quarter said that the neighborhoods where they purchased homes were about the same. Of note, however, one out of five black homebuyers reported that their post-purchase neighborhood was somewhat or much worse than where they lived prior to purchase. This is not surprising since particular housing subsidies, such as the Housing Choice Vouchers or assignments to scattered-site DHA housing units, enabled numerous minority families to reside in neighborhoods with housing that was priced substantially higher than what they could afford without assistance to purchase or rent in the private market.

Table 3 examines the experiences of our 152 minority homebuyers relative to the sustainability of homeownership.[4] When appropriate, statistics have been annualized to control for variations in the length of homeownership. By 2008, approximately 79% of Latinos and 83% of blacks had sustained their homeownership status. Further, Latino and black homebuyers had resided in their homes 23 quarters and 21 quarters, respectively, on average. By the third quarter of 2008, median home values were $165,264 for Latino homebuyers and $175,450 for black homebuyers. Over the course of their housing tenure, Latinos experienced a median gain of $28,832 in home value while blacks saw a median increase of $20,200. These gains translated into median annualized home appreciation of $4,471 (3.5%) for Latino homebuyers; $3,963 (2.7%) for blacks. By 2008, about one-quarter of Latino and one-third of black homeowners owed more on their homes than what they were worth. These home financial characteristics indicators do not systematically favor one ethnic group over the other; moreover, none of the differences was statistically significant.

By 2008, approximately 8% of Latino and 5% of black homebuyers had become landlords – keeping their original homes and generally trading up to more expensive homes. Yet, obtaining additional real estate was less frequent among minority homebuyers than witnessing

---

[4] For a further discussion of the sustainability of homeownership, see Santiago, et al. forthcoming article in *Housing Policy Debate*.

the loss of homeownership through deliberate decisions to return to renting or via foreclosure. Nearly 8% of Latino and 2% of black home-buyers had exited homeownership by the end of 2008, selling their homes and returning to renting. Another 17% of Latinos and 15% of blacks had lost their homes to foreclosures.

As in the case of pre-/post-purchase differences in neighborhood quality, there were statistically significant differences in sustainability

Table 3. Homeownership Characteristics, 2008 (All HOP Home Buyer's Club Participants during Study Period)

| | All homebuyers (N=152) | Latino (N=96) | Black (N=56) |
|---|---|---|---|
| Average number of quarters of homeownership from TOP to 2008Q3 | 22.7 | 23.3 | 21.8 |
| Median home value as of 2008Q3 | $168,541 | $162,901 | $175,450 |
| Median home appreciation as of 2008Q3 | $25,100 | $28,382 | $20,200 |
| Median annualized home appreciation as of 2008Q3 | $4,200 | $4,471 | $3,963 |
| Median annualized appreciation rate | 3.1 | 3.5 | 2.7 |
| Percent experiencing negative home appreciation by 2008Q3 | 26.8 | 22.2 | 32.1 |
| Percent still in homeownership as of 2008Q3 | 79.0 | 78.6 | 82.7 |
| Percent of homeowners returning to renting by 2008 via foreclosures | 15.7 | 16.6 | 15.3 |
| Percent of homeowners returning to renting by 2008 via home sales | 5.3 | 7.8 | 1.8 |

Sources: Real Property records from the respective county real estate offices were used to assess property values at time or purchase and 2008Q3 or time of sale or foreclosure.

Note: None of the differences across groups was significant at the p.05 level.

by HOP Program status. In analyses not presented here, Latino HOP graduates had longer homeownership tenures than HOP dropouts. Compared to HOP dropouts, median annualized home appreciated rates were significantly higher for both Latino and black HOP graduates. Latino HOP graduates were significantly less likely to have negative equity in their homes than black or Latino HOP dropouts.

*Perceived Benefits of Homeownership – Retrospective Homeowner Survey and Focus Group Data*

The 114 minority participants in our *Retrospective Homeowner Survey* and 38 homeowners participating in our focus groups were, on the whole, very happy with their experiences as new homeowners. They described a number of benefits associated with homeownership (Table 4) and gave us some insight into their largest challenges both in buying their home (Table 5) and in sustaining homeownership (Table 6). These are described in detail below.

The overriding perceived benefit of homeownership falls under pride in becoming homeowners and, in particular, reaching their goal of homeownership. Approximately four out of ten minority homebuyers identified this as one of the best dimensions of homeownership. One black single parent of two described this sense of pride in accomplishing something that had never been done before in her family:

> And it's really yours. And for me it was really, really nice because of five siblings all of them, except for one, has been the first at doing something, even if it was something like having the first baby or first grandchild or something. But, of five siblings, I'm the *very, very first one* to own my own home. So, I mean to me that's better than getting a college degree or buying a brand new car. I got something big, I got a house!

According to our respondents, this sense of pride percolated to every member of the household, particularly the children. A Latino homeowner describes how owning a home has influenced his four children:

> I think that it kinda let's them know that they don't have to be caught up in a cycle of poverty. And that there is a way out if they work towards it. And by seeing how we went through it, you know, starting off $5 hour, having a bunch of little kids running around, and working my way up and stuff. Finally achieving this goal of getting myself a house, it gave

them something to look at and say you know, we don't have to be project kids. And I don't have to raise my kids in the projects. And, uh so they look at it like that and I think they also get a great sense of pride that we were able to, to pull ourselves out of it. I think that it makes them realize that they can move towards their goals as well. It seems like that's what I'm getting from my kids.

Additionally they see the effects of these feelings of pride extending beyond themselves to their extended families and their friends. As one recent homebuyer – a Latina mother of three – recounts: "My family is real proud. That was my dream to own a home. I never thought I was gonna be able to do it on my own."

Moreover, as several participants explained, the DHA homeownership program in which they participated is seen as so powerful that they feel it should be extended to other low income families across the country. One of the black homebuyers, a single parent, recalls:

I was real excited to be in this program. I think it's very interesting. I think that it can be helpful for other people, if it can spread. There's people that have been in the same situation that we were in, that think there's no hope, then why should I? You know we need to give people hope, and who better to give it to them, than folks who've been where they're at.

Further, participants recognize how the program has instilled pride, especially among single parents who have been able to realize homeownership. As one of the Latino homebuyers – a father of four – asserts:

But this program has made it possible for them (single mothers) to get a greater sense of pride - to be confident and feel like they have accomplished something themselves. And to me that is the best benefit of this program. If there's any other reason for it to go to every other state in America - that's it!

The economic benefits attributed to homeownership, such as increased equity or the house as an investment, were of lesser importance than the perceived non-economic benefits. As shown in Table 4, slightly less than 30% cited economic considerations as the primary benefit of homeownership. One out of five cited the tax benefits associated with homeownership. Although this emphasis on the non-economic benefits of homeownership is in line with those of recent Habitat for Humanity purchasers (Mitchell and Warren 1998), they are strongly at odds with those produced by Rohe and Quercia (2003), who found

Table 4. Perceived Benefits of Homeownership and Anticipated Neighborhood Changes (All HOP Home Buyer's Club Participants Completing Surveys)

| | Percent of all survey respondents | | |
| --- | --- | --- | --- |
| | All minority homeowners (N=114) | Latino homeowners (N=68) | Black homeowners (N=46) |
| *Best dimensions of homeownership* | | | |
| Pride of ownership | 42.1 | 38.2 | 47.8 |
| Control over dwelling | 33.3 | 42.6 | 19.6 |
| Stability or security that homeownership provides | 14.0 | 16.2 | 10.9 |
| Privacy | 14.0 | 13.23 | 15.2 |
| Having outdoor space for children | 11.4 | 11.8 | 10.9 |
| *Major benefits of homeownership* | | | |
| Control over dwelling | 30.7 | 32.4 | 28.2 |
| Equity gain or investment | 29.8 | 23.5 | 39.1 |
| Tax benefits | 20.2 | 13.2 | 30.4 |
| Not having a landlord | 14.9 | 10.3 | 21.7 |
| *Anticipated changes in neighborhood* | | | |
| Improved Neighborhood Quality of life | 60.2 | 49.2 | 75.6 |
| Increased property values | 68.7 | 59.7 | 77.8 |

*Source: Denver Housing Study* Retrospective Homeowner Survey. Statistics compiled by authors.

*Notes:* Percentages based on the number of respondents identifying a particular feature or benefit. Respondents could enumerate more than one feature or benefit to homeownership. None of the differences across groups was statistically significant.

that almost two-thirds of recent homebuyers graduating from Neighbor Works training cited increased home equity as the primary benefit.

This downplaying of economic benefits in our sample may seem odd, given the characteristics of the housing market in Denver, where homeowners have become accustomed to substantial and sustained home price appreciation since 1992 (Galster et al. 2003:ch. 5). Thus, one might reasonably expect that new homeowners would assume these economic benefits will continue for the indefinite future as a normal state of affairs.

However, the focus on non-economic benefits by our minority homebuyers may be more readily understood when placed within the context of subsidized housing environments. It is understandable that our sample of low-income homebuyers, who have spent considerable time in subsidized housing, would overwhelmingly cite control over one's dwelling, increased pride and self-esteem associated with realizing the goal of homeownership, increased privacy, and security of tenure as the primary benefits accrued with the purchase of their homes. Thus, it is not surprising that approximately three out of ten respondents cited control over their dwellings as the most important benefit of homeownership, given their recent experience with the rigorously monitored environment of public housing in Denver.

One of the most enjoyable experiences described by our low-income homeowners is the ability to personalize their own space without having to ask permission of the housing authority or landlord. Indeed, one out of six study participants expressed great satisfaction that they no longer had to respond to a landlord (in most cases, this was the DHA). There is a deep personal satisfaction expressed regarding decorating their own home and, most commonly, painting the walls any color they want. As one black homebuyer who has owned her home for several years explains, "Well for me the most wonderful thing is knowing that I now get to explore my sense of style and decorating. Because I can redo stuff the way I want to."

This enjoyment extends to the rest of the family. According to one of the Latino homebuyers:

> It's nice. Its made my family feel good because they can personalize their house now. They can personalize their room....When we were living in DHA you can't do nothing to 'em.

Another recent homebuyer – a Latino father of two – concurs: "Just painting the color you want, instead of being stuck with more eggshell – so I'm pretty happy."

This perceived benefit remains primary in the minds of homeowners not only during the initial years of homeownership but also in subsequent years of homeownership. Our respondents expressed this sense of control in a variety of ways:

"Knowing that it's yours and need no one's permission to make changes."

"Just being able to do anything, anytime we want."

"No inspections. Being able to do whatever in my own home."

Privacy was another perceived benefit of homeownership, cited by nearly one out of ten minority homebuyers. In contrast to their experiences in public housing, where DHA staff had access to housing units to conduct mandatory inspections or maintenance tasks, homeowners reveled in the degree to which they could maintain a sense of privacy. As a black homeowner notes, "I don't have to answer the door. You know, no more inspections. It's a pleasure knowing that not every year, someone is going to call me and come inspect my house, and I have to be there."

The sense of stability or security associated with homeownership was also identified as an important benefit of homeownership. Approximately 14% of the homeowners identified housing stability or security as a major benefit derived from their home. The importance of this, particularly for households that have experienced significant housing instability and frequent moves, cannot be underestimated. A black mother of two describes the benefit of homeownership over renting:

> [Renting] – That's not stability, that's not security. That's somebody else's stuff. They can say get out any day. And that's the other thing, you know, that as long as you are able to work, that [the house] it's yours. Nobody can tell you I don't want to rent to you anymore [and] you need to move.

Finally, 11% of the homeowners noted the heightened sense of freedom their children experienced because they now had their own backyards to play in.

### Homeowner Expectations about Property Values and Neighborhood Quality of Life

Confirming the quantitative data presented earlier, many of the 114 survey participants describe homeownership as an opportunity to move into a better neighborhood than where they lived with DHA. They speak of their new neighborhoods as benefitting them by providing a better environment to raise their children, greater safety, better schools, more space, more privacy, and shopping areas close by. Several participants referred to their neighborhoods as "up and coming" and they expressed optimism and hope that their neighborhoods will provide a more inspiring environment for their children. With regard to changes in the neighborhood environment, one Latino father describes his family's move to Montbello, on Denver's Northeast side:

> I think mine is improving especially because the schools, for instance, are a really good sign of improvement because when your schools start improving, the kids in the neighborhood have something more to work with and to look forward to.

Some tell of the lengthy commutes they must endure in order to afford a house in a safer neighborhood, which they say is well worth it. According to a black owner who purchased a home in Aurora (a suburb of Denver):

> It's just totally disciplined where I live. I mean, it's a nice neighborhood. And I left from my neighborhood. I needed to get out of that neighborhood. I lived in that neighborhood for a very long time and I've got a son that's a product of his environment, you know what I'm saying? And when he comes in my house, you know, he's out of there, he doesn't have to be over in the 'hood, you know. And where I live now, yeah, I have to drive a long distance to work. The job was only like ten minutes away before, and now I'm like 45 minutes away and there are three highways to get there. But I don't mind because I know when I go home it's like peace and quiet.

Some of the benefits associated with living in the new neighborhood have been expressed in terms of home maintenance and general neighborhood upkeep. According to our study participants, 85% of the homes in their neighborhood were well maintained and repaired. Further, they estimated that approximately 40% of neighboring homeowners had made major improvements to their homes within the past few years. As a result, most minority homeowners expressed considerable optimism about increasing property values and quality of life within their neighborhoods (see bottom panel of Table 4). Prior to the downturn of the regional housing market in 2008, nearly eight out of ten black and six out of ten Latino homebuyers expected that property values in their neighborhood would continue to rise over the next several years. Indeed, a number of the homeowners reported a doubling of their property values within a year or two of purchase. Their observations are confirmed by Galster et al.'s (2003) findings, which suggest that even the poorest neighborhoods in Denver witnessed substantial gains in property values during the decade immediately preceding the recent retrenchment in the housing market. Reasons cited by respondents for the anticipated as well as actual growth in property values include the quality and upkeep of homes, the benefits of a strong local economy, and substantial economic development activities occurring both within as well as in close proximity to the neighborhood.

When asked about their expectations regarding neighborhood quality of life at time of survey, six out of ten minority homeowners expressed optimism. This varied considerably by ethnicity: while nearly 80% of black homeowners expected quality of life to improve in the neighborhood, only 49% of Latino homebuyers believed it would. In contrast, about 40% of Latinos and 20% of blacks thought it would stay the same, and 10% of Latinos felt that it would decline. This suggests that minority homebuyers were not economically constrained to purchase only in distressed and declining neighborhoods.

*Challenges of Homeownership*

While there are several common challenges to homeownership for low-income, minority homebuyers, those most often cited by minority participants are the need for costly repairs to the house, worries about the precarious nature of their employment accompanied by the potential inability to pay their mortgages, and ongoing concerns about the rising costs of utilities. When asked about what worried them the most as homeowners, nearly 80% of the study participants expressed being concerned about their ability to keep up with rapidly rising utility costs (see Table 5). The frequency of this concern is substantially higher than in prior studies (cf. Rohe and Quercia's 2003 estimate of only 25%). For a number of HOP homebuyers, utility costs were significantly higher than what they had anticipated. As one of the Latino homeowners who bought a spacious house to accommodate his large and growing family remarks:

> I had never expected a Public Service bill quite as large as this big house would give me. I mean, my Public Service bills are averaging $250 bucks a month. And so that was a little bit of surprise. I didn't expect the water bill to be quite as much as it was either.

For some, these unexpected additional costs have led them to prioritize payments or to engage in what this Latino homeowner describes as "creative budgeting":

There have been times when I have missed paying a Public Service bill. You go through [them] and you say, 'OK, throw them up in the air and whichever one God takes, we take. He didn't take none of them so I didn't pay that month at all. I just had to figure out another way of budgeting it. There were times when I had to skip a payment and make it up later, but I never gave up the mortgage. I never gave up the important things. The Public Service is important but you can kinda get away with sliding a month here and there with them. As long as you go make it up. And so I've had to do that, a little bit of, I guess you can call it, creative budgeting to make it work. I'm just living and hoping that my next raise comes up as soon as possible.

Table 5. Anticipated Concerns and Actual Challenges about Home-ownership (All HOP Home Buyer's Club Participants Completing Surveys)

|  | All minority homebuyers (N=114) | Latino homebuyers (N=68) | Black homebuyers (N=46) |
| --- | --- | --- | --- |
| *Anticipated concerns re: homeownership* | | | |
| Rising utility costs | 77.0 | 80.6 | 71.1 |
| Home maintenance and repairs | 74.0 | 77.6 | 68.9 |
| Paying mortgage on time | 62.0 | 62.7 | 53.3 |
| Declining quality of life in the neighborhood | 58.0 | 58.0 | 62.2 |
| Rising property taxes | 54.0 | 49.3 | 57.8 |
| Stress of homeownership | 51.0 | 53.7 | 37.7 |
| Declining property values | 36.0 | 38.8 | 33.4 |
| *Actual challenges re: homeownership* | | | |
| Cost/Efforts associated with regular maintenance and upkeep | 28.9 | 25.0 | 34.8 |
| Paying mortgage payments | 18.4 | 19.1 | 17.4 |

Table 5.  (*Cont.*)

|  | All minority homebuyers (N=114) | Latino homebuyers (N=68) | Black homebuyers (N=46) |
|---|---|---|---|
| Paying utility payments | 13.2 | 16.2 | 8.7 |
| None | 14.0 | 16.2 | 10.9 |
| *Major costs associated with homeownership* | | | |
| Upkeep of home | 27.2 | 29.4 | 23.9 |
| Remodeling/home improvements | 26.3 | 25.0 | 28.3 |
| Paying mortgage | 20.2 | 22.0 | 17.4 |
| Paying utilities | 14.0 | 11.8 | 17.4 |
| None | 7.9 | 7.3 | 8.7 |

*Source: Denver Housing Study* Retrospective Homeowner Survey. Statistics compiled by authors.

*Notes:* Percentages based on the number of respondents identifying a particular concern, challenge or cost. Respondents could enumerate more than one feature or benefit to homeownership.
None of the differences across groups was statistically significant.


The second most frequently cited worry concerned home maintenance and repairs, particularly in terms of the ability to address any unexpected, emergency home repairs. These new homeowners were particularly aware of the devastating financial consequences that such emergency repairs could have on their households. Indeed, one-third of first- and second-year homeowners had experienced unexpected problems, particularly with heating and plumbing systems. As one black homeowner related, "The first week I moved in, the downstairs flooded. This [recurred] six times in one year."

Other minority homeowners recount their rude introduction to home repairs:

> The second day, my toilet backed up, the microwave died, the heater broke and the washer plugs didn't fit the circuit.

> I moved in December and in January, my heater went out. It was inspected and it was checked out as being good but it was the main board and you can't really check that out you know, so that went out. So here

> I am … heater's out, it's January, freezing cold and I have to do something
> to get it fixed. So right away I have to go into the savings that I had set
> aside to live off of in case I was ever to get unemployed for any reason.
> The first thing I did after the furnace went out was went out and found
> me a really good home warranty program where they would cover all of
> my appliances and heater, air conditioning all that good stuff and uh, and
> as far as paying on that right away and that's helped me a lot because
> everything has gone out since then.

Such worries about repairs were exacerbated because homeowners
could not pass them on to someone else, as they could when they were
renting. As one black homebuyer describes:

> For [my worry] it's just the usual stuff – home repairs. God, I hope some-
> thing doesn't break because I can't afford to fix it. It's something impor-
> tant, too, like the hot water heater or the furnace…. It doesn't change that
> I'm happy. I own my own place. But, you can't just call the landlord and
> say, 'Look, its broke, it needs to be fixed.' It's like we can't not pay these
> house repairs. You have to figure out, where do I pull this money from?
> How do I pay for this?

Another black homeowner – a single mother of two – expressed concerns about home repairs within the context of job security:

> Do I want to get myself into that debt, do I want to put myself out there?
> If I feel like that right now even if I take out a loan to pay for that stuff
> (repairs) right now, what if I don't have a job? Am I going to be able to
> pay for that, am I going to be able to keep my job, and keep my place?
> You know, that's my biggest worry.

Other homeowners echoed concerns about the ability to pay for such
real or anticipated emergency repairs, underscoring the vulnerability
of their homeownership. Alternatively, they are confronted with the
challenge of making necessary repairs while keeping their mortgage
payments current. As one Latino homeowner relates, "The biggest
challenge for me has been to replace my furnace and pay my mortgage
at the same time."

    Concern over their ability to keep up with mortgage payments both
in the short- and long-term was expressed by 62% of homeowners.
This black homeowner described the sense of financial insecurity
experienced by low-income homeowners:

> One of my big worries right now is, um, am I gonna be able to keep it.
> Right now I still have some money for backup. But, when my money
> runs out, am I gonna have enough money, because I was getting like,
> child support, you know. Eight hundred dollars, about $850 dollars a

month, you know, which, you know, enabled me to qualify for buying my house.

For a number of our homeowners, concerns about timely mortgage payments were accentuated by fears of actual or impending job loss. Several Latino homeowners highlight these concerns:

> It's hard, yeah. I was unemployed for two months. And during that whole two months it was pretty stressful just trying to make sure I got my mortgage payment paid and all my bills.

> I work for the city, and it's kinda shaky. We may have to be laid off… What if I don't have a job? Am I going to be able to pay for that? Am I going to be able to keep my job, and keep my place? You know, that's my biggest worry.

Many of the homeowners we interviewed identified that making mortgage and utility payments on time were major challenges. For some of our respondents, making timely mortgage payments had become a juggling act, choosing among creditors. As one black homeowner underscores:

> Not the mortgage payment because that's the first thing I pay now. Everybody else might be on hold. The cable, the phone …somebody but, I'll always make sure I pay my mortgage and my HOA [Home Owner Association fees] on time every month. Everybody else, they might get a piece or a portion but that's what I make sure I pay.

Concerns about rising property taxes and concomitant increases to insurance and house payments were expressed by 54% of our homeowners. Just as homeowners were pleasantly aware of increasing property values, they were painfully aware of the consequences in terms of higher property tax burdens. One homeowner describes her experience of rising house payments on a home that has nearly doubled in value since time of purchase:

> So it goes up [the house payment] …that's automatic. It went up because they didn't take enough for my property insurance. Now I'm having to pay $32 more because of that. So now my house payment went up. Well, you guys are going to laugh, but to me it's a lot of money, you know.

Other concerns articulated by minority homeowners were the inability to handle the stress of homeownership (51%) and worries about declining property values (36%) – both concerns were expressed in interviews conducted prior to the recent deflation of the housing market.

When asked about the challenges that they faced in keeping their homes, one out of six homebuyers stressed that they had not encountered any challenges. Among buyers who found homeownership to be challenging, the challenges that were mentioned closely matched the concerns expressed by homebuyers. Approximately 30% of the participants reported that their biggest challenges were associated with the expense as well as effort needed to maintain their homes. Nearly one out of five talked about the challenges of making their mortgage payments. Slightly less than one out of six indicated that paying their utilities was the biggest challenge they faced as homeowners. As one might expect, all of these issues were mentioned as the major costs associated with homeownership. Nonetheless, these were costs minority homebuyers were willing to incur in order to purchase and then keep their homes.

Given the economic vulnerability of our sample homebuyers, we asked them to identify the factors that contributed to the sustainability of homeownership. Their responses are summarized in Table 6. One out of five minority homebuyers cited employment stability – having

Table 6. Factors Contributing to the Sustainability of Homeownership (All HOP Home Buyer's Club Participants Completing Surveys)

| | Percent of all respondents | | |
| --- | --- | --- | --- |
| | All minority homeowners (N=114) | Latino homeowners (N=68) | Black homeowners (N=46) |
| *Factors contributing to sustainability* | | | |
| Employment stability | 20.0 | 22.6 | 20.3 |
| Sense of ownership | 16.6 | 14.0 | 20.3 |
| Making payments on time/making extra payments | 8.9 | 8.6 | 9.4 |
| Inheritance for children | 7.6 | 14.0 | 1.3 |
| Desire to keep home | 6.4 | 5.3 | 7.8 |

*Source: Denver Housing Study* Retrospective Homeowner Survey. Statistics compiled by authors.

*Notes:* Percentages based on the number of respondents identifying a particular factor contributing to sustainability. Respondents could enumerate more than one factor. None of the differences across groups was statistically significant.

and keeping their jobs – as the primary factor enabling them to sustain homeownership. Slightly less than one out of ten reported that continuing homeownership status was tied to paying their mortgage on time or even accelerating their mortgage repayment. Yet there were several noneconomic factors that study participants recounted as enhancing the sustainability of homeownership. For about 17% of the homebuyers, the sense of ownership was linked to their strong desire to keep their homes. Further, this desire often was motivated by the interest in leaving an inheritance for their children.

*Making the Transition from Subsidized Householder to Homeowner*

Perhaps one of the more difficult aspects of homeownership for some low-income homebuyers was the dramatic shift in status, particularly as it related to their ability to access alternative sources of support, even though one's economic status might not have changed sufficiently to foster complete autonomy. This situation is eloquently described by one of the Latino homeowners:

> We're all struggling to get to this point where we can buy our house and then when we finally buy our house it's like you just get dropped and no longer get assistance from anybody. Like you were with your, with these people who could help you get your plumbing fixed. They're looking at you no longer as somebody who is a low-income housing tenant. Now they're looking at you as a homeowner and an employed homeowner, which obviously you have to be. So, therefore you don't qualify for a lot of this stuff anymore when in actuality we are still struggling and are still barely living off of our income. In other words, we're still trying to make ends meet. We're still trying to keep paying those bills and we basically are still low income. It's just that now we're low income with our own house.

> We're a homeowner so therefore you don't qualify anymore. You know I mean it happens with everything, with everything you can think of. Like, for instance, even assistance for kids going to classes, going to school and stuff. You don't qualify. You know, for getting help to fix your house you don't qualify. You know, so for a lot of us, and I think especially a lot of the single women that are trying to make it on their own, they still need that help. They still need that assistance to have somebody come in and fix their plumbing or do some drywall work for them. Or replace a toilet. You know, stuff like that. There's things that are gonna go wrong with your house. And you know we succeeded, we got us a house. But …does that really mean that we are so completely free of being a low-income family that we no longer should qualify for any type of help? But you know to have some (neighborhood development corporation) or

any of these other ones available to say, 'OK. Yeah, this is a person who just got into their house. They're not rich. You know they're still struggling. They still need assistance. And just because they've got a house doesn't mean they can afford to go out and pay a couple of thousand bucks to get their plumbing fixed.'

In sum, our respondents were well attuned to the challenges they faced as low-income homeowners. Although many of them have had to weather some substantial difficulties during their tenure as homeowners, they also have demonstrated resiliency and creativity in their responses to these challenges. Nonetheless, their experiences underscore their vulnerability, particularly in times of unanticipated or additional housing expenses. However, aside from adjusting to the financial costs of homeownership, including mortgages and home repairs, the transition from public housing to homeownership generally has been a positive one. Our participants have expressed the sheer joy in being homeowners in the following passages:

> So far its been a really good experience you know (moving from housing to homeownership), and that was something that needed change because when you're around people who live differently and see life through a different perspective and you know, have different values and, sometimes it does make a difference on your children because they think 'well, why can't I do that?' So for us it's not really secluding them from that, but getting in a better environment. (Latina homeowner)

> So far it's a blessing. It's wonderful. It's divine. It's so great because I've been living in low housing ever since my son was 6 months old and then we got into Section 8 just when I got laid off my job. And so now to own a home it's like it is grand, it's glorious, it's audacious. I mean, you just can't put words to it. It's like it swells you up inside because it's saying like yes, you know, 'I did this you know through the grace of God. I did this in order to better my lifestyle to better my son's lifestyle to let him know that whatever you set your mind to, whatever goal you have, you can accomplish it.' (black homeowner)

*Housing Maintenance, Upkeep, and Improvements*

Given their heightened economic vulnerability, one might expect that these low-income homeowners would often forego home maintenance and repairs. However, we discovered that, despite their financial constraints, our homeowners were committed to maintaining and often remodeling their homes. Further, these stated commitments were backed by specific actions. The results of their activities are summarized in Table 7.

When asked about home maintenance expenses, 91% of homeowners indicated they had incurred such expenses during the 12 months prior to their interview. These homeowners had paid, on average, $500 on home maintenance during that time period. The median expenditure for such home maintenance costs since time of purchase was

Table 7.  Post-Purchase Maintenance, Repairs, and Home Improvement Expenditures (All HOP Home Buyer's Club Participants Completing Surveys)

|  | All minority homeowners (N=114) | Latino homeowners (N=68) | Black homeowners (N=46) |
|---|---|---|---|
| *Home maintenance* | | | |
| Median expenditures for home maintenance over the duration of homeownership | $1,000 | $1,275 | $2,638 |
| Median annualized expenditures for home maintenance | $195 | $147 | $325 |
| Percent who incurred home maintenance costs during the 12 months prior to interview | 90.8 | 89.5 | 90.5 |
| Average amount spent on home maintenance during the 12 months prior to interview | $500 | $500 | $600 |
| Percent who borrowed or refinanced these home maintenance costs | 22.0 | 22.8 | 20.9 |
| Average amount borrowed for home maintenance costs | $25,000 | $26,000 | $20,000 |

*(Continued)*

322     ANNA MARIA SANTIAGO ET AL.

Table 7. (*Cont.*)

| | All minority homeowners (N=114) | Latino homeowners (N=68) | Black homeowners (N=46) |
|---|---|---|---|
| *Percent of homeowners who replaced* | | | |
| Plumbing | 56.0 | 59.6 | 51.2 |
| Windows and doors | 42.0 | 45.6 | 37.2 |
| Water heaters | 21.0 | 21.1 | 20.9 |
| Roofs and gutters | 21.0 | 24.6 | 16.3 |
| Heating systems | 20.0 | 22.8 | 16.3 |
| Driveways | 19.0 | 24.6 | 11.6 |
| Cooling systems | 17.0 | 15.8 | 18.6 |
| Porches | 15.0 | 15.8 | 14.0 |
| *Minor home repairs* | | | |
| Median expenditures for minor home repairs over the duration of homeownership | $365 | $450 | $235 |
| Median annualized expenditures for home repair costs | $82 | $84 | $71 |
| Percent who incurred minor home repair costs during the 12 months prior to interview | 57.9 | 61.4 | 53.1 |
| Average amount spent on home repairs during the 12 months prior to interview | $700 | $650 | $700 |
| Percent who borrowed or refinanced to make these minor home repairs | 4.0 | 5.3 | 2.3 |
| Average amount borrowed for minor home repairs | $27,500 | $30,000 | $25,000 |

Table 7.  (*Cont.*)

| | All minority homeowners (N=114) | Latino homeowners (N=68) | Black homeowners (N=46) |
|---|---|---|---|
| *Percent making the following minor repairs* | | | |
| Interior painting | 64.0 | 66.7 | 60.5 |
| Flooring | 45.0 | 47.4 | 41.9 |
| Exterior painting | 29.0 | 38.6 | 16.3 |
| Other interior repairs | 22.0 | 22.8 | 20.9 |
| Other exterior repairs | 12.0 | 15.8 | 7.0 |
| *Major home Improvements* | | | |
| Percent who made major home improvements since home purchase | 12.2 | 14.5 | 9.3 |
| Median expenditure on major home improvements | $1,750 | $1,350 | $2,250 |
| Annualized median expenditure on major home improvements | $164 | $148 | $186 |
| Percent who borrowed or refinanced to make major home improvements | 11.1 | 12.5 | 9.1 |
| Median amount borrowed or refinanced to make major home improvements | $25,000 | $14,500 | $25,000 |

*Source: Denver Housing Study* Retrospective Homeowner Survey. Statistics compiled by authors.

*Notes:* Differences across groups were not statistically significant.

$1,000. When we control for homeownership tenure, we find that the median annualized expenditure for home maintenance was only $195. Nonetheless, more than one in five homeowners had significantly higher expenditures that forced them to seek loans to finance these home maintenance costs. For those who did borrow money for these expenses, the average amount borrowed was $25,000. These higher-end borrowers needed to cash in on the equity accrued on their homes; securing home equity lines of credit was the primary source of monies for these maintenance costs.

Plumbing was the most frequently cited home maintenance item, where more than half of the study participants replaced plumbing during their homeownership tenure. Repairing or replacing windows and doors was the next-most common post-purchase maintenance activity. Such repairs were cited by 42% of the homeowners. One out of five homeowners reported repairing or replacing water heaters, roofs and gutters, heating systems or driveways since purchasing their homes. About one in six replaced cooling systems or porches.

Minor home repairs also were consistently made by study home-owners. During the 12 months prior to the survey, nearly 60% of the homeowners had made minor home repairs. The median amount spent on such repairs during that 12-month period, as reported by survey respondents, was $700. Interior painting (64%), flooring (45%) and exterior painting (29%) were the most common repairs made by study participants. However, when we assessed the itemized home repair costs made during their homeownership tenure, we found that these costs actually averaged $365; the median annualized expenditures for minor home repairs were $82. However, 4% of the homeowners reported borrowing to pay for these expenses, and for them the average amount borrowed was sizeable ($27,500). As in the case of home maintenance, the primary source of financing for home repairs was home equity loans.

About 12% of the homeowners in our study made major improvements to their homes since time of purchase. Improvements ranged from additional bedrooms or bathrooms, to decks, patios, garages, driveways, and fences, to water treatment systems. On average, the median home improvement expenditure over the course of homeownership was $1,750; the annualized median expenditure on home improvements was $164. Slightly more than one out of ten borrowed money to finance these major home improvements. Of those borrowing or refinancing for such improvements, the median amount borrowed was $25,000 and financing was secured by drawing down on home equity.

The investments made to maintain, repair and improve the home by our minority homebuyers are indeed significant when put into context. Combining all these expenditures, we find that the minority homebuyers in our study invested, on average, $2,501 on the upkeep of their homes since purchase. Slightly less than one in four had invested less than $500 over the entire period of homeownership. The comparable percentage for a 1998–1999 national sample of very low-income homeowners was 45%, (Belsky 2002). Indeed, the median *annualized* investment in maintenance, repairs, or major improvements was $500 for minority homeowners in the study.

Thus, among this group of minority homeowners there is clear evidence that they have invested considerable effort and resources in the maintenance and improvement of their homes. Nonetheless, this has come at significant financial strain to many of these homeowners, who have found themselves borrowing against current and future equity of their homes in order to finance these endeavors. The incidence of debt financing of these home investments appears on par with that observed by Rohe and Quercia (2003), however.

### Growth of Non-Housing Assets

For most minority homeowners participating in the survey, their primary asset was their home. Indeed, for nearly one in five homeowners, their home was the only asset they held. Median housing wealth for survey participants was $24,950 but varied considerably by ethnicity. Median housing wealth was $20,100 for black homeowners but $32,500 for Latino homeowners. Since becoming homeowners, 80% of our study respondents did accrue some, albeit modest, amounts of non-housing assets. Minority homeowners accrued, on average, $3,350 in non-housing assets since time of home purchase. The median value of the assets held by Latinos was $4,250; the comparable figure for blacks was $2,665. The annualized median value of these non-housing assets was $551, ranging from $433 for black to $686 for Latino homebuyers.

*What constitutes these non-housing assets?* As shown in Table 8, the vast majority of minority homeowners (93%) held checking accounts with relatively modest median deposits ($425). Approximately two-thirds of all minority households had savings accounts, although the median amounts in their savings accounts also were quite modest ($400). Almost two-thirds of the homeowners had retirement or pension benefits valued at $8,750. Approximately one in five homeowners held stocks, bonds, or mutual funds, with a median value of $1,860.

Outside of home equity and bank accounts, life insurance policies and vehicles were the most commonly held assets by our minority homeowners. Nearly 65% of black and Latino homeowners had life insurance; the median value of the policy was $95,000. One out of ten homeowners owned their vehicles free and clear. The median value of vehicles owned by these homeowners was $5,000. Less than 10% of our homeowners – all of them Latino HOP graduate homebuyers– held other assets, such as additional real estate or business accounts. In contrast, none of the black homeowners in our study had other real estate or business accounts.

Table 8. Housing and Non-Housing Assets Held by Minority Home-owners at Time of Survey (All HOP Home Buyer's Club Participants Completing Surveys)

| Type of assets | All homebuyers (N=114) | Latino homebuyers (N=68) | Black homebuyers (N=46) |
|---|---|---|---|
| Median home value as of 2008Q3 | $174,250 | $172,600 | $176,400 |
| Annualized median home appreciation as of 2008Q3 | $4,249 | $4,671 | $4,148 |
| *Percent who have …* | | | |
| Any non-housing assets | 82.6 | 82.1 | 81.0 |
| Percent with personal checking accounts | 92.9 | 89.3 | 97.6 |
| Median value of checking account | $425 | $400 | $431 |
| Percent with personal savings accounts | 68.4 | 67.9 | 69.0 |
| Median value of savings account | $400 | $300 | $650 |
| Percent with retirement or pension plans | 64.3 | 62.5 | 66.7 |
| Median value of retirement or pension plan | $8,750 | $9,000 | $10,000 |

Table 8. *(Cont.)*

| Type of assets | All homebuyers (N=114) | Latino homebuyers (N=68) | Black homebuyers (N=46) |
|---|---|---|---|
| Percent with money in stocks, bonds or mutual funds | 20.4 | 14.3 | 28.6 |
| Median value of stocks, bonds or mutual funds | $1,860 | $2,000 | $1,710 |
| Percent with life insurance policies | 64.3 | 66.1 | 61.9 |
| Median value of life insurance policies | $95,000 | $100,000 | $105,000 |
| Percent with vehicles owned free and clear* | 70.4 | 75.0 | 64.3 |
| Median value of vehicles owned free and clear | $5,000 | $5,000 | $5,000 |
| Percent with additional real estate* | 6.1 | 10.7 | 0.0 |
| Median value of additional real estate | $217,000 | $217,000 | $0.0 |
| Percent with other financial assets | 4.1 | 3.6 | 4.8 |
| Median value of other assets | $13,000 | $11,750 | $13,000 |
| Median value of non-housing assets (excluding pensions and life insurance) | $3,350 | $4,250 | $2,665 |
| Median annualized value of non-housing assets | $551 | $686 | $433 |

*Source: Denver Housing Study* Retrospective Homeowner Survey. Statistics compiled by authors.

*Notes:* * Group differences in the percentage who own additional real estate or vehicles owned free and clear are significantly different at the p < .01 level.

*Growing Indebtedness beyond Mortgages*

According to our survey respondents, nearly half of the Latino homeowners reported that their financial situation had improved during the
three years prior to their interview. By contrast, a significantly smaller
share (37%) of black homebuyers had such good fortune. Moreover, a
sizable fraction of black homebuyers (38%) but significantly fewer
Latinos (8%) reported that their financial situations had gotten much
worse over the past three years. For those experiencing worsening
financial situations, growing indebtedness was one of the main contributors. Not surprisingly, black homebuyers in the study had difficulties paying their monthly bills at a significantly higher rate than Latinos
(14% compared to 5%).

As noted earlier, approximately one out of four minority homebuyers in our study incurred additional mortgage debt in the process of
maintaining or repairing their home, and one in ten incurred more of
the same by undertaking home improvements. Yet, an even more wor-
risome finding for our sample of minority homeowners has been their
increasing consumer indebtedness in addition to their mortgages (see
Table 9). More than eight out of ten Latino and black homeowners
reported holding non-housing debt at the time of their interview.
Median consumer debt was $6,900 and varied from $5,000 for Latinos
to $9,100 for blacks. The median annualized debt was $1,000 – $925
for Latinos and $1,624 for blacks. The estimated median monthly con-
sumer debt payment was $250 at the time of the survey; slightly higher
for black homebuyers.

As part of the *Retrospective Homeowner Survey*, respondents were
asked detailed questions about the debts they had accumulated over
the course of their homeownership. We found that a large fraction of
increased indebtedness was associated with items that would be considered investments (e.g., automobiles, business loans, educational
loans); such accounted for 69% of the total debt amount. However, we
also found substantial post-purchase increases in consumer debt:
credit cards (72%) were the most frequently mentioned sources of
additional debt. Loans from family or friends were reported as out-
standing debts by 12% of the HOP homeowners. With this increased
debt burden, it is not surprising that some homeowners had difficulty
paying all of their debts in a timely manner. Nearly four out of ten
homebuyers in the study reported that they had been late in making a
consumer debt payment during the 12 months prior to the interview.
Nearly one in ten reported finding it difficult to pay their monthly bills

most or all of the time. In analyses not show here, that was particularly the case for black HOP dropouts.

We investigated whether there were any statistically significant relationships between a homebuyer's increase in consumer debt and their debts incurred for either home repairs or for home improvements, but could identify none. This suggests that growing consumer debt was a general phenomenon in our sample that was not contingent on the voluntary or involuntary investments made in the home.

Thus, a sizable fraction of our sample of minority homeowners has acquired significant consumer debts in a relatively short period of time. In addition to initial mortgage payments that, for many, were on the high end of mortgage qualifying amounts, these homeowners were often burdened by mortgage debt associated with unexpected home maintenance and repair costs that further inflated their monthly mortgage payments. It is no wonder, then, that a number of these homeowners expressed concern about their ability to pay for their mortgage and their other expenses. Nor is it surprising that they were forced at times to make choices about which bills, in addition to the mortgage, were to be paid.

Rising debt has eroded the home equity of minority homebuyers. In analyses not presented here, we found that for those whose homes continued to appreciate in value through 2008 (representing three out of four homebuyers in the study), existing consumer debt was about double the amount held in non-housing assets ($6,950 in debts; $3,300 in assets). Among the nearly 25% of homebuyers whose homes had negative equity, this nearly 2:1 consumer debt/asset ratio remains ($6,600 in debts; $3,450 in assets). Their consumer debts are exacerbating the financial precariousness of these households.

### Mortgage Delinquencies, Foreclosures, Refinancing, and Predation

Previous studies underscore significantly higher rates of exits from homeownership and mortgage defaults among minority and low-income homeowners – both of which have been linked not only to economic vulnerability but also to the lack of financial literacy and victimization by predatory lenders (see the review in Galster and Santiago 2008). In this section, we summarize the experiences of our Denver homebuyers, which illustrate that, despite the financial strains they do experience, these adverse consequences proved rarely the case.

Table 9. Post-Purchase Debt Burdens of Minority Homebuyers by Ethnicity (All HOP Home Buyer's Club Participants Completing Surveys)

| | All homebuyers | Latino homebuyers (N=68) | Black homebuyers (N=46) |
|---|---|---|---|
| *Post-purchase changes in housing debt* | | | |
| Median value of mortgage at time of survey | $124,000 | $110,000 | $133,000 |
| Median monthly mortgage payment at time of survey | $1,079 | $1,064 | $1,086 |
| Percent who refinanced their home | 25.0 | 28.1 | 20.9 |
| Percent who acquired a second mortgage | 15.0 | 19.3 | 9.3 |
| Percent who obtained a home equity line of credit | 15.0 | 17.5 | 11.6 |
| Percent who consolidated debt | 28.0 | 38.6 | 14.0 |
| Percent who secured home improvement loans | 12.0 | 12.3 | 11.6 |
| Percent who incurred credit card debt to finance home repairs | 24.0 | 21.0 | 27.9 |
| Percent who made a late mortgage payment in 12 months prior to survey | 31.0 | 29.8 | 32.6 |
| Percent who were 30+ days late on mortgage payment in 12 months prior to survey | 13.0 | 12.3 | 14.0 |
| Percent with 2+ delinquent mortgage payments in 12 months prior to survey | 8.0 | 5.3 | 11.7 |

Table 9.  *(Cont.)*

| | All homebuyers | Latino homebuyers (N=68) | Black homebuyers (N=46) |
|---|---|---|---|
| Percent of current homeowners who have been threatened with foreclosure | 7.0 | 3.5 | 11.6 |
| *Post-purchase consumer debt* | | | |
| Percent who have additional debts outside of mortgage | 83.4 | 84.2 | 83.3 |
| Median consumer debt at time of survey | $6,900 | $5,000 | $9,100 |
| Median annualized debt since time of purchase | $1,000 | $925 | $1,624 |
| Median monthly debt payment at time of survey | $250 | $250 | $300 |
| *Type of non-housing debt* | | | |
| Percent with vehicle loans | 50.6 | 47.9 | 54.3 |
| Median balance on vehicle loans | $7,000 | $6,000 | $7,000 |
| Percent with credit card debts | 72.3 | 70.8 | 74.3 |
| Median balance on credit cards | $2,050 | $2,000 | $2,550 |
| Percent with personal loans | 10.8 | 14.6 | 5.7 |
| Median balance on personal loans | $4,000 | $5,000 | $2,300 |
| Percent with student loans | 33.7 | 27.1 | 42.9 |

*(Continued)*

Table 9. *(Cont.)*

|  | All homebuyers | Latino homebuyers (N=68) | Black homebuyers (N=46) |
|---|---|---|---|
| Median balance on student loans | $12,000 | $10,000 | $12,000 |
| Percent with medical bills | 24.1 | 20.8 | 28.6 |
| Median balance on medical bills | $1,000 | $350 | $1,750 |
| Percent with legal bills | 1.2 | 0.0 | 2.9 |
| Median balance on legal bills | $2,000 | $0.0 | $2,000 |
| Percent with loans from family or friends | 12.0 | 10.4 | 14.3 |
| Median balance on loans from family or friends | $800 | $250 | $1,400 |
| Percent with store loans | 12.0 | 12.5 | 11.4 |
| Median balance on store loans | $1,050 | $1,050 | $1,625 |
| Percent with other loans | 10.8 | 12.5 | 8.6 |
| Median balance on other loans | $9,000 | $5,150 | $10,000 |
| Percent having difficulty paying monthly bills most or all of the time* | 9.0 | 5.3 | 14.0 |
| Percent whose financial situation improved over the few years prior to the survey* | 43.0 | 47.4 | 37.2 |
| Percent whose financial situation worsened over the few years prior to the survey* | 22.0 | 8.8 | 39.5 |

*Source: Denver Housing Study* Retrospective Homeowner Survey. Statistics compiled by authors.

*Notes:* *Differences across ethnic groups are significant at the p < .05 level.

*Mortgage Delinquencies*

Approximately one-third of the study participants made at least one late mortgage payment during the 12 months prior to their interview; only 2% of the sample reported making late payments every month during that same time period. One in eight homeowners made one delinquent payment that was more than 30 days late; almost one out of ten homeowners reported making two or more delinquent payments during the 12 months prior to the survey. This relatively low rate of delinquencies is comparable to the findings of Rohe and Quercia (2003). Although a sizable fraction of homeowners had difficulties paying their mortgages on time, only two of the homeowners who had made delinquent payments reported they had restructured their mortgage to alleviate this problem. However, only two of the respondents reported seeking assistance from DHA to address the underlying issues associated with these late payments. Others reported they were "too embarrassed to contact the authority." In the cases where the respondents sought DHA assistance, the authority helped support the homeowners with partial payments and foreclosure prevention assistance.

*Foreclosures and Exits from Homeownership*

Prior to 2007, there were only a handful of foreclosures directed against the 152 minority homeowners in the study. During the past several years, foreclosures increased dramatically in Denver with the downturn of the mortgage finance and housing markets. Approximately three-quarters of foreclosures occurred to homebuyers in 2007 and 2008 – periods when the mortgage crisis was at its peak in Denver. By the end of 2008, 16% of the homeowners in the study had already experienced a foreclosure. Moreover, an additional 7% of all survey respondents who were still homeowners reported being threatened with foreclosure, underscoring their economic vulnerability. Despite this heightened vulnerability and the sizeable fraction of homeowners who have made late payments on their mortgages in the past, approximately 85% of minority homeowners reported that they had not developed any strategies to prevent foreclosures. For the few homeowners who did, their self-styled strategies involved: "paying the mortgage on time," "making sure they maintained their employment," "budgeting," and "selling their homes." However, about 9% of Latino homebuyers and 4% of black homebuyers reported restructuring their debt in regards to averting foreclosure.

*Refinancing*
By 2008, 28% of Latino and 20% of black homeowners in our study had refinanced their homes. While home repairs and major improvements drove part of this refinancing – about one in three respondents borrowed to finance these repairs – other homeowners used refinancing as a means of obtaining lower interest rates or paying off second mortgages to DHA or other home purchase programs. As we will see below, none of these refinancings was unnecessarily undertaken at the urging of predatory lenders.

*"Predatory Lenders" and Debt Purveyors*
We included several questions regarding exposure to predatory lenders and other purveyors of debt in the Retrospective Homeowner Survey and our focus groups with homeowners (Renuart 2004). All of the homeowners who responded to our survey reported receiving numerous unsolicited offers for loans, refinancing, and/or additional credit, or offers to purchase their homes. Other unsolicited offers were for debt or credit consolidation, second mortgages and mortgage insurance. All of the homeowners in the sample reported that they threw away or refused these unsolicited offers.

Homeownership has expanded and improved credit for the majority of the homebuyers in the study. For many, better credit has been liberating (as one Latino homebuyer exclaims: "Qualify for credit cards, oh yeah!") and has allowed them to make necessary improvements to their homes, seek further education, and refinance their homes with lower interest rates. Others, however, express consternation at the flood of unsolicited offers of credit that tempt them to get into consumer debt. In some cases, the increased access to credit is portrayed as a benefit to low income homeowners who have previously experienced very few options. In worst-case scenarios, expensive or even predatory lending practices can penetrate their precarious financial positions and harm their homeownership sustainability. For example, one black homeowner reported that she was given the offer of overdraft protection that she could use in case she didn't get paid and was at risk of being late on her bills. She was not aware that the practice of offering overdraft protection has been used to charge greater fees to bank customers:

> I got called in on my checking account to check something and they offered me a VISA through my bank for overdraft protection on my checking account. So I was so excited (and thought) hopefully they'll give a $1000 credit limit so that I can at least cover my mortgage and HOA

[Home Owners Association fees] for a month in case of some big snafu happens and I don't get my check right away. You know it won't bounce, so I won't be late. I looked up. They done gave me one for 3 grand.

Homeowners also are susceptible to predators who disguise their scams behind refinancing offers. As one black homeowner – and HOP dropout – describes:

The ARM matured; went up like $300 on the $112,000 [mortgage]. Somebody called claiming to be the original financier and asked if I wanted to refinance.

Turned out to be a scam. I got behind [in my mortgage payments] because of the alleged refinance. Paid for an appraisal and didn't make the August or September payment because I had the appraisal done.

Another black homeowner described how her new access to credit has substantial risks for increased consumer debt: "Oh, the credit cards be coming. You read that fine print, you know that … first 6 months zero interest, and then all of a sudden after that it's like …"

Others also acknowledged the powerful enticement of easy access to credit that opened up as a result of homeownership. As one black homeowner remarked:

Before I got into the [HOP] program. I couldn't even go into Sears and get a department store credit card. Please – I get a new credit card offer in the mail every other day. I have people offering to sell me new cars. I've got lenders calling me. Every week I get at least ten offers in the mail to refinance my mortgage. We finance this, we finance that. We'll finance yours, we'll finance the kids.

As part of pre-purchase counseling, HOP program participants received extensive training regarding "safe debt."[5] Nevertheless, as one black homeowner describes, the relative ease by which one could fall into the trap of getting into unsafe debt:

Well, they sent me a $5,000 check in the mail. It was a real check. I looked at it and I said this is a trick and I looked at it. It said 29% interest. $5,000 with that interest, you'll end up paying back almost $9,000 and it's those

---

[5] Safe debt refers to debt acquisition processes that are intended to keep the debt ratio sound. HOP participants are taught to focus on acquiring things that will actually make more money than what was spent on them (e.g., real estate) instead of purchasing items that do not (e.g., shopping sprees, vacations). Participants also are taught to carefully scrutinize the types of loans that are being offered, to prefer fixed rate loans over variable rate loans, and to avoid more exotic loans (e.g., loans with balloon payments, interest-only loans).

types of things. If I wouldn't be smart, I would be caught up. You know what I mean. I'd be locked in. I'd be paying up the butt for that. Education that needs to go on because they give you so much credit now.

However, because of the HOP training, even the newest homeowners are aware when offers are too good to be true: "Sometimes you think you want to, but then you don't. I know I don't because I know they're gonna rip you off. I already know it."

We observed another form of predation, likely confined to inflating real estate markets like Denver, which sought to exploit a perceived lack of information on the part of our recent homebuyers. Our home-buyers received unsolicited offers to purchase their homes, generally at prices well below current property values. As one of the longer-term black owners – a mother of three – reports:

> The funny thing is, they want to buy your house, like in my case. They want to buy my house for what I paid for it almost six years ago. I don't think so! It's worth twice as much now!

Thus, the evidence here suggests that the often-cited financial pitfalls awaiting minority homebuyers have largely been avoided. Most of our homebuyers either ignored the various solicitations offered to them or questioned their authenticity. However, the homebuyers in our study repeatedly acknowledged that temptations of various sorts lurked in their environs and remarked on the ease with which less knowledge-able homeowners might be seduced into predatory loans.

### Conclusions, Implications, and Future Directions

Federal programs have long been encouraging increasingly lower-income and minority households to buy homes. But questions have been raised concerning the long-term sustainability and desirability of this impetus. Our study has attempted to engage these concerns by investigating the homeowning experiences of low-income Latino and black homebuyers who participated in the Denver Housing Authority's Homeownership Program, where 70% of them ultimately purchased their homes through the program. This sample of homebuyers is unique in the literature insofar as it is comprised of former recipients of housing subsidies who voluntarily undertook a multi-year home-ownership counseling and asset-building program. Our findings give rise to cautious optimism, even though we recognize that our sample is selective.

Our primary conclusion based on the experiences of these participants is that most conventionally articulated, worst-case fears about low-income, minority homebuyers have largely been absent. They have *not* been forced to purchase homes in severely distressed, declining neighborhoods. Even in the midst of the current housing downturn, most have not suffered depreciation of their property values and relatively few have defaulted on their mortgages. They have not let the physical conditions of their homes deteriorate. They have taken advantage of refinancing options and avoided various and numerous credit card and predatory solicitations. Few see homeowning as a negative experience or erroneous decision in retrospect. We observed no statistically significant differences in any of these outcomes between Latino and black homebuyers in our study.

Moreover, our low-income, minority homebuyers overwhelmingly have found that the best thing about their experience has been sociopsychological, not financial (even though most have witnessed home equity gains). Indeed, the non-economic benefits of homeownership–enhanced senses of control, pride, security and privacy–are apparently very important for a population that society views as on the margins. This dimension of benefit has been largely absent from prior discussions of low-income homeownership (e.g., Shlay 2006).

Nevertheless, it is also abundantly clear that owning a home is not an easy, challenge-free experience for low-income, minority homebuyers. The homebuyers in our study were surprised by the degree of unexpected maintenance and repairs that their homes required. Yet, they were tenacious in responding to these issues even when financially burdened. Many voluntarily invested in substantial home improvements. Unlike similar responses from higher-income homeowners, however, for our sample there is limited ability to incur these extra costs without taking out additional loans or refinancing mortgage debt. This creates legitimate concerns regarding longer-term financial sustainability. Such concerns are only intensified by our finding that a nontrivial segment of the homebuyers in our study drew down their home equity and increased their levels of consumer debt.

We caution the reader that our results are not likely generalizable to a broader, generic set of low-income minority homebuyers. We suspect that the generally favorable experiences reported by Latino and black homebuyers in our sample can be partly attributed to the asset-building and pre-purchase counseling provided through the DHA's HOP program and partly to self-selection effects. It is thus premature for us to draw firm evaluative conclusions about HOP. In a forthcoming strand of our research we shall evaluate comprehensively this program, following strategies pioneered by Rohe and Kleit (1997) and Rohe and Quercia (2003). However, at this point in our investigation some extensions of the program can be appropriately suggested.

Our HOP participants have indicated that the transition from subsidized tenant to homeowner is a difficult one, and several have suggested that the current program is too abrupt in assuming that participants can switch instantaneously into a regime of no supports once they sign the deed on their new home. We believe that post-purchase follow-up, training in home maintenance techniques, and financial counseling would pay handsome dividends. Numerous dangers continue to confront minority homebuyers, so sustainability remains an ongoing challenge to which public policy must pay attention.

## References

Aaronson, Daniel. 2000. "A Note of the Benefits of Homeownership." *Journal of Urban Economics* 47: 356–369.

Ambrose, Brent and William Goetzmann. 1998. "Risks and Incentives in Underserved Mortgage Markets." *Journal of Housing Economics* 7: 274–285.

Belsky, Eric S. 2002. "Rehabilitation Matters: Improving Neighborhoods one Home at a Time." *Bright Ideas* (Summer): 3–7.

Belsky, Eric S. and Mark Duda. 2002. "Anatomy of the Low-Income Homeownership Boom in the 1990s." Pp. 15–63 in Nicholas P. Retsinas and Eric S. Belsky, eds., *Low-Income Homeownership: Examining the Unexamined Goal*. Washington, DC: The Brookings Institution.

Belsky, Eric S., Nicolas P. Retsinas and Mark Duda. 2005. "The Financial Returns to Low-Income Homeownership." Cambridge, MA: Harvard University.

Blank, Rebecca. 2002. "Evaluating Welfare Reform in the U.S." *Journal of Economic Literature* 40: 1105–1166.

Boehm, Thomas P. and Alan M. Schlottman. 1999. "Does Home Ownership by Parents Have an Economic Impact on Their Children." *Journal of Housing Economics* 8: 217–232.

Boehm, Thomas P. and Alan M. Schlottman. 2003. "The dynamics of race, income, and homeownership." *Journal of Urban Economics* 55: 113–130.

Boehm, Thomas P. and Alan M. Schlottmann. 2004. "Wealth Accumulation and Homeownership: Evidence for Low-Income Households." Office of Policy Development and Research, U.S. Department of Housing and Urban Development.

Bostic, Raphael W. and Kwan Ok Lee. 2008. "Mortgages, Risk, and Homeownership among Low- and Moderate-Income Families." *American Economic Review: Papers and Proceedings* 98: 310–314.

Bowdler, Janis, Roberto Quercia, and David Smith. 2010. *The Foreclosure Generation: The Long-Term Impact of the Housing Crisis on Latino Children and Families*. Washington, DC: National Council of la Raza.

Brooks-Gunn, Jeanne, Greg J. Duncan, and J. Lawrence Aber, eds. 1997. *Neighborhood Poverty: Vol. 1 Context and Consequences for Children*. New York: Russell Sage Foundation.

Case, Karl and Maryna Marychenko. 2002. "Home Appreciation in Low- and Moderate-Income Markets." Pp. 239–256 in Nicolas P. Retsinas and Eric S. Belsky, eds., *Low income homeownership: Examining the unexamined Goal.* Washington, DC: Brookings Institution Press.

Case, Karl and Robert Schiller. 1994. "A Decade of Boom and Bust in the Prices of Single-Family Homes: Boston and Los Angeles: 1983–1993." *New England Economic Review* (March): 40–51.

Christy-McMullin, Kameri, Shobe, Marcia A., and Janet Wills. 2009. "Arkansas IDA Programs: Examining Asset Retention and Perceptions of Well-Being." *Journal of Social Service Research* 35: 65–76.

Cox, Kevin. 1982. "Housing Tenure and Neighborhood Activism." *Urban Affairs Quarterly* 18:107–129.

Dietz, Robert and Donald Haurin. 2003. "The Social and Private Micro-Level Consequences of Homeownership." *Journal of Urban Economics* 54: 401–450.

Ding, Chenri and Gerrit-Jan Knaap. 2003. "Property Values in Inner-City Neighborhoods: The Effects of Homeownership, Housing Investment, and Economic Development." *Housing Policy Debate* 13: 701–727.

DiPasquale, Denise and Edward Glaeser. 1999. "Incentives and Social Capital: Are Homeowners Better Citizens?" *Journal of Urban Economics* 45: 354–384.

Englehardt, Gary , Michael Ericsen, William Gale, and Gregory Mills. 2010. "What are the Social Benefits of Homeownership? Experimental evidence for low-income households." *Journal of Urban Economics* 67: 249–258.

Galster, George. 1983. "Empirical Evidence on Cross-Tenure Differences in Home Maintenance and Conditions." *Land Economics* 59: 107–113.

Galster, George. 1987. *Homeowners and Neighborhood Reinvestment.* Durham, NC: Duke University Press.

Galster, George. 2008. "Scholarship on U.S. Housing, Planning, and Policy: The Evolving Topography since 1968." *Journal of the American Planning Association* 74: 1–12.

Galster, George and Jennifer Daniell. 1996. "Housing." Pp. 85–112 in George Galster, ed., *Reality and Research: Social Science and U.S. Urban Policy since 1960.* Washington, DC: Urban Institute Press.

Galster, George, Laudi Aron and William Reeder. 1999. "Encouraging Mortgage Lending in 'Underserved' Areas: The Potential for Encouraging Homeownership in the U.S." *Housing Studies* 14: 777–801.

Galster, George, David Marcotte, Marvin Mandell, Hal Wolman, and Nancy Augustine. 2007. "The Impacts of Parental Homeownership on Children's Outcomes during Early Adulthood." *Housing Policy Debate* 18: 785–827.

Galster, George and Anna Santiago. 2008. "Low-Income Homeownership as an Asset-Building Tool: What Can We Tell Policymakers?" Pp. 60–108 in Margery A. Turner, Howard Wial, and Hal Wolman, eds. *Urban and Regional Policy and Its Effects.* Washington DC: Brookings Institution Press.

Galster, George, Peter Tatian, Anna Santiago, Kathryn Pettit, and Robin Smith. 2003. *Why NOT in My Back Yard? The Neighborhood Impacts of Assisted Housing.* New Brunswick, NJ: Rutgers University, Center for Urban Policy Research Press.

Goetzmann, William N., and Matthew Spiegel. 2002. "Policy Implications of Portfolio Choice in Underserved Mortgage Markets." Pp. 257–74 in Nicholas P. Retsinas and Eric S. Belsky, eds., *Low-Income Homeownership: Examining the Unexamined Goal.* Washington DC: The Brookings Institution.

Gramlich, Edward M. 2007. *Subprime Mortgages: America's Latest Boom and Bust.* Washington, DC: Urban Institute Press.

Green, Richard K. and Michelle J. White. 1997. "Measuring the Benefits of Homeowning: Effects on Children." *Journal of Urban Economics* 41: 441–461.

Grinstein-Weiss, Michal, Jung-Sook Lee, Johanna Greeson, Chan-Keun Han, Yeong Yeo, and Kate Irish. 2008. Fostering Low-Income Homeownership through

Individual Development Accounts: A Longitudinal, Randomized Experiment. *Housing Policy Debate* 19: 711–740.

Harkness, Joseph M. and Sandra J. Newman. 2002. "Homeownership For the Poor in Distressed Neighborhoods: Does It Make Sense?" *Housing Policy Debate* 13: 597–630.

Harkness, Joseph M. and Sandra J. Newman. 2003. "Differential Effects of Homeownership on Children from Higher- and Lower-Income Families," *Journal of Housing Research* 14:1–19.

Haurin, Donald R., Patric Hendershott, and David Ling. 1988. "Home ownership Rates of Married Couples: An Econometric Investigation." *Housing Finance Review* 7: 85- 108.

Haurin, Donald R., and Stuart S. Rosenthal. 2005. "The Growth of Earnings of Low-Income Households and the Sensitivity of Their Homeownership Choices to Economic and Socio-Demographic Shocks." U.S. Department of Housing and Urban Development. Washington, DC: Office of Policy Development & Research.

Haurin, Donald R., Toby L. Parcel, and R. Jean Haurin. 2002a. "Impact of Home Ownership on Child Outcomes." Pp. 427–446 in Eric Belsky and Nicholas P. Retsinas, eds., *Low Income Homeownership: Examining the Unexamined Goal.* Washington, DC: Brookings Institution Press.

Haurin, Donald R., Toby L. Parcel and R. Jean Haurin. 2002b. "Does Home Ownership Affect Child Outcomes?" *Real Estate Economics* 30: 635–666.

Haurin, R. Jean. 1992. "Patterns of Childhood Residence and the Relationship to Young Adult Outcomes." *Journal of Marriage and the Family* 54: 846–880.

Haveman, Robert and Barbara Wolfe. 1994. *Succeeding Generations: On the Effects of Investments in Children.* New York: Russell Sage Foundation.

Herbert, Christopher E. and Eris S. Belsky. 2008. "Initial Housing Choices Made by Low-Income and Minority Homebuyers." *Cityscape* 10: 61–94.

Hoff, Karla and Arijit Sen. 2005. "Homeownership, Community Interactions, and Segregation." *American Economic Review* 95: 1167–1189.

Immergluck, Dan. 2008. "From the Subprime to the Exotic: Expanded Mortgage Market Risk and Implications for Metropolitan Areas and Neighborhoods." *Journal of the American Planning Association* 73: 59–76.

Keil, Katherine and Rachel Carson. 1990. "An Examination of Systematic Differences in the Appreciation of Individual Housing Units." *Journal of Real Estate Research* 5: 301–317.

Kochhar, Rakesh, Ana Gonzalez-Barrera and Daniel Dockterman. 2009. *Through Boom and Bust: Minorities, Immigrants and Homeownership.* Washington, DC: Pew Hispanic Center (May).

Listokin, David, Elvin K. Wyly, Brian Schmitt and Ioan Voicu. 2002. *The Potential and Limitations of Mortgage Innovation in Fostering Homeownership in the United States.* Washington, D.C.: The Fannie Mae Foundation.

Locke, Gretchen, Michelle Abbenante, Hong Ly, Naomi Michlin, Winnie Tsen and Jennifer Turnham. 2006. *Voucher Homeownership Study: Volume 1 Cross-site Analysis.* Washington, DC: U.S. Department of Housing and Urban Development, Office of Policy Development and Research.

Mayer, Christopher. 1993. "Taxes, Income Distribution, and the Real Estate Cycle." *New England Economic Review* (May-June): 39–50.

Mayer, Susan E. 1997. *What Money Can't Buy: Family Income and Children's Life Chances.* Cambridge, MA: Harvard University Press.

McCarthy, George, Shannon van Zandt and William Rohe. 2001. *The Economic Benefits and Costs of Homeownership.* Washington, DC: Research Institute for Housing America, Working Paper No. 01–02.

McKernan, Signe-Mary and Michael Sherraden. 2008. *Asset Building and Low-Income Families.* Washington, DC: The Urban Institute Press.

Meyer, Peter B., Jerry Yeager and Michael A. Burayidi. 1994. "Institutional Myopia and Policy Distortions: The Promotion of Homeownership for the Poor." *Journal of Economic Issues* 28: 567–76.

Mitchell, Maxine, and S. Paige Warren. 1998. "Making Home Ownership a Reality" in *Survey of Habitat for Humanity International (HFHI), Inc. Homeowners and Affiliates*. Washington DC: Office of Policy Development and Research, U.S. Department of Housing and Urban Development.

Nothaft, Frank E. and Yan Chang. 2005. "Creating Wealth in Low-Income Communities: Refinance and the Accumulation of Home Equity Wealth." Pp. 71–102 in Nicholas P. Retsinas and Eric Belsky, eds., *Building Assets, Building Credit: Creating Wealth in Low-Income Communities*. Washington, D.C.: Brookings Institution Press.

Nesslein, Thomas S. 2000. "Owning Versus Renting: Is the Promotion of Homeownership for the Poor Good Social Policy?" Paper prepared for the 22nd Annual Research Conference, Association for Public Policy Analysis and Management, Seattle WA, November.

Pitcoff, Winton. 2003. "Has Homeownership Been Oversold?" *National Housing Institute's Shelterforce Online* 127.

Pollakowski, Henry O., Michael A. Stegman and William M. Rohe. 1991. "Rates of Return on Housing of Low-and-Moderate-Income Owners." *AREUEA Journal* 19: 417–25.

Poterba, James. 1991. "House Price Dynamics: The Role of Taxes and Demography." *Brookings Papers on Economic Activity* 2: 110–126.

Reid, Carolina Katz. 2004. "Achieving the American Dream? A Longitudinal Analysis of the Homeownership Experiences of Low-Income Households." PhD dissertation, University of Washington, Department of Geography.

Renuart, Elizabeth. 2004. "An Overview of the Predatory Lending Process." *Housing Policy Debate* 15: 467–502.

Retsinas, Nicolas P. and Eric S. Belsky, eds. 2002. *Low Income Homeownership: Examining the Unexamined Goal*. Washington D.C.: Bookings Institution Press.

Retsinas, Nicolas P. and Eric S. Belsky. 2005. "Building Assets, Building Credit: Creating Wealth in Low-Income Communities." Washington D.C.: Bookings Institution Press.

Rohe, William M. and Victoria Basolo. 1997. "Long-term Effects of Homeownership on the Self-perceptions and Social Interaction of Low-income Persons." *Environment and Behavior* 29: 793–819.

Rohe, William M. and Rachel Garshick Kleit. 1997. "From Dependency to Self-Sufficiency: An Appraisal of the Gateway Transitional Families Program." *Housing Policy Debate* 8: 75–108.

Rohe, William and Michael Stegman. 1994. "The Impact of Home Ownership on the Social and Political Involvement of Low-Income People." *Urban Affairs Quarterly* 30:152–172.

Rohe, William and Leslie Stewart. 1996. "Home Ownership and Neighborhood Stability." *Housing Policy Debate* 7: 37–81.

Rohe, William M. and Harry L. Watson, eds. 2007. *Chasing the American Dream: New Perspectives on Affordable Homeownership*. Ithaca, NY: Cornell University Press.

Rohe, William, George McCarthy and Shannon van Zandt. 2000. *The Social Benefits and Costs of Homeownership*. Washington, DC: Research Institute for Housing America, Working Paper no. 00–01.

Rohe, William M., and Roberto G. Quercia. 2003. "Individual and Neighborhood Impacts of Neighborhood Reinvestment's Homeownership Pilot Program." Center for Urban and Regional Studies, University of North Carolina at Chapel Hill.

Rohe, William, Roberto Quercia and Shannon van Zandt. 2002. *Supporting the American Dream of Home Ownership: An Assessment of the Neighborhood Reinvestment's Home Ownership Pilot Program*. Chapel Hill, NC: Center for Urban and Regional Studies, University of North Carolina.

Rohe, William, Shannon van Zandt, and George McCarthy. 2002. "Home Ownership and Access to Opportunity." *Housing Studies* 17: 51–62.

Rossi, Peter H. and Eleanor Weber. 1996. "The Social Benefits of Homeownership: Empirical Evidence from National Surveys." *Housing Policy Debate* 7: 1–35.

Santiago, Anna M., and George C. Galster. 2004. "Moving from Public Housing to Home Ownership: Perceived Barriers to Program Participation and Success." *Journal of Urban Affairs* 24: 297–324.

Santiago, Anna M., George C. Galster, Angela A. Kaiser, Ana H. Santiago-San Roman, Rebecca A. Grace and Andrew T.W. Linn. 2010. "Low Income Homeownership: Does It Necessarily Mean Sacrificing Neighborhood Quality to Buy a Home?" *Journal of Urban Affairs* 32: 171–198.

Santiago, Anna M., George C. Galster, Ana H. San Roman, Cristina M. Tucker, Angela A. Kaiser, and Rebecca A. Grace. 2009. "Sometimes It Just Becomes Too Much: Why Participants Drop Out of Homeownership Counseling Programs." Paper presented at the Annual Meetings of the Association for Public Policy Analysis and Management (November).

Santiago, Anna M., George C. Galster, Ana H. San Roman, Cristina M. Tucker, Angela A. Kaiser, Rebecca A. Grace, and Andrew T.H.. Linn. 2010. "Foreclosing on the American Dream? The Financial Consequences of Low-Income Homeownership." *Housing Policy Debate* 20: 707–742.

Sherraden, Michael. 1991. *Assets and the Poor: A New American Welfare Policy.* Armonk, NY: M.E. Sharpe.

Shlay, Anne B. 2006. "Low-Income Homeownership: American Dream or Delusion?" *Urban Studies* 43: 511–531.

Smith, Lawrence B. and Michael H.C. 1996. "The Relative Price Differential Between Higher and Lower Priced Homes." *Journal of Housing Economics* 5: 1–17.

Smith, Barton A. and William P. Teserak. 1991. "House Prices and Regional Real Estate Cycles: Market Adjustment in Houston." *AREUEA Journal* 79: 12–37.

Stegman, Michael A., Roberto G. Quercia and Walter Davis. 2007. "The Wealth-Creating Potential of Homeownership: A Preliminary Assessment of Price Appreciation among Low-Income Home buyers." Pp. 271–292 in William M. Rohe and Harry L. Watson, eds., *Chasing the American dream: New perspectives on affordable homeownership*. Ithaca, New York: Cornell University Press.

Stegman, Michael A., Roberto G. Quercia, George W. McCarthy, Michael Foster and William M. Rohe. 1991. "Designing Better Homeownership Assistance Programs Using the Panel Study of Income Dynamics (PSID): An Exploratory Analysis." *Journal of Housing Research* 2: 39–85.

Turner, Tracy M. and Marc T. Smith. 2009. "Exits from Homeownership: The Effects of Race, Ethnicity and Income." *Journal of Regional Science* 49: 1–32.

U.S. Department of Housing and Urban Development. 2002. *Barriers to Minority Homeownership*. Washington, DC.

Van Order, Robert and Peter Zorn. 2002. "Performance of Low-Income and Minority Mortgages." Pp. 322–47 in Nicholas P. Retsinas and Eric S. Belsky, eds., *Low-Income Homeownership: Examining the Unexamined Goal*. Washington, DC: Brookings Institution.

Vartanian, Thomas P. 1999. "Childhood Conditions and Adult Welfare Use: Examining Neighborhood and Family Factors." *Journal of Marriage and the Family* 61: 225–237.

Wiranowski, Mark. 2003. "Sustaining Home Ownership through Education and Counseling," in *Fellowship Program for Emerging Leaders in Community and Economic Development*. Neighborhood Reinvestment Corporation, Joint Center for Housing Studies of Harvard University.

Wolfe, Rachael A. and Seth Ovandia. 2009. "Not Getting their Money's Worth: African-American Disadvantages in Converting Income, Wealth, and Education into Residential Quality." *Urban Affairs Review* 45: 66–91.

# INDEX

www.ingramcontent.com/pod-product-compliance
Lightning Source LLC
Chambersburg PA
CBHW060023030426
42334CB00019B/2154